# Register Now
## to Y

Your print purchase of *A Clinician's Guide for Treating Active Military and Veteran Populations With EMDR Therapy* **includes online access to the contents of your book**—increasing accessibility, portability, and searchability!

**Access today at:**
http://connect.springerpub.com/content/book/978-0-8261-5283-9
or scan the QR code at the right with your smartphone
and enter the access code below.

D84SUJ8C

*Scan here for quick access.*

**If you are experiencing problems accessing the digital component of this product, please contact our customer service department at cs@springerpub.com**

View all our products at springerpub.com

**E. C. Hurley, DMin, PhD,** is a retired Army colonel with 33 years of military service in the U.S. Army and Army Reserve beginning with the rank of private during the Vietnam era and retiring with the rank of colonel three decades later. His military awards include the Army Meritorious Service Medal (awarded three times), the Bronze Star Medal, the Legion of Merit, and the Army Air Assault Badge. He was selected and trained as an EMDR trainer by Francine Shapiro, PhD. As a licensed psychotherapist since 1980, he is trained in the major orientations of psychotherapy. He is a diplomate with the American Academy of Experts in Traumatic Stress, an approved supervisor with the American Association for Marriage and Family Therapy, and an approved consultant and trainer with the EMDR International Association (EMDRIA) and the EMDR Institute, as well as a member of the American Psychological Association and the Psychological Society of Ireland. Dr. Hurley holds graduate degrees in pastoral counseling, counseling psychology, and clinical psychology with the Doctor of Ministry in pastoral counseling and a PhD in clinical psychology.

Dr. Hurley is the executive director of EMDR-Tennessee and the founder of Soldier Center. He provides EMDR basic trainings at Soldier Center and various other locations, including virtual online trainings for EMDR basic and advanced trainings. Dr. Hurley is the 2005 recipient of the Elizabeth Stryker Volunteer of the Year award presented by the EMDR Humanitarian Assistance Program (EMDR-HAP) and, in 2019, was presented the Francine Shapiro Award, the highest award the EMDRIA bestows. He is a member of EMDR's Council of Scholars, a group of international EMDR leaders. He is author of the chapter "EMDR Therapy in the Treatment of Military Sexual Trauma" in the book *Treating Military Sexual Trauma*, edited by Lori Katz (2015) and the co-author of a chapter on EMDR therapy in the publication *PTSD Case Book* (2015) published by the American Psychological Association. His published research includes *Effective Treatment of Veterans With PTSD: Comparison Between Intensive Daily and Weekly EMDR Approaches*, which compares EMDR intensive daily treatment with weekly sessions.

# A CLINICIAN'S GUIDE FOR TREATING ACTIVE MILITARY AND VETERAN POPULATIONS WITH EMDR THERAPY

E. C. Hurley, DMin, PhD

Springer Publishing Company, LLC
11 West 42nd Street, New York, NY 10036
www.springerpub.com
connect.springerpub.com/

*Acquisitions Editor:* Kate Dimock
*Compositor:* S4Carlisle Publishing Services

*ISBN:* 978-0-8261-5822-2
*ebook ISBN:* 978-0-8261-5823-9
*DOI:* 10.1891/9780826158222

20 21 22 23/ 5 4 3 2 1

The author and the publisher of this Work have made every effort to use sources believed to be reliable to provide information that is accurate and compatible with the standards generally accepted at the time of publication. The author and publisher shall not be liable for any special, consequential, or exemplary damages resulting, in whole or in part, from the readers' use of, or reliance on, the information contained in this book. The publisher has no responsibility for the persistence or accuracy of URLs for external or third-party Internet websites referred to in this publication and does not guarantee that any content on such websites is, or will remain, accurate or appropriate.

**Library of Congress Cataloging-in-Publication Data**
**E. C. Hurley:** https://orcid.org/0000-0002-0885-839X

Names: Hurley, E. C., author.
Title: A clinicians guide for treating active military and veteran
  populations with EMDR therapy / E.C. Hurley.
Description: New York : Springer Publishing Company, [2021] | Includes
  bibliographical references and index.
Identifiers: LCCN 2020041708 (print) | LCCN 2020041709 (ebook) | ISBN
  9780826158222 (paperback) | ISBN 9780826158239 (ebook)
Subjects: MESH: Eye Movement Desensitization Reprocessing–methods | Stress
  Disorders, Traumatic–therapy | Military Personnel–psychology |
  Veterans–psychology | Medical History Taking–methods | Practice Guideline
Classification: LCC RC552.T7 (print) | LCC RC552.T7 (ebook) | NLM WM
  425.5.D4 | DDC 616.85/2106–dc23
LC record available at https://lccn.loc.gov/2020041708
LC ebook record available at https://lccn.loc.gov/2020041709

Contact sales@springerpub.com to receive discount rates on bulk purchases.

*Publisher's Note:* **New and used products purchased from third-party sellers are not guaranteed for quality, authenticity, or access to any included digital components.**

Printed in the United States of America.

This book is dedicated:

To Francine, whose healing gift of EMDR therapy has allowed me to
serve others—a dear friend and mentor,

To Nancy, whose love and support has encouraged me to use my gifts in
so many corners of the world and continues to share life's journey,

To my children Michael and Andrea who fill a dad's heart with love,

To the staff at Soldier Center,

To colleagues worldwide who share our compassion for humanity,

And, to all who have worn the uniform both now and in the past—
I salute you.

E. C. HURLEY
SOLDIER CENTER
CLARKSVILLE, TENNESSEE

# CONTENTS

## Appendices

# PREFACE

I have been a soldier for most of my life. The military's core values, culture, and mission-driven approach to life are as much a part of me as the air I breathe. My military experience and clinical training while in the military allowed me to develop my clinical skills in providing psychotherapy to soldiers and their families at various military installations throughout the United States, Europe, Korea, and combat zones in southwest Asia. I have met with soldiers in the barracks after duty hours as well as during their full-blown panic attacks as they were rushing to find shelter in a bunker while the base was under attack. Sharing these experiences developed within me a comradery with a deep respect for those who serve the nation as well as their families who support them. It is my belief that military personnel, veterans, and their families deserve effective treatment in a timely manner. My goal is to provide the most effective treatment possible as well as train other mental health providers to do the same.

The military is a way of life. Its culture and values become ingrained in the lives of those who serve the nation. How clients demonstrate these has a diagnostic feature as I observe veterans entering my office. Do they exude confidence in their ability to maintain their security in my office, or are they extremely hypervigilant as if every sound or movement is a potential threat? Do they feel out of control due to the severity of their pathological symptoms? Can they be present enough to maintain their military bearing? I observe servicemembers, in spite of being wounded, walking erect, straight, individuals who have led others in combat. I respect these individuals for their service to the nation as I learn of their contributions. I realize at another time in life that any of these servicemembers could have been my platoon sergeant, functioning as a noncommissioned officer (NCO) who knows the names of each member of my family and the birthdates of each of my children, who takes to heart the responsibility of bringing each soldier home alive. This helps me to understand a client's struggle between their current wounded condition and the accomplishments they have achieved in healthier times of the past. The understanding validates my respect for the client as I, their therapist, identify the client's treatment goals, that is, their reason for being in my office. Persons who have served in the military know rank is appointed; however, respect is earned among warriors. As we establish rapport in the treatment session, there is an awareness that we share similar core values and belief in "mission first." Now, the client is the focus of my mission as I muster the best I have to offer in providing the client's psychological healing. One of the highest honors is for this military client to know their therapist can be trusted to have their "six" during the treatment process. A veteran who had told me, "Suicide is always an option" ended the session by stating, "Doc, I don't want you to give up on me." In response I stated, "I won't give up on you if you don't give up on me." To which he responded, "Roger!"

**Translating Military Experience and Clinical Skills Into Effective Treatment**—Following the attack on September 11, 2001, military core values were operationalized as the mission tempo was implemented for U.S. military personnel. Within a few months downrange—in combat—soldiers began to return, exhibiting symptoms of acute stress and simple posttraumatic stress disorder (PTSD). As they returned home for 2 weeks of rest and relaxation (R & R), the number of personnel exhibiting stress-related symptoms began to increase. The first soldier I treated after 6 months in combat came home for his R & R. He stood in my office having been home 3 days. His spouse told him to "go see Hurley" since I had been the therapist who provided couples therapy with them prior to the deployment. A common complaint expressed by several spouses indicated the soldier-husband was irritable, argumentative, emotionally distant, experiencing nightmares, and socially withdrawn.

The soldier arrived early for his appointment, displayed agitation as he waited in the waiting room, then entered my office with a short greeting. Having been in my office 6 months prior, he located a chair and seated himself as he began to explain the complaints his wife described to him. Within minutes, the soldier had jumped up and began pacing across my office. With an elevated voice, almost shouting, he began blaming his spouse, children, the U.S. Army, almost anyone and anything else. He found it difficult to be seated. Although I had been trained in most models of psychotherapy, I had difficulty communicating with the solider while he was pacing across my office ranting and yelling. My commitment to offer the best treatment possible collided with the soldier's psychological wall of anger, blame, and hypervigilance. The soldier taught me: *Talk therapy doesn't work when the client is so dysregulated, they can't listen!* Out of my desperation to find an effective treatment approach, I registered to attend a training in Eye Movement Desensitization and Reprocessing (EMDR) therapy that weekend. I had been skeptical of EMDR therapy for several years, but nothing else I had in my clinical toolbox was working!

On Tuesday of the following week, I saw the soldier again. Just back from my basic EMDR therapy training, I used a relaxation technique, the Safe/Calm Place, to assist in his affect regulation. The soldier remained calm and focused as I encouraged him to use the relaxation technique regularly. The last part of the session I introduced him to EMDR therapy as being a possible treatment if he was willing to give it a try. In the follow-up session on Thursday of that week, I treated the soldier's disturbing memory of a single-incident combat-related event involving soldiers being killed when his convoy hit an improvised explosive device (IED). His subjective unit of disturbance (SUD) dropped from a 9 to a 0 within the 50-minute session. The positive thought (validity of cognition) he wanted to believe about himself, "I am A-OK now!" increased from a 3 to a 7, the highest rating he could give to how true the belief felt to him. We did the body scan, looking for any somatically stored material unconsciously related to the memory. Body sensations in his stomach and chest cleared away. The following Monday was his third EMDR session. When I walked to the waiting room to meet the soldier, his wife was there. I had never met her. She told me, "I just wanted to stop by and thank you! I don't know what you are doing with my husband, but whatever it is, it is working—I have him back the way he was before he went to Iraq!" We shared the joy associated with the treatment outcome as the soldier and I entered the treatment room. That session we focused on the trigger related to the IED incident. Unexpected noises set him off. True to the EMDR therapy third-prong approach, I treated his trigger, the reaction to loud noises. On Friday, before he was to return to Iraq, the future template was used to prepare him for his return to duty in Iraq. In retrospect, I sought EMDR training out of my desperation to provide an effective evidence-based treatment for the solider. The wife's response to his treatment energized my commitment to using this therapy. Within 3 months of being trained in EMDR therapy, I decided to specialize in using the therapy to treat military personnel with PTSD. As multiple deployments began with repetitive exposure to life-threatening events, clinical presentations became complex PTSD. As this happened, my specialization began to focus on treating complex PTSD and moral injury with EMDR therapy. Being trained in EMDR therapy changed my professional life!

As my private practice developed into a community-based treatment center, Soldier Center, with all clinical staff trained in EMDR therapy, the center became an EMDR treatment center for military and veteran populations. At the encouragement of Dr. Francine Shapiro, PhD, I developed a 5-day EMDR intensive treatment program providing two EMDR therapy sessions daily for 5 days. As the clinical cases became more complex with soldiers taking part in multiple deployments, I expanded the intensive treatment from 5- to 10-day treatment. Active duty warrior transition units (WTUs) began to regularly refer personnel with psychological wounds as did family members of veterans with PTSD looking for effective treatment.

After serving a number of years as an EMDR trainer, I was asked to serve as the EMDR Institute trainer to the U.S. Army Medical Command (AMEDD) where I trained U.S. military personnel throughout the world in EMDR therapy. My training has now expanded as an EMDR Institute regional trainer as well as training all branches of the U.S. military. I provide EMDR advanced trainings covering topics such as "treating complex PTSD and dissociative exhibitions with EMDR therapy," "treating adults abused as children with EMDR therapy," "treating military sexual trauma (MST) with EMDR therapy," and "treating moral injury and suicidality with EMDR therapy," while an EMDR externship at Soldier Center and a certification track allow EMDR therapists to pursue the designation of "EMDR Military Specialist" offered through Soldier Center.

**Goal of the Book**—This book is the result of my 30+ years of military service and extensive experience as an EMDR therapist, EMDRIA-approved consultant, and an EMDR-approved trainer who specializes in training mental health providers who treat military and veteran populations. The overall goal of the book is to provide a resource for empowering EMDR-trained therapists to provide the most effective treatment available to our military and veteran populations who bring with them a wide range of clinical rules of engagement in the therapist's office. My hope is the book fills the void of many therapists who are trained in EMDR therapy but wish they had a "go-to" manual on how to deal with unique treatment issues in treating military personnel and veterans. The author translates how to present clinical psychotherapy material into an approach that enables this special population to understand and willingly engage in treatment.

**Distinguishing Features**—The book includes a lifetime of lessons learned in working with military personnel and veterans. It includes a paradigm for evaluating the military personnel and veteran's initial clinical presentation in the opening minutes in your office. The book describes how to use nuances of the military culture to present a motivating treatment plan. Numerous case examples are provided to illustrate intervention strategies across the treatment spectrum while treating military personnel and veterans. Illustrations range from single-incident traumas to complex PTSD and moral injury. Case studies showing my sessions at Soldier Center describe the nuances of treatment. Complex cases, including suicidality, moral injury, MST, and dissociative exhibitions, are included. Use of the EMDR eight-phase standard protocol is highlighted. Modifications for treating complex trauma are illustrated while addressing when it is appropriate to move from Phase 2 Preparation to Phases 3 and 4 in reprocessing complex trauma. Additional chapters address topics important to the military and veteran community such as treating PTSD with mild to moderate traumatic brain injury (mTBI), moral injury, MST, suicidality, and

EMDR early intervention. A chapter addressing "When EMDR Therapy Does Not Work (With Some Therapists)" highlights those occasional, but much discussed cases when veterans were unsuccessfully treated with EMDR therapy. Often these failures can be tied to a therapist who did not follow the appropriate protocol. A review is offered of what the therapists in these cases did not do, with suggestions regarding what the therapists could have done to make the treatment successful.

**Appendices/Handouts**—(a) "An Overview of EMDR Therapy Treatment for Military Personnel/Veterans and Spouses"; (b) "Presenting EMDR Therapy to Your Client"; (c) "Establishing a Treatment Plan for Shame-Based Clients"; (d) "Target Sequence Treatment Plan"; (e) "The Three Techniques"; (f) "EMDR Case Conceptualization and Treatment Planning"; (g) "Examples of Presenting EMDR Therapy During Phase 2"; (h) "Cognitive Interweave".

**Intended Audience**—The book's intended audience consists of EMDR-trained psychotherapists who treat military personnel, veterans, first responders, and their families including therapists attending EMDR therapy basic trainings, EMDR advanced trainings, EMDRIA conferences, and online EMDR continuing education programs.

*E. C. Hurley*

# ACKNOWLEDGMENTS

This book was written over the course of a year as my wife Nancy and I shared life both in Tennessee and the west coast of County Clare, Ireland. In both locations, Nancy and I celebrated life together. Authoring this book included adopting an irregular schedule, allowing it to become normal, with my arising in the wee hours of the morning and rearranging my previous schedule over the course of several months. I want to acknowledge my appreciation for Nancy's support and encouragement in order for this book to become a reality.

Dr. Francine Shapiro, PhD, invited me to become an EMDR trainer. Francine trained me to be an EMDR basic trainer, along with a group of other colleagues who shared her understanding and guidance. I am forever appreciative of knowing Francine and her contribution of the gift of EMDR therapy in bringing effective treatment to military veterans and their families.

I am appreciative of a community of EMDR-related colleagues including EMDR therapists who serve active duty military personnel and the veteran community.

And I salute those active-duty military personnel and veterans who have trusted me to be their therapist. I am honored to have been able to spend time with them during their healing journey. I honor and respect them.

# TREATING MILITARY PERSONNEL AND VETERANS WITH THE EMDR EIGHT-PHASE APPROACH

# 1

# Understanding the Military Veteran

## Introduction

Key concepts in understanding and treating military and veteran patients are included in this chapter. Understanding how combat changes a person's lifestyle, the relationship of attachment to coping with loss and grief, military core values, and suicidality among the military and veteran populations are addressed. Three key questions for the intake session are discussed. Resources for understanding military language with its acronyms are provided along with a description of the influence of Stoicism on military leaders from George Washington to the present military commanders. Clinical issues such as dissociative distortions and compartmentalization are addressed for assisting the therapist in delivering effective treatment to a wide range of clinical presentations. The goal of this chapter is to enhance the EMDR therapist's understanding of the military population and how to use the understanding to achieve significant treatment results.

## Learning Objectives

- Review unique aspects of the military culture such as behavioral patterns, leadership, and attachment styles.
- Identify the strengths of EMDR therapy in treating the military and veteran populations.
- Review the military's core values within each branch of service in the United States and Canada.
- Identify the leadership philosophy among military personnel such as Congressional Medal of Honor recipient Admiral James Stockdale and Marine Corps General James Mattis.

# UNDERSTANDING THE MILITARY AND VETERAN CLIENT

## DUTY, RESPONSIBILITY, AND AUTHORITY IN THE MILITARY

Military culture is structured around duty, responsibility, and authority enacted by military personnel. A duty is something a servicemember must do by virtue of their assigned position. Duty has a legal or moral obligation. Service personnel are trained to perform their duties beginning with their entry-level advanced training. Duties vary for each rank. Some duties are based on rank, whereas others are determined by assigned position. For example, a salute is an outdoor exchange of greeting. It is a courtesy rendered as the senior ranking person receives the salute from the junior. There are three types of duties: specified, directed, and implied. Specified duties are outlined in the Uniform Code of Military Justice (UCMJ), field manuals, and regulations. Directed duties are designated tasks assigned by a command authority such as a sergeant of the guard or charge of quarters (CQ). Implied duties are usually individual responses assumed by the individual without written directives.

Responsibility is based on a person being accountable for what a servicemember does or fails to do. This includes the completion of one's designated duty. A cook is responsible for ensuring military personnel have food for meals; a bomb disposal expert (EOD) is responsible for assessing a potential for deactivation; and a military aviator is responsible for being fit to fly the next mission. Responsibility is held at all command levels. All servicemembers are responsible for keeping physically fit. Military leaders such as noncommissioned officers (NCOs) are responsible not only for their individual duties, but also to ensure the success of those they lead. The same is true for officers in command. Commanders also have the collective accountability for the performance of duties within their command in order to be mission ready. It is the power of leaders to direct those servicemembers to take action within their area of responsibility. General officers and Navy flag officers (admirals, vice admirals, and rear admirals) have responsibility for ensuring those units under their command are mission ready to accomplish their designated tasks.

## RANK HAS ITS MEANING AND PRIVILEGE

RHIP in the military means "rank has its privilege." A common saying during the Vietnam era was "God must love Privates because there are so many of them!" In some overseas bases, a Marine has to hold the rank of sergeant or higher before they can own a vehicle. The enlisted Joes (junior ranks E-1 - E-4) catch much of the extra duties.

Understanding the military rank structure can be important for therapists. Recently, while providing EMDR consultation, a consultee described her client as being a seaman who was avoiding engaging in his treatment. Generally defined, a seaman is a mariner or sailor. More specifically, in many navies of the world, seaman is used to designate a rank, one of the lowest ranks in the Navy. Use of the word "seaman" led me to believe the client was a young Navy enlistee with limited life experience. On further inquiry, she indicated her client was an E-9. Enlisted ranks in the U.S. military range from the lowest rank (E-1) to the highest enlisted rank (E-9). An E-9 in the U.S. Navy is a Master Chief Petty Officer, one of the most senior ranking NCOs in the service. A Navy Master Chief engaged in therapy usually means he is serious about being in the therapist's office; otherwise, he would not be seeking treatment. The perceived avoidance is more likely that of a salty NCO who has a cautious approach to evaluate the treatment options.

## MILITARY LANGUAGE AND ACRONYMS

The military uses a unique vocabulary to describe much of its equipment, concepts, and operations. Add to this unique vocabulary the ever-increasing list of acronyms, and the most seasoned servicemember can be confused by some of the language. For example, the military name for restroom is "latrine" in the U.S. Army and "head" in the Navy and Marines. An eating facility is referred to as the "mess," "mess hall," or "dining facility." Meals for consumption in the field are known as "MREs" meaning "Meals, Ready to Eat." "Stand to" is the time when combat troops living on a base arise early and position themselves around the perimeter of the base to diligently look into the darkness of early dawn watching for any moving silhouette indicating the enemy is about to attack. As the sun rises and it is clear there is no threat, the command is given to "stand down" meaning go about your regular daily routine. I frequently use these terms in working with hypervigilant servicemembers, illustrating there are times to be "on guard" and other times to "let down our guard." We are not designed to stay on guard permanently.

"Chest candy" refers to the ribbons and medals worn on a uniform. In the Air Force, an "Eagle Keeper" refers to the maintenance crew serving an F-15 fighter. A "5-sided puzzle palace" is reference to the Pentagon. "Black" on ammunition, water, or fuel indicates the resource is gone. "Ate-up" refers to a servicemember who doesn't understand regulations at all, or who follows regulations so closely they disregards the context of the situation. Military organizations also use the phonetic alphabet for clarification in communication. All U.S. and NATO (North Atlantic Treaty Organization) bases use a phonetic alphabet to avoid confusion with specific words. Resources with the military glossary of words are readily available online (www.military.com/join -armed-forces/glossary-of-military-acronyms.html and www.military .com/join-armed-forces/military-terms-and-jargon.html).

## ATTACHMENT IN THE MILITARY

Attachment is an important component in understanding military interactions among servicemembers. An infantry soldier said to me, "I would not want my family to know this, but I am closer to my guys than I am to my own family!" This statement is common among veterans who served in combat. Living in a combat zone produces core life-or-death survival needs. Survival arouses the basic attachment needs that exist in a person from birth. Attachment theoretically provides the framework for affect regulation, interpersonal skills, and social support responses. A person's primal survival questions include: "Who can I count on to protect me?" and "Is there someone attentive to my needs?" These statements are often expressed by the question "Who has my six?", meaning "Who is looking out for me?" Military personnel live with these questions during the carrying out of their duties. The military community provides a place where basic needs such as food and shelter are provided along with a ready-made community of persons who become responsible for the survival of each other. Relational connections become integrated with the basic needs for survival and safety. The combat environment is a place for attachment to occur among persons who depend on each other for survival. During combat, servicemembers fight for the survival of each other. Military leadership is responsible for the care of those subordinate members of the unit.

Servicemembers identify those persons whom they can count on, those who "have their six," that is, protect their back. Attachment bonds develop between an individual and those who share survival responsibilities. During intense military missions, an individual's attachment style is superseded, at least in part, by the military actions each servicemember is trained to perform. Performance during the mission defines the social acceptance of each person. Being trained in the appropriate response avoids much of the interpersonal drama that might be obvious at more normal times. The defense of the team/unit intensifies the attachment bond among members. Persons who enlisted in the military find the military structure provides an almost ideal attachment experience with its provisions of basic survival needs including physiological, safety, and a sense of belonging. The strength of attachment bonds influences the degree of interpersonal connection among members as well as the intensity of grief and survival guilt when friends are killed.

Campbell, Ryan, Wright, Devore, and Hoge (2016) describe combat attachment with its intense adrenalin-producing experiences as addictive. Attachment is enhanced as the veteran becomes addicted to the feelings of excitement or euphoria and physiological hyperarousal in connection with mission operations shared with the team. The arousal pattern becomes cyclical in reexperiencing memories of exciting adrenalin-producing events followed by times of emotional numbness, guilt, and overall feeling down. There is a social component to the adrenalin rush numerous military personnel share following a combat tour.

Journalist Sebastian Junger, co-director of the film *Restrepo* and author of *Tribe* (Junger, 2016), wrote about the alienation many veterans experience on returning from war in comparison to the bond experienced by soldiers in combat. He suggests the rate of posttraumatic stress disorder (PTSD) among military personnel is caused more by the loss of attachment bonds among servicemembers returning home than the intensity of their combat trauma. Research by Escolas et al. (2012) found attachment styles were correlated with PTSD after deployments. Once home, secure attachment styles among veterans were associated with fewer reported symptoms of PTSD. It is suggested that attachment may be associated with protection from PTSD.

The military structure with its defined organization, roles, duty responsibilities, and boundaries removes much ambiguity to the sense of belonging. Military personnel wear badges and patches to uniform clothing indicating they belong. Strong cohesion is developed within units who endure both intensive training and danger. Unit cohesion has been correlated with less mental health pathology (Junger, 2016).

Anniversary dates and occasions when members of the unit were killed become embedded in servicemembers' personal awareness. Wrist bracelets and tattoos memorialize the life of persons lost in combat noting the date the loss happened. The strength of attachment bonds correlate with the severity of grief at the time of loss. Many veterans carry unresolved grief due to the loss of their military friends. Guilt and anger are often components of grief. Unresolved grief is often managed with avoidance until the anniversary dates of their death. Frequently, on anniversary dates veterans review their photos and watch YouTube videos of combat operations and contact their buddies to discuss those times together. Family members and therapists learn to prepare for these dates while assisting the veteran to address the loss in healthy ways. Unresolved grief is one of the most common psychological wounds among veterans. If left unresolved, the grief becomes normalized as part of the servicemember's life experience. The wounds of unresolved grief can be numerous among our servicemembers. Therapists treating these populations learn to identify losses in the person's life, including anniversary dates when friends were killed, as part of the client's initial history-taking phase. Persons medically retired may grieve over the loss of identity in a warrior culture, while struggling with physical and psychological limitations.

Members of the military population learn of the culture during basic training. The military environment influences every servicemember to: (a) take initiative (lead, follow, or get out of the way!); (b) be responsible; (c) be competitive in pushing oneself to the limit; (d) place teamwork before individual needs; (e) maintain military bearing; (f) pay attention to detail; (g) maintain uniformity; (h) remember that individual mistakes cost everyone; (i) be ready for quick action; (j) note that punishment for screwing up may include the entire team; (k) obey (follow orders); and (l) learn to manage caustic comments.

Combat veterans exhibit common survival characteristics. When entering a room, many prefer to sit facing the door with their back to the wall. A number of infantry soldiers describe their plan to respond to any threat before they are seated in a room. Using risk assessment, they assess the risk level and have a response plan in case they are attacked. In office waiting rooms and public places, veterans monitor the activities continually evaluating the threat level—always with a plan in case an attack happens.

Military bearing describes how a servicemember carries themselves, straight and erect, as well as the briskness of the walk. Servicemembers are taught in basic training (boot camp for Marines) to always walk at a brisk pace as if you have somewhere to go. Present yourself as a person on a mission. In fact, basic training usually begins with the recruit having to run everywhere when they are outdoors. The pace of walking is ingrained in everyone who has served in the military. Years later, while walking with a nonmilitary partner, the partner notices the veteran does not slow down when walking, even when accompanying a partner to social engagements. Veterans, when aware, often work to slow down, but find themselves spontaneously walking faster again.

Present awareness and risk assessment of the current situation is a part of military life. The more threatening a veteran perceives the situation, the more vigilant or hypervigilant their response will be. Some persons regulate the anxiety of exposure in public places by monitoring their social activities. Feeling in control of the situation eases anxiety. If the effort to monitor their activity becomes too challenging, the veteran will likely socially withdraw as a means of controlling the environment. This means avoiding unnecessary shopping or shopping in the early hours of the morning when the least number of shoppers are present. Avoiding shopping malls or supermarkets is a strategy for narrowing the circle of activity in order to maintain security. If the amount of stimuli lessens with social withdrawal, the servicemember feels more in control of the situation. In one case a senior NCO, now living back in the states but suffering with severe psychological wounds due to multiple combat deployments, refused to leave his apartment to buy groceries. Instead, he ordered diet meals from Jenny Craig, which were delivered to his apartment. The NCO felt secure enough to function in his duties while at his assignment on base but not in open shopping areas. Shopping areas reminded him of the danger of open marketplaces where suicide bombers would kill people. His perceived risk in a public marketplace was more than he was willing to endure even when back home. He was easily triggered when seeing someone whose clothes reminded him of his combat environment.

Veterans, especially persons with stress-related difficulties, prefer routine activities rather than novel situations since new situations require additional psychological strain in conducting risk assessment. Seeking treatment can be a stressful experience. Meeting a new person such as a receptionist and therapist as well as monitoring the threat level in a strange environment, such as a waiting room, can be fatiguing for a person suffering with complex trauma. The threat level of a waiting room is further enhanced with the awareness that veterans have killed themselves at Department of Veterans Affairs facilities, a place where veterans seek help. Predictable routines reduce stress; the possibility of unpredictable events happening adds to the stress.

Military personnel tend to arrive for their appointment early. They are taught that arriving at the time of the appointment means they are late; therefore, they need to arrive 15 to 20 minutes early. There have been many couples who argue when the partner did not understand this rule and prepared to arrive just at the time of the appointment. Couple spats also occur when the soldier places the head gear (cap) and gloves at a place only to find they have been moved the following morning when it is time to leave for morning formation. The soldier reacts as if the situation is a matter of life or death because down range, in a combat environment, time can determine life or death. Taking unnecessary time to hunt for equipment can be a matter of life and death down range when under attack.

Veterans, back from combat, express few emotions, except for anger. Warriors on combat missions consider anger as a gift. It allows the warrior to feel empowered. Other emotions get in the way of this functioning, so they are turned down during deployments. In relationships back home, the partner may begin to question if they are still loved based on the servicemember's lack of emotional expression. The servicemember, oblivious to the emotional distancing, continues to maintain the same response exhibited during the past year of deployment. This is an attempt to maintain a sense of normalcy. The stressors associated with the need to adapt and adjust now that the servicemember is home frequently contribute to the military client's wish to be back over there, a place where life did not require so much adjustment. "It was easier there!"

Returning home requires learning another routine, adjusting to time differences, and remembering to be attentive to other people's feelings. When faced with life or death every day, the concept of someone getting their feelings hurt may seem pathetic to the warrior! It is too far up Maslow's hierarchy of needs to contend with in combat. You can't just say something straightforward any longer because those you care about will get their feelings hurt—then you have to expend more time and effort making amends! This can be exhausting for the servicemember and family members. The degree of stress from combat missions determines how stressful returning home can be for the servicemember. For some persons, returning home is a well sought dream for returning to loved ones. Others, particularly those with psychological wounds from repetitive exposure to combat, find daily living back home can be emotionally challenging. Many servicemembers believe the daily routine in combat was easier. An infantry sergeant told me, "The Army taught me my job in the infantry was to put as many rounds as possible down range. Now that I am home, I want to have some positive conversation with my wife. We sit down to talk and then, the first thing we disagree on, I lay down overwhelming suppressing fire verbally. Next thing I know, she is mad, won't speak to me and I am left questioning, 'what did I just do?'"

UNDERSTANDING THOSE WHO RUN TOWARD DANGER

> *"When we go into battle, I will be the first one to set foot on the field, and I will be the last to step off. And I will leave no one behind. Dead or alive, we will come home together. So help me God."*
>
> —LT. CO. HAL MOORE, AUGUST 1965, FORT BENNING, GEORGIA

This statement was made by then Lieutenant Colonel Hal Moore when addressing his soldiers at Fort Benning, Georgia, before deploying to Vietnam. Military personnel and first responders are sometimes identified as *those who run toward danger rather than away from it!* It is a person's core values and mental focusing that allows them to accomplish the mission while managing emotions. They focuses on the assigned duty while ignoring emotions that could interfere with the mission. *The mission comes first! Thoughts or feelings are not as important as accomplishing the mission.* This approach allowed firefighters to run into New York City's collapsing twin towers on 9-11. It was also present in military officers such as Lt. Colonel Moore, battalion commander of the 7th Cavalry, who would later lead his troops in an extensive battle at la Drang, Vietnam. The same core values continue to guide servicemembers today. Sky Soldiers with the 173rd Airborne Brigade had the mission of maintaining a forward operating base (FOB) in the Korengal Valley of Afghanistan, a place considered one of the deadliest in Afghanistan. They held their ground in spite of being daily rocketed, mortared, and shot at throughout their entire mission. Numerous service personnel from all branches of the military confront these challenges routinely.

Providing effective treatment to military and veteran populations provides therapists the opportunity to learn about the uniqueness of their clientele. Establishing rapport is multidirectional; the client in your office is attempting to understand you and your work environment while at the same time you are working to develop a therapeutic relationship. It is important to recognize how difficult it is for your client to be in your office. Your office is familiar terrain to you; however, it is unchartered territory to your client. Unfamiliar areas are considered a threat to one's well-being until proven otherwise. Negotiating the security of your office is important to your client.

## MILITARY CORE VALUES

Understanding what molds the character and influences the essence of the military women and men in your office is an important part of your clinical preparation. The military culture molds character. This process begins for military personnel at the induction center as every new inductee takes the Oath of Enlistment. All U.S. military personnel swear to support and defend the Constitution. The Constitution is the source of the military's authority as represented by the American people, those duly elected and appointed representatives, and the officers in command, as well as other personnel entrusted with executing orders. The first oath of enlistment was established in 1775. Today's military oath of enlistment was established on October 5, 1962, which replaced some of the original wording contained in the 1775 and 1780 editions. Listed here is the oath of office for enlisted military servicemembers:

> I, _____, do solemnly swear (or affirm) that I will support or defend the Constitution of the United States against all enemies, foreign and domestic; that I will bear true faith and allegiance to the same; and that I will obey the orders of the President of the United States and the orders of the officers appointed over me, according to regulations and the Uniform Code of Military Justice. So help me God.

> U.S. ARMY CENTER OF MILITARY HISTORY (N.D.)

Both enlisted and officer oaths require the person to swear (or affirm) they will defend the Constitution of the United States, to adhere faith and allegiance to it, and obey the orders of the president and superior officers in accordance with the UCMJ. This swearing in occurs before the person begins basic training. Basic training immerses a person into a military community where physical development, introductory knowledge of military traditions and culture, and military skill development are provided.

Military servicemembers are held to high standards. The military culture is based on tradition, ethos, values, and the structure and leadership of the military organization. Subcultures represented by the various branches of service evolve from national goals. Each branch of the military has its own history, rules, regulations, operating procedures, and perspectives.

Ethos is the spirit or national character from which values emerge. For example, the ethos of the U.S. Army is identified by the following statements: (a) I will always place the mission first; (b) I will never accept defeat; (c) I will never quit; and (d) I will never leave a fallen comrade (U.S. Army, n.d.-b).

On an individual level, core values provide the structure for servicemembers to move into action, while the mission requirement fuels the motivation, and mental processing presents the means to accomplish the mission. Those same values establish a person's priority both on duty and off duty. Priorities influence the use of a person's time, what they do, the interaction with other persons with whom they spend their time, and how they define the relationships. Values clarify what is acceptable and expected for individuals and those units they serve. Later in life, when a person reviews their military service, they use the same values to evaluate their service. The servicemember becomes acculturated to the military values as they are lived 24/7 in the military environment. Servicemembers live and breathe the values. Common guidance and unit cohesion is integrated into the entire unit as its members subscribe to those core values.

Each branch of the military has its own list of core values (Table 1.1). The values provide an organizational structure in the training and de-

## TABLE 1.1 Core Values: Branches of Military Service in the United States and Canada

| U.S. Army | U.S. Navy/ U.S. Marines | U.S. Coast Guard | U.S. Air Force | Canadian Forces |
|---|---|---|---|---|
| • Loyalty | • Honor | • Honor | • Integrity first | • Integrity |
| • Duty | • Courage | • Respect | • Service before self | • Loyalty |
| • Respect | • Commitment | • Devotion to duty | • Excellence in all we do | • Courage |
| • Selfless service | | | | • Stewardship |
| • Honor | | | | • Excellence |
| • Integrity | | | | |
| • Personal courage | | | | |

*Sources*: Department of National Defence and Canadian Forces. (2012). *Code of values and ethics*. Retrieved from http://www.forces.gc.ca/assets/FORCES_Internet/docs/en/about/code-eng.pdf; U.S. Air Force. (n.d.). *Air Force core values*. Retrieved from https://www.airforcemomsbmt.org/AirForceCoreValues.htm; U.S. Army. (n.d.-a). *Army core values*. Retrieved from https://www.army.mil/values; U.S. Navy. (2009). *U.S. Navy core values*. Retrieved from https://www.navy.mil/navydata/nav_legacy.asp?id=193; U.S. Coast Guard. (n.d.). "Introduction". Retrieved from https://www.gocoastguard.com/family-and-friends/the-helmsman/introduction.

velopment of its members. While the EMDR therapist interacts with the client's clinical presentation, much of the unspoken attitudes and expectations are driven by the core values taught and lived within the military culture. Most veterans judge themselves by the standards of the core values.

The task of training hundreds of thousands of military personnel to perform their duties in a specific manner begins with entry-level training including character development along with combat skill development. Each branch of the military, from every nation, has its own standards and core values. For example, the U.S. Army lists seven core values. The U.S. Navy, Marines, Air Force, and Coast Guard each embrace three core values. There are five core values listed by the Canadian armed forces. Entry-level basic training introduces military personnel to the core values of their service branch. Those values assist in establishing priorities and accomplishing effective decision-making, mission readiness, and performance standards. Later, during periods of transition, those ethical guidelines represented by the core values are used to provide guidance.

Guidelines provide direction to military personnel for managing situations within their military experience. They also provide a tension between the ideal and the daily challenge of life amidst the chaos of combat. The Armed Forces Code of Conduct (U.S. Government Printing Office, 1958) was developed following the Korean conflict when the Pentagon learned that as many as three out of five American prisoners of war (POWs) may have cooperated with the enemy. Later, during the Vietnam War, POWs such as James Stockdale, a Navy pilot shot down and held captive in the Hanoi Hilton POW camp for 7 years, described how aspects of the Code of Conduct were challenging to maintain where he was imprisoned. The directive to only provide "name, rank, and serial number" was difficult for many prisoners who were tortured at the Hanoi Hilton prison camp. The enemy used forced confessions against the American war effort. Jeremiah Denton, another naval aviator held captive for more than 7 years in North Vietnam, was forced to make anti-American statements all the while using the blinking of his eyes to send a Morse Code message "torture." POWs were caught between the ideal values of their military training and coping with some of the most inhumanly inflicted pain imposed by their captors. Military core values have been emphasized, particularly following the moral failures of My Lai during the Vietnam War and the moral crisis at Abu Ghraib prison during Operation Iraqi Freedom (OIF). The war policy during OIF led to the "revolt of the generals" when more than 20 American generals defied military tradition to publicly criticize the administration's policy in the conducting of the war in Iraq (Sauer, 2007). Such moral crises within the military have historically required emphasizing the core values within the military branches of service. The emphasis on core values mediates the ethical and moral failures during the chaos of war. Publications such as *A Brief History of Army Values* (Center for the Army Profession and Ethic, 2018) highlight the variations in recognition of the military service branches' core values. The teaching of core values has become an important part of guiding the military force.

Core values maintain the moral and ethical climates of the armed forces. Understanding these values assists psychotherapists in understanding the military culture of their military and veteran clients.

The Canadian Armed Forces' Code of Values and Ethics, published by the Department of National Defense (DND) and Canadian Forces (CF), outlines three ethical principles for the CF: (a) Respect the dignity of all persons; (b) serve Canada before self; and (c) obey and support lawful authority.

The values and behaviors expected of members of the CF and DND include (a) integrity, (b) loyalty, (c) courage, (d) stewardship, and (e) excellence. Detailed information regarding the ethical principles and code of values is published in *Code of Values and Ethics* available online (DND and CF, 2012). Members of the CF who fail to comply with the ethical principles, values or expected behavior, or other policies outlined in the Defense Administrative Orders and Directives (DAOD) can be subject to: change of duty; release or other administrative action; or disciplinary action under the Canadian National Defense Act (Department of National Defence and Canadian Forces, 2012).

These values represent the heart and soul of every servicemember even when they are so subtle the therapist has to search to find them. Understanding the values, along with the ability to incorporate them, has the ability to strengthen the therapeutic relationship while motivating the treatment process.

## STOICISM IN THE MILITARY CULTURE

Professor Nancy Sherman, a moral philosopher with past teaching assignments at the U.S. Naval Academy, called Stoicism "the philosophy behind the warrior mind" (Sherman, 2005, p. 12). Understanding the thinking behind the warrior mind is helpful in treating the military population. Founded by the Greek philosopher Zeno of Citium in the third century BCE, Stoics came to represent a philosophical approach to life which provided followers a practical sense of self-command, self-reliance, resilience, and moral autonomy while encouraging cardinal virtues such as temperance, wisdom, and courage (Sellars, 2006). These qualities are attractive to many military personnel. Its teachings have influenced leaders ranging from the Roman emperor Marcus Aurelius and Fredrick the Great to today's military leaders.

George Washington was a student of the Stoic philosopher Cato the Younger. By the time Washington wrote his farewell address, he embedded several quotations from Cato into his speech (Stockdale, 1993). During the early development of Washington's Continental Army, Prussian officer Friedrich Wilhelm Rudolf Gerhard August Freiherr von Steuben arrived at the Valley Forge encampment to begin training soldiers in close-order drill. His strict training and discipline instilled new confidence and discipline in the demoralized army. The philosophical ideas and military theories of Fredrick the Great and his army were modeled to the fledgling Continental Army of the United States by von Steuben. Since von Steuben did not speak English, his manual of drill was written in French and translated into English by Alexander Hamilton and Nathanael Greene. The Prussian drills outlined in the manual provided organization structure as well as guidelines in executing a standard of living. Under von Steuben, Washington's shoeless soldiers practiced battle drills of firing and reloading their weapons until it became second nature, what we know today as muscle memory (von Steuben, 2018; Lockhart, 2008). The military successes learned under the Stoic king Fredrick the Great were taught to young America's Continental Army.

Both Fredrick the Great and Marine general James Mattis were known to carry copies of Marcus Aurelius' *Meditations* (Duncan, 2017) with them during military operations. Marine General James Mattis, the former U.S. Secretary of Defense, immersed himself in the philosophy of Marcus Aurelius with regular readings in the *Meditations* (Ricks, 2017). Like Fredrick the Great, General Mattis was known to carry a copy of *Meditations* with him on all his deployments including carrying it while leading Marines into battle in Iraq during OIF (Poser, 2018; Ricks, 2017). Even in the first nights of the military's push into Iraq, at the beginning of OIF in 2003, the general was known to clear his mind during a 4-hour rest break by reading from Marcus Aurelius' *Meditations*. Those who spent time with General Mattis learned he was fond of the writings of Shakespeare, Aurelius' *Meditations*, the Prussian military theorist Carl von Clausewitz, and the Chinese military strategist Sun Tzu (Dilanian, 2010). The *Meditations* was listed in General Mattis' recommended reading for leaders (Sicard, 2017).

Medal of Honor recipient James Stockdale, a U.S. Navy pilot shot down over North Vietnam and held prisoner in Hanoi for over 7 years, gave credit to the Stoic philosopher Epictetus' *Enchiridion* for helping him survive his prison torture 15 times, with 4 years of placement in solitary confinement, and being in leg irons for 2 years. Later promoted to Navy vice admiral and recognized as one of the Navy's most highly decorated officers in history, Stockdale recalled thinking, "I'm leaving the world of technology and entering the world of Epictetus" (Stockdale, 1995, p. 7) as his aircraft was shot down and he parachuted to a North Vietnamese village where he was severely beaten and taken prisoner. Stockdale credited Epictetus' teachings in *Enchiridion* for his survival as a POW.

Stockdale identified with Epictetus as he was placed in leg irons as a POW similar to Epictetus suffering with a disabled leg. While Epictetus wrote nothing, his assistant Arria recorded "Sickness is a hindrance to the body, but not to your ability to choose, unless that is your choice. Lameness is a hindrance to the leg, but not to your ability to choose. Say this to yourself regarding everything that happens, then you will see such obstacles as hindrances to something else, but not to yourself" (Stockdale, 1993).

The basic teachings of Stoicism that influence military culture include:

- Stoicism teaches a person to recognize what they can change and what they have no control over.
- Stoicism emphasizes the situation is not the problem but a person's judgment of the situation.
- Stoicism teaches concentration on what a person can control. It is referred to as the "cultivation of the 'inner citadel' of the soul."
- The early Stoics took a hard line on emotions while later Stoics took a more moderate recognition of them (Farnsworth, 2018). Stoics do not reject emotions but whether passions interfere with good judgment. Distinguishing the difference between emotions and passions, the Stoics view the issue as whether emotions unseat reason. Do they blur the perspective leading the person to make misjudgments? Though a skeptic, Seneca did not dismiss emotions if they were controlled by reason. He did consider anger to be a blight on the human race.
- Fear was viewed as a feeling which could sometimes interfere with reason and judgment. Fear is viewed as making situations worse by interfering with our judgment and causing us to think and do foolish and cowardly things. It spoils the pleasure of the moment. From the Stoic perspective, fears are opinions about what is yet to come.
- Stoics consider overcoming the fear of death important. Death is an inevitable event along the continuum of life. What we must overcome is not death but the way we think about it (Seneca, 2004, *Epistles*, 82.15–16). Freedom from the fear of death is considered a central goal by many Stoics.
- Grief was viewed by Seneca as an unavoidable response to loss. He felt it natural and appropriate to have grief feelings for a while, then reason with them. The Stoic believed it was better to reason with feelings of grief than avoid them or distract oneself (Seneca, 2015, *Consolation to Helvia*, 16.1). Emotions born of grief were seen as ungovernable.
- Stoics seek to avoid adversity like anyone else would do. Adversity is a fact of life—it comes regardless. The goal is to view adversity correctly so a person's peace of mind would not be destroyed by its arrival.

Military personnel exhibit characteristics that are sometimes described as being Stoic. In general, military lifestyles often imply a person to be self-contained, downplay emotions, and focus on doing one's duty. Such characteristics are integrated into the military lifestyle of most militaries worldwide. Beyond this generic philosophical description of military characteristics, it is recognized that military leaders have publicly endorsed Stoicism as being recommended reading for officers (General James Mattis) as well as teaching resiliency for POWs (James Stockdale) and soldiers in combat (Peter Ryan). The philosophy offers guidelines to military personnel regarding how to maintain a keen perspective on what matters even in the heat of battle, how to handle emotions and passions, and how to be the master of one's own actions.

It is suggested the philosophy of Stoicism can empower a person to be more resilient and at peace with themselves (Nauvall, 2019.). Stoicism teaches a person to recognize a sense of dignity even when stripped of most resources in their experience as demonstrated by the imprisonment of POWs such as James Stockdale. The external environment does not control a person's sense of well-being. It is mind over matter as the soldier cannot control the situation, but the soldier can control their response to the situation. The philosophy reduces the sense of vulnerability while endorsing a person's robust will to succeed. It's the "can-do" attitude with the ability to "suck it up and drive on" attitude that is embraced by the warrior. McMaster, retired U.S. Army general and former National Security Advisor, suggested the development of Stoic-like resilience and fortitude for self-control can offer significant value in reducing combat stress (McMaster, 2008). The appeal of Stoic philosophy among military leaders can be evidenced in the basic teachings which, when applied to military missions, assist military personnel in maintaining a clear focus on areas they can influence.

## CLINICAL ISSUES FOR UNDERSTANDING THE VETERAN

### COMPARTMENTALIZATION AND SURVIVAL ON THE BATTLEFIELD

Compartmentalization is a psychological coping strategy, a dissociative response to manage mental discomfort and anxiety created by a person's conflicting internal views. It allows conflicting views to coexist by inhibiting their acknowledgment and interaction. A warrior engaged in combat cannot allow himself to recall tender moments with his children; such a mental process would impede his focus on the combat mission. Memories of times with his children are reserved for times when he has completed his duty for the day/night and feels safe enough to allow such thoughts. Even then, tender thoughts of loved ones back home can become depressing, so the warrior deals with the duality of family memories versus current reality of war by compartmentalizing those memories.

A combat veteran sat in my office agonizing over the dichotomy he felt after serving six combat deployments now that he is back in the world. When discussing the effects of combat on his life he speaks of the guilt he feels. "It is like trying to swallow glass," he says. He is a warrior whose past 12 years have been in a combat zone or preparing to go back to one. His only self-affirmation is describing his survival skills in combat. A week before he was at his local bank waiting to conduct business with the branch manager. After waiting a few minutes. watching her shuffle papers through the glass partition to her office, he impulsively walked into her office with intense anger, dropping F-bombs and accusing her of ignoring him as a customer. "I knew I had made a mistake as soon as I opened my mouth, but I could not stop or withdraw the words coming out of my mouth," the veteran stated. Describing his dual life he said, "The person I let people see – the 'Hi! How are you?' is not who I am. Who I am they don't want to know. They would be afraid of that person!"

Military personnel are required to manage very dichotomous life experiences. The life they live during a combat deployment is very different than the social life back home. Risk assessment and situational awareness are ongoing processes during deployment. Life-threatening experiences are always possibilities. When asked when he felt safe during deployment, a 12-year veteran replied "Never!" The reality of death is apparent, yet personnel learn to avoid focusing on that reality. Combat operations with close-call, near-death experiences are managed, so they are not held in the forefront of mental focus. This is accomplished through compartmentalization.

Historically, compartmentalization, referring to veterans being trapped in traumatized memories, has been recognized among combat veterans since the post-Vietnam era. Different terms have been used to describe the parts of personality structure in compartmentalization. The warrior persona was referred to as "Survivor mode" in contrast to "normal personality functioning" by Figley (1978). A decade later, Laufer (1988) called the components of compartmentalization the "war self" in comparison to an "adaptive self." The Structural Dissociation model (van der Hart, Nijenhuis, & Steele, 2006), building on the 1940 work of Charles Myers, identified the civilized, socially interactive part as the Apparently Normal Part (ANP) of self and the reactive survivor part as the emotional part (EP). These compartmentalized parts sometimes develop during childhood; at other times, compartmentalization develops during adulthood due to repetitive, life-threatening events of war. Social and psychological adjustments between life in the war zone and the routines back home can create significant adjustment problems for military personnel, similar to the veteran described previously.

When the adjustments are challenging, the servicemember sometimes longs to be back in the combat area "where things are routine."

## THREE MOST IMPORTANT QUESTIONS IN THE INITIAL SESSION

Clients who experience a lack of control in their life describe feeling more vulnerability. Emotionally they need to experience additional security. The therapist can address this important issue early in the initial session by asking the client, *"What do you need to feel secure in this room?"* Sometimes the client wishes to have the window blinds open to monitor the outside or adjust the lighting in the room. The question conveys to the client that the therapist is aware of his needs and attentive to addressing them. This question provides the building block for developing trust and rapport in the therapeutic relationship.

The second important question in the first session is, *"What do you want to change as a result of being here?"* The client's answer to this question helps develop the treatment goal. This is what brings the client in for treatment. Prior to my learning EMDR therapy, I would ask the client a similar question, "How will you know when your treatment is finished?" The EMDR treatment plan is developed around the client's reason for seeking treatment. Clients are more motivated to keep their appointment and invest in its outcome when they know each session is directly connected to their reason for seeking therapy.

A third question, as a follow-up to the previous question, also asked in the initial session is *"Would it be okay to get over this?"* This question asks about the client's motivation for treatment as well as identifying any potential secondary gain issues. On one occasion, a soldier answered me by stating she was going through a compensatory evaluation and wished to delay her treatment until she completed her evaluation. EMDR therapy will only accomplish what the client wants done (as a treatment goal). It would have been a waste of time to have treated her before she was ready for change.

## DISTORTED PERCEPTIONS

The more severe the pathology in your client, the greater the perceptual distortions the client has toward you. Learning of the dissociative experiences among military and veteran populations has taught me that many clients view me through their distorted lens. While I view myself one way, the client sees me based on their own experiences. Persons who view the world as a threat are likely to view their therapist as a potential threat in some manner. Reasons for distrust can sometimes be stronger than trust. Thus, the previous question, "What do you need to feel secure in this room?" is an important question, especially among persons with dissociative experiences who feel unable to control their own responses to being triggered. Additionally, inquiring about the success of other previous treatments is important. Clients report that the consistency of previous treatment programs has varied. While many dedicated psychotherapists work to provide effective treatment, the continuity of treatment is not always ideal. Warriors report having previously been treated at facilities where appointments were cancelled by the clinic at the last minute or met with a different psychiatrist or psychotherapist each session; these actions are likely to make clients unsure of the integrity of their treatment. Servicemembers who were previously treated with appointments 1 and 2 months apart reach the conclusion that what is offered is not effective or they are not important enough to be treated effectively. If they were previously treated unsuccessfully at other facilities, their trust and hope in your services is likely to be guarded. Inadequate treatment at other facilities diminished the client's hope in ever being effectively treated. Your sincerity, authenticity, and clinical skills will likely be viewed with uncertainty until the client experiences the benefits of your work as an EMDR therapist.

## WHEN SUICIDE IS ALWAYS AN OPTION

It is always important to check with your client regarding any suicidality. Specifically, do they have thoughts, a plan, and the means to complete the plan? If so, immediate action is needed to get the client the help they need. Veterans living with both chronic physical and psychological pain, who are desensitized to dying, and sometimes view death as a relief, a condition needing intervention as early as possible. The timing of intervention has changed in the past decades. Some veterans today will not agree to a no-harm contract, yet they need intervention. A veteran who had just been discharged from an inpatient hospital program for his third suicide attempt stated to me, "If you ask me to promise not to kill myself, I can't promise. For me, suicide is always an option!" Many military personnel with extensive exposure to combat-related deaths seem to have become desensitized to death. Some veterans report the thoughts of death provide a sense of relief, at least at times when they suffer with physical and psychological pain. Past directions of getting a no-harm contract from the client before they can be treated does not work with some members of this population. Rather, ensuring the client has adequate support networks and is open to developing hope for the future may be the best possible context to begin treatment. For example, the previously listed veteran said to me at the end of his initial session, "I don't want you to give up hope on me doc!" I replied, "I won't give up hope on you if you do not give up hope on me." He replied "Roger that!" and we proceeded with the treatment. His treatment was successful, and he is now actively engaged in community activities with his family. Hopelessness has been correlated with suicide (Beck, Kovacs, & Weissman, 1976; Beck, Brown, Berchick, Stewart, & Steer, 2006.). Effective treatment provided in a timely manner builds hope.

## CONCLUSION

The information in this chapter provides a gateway for learning about the uniqueness of the military environment, including its language, structure, and operations. It is a culture with a basic military language and the continual development of new acronyms. No one knows all the military acronyms. Instead, we learn the language we need to know for the clients we treat. Our clients teach us. Every military client has their own experience, their own history. If you are unfamiliar with the military, I encourage you to ask your client when there is something you don't understand. Persons who have a familiarity with this population are likely to find the material offered in this chapter a description of a family, sometimes challenging, at times affirming—with many memories representing a part of their life. The most difficult times are recalled with appreciation. Asking a client about their unique experiences can be empowering for the client and builds stronger bonds. This information sets the groundwork for understanding your military client through all phases of EMDR therapy.

### DISCUSSION POINTS

1. In what ways does attachment influence a servicemember's ability to self-regulate?
2. How does attachment influence a person's sense of loss?
3. Is there a core value that stands out to you as being one of the most important?
4. What core value influences a person doing what they are expected to do?
5. Why is Stoicism appealing to some military leaders?
6. What key questions are suggested for use in the initial session?
7. Is compartmentalization healthy?
8. When can you treat a veteran who says "Suicide is always an option?"

### REFERENCES

Beck, A., Kovacs, M., & Weissman, A. (1976). Hopelessness and suicide behavior: An overview. *Journal of the American Medical Association, 234*(11), 1146–1149.

Beck, A., Brown, G., Berchick, R. Stewart, B., & Steer, R. (2006). Relationship between hopelessness and ultimate suicide: A replication with psychiatric outpatients. *Focus on Psychiatry, 4*(2), 291–296.

Campbell, M., Ryan, M., Wright, D., Devore, M., & Hoge, C. (2016). Postdeployment PTSD and addictive combat attachment behaviors in U.S. military service members. *American Journal of Psychiatry, 173*, 1171–1176. doi:10.1176/appi.ajp.2015.1501297

Center for the Army Profession and Ethic. (2018). *A brief history of the army values*. Retrieved from https://caccapl.blob.core.usgovcloudapi.net/web/character-development-project/repository/a-brief-history-of-the-army-values.pdf

Department of National Defence and Canadian Forces. (2012). *Code of values and ethics*. Retrieved from http://www.forces.gc.ca/assets/FORCES_Internet/docs/en/about/code-eng.pdf

Dilanian, K. (2010, July 8). Marines' Mattis to take over Central Command. *The Seattle Times*. Retrieved from https://www.seattletimes.com/nation-world/marines-mattis-to-take-over-central-command

Duncan, A. (2017). *Stoic philosophy for military leaders*. Retrieved from https://medium.com/@alex.duncan/stoic-philosophy-for-military-leaders-baf3b8d56a90

Escolas, S., Arata-Maiers, R., Hildebrandt, E., Maiers, A., Mason, S., & Baker, M. (2012). The impact of attachment style on posttraumatic stress disorder symptoms in postdeployed military members. *U.S. Army Medical Department Journal*, 54–61.

Farnsworth, W. (2018). *The practicing Stoic: A philosophical user's manual*. Jaffrey, NH: David R. Godine Publisher.

Figley, C. (1978). *Stress disorders among Vietnam veterans: Theory, research*. New York, NY: Brunner-Routledge.

Junger, S. (2016). *Tribe: On homecoming and belonging*. New York, NY: Hachette Book Group.

Laufer, R. (1988). The serial self: War trauma, identity, and adult development. In J. Wilson, Z. Harel, & B. Kahana (Eds.), *Human adaptation to extreme stress: From the Holocaust to Vietnam* (pp. 33–54). New York, NY: Springer.

Lockhart, Pl. (2008). *The drillmaster of Valley Forge: The Baron de Steuben and the making of the American Army*. New York, NY: Harper Collins.

McMaster, H. (2008, August–September). Survival. Ancient lessons for today's soldiers. *Survival, 50*(4), 177–190. doi:10.1080/00396330802329071

Moore, H. (2011). *Vietnam War hero offers leadership lessons*. Retrieved from https://americanprofile.com/articles/leadership-lessons-list-from-vietnam-veteran

Nauvall, J. (2019). Stoicism: The ultimate guide for beginners to improve self-discipline, mental toughness, leadership, wisdom, resilience, inner peace for living a good life, based on the stoics philosophy. Self published by author Jonathan Nauvall.

Poser, J. (2018). *No better friend, no worse enemy: The life of General James Mattis*. New York, NY: Broadside Books.

Ricks, T. (2017, February 17). The tragedy of James Mattis. Retrieved from https://foreignpolicy.com/2017/02/17/the-tragedy-of-james-mattis

Sauer, M. (2007, September 27). The revolt of the generals: Generals opposing Iraq war break with military tradition. *Global Tribune.* Retrieved from https://www.globalresearch.ca/the-revolt-of-the-generals-generals-opposing-iraq-war-break-with-military-tradition/6920

Sellars, J. (2006). Stoicism (Ancient Philosophies). Vol. 1. New York: Routledge.

Seneca, L. A. (2004). *Letters from a Stoic.* New York, NY: Penguin Books.

Seneca, L. A. (2015). *Selected dialogues and consolations* (P. Anderson, Trans.). Indianapolis, IN: Hackett Publishing.

Sherman, N. (2005). Stoic warriors: The ancient philosophy behind the military mind. New York, NY: Oxford University Press.

Sicard, S. (2017, April 2). 30 Books Mattis thinks every good leader needs to read. *Task and Purpose.* Retrieved from https://taskandpurpose.com/30-books-mattis-thinks-every-good-leader-needs-read

Stockdale, J. (1993). *Courage under fire: Testing Epictetus's doctrines in a laboratory of human behavior.* Stanford, CA: Hoover Institution, Stanford University.

Stockdale, J. (1995). *Stockdale on Stoicism II: Master of my fate* (U.S. Naval Academy). Retrieved from https://www.usna.edu/Ethics/_files/documents/Stoicism2.pdf

U.S. Air Force. (n.d.). *Air Force core values.* Retrieved from https://www.airforcemomsbmt.org/AirForceCoreValues.htm

U.S. Army. (n.d.-a). *Army core values.* Retrieved from https://www.army.mil/values

U.S. Army. (n.d.-b). *Lifestyles: Living the Army values: Ethos.* Retrieved from https://www.goarmy.com/soldier-life/being-a-soldier/living-the-army-values.html

U.S. Army. (2011). *Warrior ethos.* Retrieved from https://www.army.mil/article/50082/warrior_ethos

U.S. Army Center of Military History. (n.d.). *Oaths of enlistment and oaths of office.* Retrieved from https://history.army.mil/html/faq/oaths.html

U.S. Coast Guard. (n.d.). "Introduction". Retrieved from https://www.gocoastguard.com/family-and-friends/the-helmsman/introduction

U.S. Government Printing Office. (1958). *Code of conduct for members of the armed forces of the United States.* Washington, DC. Retrieved from https://www.archives.gov/federal-register/codification/executive-order/10631.html

U.S. Navy. (2009). *U.S. Navy core values.* Retrieved from https://www.secnav.navy.mil/Ethics/Pages/corevaluescharter.aspx#:~:text=As%20in%20our%20past%2C%20we,continue%20to%20guide%20us%20today.

van der Hart, O., Nijenhuis, E., & Steele, K. (2006). *The haunted self: Structural dissociation and the treatment of chronic traumatization.* New York: W.W. Norton & Co.

von Steuben, F. (n.d.). A letter on the subject of an established militia and military arrangements: Addressed to the inhabitants of the United States. New York, NY: Sabin Americana.

# 2

# Introducing EMDR Therapy to Your Client: Gateway to History-Taking

## Introduction

This chapter provides a prelude to EMDR Therapy's History-Taking. As a gateway to history-taking, it provides the necessary opportunities in establishing the groundwork for effective therapy. It may require 15 minutes or two sessions, depending on the complexity of the client's symptoms. This period begins with the initial client–therapist meeting and continues until the beginning of Phase 1 History-Taking. Successful negotiation of this period allows for addressing the client's security needs; the ability to feel in control of their response; establishment of mutual respect; the beginning of the client-centered, therapist-directed approach; the beginning of trust and rapport; and addressing what the client wants to be different by being at your office (treatment goals), The development of trust and rapport begins here. These are all important components of establishing the necessary basis for effective EMDR therapy.

## Learning Objectives

- Discuss establishing a meaningful therapeutic environment for effective EMDR therapy.
- Identify the roles of mutual respect, trust, and rapport in the treatment of the veteran and military populations.
- Review case examples for establishing an effective treatment environment among veterans with avoidance issues and suicidal thoughts.
- Learn effective approaches in identifying the client's treatment goals.

## THE GATEWAY TO TREATMENT

The chapter highlights the gateway for establishing effective treatment with the client. This is the introductory period for transitioning the client into treatment. It may require 15 minutes or 2 hours, depending on the complexity of the client's symptoms. Much of the EMDR therapy literature presents this period as subsumed under Phase 1 History-Taking. However, due to the importance of this period, this chapter is provided as a prelude to the history-taking process.

During this period, the following objectives are addressed: (a) the client's security needs; (b) the ability for the client to feel in control of their responses; (c) establishment of mutual respect; (d) the beginning of the client-centered, therapist-directed approach; (e) the beginning of trust and rapport; and (f) addressing why the client is in your office (treatment goals).

In reviewing meta-analyses of numerous psychotherapies, Wampold (2001) found that the alliance between therapist and client influenced the treatment outcome more than any other dynamics the therapist controlled. This chapter highlights that period of therapist–client interaction beginning with the client's arrival at your office and continuing through the introduction of EMDR therapy as a possible treatment modality. In the basic EMDR text *Eye Movement Desensitization and Reprocessing (EMDR) Therapy*, Third Edition, Shapiro (2018) addresses the client's "readiness for treatment" in her discussion of history-taking. As the developer of EMDR therapy, she, in the basic text, offers much wisdom and experience addressing these aspects of EMDR therapy. In addition, this clinician's guide for treating military, veterans, and first responders addresses the clinical challenges therapists often face during the initial intake and follow-up sessions with these unique populations.

## EVERY CLIENT NEEDS TO FEEL SECURE AND IN CONTROL WHILE IN YOUR OFFICE

In keeping with Maslow's hierarchy of basic human needs (Kenrick, Griskevicius, Neubert, & Schaller, 2010), these special population clients when seeking psychotherapy tend to function best when having a sense of self-control as demonstrated by self-regulation abilities (basic physiological responses) as well as a sense of security. First and foremost, the client must feel secure in the therapeutic environment to ensure effective treatment outcome (Courtois & Ford, 2009). The therapeutic environment is foreign territory to the new client. Some level of client anxiety is to be expected due to the uncertainty of the treatment process. The perceived threat level is in proportion to the perceived vulnerability of the client. Effective treatment requires the client to feel secure enough in your office that they are willing to be open to engage in the treatment process. Hypervigilant clients require the therapist's attention in creating a secure treatment environment. Note the client's ability to present their life experiences while self-regulating, remaining present and grounded in your office. Persons who have difficulty with self-regulation may need additional skill development prior to engaging in the processing of disturbing memories. This involves the early development of these skills even before reviewing the person's history of disturbing events. An example of developing early self-regulation is provided at the conclusion of this chapter.

Many persons who have spent time in combat areas come to believe there is no safe place. However, they need to know security can be established anywhere, even in a combat zone or therapist's office. The ability to control the environment and self-regulate needs to be addressed before a person is ready to reprocess their disturbing memories. Many military personnel and veterans are fully functioning individuals capable of caring for their personal security while self-regulating. Clients with life adjustment incidents and small "t" traumas typically operate with the ability to self-regulate and maintain their own security. Maintaining this ability, many clients manage this period uneventfully as they experience their ability to successfully monitor and control their environment. In such cases, the early period of therapist–client interaction may require 15 to 30 minutes to transition into providing a narrative of their life's experiences.

## EMDR THERAPY IS CLIENT-CENTERED AND THERAPIST-DIRECTED

Most clients know very little about the EMDR therapy approach prior to entering your office. As a client-centered approach, the therapy allows the client to experience a sense of control and mastery with its naturalistic processing of memories. Due to the client's limited understanding of the treatment, the therapist must be able to provide guidance and direction in facilitating the treatment process as well as address any questions the client may have regarding treatment. Providing clinical direction and explanation during the process enhances the client's confidence and sense of security. EMDR's treatment is a basic process allowing most psychotherapists to develop a natural confidence in the approach. The approach allows for the reprocessing of inadequately processed, maladaptively stored memories by accessing the memory and providing bilateral stimulation (BLS), thereby allowing the memory to be changed or transmuted into healthy resolution. EMDR therapy treats memories, disturbing memories which continue to interfere with a person's quality of life. The model, treatment mechanism, and methodology work to effectively resolve disturbing memories. Maintaining fidelity to the model provides an efficacious treatment outcome. While recognizing this, it is also important for the therapist to continue their development of solid clinical skills for treating complex cases.

## INFORMING THE CLIENT ABOUT THE PROCESS

Persons who have participated in traditional talk therapy may not understand the impact of each therapy session or appreciate that each session missed contributes to prolonging the outcome of their treatment goals. Nor does the client understand the efficacy of treatment with results being provided within one to four sessions for most target memories. While engaging the client, the therapist assumes the role of a clinical scout, viewing the clinical terrain and interpreting the horizon. The therapist cannot afford to assume the client knows where the treatment is going. Describe and interpret each step of the way for the client, particularly during treatment of the first target memory. In this manner, the therapist sets the pace, maintaining an appropriate tempo or cadence in the treatment process. This is not a passive process. Time is translated as healing opportunities. While each client and session is unique, the therapist maintains the tempo of the process and describes the destination for the client who has never traveled the road to healing.

## PRESENT ORIENTATION VERSUS PAST EVENTS WITH COMPLEX DISTURBING LIFE EVENTS

What is identified as small "t" traumas are dramatic, but they are not life-threatening events. The client suffering adverse life events frequently presents with a calm ability to self-regulate. These clients maintain a sense of controlling their responses during the session. Initially, there is a brief period of social interaction before the therapist moves the discussion to how past events influence current experiences. Even with the small "t" events, Mol and colleagues (2005) found the cumulative impact of such life events can generate an equal or greater level of posttraumatic stress disorder (PTSD) symptoms as those large "T" events. More complex trauma, the large "T" events, often require additional preparation during this period. This initial period, working with more complex symptoms, requires the initial in-session focus to be on the security and stability of the present therapeutic experience. It is the client's present experiences that motivate him to seek treatment related to past incidents.

Numerous researchers and clinicians found the standard PTSD categories did not recognize the severe psychological harm associated with prolonged and repeated exposure to traumatic events. This is apparent among many military personnel with multiple combat deployments. The International Society for Traumatic Stress Studies (ISTSS) task force recognized a more severe or complex category of PTSD.

Included are the core symptoms of reexperiencing, avoidance/numbing, and hyperarousal with (a) disturbances in self-regulatory capacity; (b) disturbances in relational capacities; (c) alternations in attention and consciousness (such as dissociation); (d) adversely affected belief systems; and (e) somatic distress or disorganization (ISTSS Expert Consensus Guidelines for Complex PTSD, 2012). Herman (2015) described the etiology of complex PTSD as resulting from repeated or prolonged exposure to interpersonal trauma with no means of escape.

Research conducted with the New Jersey National Guard, published in the *American Journal of Public Health* (Kline et al., 2010), found military personnel who had been deployed to combat zones multiple times were more than three times as likely to screen positive for PTSD and major depression in comparison with soldiers with no previous deployments. EMDR therapists treating these populations witness the varying dimensions of symptom complexities exhibited by clients with multiple deployments. With this in mind, persons suffering with more complex trauma often have difficulty in the areas of security and self-regulation. Since military personnel are trained in situational awareness and conducting risk assessment, these fundamental military concepts can be helpful in establishing client-centered treatment. For clients who are hypervigilant, it can be helpful to let them know you are responsible for the security in your office. Inform the hypervigilant client it is your area of responsibility, your AOR. Inquire about any concerns they might have to ensure they are secure enough to address any therapeutic work that is needed. Ensure the client that you will work with them to ensure they have the ability to self-regulate, developing their sense of self-control as part of their preparation for treatment. Any insecurity that impedes treatment progress needs to be identified as the client recalls when they were first learned and included as early target memories for treatment in the client's treatment plan.

## EMDR THERAPY IS A CLIENT-CENTERED, THERAPIST-DIRECTED APPROACH

Recognizing the uniqueness of the individual is the basis of this approach. It is not a one-size-fits-all approach, but instead focuses on learning the concerns and needs of each person. During this initial period, the therapist observes the client's stabilization, integrative capacity, affect tolerance, and motivation for change (Hensley, 2016).

Treating clients with complex traumatic stress disorders is different than treating persons suffering with small "t" adverse life experiences. Clients with complex stress-related symptoms must be firmly grounded in the present before the therapist can treat the past. The more reactive the client is, with being triggered and having dissociative exhibitions, the more out of control and insecure they feel. This determines the amount of time necessary before the client is ready to begin EMDR therapy Phases 3 to 8. Some veterans with severe symptoms may need two or more sessions before they can provide a narrative account of their history. There are clients who need to develop self-regulation skills before they can manage the level of affect related to their clinical history. It is often helpful for the therapist, when treating complex clinical presentations, to collaborate with the client regarding what they are able to discuss during this process. In such cases, it is helpful to let the client know what areas the therapist is wishing to explore and gain their consent for discussion; for example, asking, "I would like to get an overview of your military deployments, are you okay with discussing these now?"

Key statements and questions asked during this part of the introduction include:

1. What do you need in order to be secure in this room?
2. I would like to learn some of the things you think would be important for me to know about you and your reason for being here.
3. How has life been for you, overall—from childhood to now?
4. What concerns do you have about being here?
5. Are there things you are not ready to talk about yet?
6. What do you wish to resolve as a result of being here (treatment goals)?
7. What questions do you have of me?

## PSYCHOLOGICAL CONTAINMENT

Psychological containment provides for a sense of safety and security. Trauma survivors must experience a sense of containment before beginning disclosure of their experiences. Avoid creating a sense of vulnerability by pacing the client's disclosure as the client opens up (Muller, 2018). It is helpful to ask those clients suffering with complex symptoms and active triggers, "What do you need in order to feel secure in this room?" Persons who self-regulate adequately are likely to view the clinical environment as sufficiently secure. Clients who are frequently reactive and easily triggered often feel their life is out of control with activated security concerns in the treatment room. This may require the client to be able to monitor the environment by keeping window blinds open or checking a door that permits access to the room.

## PACING THE DISCLOSURE OF INFORMATION

As the client indicates their readiness for treatment, they move from focusing on the present orientation to identifying what has happened in the past. This is the time when anxious, newly trained EMDR therapists tend to focus more on correctly introducing EMDR therapy rather than enjoying the social interaction in meeting the client, then identifying the presenting issues, followed by offering EMDR therapy as a solution to the client's reason for seeking treatment. Seasoned therapists will view this transition as a social shift in moving the client toward the EMDR treatment process.

This is a period of social interaction with the initial goal of helping the client to be comfortable meeting with you, the therapist, in your treatment room or office. Once the client's comfort is established, the therapist transitions the client toward identifying treatment goals. Observing the client's ability to self-regulate and interact socially, as they claim their personal space in the office. The therapist is tasked with providing a secure environment for the client to develop treatment goals in a secure environment prior to pursuing intense psychological treatment.

### The Therapist Assists Clients in Pacing Their Disclosure of Disturbing Events So That They Do Not Overwhelm Themselves

For all therapists, the initial focus of this period begins with the *present* interaction between therapist and client. The present get-acquainted orientation provides a pacing where relationships are established before the disclosing of distressing information later in the session. When done adequately, the present orientation with the therapeutic relationship prevents the client from feeling he has "spilled his guts" too early in the process, which can result in a profound sense of vulnerability. Therapists need to monitor the amount of time taken by the client's discussion of their experiences. If most of the session's time is spent with the client regurgitating disturbing memories, it is important to ensure the client "comes up for air" or takes enough time focusing on the present to ensure they are present rather than wandering in the memory. Ensure there is a balance between the client's narration of disturbing events and in the presentation. Ensure the client maintains present awareness and does not overwhelm themselves with recounting disturbing life events. This can be done by asking, "What did you learn from those experiences?" or "Can you recall positive or humorous events from that period?" If necessary, ensure there is enough time for the client to recall such positive events before closing the session.

Personnel who have internalized their experiences or avoided emotions may, out of desperation, allow themselves to open up and become willing to tell their story as a means of seeking help. Dysregulated clients need safety and grounding. In such cases, the therapist can assist the client, ensuring the entire session is not devoted to the review of distressing memories. In most cases, the therapist will typically observe the client smiling and recalling positive experiences as well as those disturbing memories. Regulated clients need to feel secure and welcomed. Both regulated and dysregulated clients need to know they are respected in their efforts to seek resolution of their presenting issues. Seasoned therapists engage in this period as a natural process of social interaction with the goal of meeting, greeting, establishing the client in the treatment environment, and moving the client toward Phase 1 History-Taking.

MY BASIC RULE IS TO ALLOW THE CLIENT TO IDENTIFY WHAT BRINGS THEM IN FOR THERAPY, THAT IS, THEIR TREATMENT GOALS, THEN INTRODUCE EMDR THERAPY AS AN EFFECTIVE MEANS FOR ACHIEVING THE GOAL (FIGURE 2.1).

Connecting the client's reason for being in your treatment office with the treatment you offer is a natural progression. Most clients seek treatment to improve their quality of life. The greater the psychological pain, the more desperate the client is in locating effective treatment in a timely manner. Many clients have heard of EMDR therapy from peers or other therapists. Often clients are referred to me or the staff at Soldier Center specifically for EMDR therapy. Some were treated in inpatient programs or by referring EMDR therapists at other locations.

COPING MECHANISMS EXIST FOR A REASON. DON'T REPLACE AN AVOIDANCE TECHNIQUE UNTIL THE CLIENT IS ABLE TO REPLACE IT WITH SOMETHING HEALTHIER OR STRONG ENOUGH TO PROCESS THE DISTURBING MEMORY.

Levels of clinical resistance and avoidance or acceptance and disclosure are determined during this period of establishing a therapeutic alliance. The therapeutic relationship building has sometimes been referred to as a clinical "visit." Other therapies sometimes call this "joining with the patient/client." The client's motivation for treatment is first observed during this period. Avoidance strategies are sometimes revealed as a demonstration of the client's ambivalence to the process. Such strategies are often developed as a coping mechanism for emotional survival. Later, when the client is ready to begin reprocessing target memories, those avoidance responses can be addressed. At that time, it should be recognized that attempts to challenge avoidance can be met with resistance. When the therapist challenges the client's

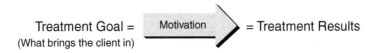

Treatment Goal =    Motivation    = Treatment Results
(What brings the client in)

FIGURE 2.1 From goals to results.

survival strategies, the client usually wins! A number of strategies can be useful in addressing avoidance including Manfield's Flash technique (Manfield, Lovett, Engel, & Manfield, 2017) and Knipe's avoidance technique (Knipe, 2015), as well as targeting the memory when the client first learned to avoid such situations. The latter involves targeting the initial memory when the client first learned to use avoidance as a coping defense.

## MUTUAL RESPECT STRENGTHENS THE BUILDING OF TRUST AND RAPPORT

The establishment of mutual respect facilitates this process. During my early years as a psychotherapist, I learned the importance of establishing mutual respect in the therapeutic relationship. Looking for something positive, which I could respect in each of my clients, facilitates my clients' trust and acceptance of me as their therapist. I learned identifying what I respect in a client ensures I have a respectful relationship with them. And, expressing my appreciation to the client facilitated a mutual ground of rapport between myself and the client. In spite of differences, the common ground between the therapist and client allows us to be human beings with a mutual contract for the client's healing.

Military personnel, veterans, and first responders typically maintain high standards in their duty performance. It is easy for them to arrive at your office judging their duty performance mercilessly, feeling inadequate while projecting a strong image. Your client may view seeking help from a mental health provider as a sign of weakness. Regardless of your model for engaging your clients, I suggest that mutual respect and meeting with supportive, nonjudgmental acceptance is required to provide effective treatment to these populations. A brief statement to the client can work wonders—recognizing how difficult it can be when someone who serves others seeks care for themselves. The therapist can further acknowledge it is always challenging to meet a stranger and begin to disclose personal issues. Assurance of confidentiality accompanied with a statement that you work with many others, just like your client, helps you recognize both the challenge and the importance of seeking help so they can reclaim their life. I consider this time of client–therapist interaction "the visit." There are a number of challenges during this initial engagement:

1. Initially engaging the client in a manner that allows the therapist to assess the client's interaction with the therapist, particularly related to motivation, self-regulation, and expectations.
2. Adjusting your response to the client based on their presenting attitude.
3. Learning what has influenced the client's presenting attitude. Has

the client heard positive things about you and/or the therapy you provide? Has the client had previous treatment? If so, was the outcome positive or a disappointment?

4. Observe the client's clinical presentation. Is he talkative and socially engaging or more restrained verbally? Do their hands or legs shake while engaging in conversation with the therapist?

5. Evaluate the client's level of disclosure. Does the level of disclosure reveal the level of trust in the treatment?

6. Assisting the client to pace their level of disclosure for Phase 1 History-Taking.

7. Is the client demonstrating avoidance strategies? If so, what is the client avoiding and protecting?

8. Is the client hyper- or hypovigilant? What is the source of either of these?

As a therapist, I want to understand the concerns of the client. In the initial minutes of meeting the client I state, "I want to learn about you and what brings you into my office. What do you need in order to be secure here? How has life been for you? What do you want to change by being here?" And, "Are there any concerns I need to know about you being here?" Sometime during the initial meeting, I will ask, "Are there things you are not yet ready to discuss with me?"

The EMDR therapist provides an appropriate setting for effective treatment with the new client providing for a sense of security and direction. Additionally, clients who have been long-term consumers of psychological services may have limited awareness of the efficacy of EMDR therapy in changing their lives. The therapist sets the tone and direction of EMDR therapy and cannot assume the client understands the treatment process with this model of therapy. Educating the client regarding the EMDR therapy process is essential.

The following case examples demonstrate the introduction of EMDR therapy. The first case illustrates the therapist's authenticity required in treating an avoidant client (Case Study 2.1). The next case (Case Study 2.2) illustrates the helpfulness of introducing self-regulation skills to the client in the first session. In these cases, both clients attend their first sessions experiencing anxiety. Their ability to diminish the anxiety felt in their bodies with the use of six to eight slow repetitions of BLS helps them feel they can immediately benefit from what the therapist has to offer beginning in the first session. The use of slow BLS also provides a positive introduction to EMDR therapy's use of BLS. This is often referred to as "front-loading" the use of techniques normally used in EMDR's Phase 2 Preparation phase.

## CLINICAL EXAMPLES

### CASE STUDY 2.1: THE AVOIDANT VETERAN

The veteran presented accompanied by his spouse. On initial presentation, he indicated he did not want to change; he wanted someone to address his spouse's complaints about his need to change. Upon learning the veteran did not wish to change, the therapist suggested he could not be helpful since all psychotherapies require the client's desire to change. Invitation was extended for him to return should he ever desire to change aspects of his life. He returned 3 weeks later (he had 2 weeks of outpatient surgery which delayed his return).

Client:      I brought my wife with me so she can tell you what is wrong with me.

Therapist:   I prefer to learn this information from the client who knows their issues.

Client:      I am happy with who I am, it's her who is always complaining about things being wrong with me!

Therapist:   Is there anything you want to change?

Client:      No! I just want to get her off my back!

Therapist:   Well, I don't have much success treating persons who have nothing they want to change. To attempt this would be a waste of your time and mine. If, sometime in the future, you decide you want to work on your issues, give me a call and we can schedule a time.

*** Three weeks later the veteran showed up at my office.***

Client:      When I left your office the last time, I told my wife "That's the kind of guy I want to work with—he's a straight shooter."

Therapist:   It is good to see you back here and ready to work on your issues. Let's talk about your life experiences—what brings you in—and what you wish to change by being here in my office.

*** Next: Phase 1 History-Taking began***

* * * * * * * * * *

CASE STUDY 2.2: INTRODUCING EMDR THERAPY TO HIGHLY ANXIOUS CLIENTS—FEARFUL OF PSYCHOTHERAPY

Phase 1 With a Modified Safe/Calm Place

The client is a 28-year-old E-5 NCO in the U.S. Army. He presents with clinical complaints of being anxious, insecure, and highly reactive in relationship with his significant other. He identified memories of three disturbing events: (a) walking into a room where he discovered his father sexually involved with his mother's best friend; (b) his wife abandoning him with no notice while he was assigned in Korea, taking the children and furniture and relocating to another state without notice; (c) the combat death of his best friend who he escorted back to the states for burial. Due to the client's high level of anxiety, a focus on body sensation and modified Safe/Calm Place was used to enhance the client's awareness of his ability to self-regulate.

Therapist:   So tell me what brings you in, David.

Client:   I got back from Afghanistan March 17th. This is my third overseas assignment and the time I've been back, I've had like non-stop arguments with my intimate partner. That's not me. I wake up in the middle of the night. You know, seeing the crap that I saw in Afghanistan, seeing my buddy that was killed back in 2006.

* * * * (Detailed History-Taking continued … ) * * * *

I've had a lot in the past 3 years. I think I need to get a lot of it off my chest and shoulder so I can start acting back to the way I used to be, just casually going about my day, having a good time. And my girlfriend, she's in the military too. We want to eventually start a family.

So I called Army OneSource and my chaplain hooked me up with your card.

* * * * * * * * *

* (35 minutes of identifying his life experiences and concerns—before introducing Safe/Calm Place) *

* * * * * * * * *

Client:       Like I said, I just got to get all of this stuff off my shoulder.

Therapist:    What do you do to relax?

Client:       Since I've been back, I bought a motorcycle. Now I just take off on it for about an hour, an hour or less. If I'm with my buddies, I'll go put around for about 3 hours or so—a little less than 3 hours, then come back. And just where the wind's been blowing on my face blew all my problems away for you know that amount of time and a little bit afterward.

              Then, I'm just like, what's going on? This is, you know, is she doing something wrong? I'm trying to call my kids and my ex-wife won't answer and she holds my kids over my head and stuff.

Therapist:    So, can you feel the anxiety in your body at times?

Client:       Yeah, bad.

Therapist:    Are there some places that you notice it in your body?

Client:       To be honest with you, I feel pressure on my chest, shoulders tensing up, my back tenses up and then I feel crawling on my neck, and then I get a headache.

Therapist:    One of the approaches I use is based on eye movement. It has been determined that getting the eyes to move sort of like when we are in our deepest sleep, we call that REM sleep for rapid eye movement. While we are in our deepest sleep, our eyes are moving and we think that's probably a sign that the brain is processing memories, material from the day.

So one of the things that helps to relax is eye movement. So one of the things I would like to check out with you, if I just move my fingers sort of slowly like that about, oh, about 12 times or so, and it helps the body, the nervous system to relax. And so I just like, if it's okay with you, to have your eyes follow my fingers. Let's just try that and see how that works.

Therapist: I'm just going to scoot my chair a little closer to you over to the side and. …

Client: You want me to follow?

Therapist: Yes, what I'll do is I'll just move my fingers and your eyes will just automatically follow because my fingers are going to be sort of in front of your face up here. And when I move my fingers, you're either going to follow or they do that naturally, so you don't have to work at following my fingers.

It's a sort of a normal thing to do, you know, if something gets in my face and moving, my eyes typically follow. But there's something about eye movement that helps the nervous system. If it's done at a certain speed, it helps the nervous system calm down. So I just want to try that out with you.

And if you would just sort of focus on the sensation where you feel the anxiety, where would you describe what you're feeling right now?

Client: Well. it's a little bit on my chest.

Therapist: Okay. So what I'm going to do is not hypnosis or anything like that. You're totally aware.

You're in control. Should something come up and you need to stop, just give me a stop signal and

|  |  |
|---|---|
|  | we stop. And a stop signal can be a halt or referee time-out signal. Some people just turn their head away. Is there a particular signal that you want to use? |
| Client: | I'll just hold my hand up. |
| Therapist: | Okay, that will be fine. Now, what I'm going to do is start with my hand back here and move it forward and I'll just stop at a distance that's comfortable for you. |
|  | I just need to align my finger sort of like in front of your eyes there. Okay, is that comfortable for you? Now, in terms of eye movement, I can do side to side, we call that horizontal. I could just go just like that doing side to side. |
|  | Or, I can do what we call diagonal, going in that direction like that, or I can go in that direction. Is one of those more comfortable for you? |
| Client: | Side to side. |
| Therapist: | Okay. Alright, so I'm just going to do a few sets of eye movements and ask you just to notice where you feel that anxiety. |
|  | I'm just going to do a few sets and I'll stop and just ask you to notice what you sense. Okay? Just focus on the anxiety and your eyes sort of automatically follow my fingers. Just focus on what you feel now (eight passes of bilateral stimulation). |
|  | What do you notice now? |
| Client: | There is not a lot of weight on my chest now. |
| Therapist: | Okay. Let's do another set (eight passes of bilateral stimulation). |

And what do you notice now?

Client:        Just sitting here.

Therapist:     So how would you describe just sitting here now
               with what you were feeling 10 minutes ago?

Client:        A little more comfortable. Some thoughts in my
               head. They are not all the time constant thinking
               like it has been.

Therapist:     Good. So, I want to move from that to doing a
               relaxation exercise. This is something you can use
               between sessions. Can you think of a place that
               seems, that feels secure and calm to you? It can be
               either a real or imagined place. Some people think
               of being by the ocean with the waves coming in;
               others think being by a mountain stream. Others, it
               might be a room at the house. Is there a particular
               place that comes to your mind?

Client:        The top of the mountain that me and my buddies
               used to go and hang out and just sit. It overlooks
               the valley.

Therapist:     Good. So let me ask you just to take a minute to
               pull up a mental picture of that. The details of
               sitting there, what you notice. Once you get that
               mental picture, just describe it to me, okay?

Client:        We sit on the top of a mountain, literally on the top
               of a mountain. Directly in front of us you have a
               town. Off in the distance, to my right, you can see
               another town, and in the distance, to my left, is
               another village where I am from. There is a partial
               lake between them. Everything is all green grass,
               fields, farmland. There are just roads leading in
               and out of the mountains.

Therapist:     So let me ask you as you describe being there and
               think it, describe any other details that might come
               to mind.

Client:        The smell of the outdoors. The fresh air; the breeze
               you get while you're up there so high up that you

won't get when you are down low. (Pause.) The fact that you're so high up that you're just on top of everything.

Therapist:  Good. So as you imagine being there, what emotion or body sensation do you notice now as you think about being there?

Client:  Relaxing. Open-minded. Carefree.

Therapist:  So just focus on that and I'm just going to do eye movement as you focus on being there, relaxed, carefree. (Therapist provides seven passes of eye movement.)

Just take a deep breath. Fill your lungs with air. Exhale and let it all go. And what do you notice now?

Client:  Calm, relaxed. (Client's body appears to be relaxing.)

Therapist:  So as you think about the sense of being calm and relaxed and being there on top of the mountain, is there a word you could use to remind you of this place and your feeling relaxed? Sort of a cue word?

Client:  Open-minded.

Therapist:  Okay, just notice what you're feeling and the word "open-minded" (eight passes of eye movement provided).

Take a deep breath, let it all go. What do you notice now?

Client:  It is not as bad as it should be. I feel really relaxed, calm.

Therapist:  So let me ask you just to notice, you just say that word "open-minded" out loud.

Client:  Open-minded, carefree place. Just relaxed.

Therapist:     As you say that word, what do you notice in your body?

Client:        Just relaxed.

Therapist:     Good, good. So I'd like to do a little experiment. I'd like to ask you to think of something that's just a little annoying, not a big thing but something that's mildly annoying, and when you get it in mind, just let me know.

Client:        Okay.

Therapist:     Just say out loud the word "open-minded."

Client:        Open-minded.

Therapist:     What happened? What do you notice in your body?

Client:        Just let it go.

Therapist:     Good. So this is a relaxation exercise and the key-word is "open-minded" and I would encourage you to practice that each day between the sessions when you want to relax; just practice relaxing, but remember being on the top of that mountain and just saying the word "open-minded," okay? And this is a way of helping you begin to relax.

               You can use any time: when you're at work, driving, or at home. Just try that out on a daily basis: Say the word, think about being on top of the mountain, and the word "open-minded." Allow yourself to experience that level of relaxation. And so we will be working on doing some relaxation and then we're going to work on, probably in about the second session, we will discuss more in our next meeting, but I will talk with you about a therapy that will help you to get rid of those issues causing the nightmares and problems. So you have the memories of what happened, but the emotional charge will not be there. Does that sound like what you are seeking?

Client:        That sounds like an awesome plan.

Therapist:     Now, before we stop today, I'm going to ask you to take a minute to fill out a questionnaire. This will help me to understand where you're at in terms of some of the issues you've talked about in terms of PTSD.

## CONCLUSION

This chapter discusses the importance of establishing (a) the client's sense of security in your office; (b) the client's feeling in control to self-regulate; (c) leadership and direction with the client-centered, therapist-directed approach; (d) the client's treatment goals (what brings them in); and (e) mutual respect as part of establishing trust and rapport.

### DISCUSSION POINTS

1. How was trust and rapport established in Case Study 2.1 with the client avoiding treatment by stating he was only present to placate his wife with her complaints?
2. Why did he return requesting treatment 3 weeks later?
3. In Case Study 2.2, front-loading the client's self-regulation using body sensations and the Safe/Calm Place, was the process related to the client's presenting symptoms?
4. Did the relaxation help with the client's positive anticipation of future sessions?
5. From the AIP perspective, what past events appear to have influenced his present triggers?
6. What other options might have been used if the client reported difficulties viewing himself at a Safe/Calm Place?
7. How was trust and rapport maintained?
8. Did the soldier demonstrate an openness for full disclosure?

### REFERENCES

Cloitre, M., Courtois, C., Ford, J., Green, B., Alexander, P., Briere, J., et al. (2012). The ISTSS expert treatment guidelines for complex PTSD in adults. Retrieved from https://www.istss.org/ISTSS_Main/media/Documents/ISTSS-Expert-Concesnsus-Guidelines-for-Complex-PTSD-Updated-060315.pdf

Courtois, C., & Ford, J. (2009). *Treating complex traumatic stress disorders (adults): An evidence-based guide*. New York, NY: Guilford Press.

Hensley, B. (2016). *An EMDR therapy primer: From practicum to practice*. New York, NY: Springer Publishing Company.

Herman, J. (2015). *Trauma and recovery: The aftermath of violence from domestic abuse to political terror*. New York, NY: Basic Books.

Kenrick, D., Griskevicius, V., Neubert, S., & Schaller, M. (2010). Renovating the pyramid of needs: Contemporary extensions built upon ancient foundations. *Perspectives on Psychological Science, 5*(3), 292–314. doi:10.1177/1745691610369469

Kline, A., Falca-Dodson, M., Sussner, B., Ciccone, D. S., Chandler, H., Callahan, L., & Losonczy, M. (2010). Effects of repeated deployment to Iraq and Afghanistan on the health of New Jersey Army National Guard troops: Implications for military readiness. *American Journal of Public Health, 100*(2), 276–283. doi:10.2105/AJPH.2009.162925

Knipe, J. (2015). *EMDR toolbox: Theory and treatment of complex PTSD and dissociation*. New York, NY: Springer Publishing Company.

Manfield, P., Lovett, J., Engel, L., & Manfield, E. (2017). Use of the flash technique in EMDR therapy: Four case examples. *Journal of EMDR Practice and Research, 11*(4), 195–205. doi:10.1891/1933-3196.11.4.195

Mol, S., Arntz, A., Metsemakers, J., Dinant, G., Vilters-Van Monfort, P., & Knottnerus, A. (2005). Symptoms of post-traumatic stress disorder after non-traumatic events: Evidence from an open population study. *British Journal of Psychiatry, 186*, 393–399.

Muller, R. (2018). *Trauma and struggle to open up: From avoidance to recovery and growth*. New York, NY: W. W. Norton.

Shapiro, F. (2018). *Eye movement desensitization and reprocessing (EMDR) therapy: Basic principles, protocols, and procedures* (3rd ed.). New York, NY: Guilford Press.

Wampold, B. E. (2001). *The great psychotherapy debate: Model, methods, and findings*. Mahwah, NJ: Lawrence Erlbaum Associates.

# 3

# EMDR Phase 1: History-Taking Among the Military/Veteran Populations

## Introduction

Treating military, veteran, and first responder populations requires an ability to establish and maintain client rapport and evaluate the client's selection criteria, while guiding the client through essential areas of information gathering, culminating in developing an effective treatment plan. Building on the basic EMDR History-Taking approach, integrated with its application to these unique populations, this chapter is designed to prepare the therapist for an advanced level of clinical applications ranging from initial greetings to finalizing the treatment plan for personnel who run toward the danger. A section on conducting History-Taking with complex cases is included.

## Learning Objectives

- Develop and maintain trust and rapport.
- Gather psychosocial and medical history.
- Evaluate if the client meets criteria for treatment.
- If client meets criteria for treatment, develop a treatment plan and case formulation for members of unique populations who serve their communities and nation.

## PHASE 1: HISTORY-TAKING

### PSYCHOSOCIAL HISTORY

EMDR therapy's approach includes the therapist gathering a broad bio-psychosocial history. The purpose of the History-Taking (Phase 1) includes three actions: (a) gather the client's background history; (b) evaluate the client's suitability for EMDR treatment; and (c) identify those target events in the client's life, both positive and negative (EMDR Institute Basic Training Course (a and b), 2017; Hensley, 2016).

Once the client's security concerns are addressed, the therapist begins by identifying the presenting symptoms the client wishes to resolve. This is what brings the client in for treatment, the treatment goals. Learning of the client's life history, the therapist asks, "What are the earlier life experiences which established the groundwork for the current clinical symptoms?" Once those earlier life experiences are identified, they become a part of the developing treatment plan.

1. What brings you in today?
2. What earlier life experiences set the groundwork for the current presenting symptoms?
3. Develop a treatment plan around the unresolved memories of those experiences.

From the adaptive information processing (AIP) approach we view the past as being present in influencing the client's life. It is those inadequately processed, maladaptively stored memories that are the basis of the presenting pathology (Shapiro, 2018). Since EMDR therapy addresses both healthy and dysfunctional memories, understanding the client's background includes collecting a list of those healthy memories that provide the client a sense of accomplishment or success when recalling those positive memories. Memories of positive experiences are included in the client's resource list. The resource list provides an indication of the number of positive experiences a person has encountered through their life. I have found that a significant number of positive experiences, called resources, usually translate to stronger resiliency and better problem-solving skills. EMDR therapy requires the client to have at least one resource for the therapy to work. If no other resources are available, the client–clinician relationship can be used to provide the positive traction needed for the clinical movement forward.

Ask the client if there are things they are not ready to talk about yet. An advantage of EMDR therapy is the ability to treat a disturbing memory without the client needing to disclose a lot of information. In fact, I have treated military intelligence officers with posttraumatic stress disorder (PTSD). Everything about their exposure to trauma is classified and cannot be divulged including the location and description of the incident. Since it is the client's own brain doing the processing, all I need is two words, any two words, with one meaning there is no change in the memory and the other word meaning the memory is changing after a set of bilateral stimulation (BLS).

History-Taking includes compiling a list of memories associated with disturbing events in a person's life. These are memories that continue to disturb the client when they are reminded of the past experience. This is the list of disturbing memories which, when activated, can interrupt the client's state of calmness. Out of the reservoir of those disturbing memories, we identify those memories that provided the earlier groundwork for the presenting symptoms which initially brought the client to your office seeking help. The three techniques—(a) Direct Question, (b) Floatback, and (c) Affect Scan—can be used with the presenting symptom(s) to search for earlier similar life experiences.

## DIRECT QUESTION

The Direct Question technique uses the current presenting symptom and directs the client's attention back to similar experiences earlier in life, as early as childhood. Examples include:

*Does this remind you of similar incidents earlier in your life, perhaps as early as childhood?*

*When did you first come to think of yourself in this manner?*

*Do you recall when you first began to believe this about yourself?*

## FLOATBACK

The Floatback technique pairs memories connected to the client's current experience of the problem with memories of past experiences using the client's negative belief about themselves. For example:

*As you bring up the recent experience of _____, notice the image that comes to mind and the negative thoughts you have about yourself (repeat the NC) along with any emotions and sensations, and let your mind floatback to an earlier time in your life when you might have felt this way before and just notice what comes to mind....*

## AFFECT SCAN

The Affect Scan has proven its usefulness at times when earlier memories are not readily accessible or in circumstances when the client has difficulty identifying negative thoughts or words related to thoughts or feelings about themselves. The Affect Scan can also be helpful during reprocessing when the client becomes stuck in an emotional state and reprocessing stops.

An example of an Affect Scan question is:

*Hold the experience in mind, the emotions and sensations that you're having now, and allow yourself to scan back to an earlier time you experienced something similar....*

These three techniques—Direct Question, Floatback, and Affect Scan—are used both in Phase 1 History-Taking and during the reprocessing phases (Phases 4–6) to check for feeder memories when reprocessing stops after changing the mechanics and the TICES (target = image, cognitions, emotions, and body sensations).

Motivation is an important factor in any treatment approach. The client's motivation reflects directly with their keeping appointments, arriving on time, and personal investment in the treatment process. During History-Taking, the therapist's explicitly connecting the client's treatment goals with the therapy approach enhances the client's motivation. Those who have been previously treated unsuccessfully need to know the EMDR therapy approach is different from other models of therapy. Explain your approach is designed to resolve their presenting issues.

The establishment of trust is defined by what both therapist and client bring to treatment. It may have been an issue developed from childhood or more recently surfaced during military service. Lifelong experiences can originate with childhood attachment deficits relating to insecure or disorganized attachment or neglect from which the client learned not to depend on anyone. More recent military service can sometimes perpetuate loss of trust due to poor military leadership as well as acts of betrayal such as military sexual assault. The client may have learned not to trust one's judgment due to combat experiences, that is, when the situation happened the attack occurred. Many veterans returned from combat believing there is no safe place anywhere. In spite of the lack of trust, wounded persons may still seek care for their wounds. When this is the case, the EMDR therapist is required to recognize the client's trust concerns and respond accordingly. Extra effort must be taken to ensure the client's concerns are recognized and appropriate responses provided with authenticity.

Rapport is developed as the therapist's response to the client's needs is recognized and addressed. The therapist's response determines the degree of rapport as well as the enhancement of the client's motivation. Sound rapport does not occur automatically but is evaluated in each session. First, no effective treatment is ever accomplished until the client feels some sense of security. Asking the question "What do you need in order to feel secure in this room?" informs the client that her needs are considered while, at the same time, addressing the first step in rapport development and establishing the client's readiness for treatment. Secondly, sound rapport includes authenticity between clinician and client. Being real, no pretense, is valuable. Mutual respect is a requisite. These are necessary ingredients for trust and rapport in the clinical relationship. Silver and Rogers (2002) acknowledge the veteran may be hesitant to share information until a stronger relationship is developed.

## EMDR CLIENT SELECTION CRITERIA

### CLIENT STABILIZATION

Suicide rates are high among military personnel, veterans, and first responders. It is important for therapists to assess suicidality among clients. Three questions are important to ask clients: (a) Do you ever think of hurting yourself or killing yourself?; if the answer is yes, the second question is: (b) Do you have a plan to kill yourself?; if the answer is yes, then assess: (c) Do you have the means to kill yourself? Remember: *thought, plan,* and *means* are the key areas for assessing suicidality. Stabilization of the client is necessary if an affirmative answer is given to all three questions including consideration for hospitalization. There are veterans suffering with chronic physical and psychological pain who have said to me, "Suicide is always an option, Doc. If you ask me to promise not to kill myself I can't do that!" This was a person who had been hospitalized for suicidality on three occasions; each hospitalization was for 90 days. A few decades ago graduate students were taught that a "no-harm" contract was necessary in order to treat such a person. My ethical dilemma was: If I don't treat him, he will not receive help and likely will succeed in a future suicide attempt. Perhaps effective treatment can generate hope as a source of coping and healing. In fact, at the end of the first session the veteran stated, "I don't want you to give up on me, Doc." I replied: "I won't give up on you if you don't give up on me." The veteran replied, "Roger!" That was the best no-harm contract I could have received. The veteran was suffering with complex PTSD with auditory and visual intrusions from his last firefight. If he was awake, he was experiencing those intrusions. He was treated with EMDR therapy and continues to live now—many years later.

Assessment for homicidality is also important. Most personnel are more likely to hurt themselves rather than others; however, it is important to access for this possibility. The duty to warn is well recognized in the United States since the *Tarasoff* decision of the Supreme Court of California in 1976 (Felthous, 2006).

### SUPPORT NETWORKS

Internal and external support networks strengthen the client's functional abilities. Internally the client demonstrates their ability to sustain themselves psychologically with self-efficacy. Externally, the client is evaluated for a social support network of family and friends who can provide support between treatment sessions. These are persons the client would turn to when destructive ideation toward oneself or others occurs. The network provides a resource for support and problem-solving abilities.

## DISSOCIATION

Military and veteran personnel represent a broad spectrum of dissociative exhibitions. "Dissociation" is a term describing the person's disconnection from reality and, sometimes, a disconnection to parts of the client's self. Dissociation is described as a disruption or impairment to the normal integration of thoughts, feelings, and personal experiences (Berstein & Putnam, 1986; Waelde, Silvern, Carlson, Fairbank, & Kletter, 2009). While EMDR therapy requires the client to maintain dual awareness, a dissociative response moves the client toward becoming lost in the memory with no present awareness. Dissociation is viewed from the AIP perspective as personality configurations caused by insufficiently processed memories. They contain parts of traumatic memory containing emotions and physical sensations associated with specific events. Dissociated states can include perceptions, attitudes, beliefs, and emotional responses to situations and people (Shapiro, 2018). Clients suffering with complex PTSD exhibit more severe pathology; sometimes they demonstrate dissociation while seated in the waiting room. With minimal sleep from the previous night, while experiencing night terrors, they have limited physical and emotional energy. The client may sit in the waiting room and find themselves jerking as they lose present awareness, lost in the trauma memory, then returning to reality. In these cases the trauma memory is intruding without any clinical stimulation.

EMDR-trained therapists need clinical skills to work with clients ranging from mild adverse life experiences and simple PTSD to the more severe complex PTSD with dissociation (Figure 3.1).

I once described the dissociative experience to a veteran as a person becoming disconnected from reality, losing present awareness. The veteran returned home, set his alarm for 10 minutes, and made a mark on his note pad each time he came back to present awareness. He had seven marks on his paper at the end of 10 minutes, indicating he had

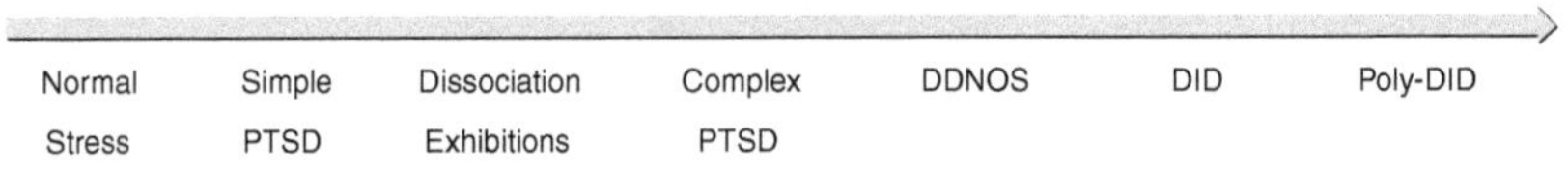

| Normal | Simple | Dissociation | Complex | DDNOS | DID | Poly-DID |
|--------|--------|-------------|---------|-------|-----|----------|
| Stress | PTSD | Exhibitions | PTSD | | | |

FIGURE 3.1 Range of dissociation diagram.
DDNOS, dissociative disorder not otherwise specified; DID, dissociative identity disorder.

dissociated and returned to present awareness on seven occasions during the 10-minute period. For a number of veterans who have been repetitively exposed to traumatic events, these dissociative responses have become common. Repetitive exposure to life-threatening events such as combat deployments can create fragmented disturbing memories. EMDR therapists who treat veterans must be prepared to address dissociative exhibitions during sessions. EMDR therapy requires the necessary clinical adjustments for the client to maintain dual awareness, that is, recalling the past event while maintaining present awareness. Remember, EMDR therapy only works if the client can maintain dual awareness.

The Dissociative Experiences Scale–II (DES-II; Carlson & Putnam, 1993), a self-administered measure, is recommended for assessing the client's propensity to disengage from present reality during treatment. In fact, Shapiro recommended every EMDR therapist intending to initiate EMDR therapy should first administer the DES-II (Shapiro, 2018, p. 96). While the DES-II is not intended as a diagnostic measure for Dissociative Identity Disorder, it does provide an adequate screening for a range of dissociative issues. The scale is based on the concept of dissociation being on a continuum ranging from normal dissociation experienced when reading a book, daydreaming, or viewing a movie to pathology such as depersonalization or derealization. While a score of 30 on the DES-II is considered an optimal cutoff score for maximizing the accuracy of the instrument predictions (Carlson & Putnam, 1993), a score of 30 or more is suggested to be a red flag indicating the need for further exploration of pathology with the client. Reviewing the 28 questions with the client can assist. Most veterans and active military personnel treated by this author have DES-II scores ranging from 20 to 80 with EMDR treatment still administered successfully. Higher scores on the DES-II typically mean the EMDR therapist must provide more effort in keeping the client grounded and present during the reprocessing phases (Phases 4–6). Techniques for keeping the client within the window of tolerance, maintaining dual awareness, are further reviewed in subsequent discussions.

## MEDICAL CONDITION: HISTORY AND CURRENT HEALTH

There was a time, a few decades ago, when military personnel were required to be in sound physical health in order to serve on active duty in the military. Such assumptions can no longer be made. Years of combat operations have left members of the force with numerous physical and psychological impediments. Both active duty and veteran populations include persons who suffer with chronic physical and emotional pain. The criteria for EMDR treatment require persons to be healthy enough to manage the physical demands of the EMDR treatment process. Veterans who suffered combat trauma more than 40 years ago, who have since undergone quadruple bypass surgery, are frequently treated with EMDR therapy in spite of their medical history. It is not just the medical history but one's current medical condition that also needs to be evaluated. It is necessary to ensure the client can endure the intense processing of memories with minimal risk of physical reactions such as seizures, heart attacks, or a stroke. Any doubt regarding this matter should be verified by the client's physician. Persons who have experienced severe abuse backgrounds require special consideration before proceeding with treatment. They may require additional self-regulation skills as they develop a comfortable level of interaction with the therapist.

A client should be healthy enough to endure the emotional distress of processing a disturbing memory. Histories of epilepsy, respiratory distress, or a cardiac condition should require a physician consult or clearance. If in doubt, clearance from a physician is warranted. While many pregnant clients are treated successfully, the therapist should discuss the effects of emotional arousal on the client as well as the unborn as treatment is considered. Any history of miscarriages should be taken into consideration.

## NEUROLOGICAL WOUNDS/TRAUMATIC BRAIN INJURY

As an EMDR therapist, I was treating military clients with undiagnosed traumatic brain injuries (TBIs) for some time before the military began to screen for neurological wounds. While diagnosing for PTSD, soldiers would acknowledge being impacted by a bomb blast from an improvised explosive device (IED) or as a special operator who placed numerous explosive charges on structures to breach entry. EMDR therapy treats the psychological trauma associated with the brain injury; it will, of course, not improve the physical nature of the wound. There are varying reports on the use of eye movement (EM) with treating TBIs. EMDR therapy is effective in treating the psychological trauma associated with mild to moderate TBI. Numerous clients I have treated, suffering with TBIs, had difficulty with EM as a treatment modality. Psychology colleagues in the Israel Defense Force reported minimal difficulty using EM in treating soldiers with TBI in the defense force. Perhaps the use or avoidance of EM, when there is a TBI, is determined by the location of the brain injury. I have treated hundreds of military personnel and veterans with a TBI without any treatment difficulties. Consultation with a physician is always appropriate when there is a concern that EMDR processing might contribute to neurological difficulties.

Numerous PTSD symptoms are similar to TBI symptoms. Overlapping symptoms include fatigue, sleep problems, memory problems, trouble focusing attention, depression, anxiety, and irritability (Henderson, 2016; Lew et al., 2008). A number of special operators I have treated with EMDR therapy for PTSD suffered with anger/irritability problems and emotional numbness with lack of empathy, having experienced years of frontal blasts with damage to their mirror neurons.

Anecdotally, the first soldier I treated, using EMDR therapy to treat his PTSD, who also had been diagnosed with a TBI, began to jerk his head and upper torso as I administered the first few sets of BLS. I immediately became concerned if the BLS was negatively impacting his TBI. Before I could ask about the reason for the jerking, the infantry sergeant stated, "I am dodging bullets!" He was processing the memory of a firefight. The memory contained peri-traumatic dissociation where time was perceived as slowing down and distance distorted. In his memory he was dodging bullets with the appropriate response of jerking to avoid being shot. We continued processing and within 50 minutes the memory of the firefight had been completed reprocessed.

## MEDICATIONS

When asked about medication as part of the selection criteria, I have come to believe "if a client can walk a straight line and talk without slurring, they can be treated with EMDR therapy." I am not referring to addiction, but the level of sedation. As Shapiro (2018) noted, there are no medications that appear to totally inhibit EMDR processing. Whether or how much a medication influences the process is determined by how sedated the neurological system is as a result of the medication. The dosage amount is of particular concern in assessing the impact of medications. Clinicians who treat the veteran population know that most veterans seeking treatment are on some medication. Waiting until a client is free of medication is unrealistic. Some medications can mask the unresolved material associated with the targeted memory. Following EMDR treatment, it is wise for the client to have a medication evaluation. As the medications are reduced or eliminated, a follow-up EMDR reevaluation should occur to ensure all targeted memories are completely processed. It is possible that a significant level of disturbance can return until the reevaluation following medical evaluation is complete, therefore allowing for total reprocessing of all disturbing material. For example, when treating a client who is medicated with benzodiazepine, the effects of the medication are likely to mask some of the residual processing. Due to medication, the client can report a subjective unit of disturbance (SUD) of 0 while on medication, but when the dosage is diminished or terminated, residual unprocessed material may increase the SUD level. Therefore, a treatment plan needs a reevaluation once the medication is reduced. Residual material can then be processed, allowing any previously masked material to be successfully treated.

## TIMING

Providing effective treatment in a timely manner is an ethical necessity for providers. There are providers serving some agencies who diligently work to provide continuity of care in spite of scheduling schemes, established by nonclinical administrators, which limit the frequency of care. This is a challenge for many dedicated providers. Lack of continuity results in subdued motivation by the client, loss of momentum in achieving treatment results, and frequently an attitude of "going through the motions" of providing treatment with limited expectation for success. This is a formula for burnout to the therapist, hopelessness for the client, and loss of purpose and meaning to all concerned.

The timing of effective treatment requires coordination between the therapist and the client as continuity of treatment is assured. Once EMDR treatment begins, it is important to maintain follow-up. Working with military populations it is sometimes necessary to schedule appointments around duty requirements and temporary duty (TDY) at other locations. Special operations clients sometimes undergo treatment weekly, then deploy for several weeks or months. In such cases, EMDR treatment results are maintained over time and treatment resumes with the client's return to home duty. Such situations often require frequent treatment sessions while the client is available with time gaps during TDY and deployments. EMDR therapy can be provided in several treatment formats ranging from an EMDR-intensive program twice a day during a 10-day period to treating clients twice a week, every 2 weeks, and sometimes 2 and 3 weeks apart due to extenuating circumstances. At Soldier Center, Clarksville, Tennessee, near Ft Campbell, Kentucky, we are committed to treating clients weekly once their treatment begins. Additionally, a 10-day EMDR-intensive program (Hurley, 2018) is offered to qualifying clients.

Disturbing associated memory networks can be activated between sessions. Two days following an EMDR session with a soldier who had finished processing a target memory (TM), resulting with a 0 SUD, a validity of cognition (VOC) of 7, with a clear body scan, the soldier called my office indicating he had intrusive memories following his last EMDR session. He had forgotten to mention the intrusive memory incident during the History-Taking phase. Once activated, the memories were overwhelming him. On receiving his phone call, we agreed to meet at my office during lunch time for the reprocessing of the intrusive memory. Twenty minutes into the EMDR session the memory had faded as it lost its emotional charge—never to bother him again!

Self-regulation skills enable clients to manage disruptions between sessions. Most of the time using the cue word from the Safe/Calm Place or breathing exercises is sufficient. However, nonstop intrusions, which do not stop or diminish, are a different category. Responding when the client reaches out for support in managing intrusions can enhance trust and rapport in the clinical process.

Due concern should be given to the needs of clients following each session. There is no way of predicting how much maladaptive residual material may remain following a session. Sometimes, those associated memory networks continue to be activated between sessions. Clients need contact information to ensure they have necessary support between appointments. Appointments should be scheduled to allow the client periods for recovery following a session. In no way should a client leave your office immediately following, or in the midst of, an intense processing session without appropriate self-regulation measures in place. Sufficient time is needed at the end of a session for debriefing, giving them time for stabilization, regaining their equilibrium as needed. The EMDR therapist has a repository of self-regulation techniques introduced in the Preparation phase. One soldier, who had processed a rather gory scene of finding fellow soldiers decapitated, had processed successfully, yet was still highly stimulated at the end of the session. Using the cue word from his Safe Calm Place helped him calm down to some extent. At the beginning of the session, while pulling up pictures on his phone, the client had shown me a picture of his two sons dressed in camouflage in preparation for a father–sons paintball game. He laughed and was proud of how he had dressed his sons. So, at the end of the session, after using the Calm Safe Place exercise, I asked him to show me the picture of his sons again. The soldier began to laugh, recounting how much fun he had with his sons the previous weekend. This was sufficient for his achieving a calm state ready to leave my office.

## EMOTIONAL DISTRESS AND SELF-REGULATION

EMDR clients should be able to endure high levels of emotional disturbance, which can occur throughout the eight phases of EMDR treatment. The EMDR therapist, while building trust and rapport, develops an attunement with the client. Attunement allows the client to find strength and assurance with the therapist to endure any level of discomfort inherent in the treatment process. As an EMDR therapist, I assure the client, "Nothing is going to happen in this session but what you and I together can handle! I have your six!" I can make this statement authentically as I have learned and developed clinical skills to treat military and veteran clients with the commitment "what I need know, I will learn in order to provide effective treatment to those who serve." Advanced EMDR trainings and consultation allow the development of the required skills.

Is the client comfortable with intense emotions? History-Taking includes learning how the client's family of origin managed emotions. Were there spoken/unspoken rules about dealing with emotions? How could the client tell when a member of the family was mad or sad? Did they ever attend funerals before the military? Answers to these questions assist in learning the client's attitude toward being emotional.

EMDR therapists must develop affect tolerance. Developing the ability to "sit with the client's affect" is mandatory. How does the client deal with affect as they describe deeply emotional events? If they become upset describing their history, do they have the ability to calm down?

## SECONDARY GAINS AMONG MILITARY AND VETERAN POPULATIONS

Many persons who serve in the armed forces consider their military service to be one of their best life experiences. For many, military service provides opportunities to excel both mentally and physically. It can be exhilarating to feel as if one's body could adapt to almost any physical challenge. The transition from such achievement to being told you are no longer capable of performing your duties and therefore are being medically boarded out of the military can be devastating for many. It is a significant stressor. Veterans with physical and mental health wounds live in such a world, where the military told them they were being separated from duty due to their inability to adequately perform any longer. Transitioning from actively performing their duty to being judged as incapable of performing the duty is no easy task. It is the extent of the disability that determines one's financial survival. By the time a wounded veteran begins to receive compensation, the sense of dependency on the system's compensation has been established. The concept of getting better means a diminishing of dependence and financial compensation. The fear of losing financial support if the veteran gets better can create an unspoken resistance to healing for some veterans. Occasionally a client has told me, "I am in the process of being med boarded, let me wait until I am evaluated for my compensation before I begin treatment." The concept of being treated with an effective treatment that can help a person reclaim their lives can seem very foreign to the client. At Soldier Center, we have treated veterans who were previously treated three and four times in federal systems with limited outcome results. Veterans who were unsuccessfully treated at previous times and locations frequently lose hope that any approach can help them. Some show up for treatment because a friend or family member learned about EMDR therapy and told them to give it a try. During such occasions, it is the EMDR therapist's responsibility to enhance the veteran's hope in effective treatment. Enhancing the client's hope can be approached by pointing out the difference EMDR therapy provides in comparison to other treatment models. Viewing videos on webpages such as "what-clients-say-EMDR," and using the resource development and installation (RDI) technique asking the client to recall an earlier time when they accomplished a challenging task successfully can offer hope again.

Some other veterans who have lived with a diagnosis for years have embedded their diagnosis with their identity. The prospect of no longer being a veteran "with PTSD" can leave a veteran struggling to have a new identity. These veterans sometimes ask, "Who am I if I am not a veteran with PTSD?" They are sometimes concerned about fitting in with others in their social group at the local Veterans Affairs center if they lose their diagnosis. It can be helpful to remind veterans they are the same—no one can take away their identity as veterans who were wounded; it just doesn't have to control who they are in the present and future. Many veterans eagerly seek healing for their psychological wounds as they endorse a hope for an improved quality of life. Asking the veteran "What would it be like if you got over these symptoms (nightmares, flashbacks, triggers, etc.)?" can help identify secondary gain issues. Enhancing hope for effective treatment is a great antidote.

## DRUG AND ALCOHOL ABUSE

Persons in recovery from substance abuse need a support system in place to ensure their recovery during the distressing times of processing disturbing memories. Often the substance use began as a means of self-regulating. Alternate means of self-regulating need to be in place as the client begins treatment. Popky's DeTUR urge reduction protocol (Shapiro, 2005) treats persons in recovery by first strengthening a positive state, enhancing their ability to manage their addiction, then treating those disturbing memories as the basis of the addiction. For persons not in a recovery program, Popky begins with treating the disturbing memories as there is no recovery state to jeopardize.

## EYE MOVEMENT DIFFICULTIES

Under no circumstances should EM, as a form of BLS, be continued if the client reports discomfort. EMDR therapy recognizes three forms of BLS as effective in processing memories, that is, EM, tactile, and auditory. If there is discomfort in EM, the therapist should use another modality. Clients who wear bifocals or trifocals should be invited to try BLS with their glasses removed. As long as the eyes are moving, the reprocessing works. The same applies with contacts. While many clients wear soft lenses and are able to engage in EM without difficulty, the client should be informed regarding wearing contacts during EM and invited to bring their contact case with eye solution in case they prefer to remove their contacts during the treatment session.

## MORAL INJURY ISSUES IN HISTORY-TAKING

A brief introduction to the concept of moral injury is provided here, in this History-Taking discussion, for the sake of conceptualizing moral wounds as part of case conceptualization and treatment planning. The construct "moral injury" was created by mental health researchers in the Department of Veterans Affairs to describe a person's moral injury as a violation of personal values either by acts of commission or omission (Litz et al., 2009; Maguen & Litz, 2012). Prior to this development, both moral philosophy (Rickaby, 2018) and theology had its concept of moral or just war (Walzer, 2015). Each discipline has its own perspective of the same wound. There are philosophical, spiritual, and psychological aspects of humanity's wounds when conflict leads men and women to inflict hurt and death on each other. What is represented by the label "moral injury" is not new. Historically, military personnel have returned from battlefields haunted by the deeds of war. For centuries, soldiers of all military branches returned home from battle seeking their own inner peace, acceptance within their communities, and absolution and forgiveness when necessary. Each community has its leaders to provide such. When terrorism has been used by groups, it is by nature the infliction of horrible acts upon people in such horrendous manner that it can overwhelm the normal functioning of humanity, leaving survivors and witnesses haunted by what happened.

Moral injury is not PTSD. It results in the person experiencing guilt and shame. EMDR therapy is effective in treating moral injury by targeting the source of their moral wounds. Persons who have shame-based childhoods readily find something to emotionally reinforce their long-established sense of worthlessness. Treating moral injury with its shame and guilt is discussed in detail later in this book.

## HISTORY-TAKING WITH CHALLENGING CASES

### SELF-REGULATION DURING HISTORY-TAKING

Sometimes it is necessary to train the client with relaxation exercises before beginning the History-Taking process for persons who have difficulty with emotional regulation when describing their disturbing memory narratives. This is in essence moving Phase 2 Preparation to become the first phase of EMDR therapy, enabling clients who are easily activated to self-regulate. Teaching them to do breathing exercises, do their own tapping such as the Butterfly Hug (sometimes referred to as "tactical tapping"), or tapping on their legs often helps the client to feel more in control. And, of course, using the Safe/Calm Place with a cue word can be helpful for many clients.

### FOR HIGHLY ANXIOUS CLIENTS

Ensuring the client has a sense of security while in your office is important. Asking the client, "What do you need in order to feel secure in this room?" is helpful for clients. Additionally, Mr. Gene Schwartz, an EMDRIA-approved consultant and colleague who treated veterans within the Department of Veterans Affairs for 30 years, reports teaching the "stop signal" to veteran clients when they first enter the office as a means of enhancing their sense of security. This can be particularly helpful for highly anxious clients.

## MODIFYING THE STANDARD PROTOCOL: TARGETING A MEMORY BEFORE COMPLETING HISTORY-TAKING

An Army noncommissioned officer (NCO; E-7) sought treatment for his PTSD. He had completed seven combat tours serving a minimum of 1 year in each deployment. He referenced his current locations by referring to his combat tours. When describing the Smoky Mountains of east Tennessee, it reminded him of the mountains of Afghanistan. The flat river bottom land of west Tennessee, along the Mississippi River, reminded him of the Tigris River regions. He described his struggle to interact with persons back in the United States. He stated, "The person my neighbors see when I wave to them as I leave my house is not the person I am. If they saw the person I am, it would scare them!" Due to his dissociative responses during three sessions of History-Taking, he could not disclose any information beyond his number of deployments and their location without becoming highly activated. When I described dissociation as getting lost in the memories while losing one's present awareness, he described every morning was like that for him as he would sit on his back deck enjoying a cup of coffee as the dissociative experiences would come rolling in like a fog to his location. He would become lost in his memories repetitively while regaining present awareness intermittently.

Using relaxation exercises and RDI (Korn & Leeds, 2002) provided limited assistance with his dissociative episodes. Following his History-Taking sessions, he described needing to rest in his vehicle for an hour after each session before driving. During his fourth treatment session, he stated, "I came to you to be treated for my PTSD; this is my fourth appointment and you have yet to begin treating me!" Recognizing his impatience and limited tolerance, I replied, "How about next week?" At this point I knew I could get him into processing with some limitations. The next week the sergeant first class arrived. I asked him, "Are you ready to work on a disturbing memory connected with your PTSD?" He replied affirmatively. I asked:

"Is there a disturbing memory, one that bothers you when you are reminded of it, yet you feel you can manage getting through processing it today?"

He identified what he called the least disturbing memory. It had a SUD of 8 out of a possible high of 10. I reminded him of his relaxation exercise, asked for the cue word, told him he was in control of the process, asked for his stop signal, and entered into the Assessment phase. The Assessment questions significantly activated his memory of an Iraqi girl about 8 years of age, wearing a suicide vest. The girl was walking in the middle of the intersection when the vest was remotely detonated. He watched in horror as he viewed the girl disappearing before his eyes. I used the TICES to change his view: "View the scene as looking through a plexiglass window, you can see it but it can't get to you." He is using the tappers and I began altering the speed and intensity of the sensation. I use ongoing cognitive interweaves to keep the client present: "stay with me!" "It's a memory from the past. It's over! Take a breath; take another breath!" We continue with reprocessing. The client worked to maintain dual awareness. I keep him mostly in the present—the processing continued. At the end of an hour the client's SUD has dropped to a 1½. He stated the number represented his sadness (grief) over the death of an innocent girl. We ran out of time. It was an incomplete session with Phase 4 completed. We completed the Installation (Phase 5) and Body Scan (Phase 6) the following session.

Following the successful completion of resolving the first TM, the sergeant was more confident of the EMDR treatment process and his ability to get through the process. Subsequently, he was able to provide an overview of the disturbing memories in each combat deployment. He was quick to respond that there were no childhood memories he wished to address. We began the treatment plan focusing on each TM he identified as we met twice a week to expedite his treatment.

## WHEN SHAME DISTORTS THE PSYCHOSOCIAL HISTORY

A consultee described her attempt to gather a psychosocial history from a veteran who suffered with a low sense of self-efficacy. He was self-deprecating with a systemic sense of worthlessness. When attempting to identify disturbing memories of events he had experienced, he could only identify incidents where he caused disappointment and emotional pain to others. With a low sense of worth, the veteran could not identify one incident where he had experienced emotional pain based on what others had done to him. If a person believes they have no rights and no value as a human being, they cannot be disappointed or harmed. He felt he had received what he deserved. This is the result of systemic chronic shame.

Shame is a multifaceted human experience that can shut down the treatment process. Cognitively the shame-based person believes themself to be worthless. Worthlessness with its numerous expressions is a common belief adopted by persons in shame-based families. When in the shame state, they tend to be sad, with nauseated visceral body sensations. In treatment they maintain gaze aversion with a self-blame perspective.

Military life provides an escape from the emotional pain of shame. The physical challenges provide a healthy outlet for the internalized anger accompanying shame. Promotions, as well as awards with uniform patches and badges, provide a chance to offset the shame. Being passed over for promotion or unplanned discharge such as a medical board can enhance a person's shame with a sense of "not being good enough" or "not measuring up." Shame enhances psychological and physical pain. Persons suffering with shame have been highly correlated with dissociative exhibitions (Talbot, Talbot, & Xin Tu, 2004).

Herman (2007) suggested disorganized attachment and disrupted communication as an unrelenting source of shame and dissociation. Insecure attachment creates a vulnerability leaving the person to feel inadequate unless they are performing perfectly to earn acceptance. Persons who grow up in shaming families feel worthless and tend to beat up on themselves. They don't believe they are worth deserving expressions of nurture, love, or positive regard. They have difficulty objectively knowing if they were slighted of basic psychological needs, that is, nurture and affection. Therefore, it is easier for them to identify the pain of disappointing others than their own pain of being neglected or hurt. They believe if a person is worthless, they deserve to be disappointed or hurt. They have difficulty believing they have a right to object to being ignored or abused as a child. Shame-based persons have difficulty identifying a history of mistreatment or neglect. They have difficulty identifying appropriate TMs since severe shame-based clients do not have enough self-esteem to recognize they have been wounded. Rather, they believe they are worthless, while further enhancing their shame by noting their disappointment to others. The pain they recognize is not their pain for being wounded but the pain of disappointing others.

Shame-based persons are susceptible to the wounds of moral injury. They tend to beat up on themselves and readily accept responsibility for the loss of life believing they should have done more or failed to prevent observed actions of commission. Shame-based persons will find a way to accept blame and inhabit their emotional pain. Knipe (2009) suggested some clients have lifelong convictions of their own worthlessness. He referred to this ongoing condition as "shame is my safe place" while reflecting on the client's comfort with shame-based discomfort. The pain of shame can create an avoidance of the processing of grief, guilt, or moral injury as there may be little motivation to lift the pall of despair without due preparation.

History-Taking questions that can help clients identify appropriate TMs include:

- Do you remember the time when you first began to believe you are different? Worthless?
- Do you remember those times you felt that sick feeling in your gut? How did you manage that feeling?

- When did you learn to "beat up on yourself?"
- What incidents/events taught you that you are different or worth-less?
- How do those memories impact you now?
- If you rated how much those memories bother you now, 0 to 10, what number would you give each?

Answers to these questions can be targets for treatment as the shame base is targeted and processed. Guilt and moral injury will often spontaneously remit during reprocessing. However, when shame is embedded into the person's personality structure, the origin of shame and lifelong events reinforcing the shame may have to be targeted early in the treatment plan in order to resolve the moral injury.

## CASE CONCEPTUALIZATION AND TREATMENT PLANNING

History-Taking provides the opportunity to gain a complete clinical picture of the client before beginning EMDR treatment. Shapiro (2018) notes the therapist must distinguish between dysfunctionally stored memories, which need reprocessing, and problems, which should be addressed by psychoeducation, stress management, or problem-solving.

### CASE CONCEPTUALIZATION

Based on EMDR's theoretical approach, the AIP model (Shapiro, 2018): (a) Memory networks are the basis of pathology and health. EMDR therapy treats both healthy and unhealthy memories. (b) The past is present. Memories of the past are used to provide meaning while interpreting the present. (c) Healthy memories can be used as resources to remind the client of achievements, accomplishments, and memories of positive interactions with persons who enhanced their sense of worth as a person. (d) Unhealthy memories are the basis of pathology since they are inadequately processed, maladaptively stored memories that continue to elicit an emotional charge in the client when recalled. (e) When an experience is successfully processed as a memory, it is adaptively stored, integrating with other similar experiences regarding self and others. (f) What is useful is learned and stored to be used in the future. What is no longer useful is discarded. (g) BLS activates the targeted memory, allowing it to be changed and transmuted into healthy, adaptive resolution.

EMDR therapy treats memories. More specifically, EMDR therapy treats memories of disturbing events/incidents that continue to distress the client when the memories are recalled. The treatment process consists of identifying the TM, then accessing the memory and providing BLS; the memory is transmuted, or changed, to adaptive resolution.

There are eight phases in the EMDR approach with standard steps. EMDR therapy is a three-prong approach, treating memories of past events, present triggers, and providing a future template where clients see themselves effectively managing their triggered responses in the future.

## DEVELOPING A TREATMENT PLAN

In developing an EMDR treatment plan, the therapist decides if the treatment is going to be *time-limited, symptom-reduction,* or *comprehensive treatment.* Symptom reduction is focused on addressing specific symptoms or disorders such as PTSD treatment in a time-limited format or research program. Treatment for many active duty personnel and veterans is considered time-limited due to the limited number of sessions authorized by referring agencies such as TriCare and the Department of Veterans Affairs programs. Comprehensive treatment is an extended treatment program that addresses an extensive period of adverse life experiences. On one occasion, a client was referred to me by a corporate headquarters for treatment of a store clerk whose life had been threatened by a store robbery. Based on the referral information, I assumed the treatment would be for a single incident trauma, that is, a store clerk being threatened with death if she did not open the safe on the store premises. On arrival, I learned the client has a long history of traumatic life experiences beginning from 6 years of age. The client was in her 50s. Even with EMDR's accelerated process, it would take 2 to 3 years to treat all the person's disturbing life experiences. The referral source, her employer, was only willing to pay for treating the store robbery incident. So, in the History-Taking session, the anticipated treatment plan changed from time-limited, symptom-focused to comprehensive treatment. I treated the client for disturbing memories related to the incident using EMD(r) where I repetitively took the client back to target every couple sets of 30-35 repetitions of bilateral stimulation (BLS) during reprocessing. This provided for reprocessing but limited access to other associated memory networks.

Graduate education with professional practicums and internships train psychotherapists in seeking a history of the client's life. Most therapists develop a History-Taking approach based on their professional discipline and training. Psychologists, psychiatrists, social workers, licensed professional counselors, and licensed marriage and family therapists each develop an approach based on their clinical orientation and therapeutic approach. Therapists, sometimes, incorporate the use of genograms and timelines as additional resources for History-Taking. Use of these additional aids is often determined by the amount of time the therapist has available to devote to gaining additional information. Training in EMDR therapy teaches therapists to use a broad psychosocial approach to History-Taking, culminating in the development of two lists:

(a) a resource list containing memories of positive experiences and accomplishments and (b) a list of disturbing memories, which when the memory of an experience is recalled it continues to upset the person.

Each client reveals their history differently. Some individuals spontaneously provide much detail of the symptoms, their duration, and the origin of the event(s) associated with the presenting issue. Other clients are more subdued and vague in disclosing information, thus requiring more intentional questioning to gain the necessary information. Sometimes clients identify incidents/events that are clustered around symptoms, issues, sensations, or beliefs. Survivors of military sexual trauma (MST) may report incidents connected by safety/betrayal issues going back to early childhood safety issues. Shame-based clients sometimes identify similar events associated with the negative cognitive "I am worthless" or the visceral stomach sensations when a shame attack occurred. While developing the treatment plan, the therapist can identify the treatment goals by asking: "What brought you in?" or "What do you want to change as a result of being here?" These questions establish the basic treatment goal while emphasizing the expectation that the therapist expects change to happen. Next, while gathering a broad psychosocial history from the client, the therapist searches for answers to "What past experiences in the client's life set the groundwork for the client's current pathological symptoms?" This list becomes the basis for the treatment plan using the three-prong approach for treating past events, present triggers, and establishing a future template out of each identified trigger. The question "Are there more recent examples of the client's presenting problem?" helps identify other associated experiences in the client's life.

Listed in the text that follows are questions that can assist in expanding the case conceptualization for the client. This includes gathering information from past events, current triggers, and the future—EMDR therapy's three-prong approach. The six questions are followed by a case example.

## TREATMENT SEQUENCE PLAN

The chronological sequence is often a natural progression with the EMDR three-prong approach of chronologically treating past memories, starting with the Touchstone event, if one is identified. Then treating the identified current triggers. Remember, following the treatment of each trigger, using EMDR Phases 3 to 8, a future template is provided enabling the client to see themselves effectively managing a situation similar to the trigger in the future. Seldom do I begin with the sequence of treating the worst memory first.

When treating clients with complex trauma, such as complex PTSD, I find it helpful to sequence the TMs starting with the easiest memory first, then sequencing the treatment of the next easiest memory, and continuing until the most challenging memory is treated last. This sequence for complex trauma allows the client to experience the EMDR process with the disturbing memory they are most likely to manage. It builds the client's confidence in their ability to complete treatment while introducing them to the EMDR treatment process.

## CASE CONCEPTUALIZATION AND TREATMENT PLANNING

The following six questions, integrated into the broad psychosocial approach, can be helpful in gathering the important information during History-Taking. These questions are included in the EMDR Case Conceptualization and Treatment Plan form listed in Appendix F (see also Figure 3.2). In addition, the Target Sequence Treatment Plan, listing the identified TM in the sequence they are being treated, is available in Appendix D.

# EMDR CASE CONCEPTUALIZATION AND TREATMENT PLANNING

The number of sessions needed for History-Taking varies depending on whether the therapist is providing time-limited, symptom-focused,

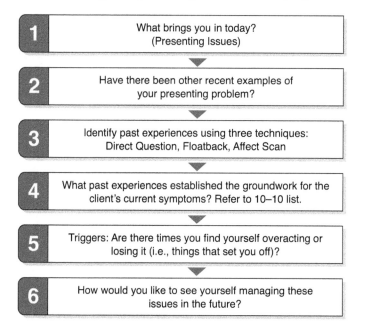

| 1 | What brings you in today? (Presenting Issues) |
| 2 | Have there been other recent examples of your presenting problem? |
| 3 | Identify past experiences using three techniques: Direct Question, Floatback, Affect Scan |
| 4 | What past experiences established the groundwork for the client's current symptoms? Refer to 10–10 list. |
| 5 | Triggers: Are there times you find yourself overacting or losing it (i.e., things that set you off)? |
| 6 | How would you like to see yourself managing these issues in the future? |

FIGURE 3.2  EMDR case conceptualization and treatment planning.

or comprehensive treatment. As a general rule, History-Taking requires one to four sessions depending on the complexity of the client's life experiences. A single incident trauma requires less time than a veteran with four combat deployments as well as a history of early childhood abuse.

I began treating military personnel and veterans using an intensive EMDR treatment model in 2006 at the suggestion of Francine Shapiro, PhD. The model allows for two EMDR sessions per day during 5- and 10-day periods. My clinical objective when I began with the 5-day treatment was to restore the client back to a level of functioning prior to their entering the military. In most cases, the number of combat traumas was the focus of the treatment. Most combat-related traumas could be identified and treated within the 5-day period by providing EMDR treatment twice a day. As multiple deployments began to produce complex PTSD cases, my goal was to accomplish the most significant healing in the amount of time available. This often meant identifying a larger list of traumatic events during History-Taking and selecting the most disturbing memories from the list, allowing them to be treated within the 10-day period. Participants were screened prior to acceptance into the treatment to ensure they could self-regulate and therefore process their disturbing memories while remaining in the window of tolerance (Siegel, 1999).

The 10–10 list provides both the resource list and the list of the 10 most disturbing memories. The 10 most disturbing memories list can be helpful while asking the question, "What previous experiences laid the groundwork for the current symptoms" to identify those disturbing memories connected to the client's symptoms. Add to those selected memories a list of current triggers and the follow-up future template as a means of providing the EMDR three-prong approach.

An example of an EMDR Phase 1 History-Taking session is provided in Case Study 3.1.

## Case Study 3.1: Initial Intake After Hospitalization Due to Suicidal Plan With Means Available

Client was hospitalized 2 weeks for suicidal intent. After multiple combat deployments, he began to experience panic attacks and uncontrollable crying in front of his soldiers. Going to the Army's Adult Behavioral Health provider embedded with his brigade, he "spilled his guts" to the mental health provider, went home that evening feeling vulnerable, and experienced another panic attack. The next morning, he returned to the Army post, had a dissociative episode, and regained present awareness with a rope in his hands with the intent to kill himself.

## Initial Meeting With Client

Therapist:  Hello! How do you prefer I address you?

Client:  Dave (name changed for anonymity) is fine.

Therapist:  Okay. I go by my initials, E. C., Echo Charlie. (Client smiles.) So, what brings you in, Dave?

Client:  I was uh (voice drops) recently in Cumberland Hall [acute care facility] (pause). My uh, … obviously, I've been talking about this for a while. At least recently as I attempted to figure out a lot of things about myself. I have come to understand that I have been suppressing a lot of things for a while. And my coping mechanism has been working and working hard. And, if I keep moving forward, I don't stop; I don't have to think, so I don't have to confront problems or issues that I have had. I have avoided dealing with them. My wife calls it the perfect storm. I just had spinal surgery. They had to replace a disc in my spine—that was in September. I just got here about a year ago. I've been in the Army 12 years, very successful, going up rank very fast. Platoon sergeant; very amped up, excited to be here. Then having back problems. I finally confronted it … I have had 3 years of taking medication and getting epidural injections and whatever therapies they were trying to work with weren't working. So, I didn't want to, but finally had to make a decision to have surgery. I went to Texas, had surgery, came back. Lost my platoon. I'm an infantryman. An infantryman who can't carry things is kinda counterproductive. It kinda hit me pretty hard, losing my platoon—watching them get ready to deploy and me not being a part of it. (Takes deep breath.) A snowball effect, I was starting to have these panic attacks, I don't know what you call them—panic, uncontrolled emotions. I would start crying and not know why. That's rare for a person like me—been deployed four times. I think of myself as very, kind of old school mentality, for lack of better terms, want to be a tough guy, you know—don't cry, always that tough guy. I would just get random emotions, crocodile tears that would just hit me, you know. I'm still struggling with that now. I mean right now I feel like crying, but that camera is on me so I am stopping myself. My heart would race, getting very, very anxious which is … I mean, I just came from being a drill sergeant in front of thousands of people and leading soldiers, having no issues. I never had a problem with fear in being in front of people. I mean, that is what I have done. It all started to change. I began to doubt myself. I have a lot of concerns with that. I decided to go see somebody. I told my first sergeant. I actually went home and cried to my wife and the next morning I got up and … it was bad timing. I had lost a friend about 5 years back who had overdosed on drugs—happened to be the same time frame. I saw a bunch of people posting on Facebook, social media … very bad timing, started to bring out emotions, it all started hitting me at the same time. I was having uncontrolled emotions, trying to do the right thing and not to show that to the soldiers, so went to talk to somebody. They started asking questions, which is their job as a therapist, and prying into stuff from previous, before my OIF deployments, I'd been through—I don't know what gave the urge now, but I decided to crack the door—let a couple of things come out. I felt very anxious about it. I think it was because of my moment of weakness. I didn't want to give that information out, but I started to, and, I made it out of that session—made it home that night and it all came out. I had a really horrible night, crying uncontrollably. I woke up, went into work the next morning. My wife knew something was really wrong. She called my first sergeant. I ended up in the parking lot. It's hard for me to say (choking up)… I thought about suicide. Which is crazy for a happily married man with two children to think like that. (Client is tearing up as he shakes his head.) I don't even know you and I'm … I'm sorry.

Therapist: No, you don't have to apologize. This is a secure place for you to talk.

Client:    So I got kinda overwhelmed. Got to the point where I was pulling out of the parking lot and actually went through a whole process of what I was going to do. Embedded behavioral health was right there on the right-hand side, the back 40 [acres—remote area of Ft Campbell] was on the other side. I was at that crossroads. Fortunately for me, I went over there. It all came out—I talked to them and went to Cumberland Hall for a couple of weeks. It's not a treatment facility, more a stabilization facility. There were some amazing doctors there. I heard about EMDR there. I had my wife go buy the book. Francine Shapiro's book is very interesting. The book seemed a little out there to me, but I did relate to a couple of stories in it very closely. Anyway, I was released. Went back to work. My stress level is still amazingly high, like to a point I feel not so much in control at times. Embedded behavioral health [on post] for whatever reason has not had an opportunity to see me. Dr. Able or Ms. Quinn talked to me about getting a recommendation off post and this is how I ended up here. I just told them whoever I do see—it had been a month and a half—and I hadn't seen anybody yet. I was getting to the point where I was starting to get cold feet. I just wanted it all to go away. Like, maybe I could just stop talking about it. But I know that is not going to get me forward in any way. I'm trying, … I'm really trying to be productive with this.

Therapist:    Good.

Client:    And figure out a way how I can get past it. It's at the point now where it's affecting me. I can't do my job. Which is at the point it's affecting my … everything. My whole life. I have dedicated the last 12 years of my life to the Army. It's done me well. I don't blame the Army for any of this. My stress level is so high I can't deal with work the way I normally could. Things that would normally bounce right off me aren't right now.

Therapist:    Sure.

| | |
|---|---|
| Client: | They become catastrophic. Even when I rationalize it in my head, it doesn't take away the feelings. |
| Therapist: | Right. |
| Client: | I mean I am sitting here right now saying [to myself] I shouldn't be emotional to a gentleman I just set down to talk with, but that doesn't stop it from happening! And this is my reality. |
| Therapist: | Yes, and this is a secure place for you to be able to do this without worrying about it. |
| Client: | Yeah. I feel that. (Nodding head "yes" with slight smile.) I mean I'm an infantryman and there's a stigma that comes along with that. There's a mentality. I've been that guy. I've said things about people who have gotten help that aren't right. Now, I'm in that boat. I can't do a lot of things I would normally do until I can find my way through that. That's what I'm trying to do. I guess more than even a career, I'm trying to save my life. |
| Therapist: | So let me get some history and talk about establishing some goals you wish to achieve in coming here. What do you want to be different as a result of being here Dave? |
| Client: | I want to get my old life back. I want to stop losing control of my emotions. Right now I feel like everything in my life is out of control. |
| Therapist: | We will work on your developing some self-regulation skills to help you manage your emotions. Then we will drain the emotional energy by using EMDR therapy to process those memories which are emotionally charged. |
| Client: | I'm ready to get started! |
| Therapist: | Okay. Good! You described the difficulty you had after leaving the therapist's office at the Embedded Behavioral Health office. **Have there been other recent examples of your having similar experiences?** |

Client:  No, I have never had an experience like that before. I am scared of going back there.

Therapist:  What about early times in your life? **When you think of that experience, does it remind you of times or events perhaps as early as childhood? (Direct Question)**

Client:  No, I don't remember any other experiences like that.

Therapist:  When you were in that experience—after leaving the therapist's office—what words would best describe a negative belief about yourself in that situation—sort of an "I am" statement?

Client:  Well, I felt out of control, scared, and worthless.

Therapist:  Do the words "I am worthless" seem to fit?

Client:  Yes.

Therapist:  So, just recall that situation and the words "I am worthless" and let your mind floatback to an earlier time when you might have had similar thoughts and experience. Don't work at it, just notice what comes up. **(Floatback technique)**

Client:  What pops up is when I lost my platoon, I felt worthless. And there was a mission we were on where I was the gunner on a Bradley. A vehicle was speeding toward us. I did what we were told to do in such a situation. Fire a round of 50 cal (50 caliber machine gun) in front of the vehicle. I fired a round in front of the vehicle, but instead of stopping the vehicle speeded up. So, I fired a round into the engine area, just as I was trained to do. The car stopped and caught fire. I waited for someone to get out of the car—no one did. So we watched the vehicle burn. After the fire burned out, and cooled off, I went to check who or what was inside. I expected it to be an insurgent with a bomb. Instead there were the charred remains of a woman and two children. That has haunted me ever since.

| | |
|---|---|
| Therapist: | Thanks for sharing this with me, Dave. **Are there also other memories with similar thoughts of "I am worthless"?** |
| Client: | Yeah, I saw a young girl, the insurgents had a suicide vest on her. I watched her cross the street and when she was near the market, the insurgent detonated the vest. I watched her dissipate into nothing. |
| Therapist: | You have witnessed some difficult scenes, Dave. |
| Client: | And, when my best friend died of an overdose. I felt I let him down. Somehow, I blamed myself that I should have prevented it from happening. Though, in my head I know better. And, when I was a teenager, I brought a lot of pain to my parents. I got into drugs causing my parents a lot of grief. |
| Therapist: | Anything else come to mind? |
| Client: | No, not really. |
| Therapist: | So, let's look at **how past experiences might have laid the groundwork for this.** |
| Client: | Well, now that we are talking about it, I can see how all these things I have kept bottled up might have caused some of this. |
| Therapist: | Seems you have dealt with loss while not allowing yourself an opportunity to grieve. There is the loss of your platoon. Loss of your best friend. Both seemed to leave you feeling worthless. Then feeling overwhelmed at the sight of the charred remains of the woman and children. Bottling up the emotions after viewing death of the little girl wearing the suicide vest. And the death of your grandfather. Let me ask you: **Are there times you have found yourself overreacting—being triggered—by sounds, smells, or situations? (Identifying triggers.)** |
| Client: | I find it difficult being around children, even my own children at times. I don't like being out in crowds. And I have problems driving sometimes if someone cuts me off. |

| Therapist: | Dave, let's take a minute to talk about how you would like to see yourself managing these issues in the future. |
|---|---|
| Client: | It is hard for me to see beyond the present with all that is going on now. As I said, when I first came in today, I would like to feel in control of my life, even if I get out of the Army, I would like to manage my life. And I would like to get over feeling worthless so often. |
| Therapist: | Based on our discussion today, let's put together a treatment plan that will help you achieve your goals. How does that sound to you? |

*Comments:* This soldier suffered with both PTSD and moral injury. He had an impressive military career. The psychological trauma from his multiple combat deployments began to be revealed through uncontrollable emotional outbursts in front of his soldiers as well as panic attacks. While distinguishing himself in combat and his overall 12-year military career, one of the most courageous deeds he accomplished was stepping forward in seeking help for his psychological wounds. He completed his treatment with EMDR therapy, relocated after discharge from the U.S. military, and lives with his wife and children.

## TREATMENT PLAN

This client demonstrated the impact of grief and loss in his life with the most recent loss of his position as platoon sergeant. The loss triggered a sense of worthlessness exacerbating his anxiety due to loss of control. Loss of his platoon represented his loss of identity as an NCO contributing to the mission readiness of his unit. This was mediated by his guilt and shame, aspects of moral injury connected with the death of the woman and children found in the burned-out vehicle. Viewing the death of the girl wearing a suicide vest contributed to his moral injury and personal sense of helplessness. The drug overdose of his best friend with its unresolved grief further added to his anxiety and depression. His intense, dissociative reaction following his initial appointment with the embedded behavioral health provider contributed to his fear of being overwhelmed in another History-Taking episode in the future. This fear fueled his avoidance of talking about his life experiences with any therapist in the future, while at the same time the client is highly motivated to reclaim his life. The client's fear of being overwhelmed again, in another therapy session, needed to be addressed first.

The treatment plan developed a target treatment sequence plan as: (a) Overwhelming experience at Embedded Behavioral therapist's intake session; (b) encounter with parents due to his drug use; (c) death of best friend; (d) death of girl wearing suicide vest; and (e) remains of the woman with two children. Then, (f) treating triggers of being around children followed with Future Template; and (g) trigger of being in crowd at the shopping mall followed by future template.

Following the EMDR therapy eight-phase standard protocol, treating the past events, present triggers, and future template, a three-prong EMDR approach was used for the treatment plan. Each TM was reprocessed resulting in a SUD of 0; VOC of 7; with clear body scan.

## CONCLUSION

Persons trained in EMDR therapy review the History-Taking phase from an AIP perspective. The basic training assumes persons with a graduate degree and mental health license (or under consultation) have been trained in basic History-Taking. This chapter supplements basic History-Taking in addressing issues relevant to military populations. Responsibility is a significant theme with this population. Highly responsible people are likely to struggle with self-imposed guilt and moral injury. They often view their world from a shame perspective. A discussion about shame is included in this chapter since the therapist will likely encounter shame in many clients' experience. Shame distorts the client's view of life as revealed in their History-Taking. Case conceptualization in this chapter is designed to prepare you, the reader, to conduct History-Taking in a manner that concludes with an appropriate, effective treatment plan specific to the military population.

### DISCUSSION POINTS

1.  Discuss treatment issues when treating a client diagnosed with PTSD and a mild TBI.
2.  What do you need to include in a treatment plan when the client is medicated with benzodiazepines or other sedatives?
3.  What score on the Dissociative Experiences Scale (II DES-II) raises a red flag during History-Taking? What range is reported eligible for treatment?
4.  What negative belief is commonly associated with a shame-based childhood?
5.  What question(s) establish the client's treatment goal(s)?

6. What is the difference between time-limited and comprehensive treatment?
7. Is moral injury the same as PTSD?
8. Does a shame-based childhood make a person more vulnerable to moral injury?

## REFERENCES

Bernstein, E. M., & Putnam, F. W. (1986). Development, reliability, and validity of a dissociation scale. *Journal of Nervous and Mental Disease, 174*(12), 727–735. https://doi.org/10.1097/00005053-198612000-00004

Carlson, E.B. & Putnam, F.W. (1993). An update on the Dissociative Experience Scale.Dissociation 6(1), p. 16–27. Retrieved from https://www.researchgate.net/publication/256295308_An_update_of_the_Dissociative_Experience_Scale

EMDR Institute. (2017a). *EMDR Institute basic training course weekend 1 of the two part EMDR therapy basic training.* Watsonville, NY: Author.

EMDR Institute. (2017b). *EMDR Institute basic training course weekend 2 of the two part EMDR therapy basic training.* Watsonville, NY: Author.

Felthous, A. (2006). Warning a potential victim of a person's dangerousness: Clinician's duty or victim's right? *Journal of the American Academy of Psychiatry and Law, 34,* 338–348.

Henderson, T. (2016). *TBI and PTSD appear similar, but treatments must differ.* Retrieved from https://www.behavioral.net/article/tbi-and-ptsd-appear-similar-treatments-must-differ

Hensley, B. (2016). *An EMDR therapy primer: From practicum to practice* (2nd ed.). New York, NY: Springer Publishing Company.

Herman, J. (2007). "Shattered shame states and their repair". Paper presented at the John Bowlby Memorial Lecture, March 10, 2007. Retrieved from http://www.challiance.org/Resource.ashx?sn=VOVShattered20ShameJHerman.

Hurley, E. (2018). Effective treatment of veterans with PTSD: Comparison between intensive daily and weekly EMDR approaches. *Frontiers in Psychology, 9,* 1–10. doi:10.3389/fpsyg.2018.01458

Korn, D., & Leeds, A. (2002). Preliminary evidence of efficacy for EMDR resource development and installation in the stabilization phase of treatment in complex posttraumatic stress disorder. *Journal of Clinical Psychology, 58,* 1465–1487.

Knipe, J. (2009). "Shame is my safe place": Adaptive Information Processing methods of resolving chronic shame-based depression. In R. Shapiro (Ed.). EMDR Solutions II. New York: W.W. Norton & Co.

Lew, V., Moore, S., Friedman, Y. J., Keane, T., Warden, D., & Sigford, B. (2008). Overlap of mild TBI and mental health conditions in returning OIF/OEF service members and veterans. *Journal of Rehabilitation Research and Development, 45*(3), xi–xvi. doi:10.1682/JRRD.2008.05.0064

Litz, B. T., Stein, N., Delaney, E., Lebowitz, L., Nash, W. P., Silva, C., & Maguen, S. (2009). Moral injury and moral repair in war veterans: A preliminary model and intervention strategy. *Clinical Psychology Review, 29,* 695–706. doi: 10.1016/j.cpr.2009.07.003

Maguen, S., & Litz, B. (2012). Moral injury in veterans of war. *PTSD Research Quarterly*, 23(1), 1–6. Retrieved from https://icds.uoregon.edu/wp -content/uploads/2011/07/Maguen-LItz-2012-Moral-Injury-review.pdf.

Rickaby, J. (2018). *Moral philosophy: Ethics deontology and natural law.* New York, NY: Franklin Classics.

Shapiro, F. (2018). *Eye movement desensitization and reprocessing (EMDR) therapy: Basic principles, protocols, and procedures* (3rd ed.). New York, NY: Guilford Press.

Shapiro, R. (2005). *EMDR solutions: Pathways to healing.* New York: W.W. Norton & Co.

Silver, S., & Rogers, S. (2002). *Light in the heart of darkness: EMDR and the treatment of war and terrorism survivors.* New York: W.W. Norton & Co.

Siegel, D. (1999). *The developing mind: How relationships and the brain interact to shape who we are.* New York: Guilford Press.

Talbot, J.A., Talbot, N.L. & Tu, X. Shame-Proneness as a Diathesis for Dissociation in Women with Histories of Childhood Sexual Abuse. *J Trauma Stress* 17, 445–448 (2004). https://doi.org/10.1023/B:JOTS.0000048959.29766.ae

Waelde, L. C., Silvern, L., Carlson, E., Fairbank, J. A., & Kletter, H. (2009). *Dissociation in PTSD.* In P. F. Dell & J. A. O'Neil (Eds.), Dissociation and the dissociative disorders: DSM-V and beyond, 447–456.

Walzer, M. (2015). *Just and unjust wars: A moral argument with historical illustrations.* (5th Ed.). New York: Basic Books.

# 4

# EMDR Phase 2: Preparing Veterans for EMDR Therapy

## Introduction

This chapter is designed to introduce the therapist to numerous therapeutic applications and an evaluative clinical template, all designed to prepare clients for EMDR's processing as early as possible. When managed successfully, the client is prepared to address those disturbing memories—the basis of their pathology. Preparation skills presented range from treating first responders who don't feel, soldiers who can't stop shaking (due to surviving a JDAM 2,000-pound bomb accidentally on their position) to experiencing racing thoughts and auditory and visual intrusions. This chapter reviews strategies for developing self-regulation skills across the clinical spectrum including persons needing extended preparation—all with the goal of getting clients into reprocessing as early as possible.

## Learning Objectives

- Discuss introducing EMDR therapy to the military, veteran, and first responder populations.
- Introduce the three modalities of bilateral stimulation (BLS) in setting up the mechanics.
- Review the basics of informed consent with various clinical presentations.
- Introduce relaxation techniques for a variety of clinical needs.
- Identify extended preparation procedures.
- Use blended preparation with complex cases.

## PREPARATION

EMDR therapy's Preparation phase is organized as a means of transitioning the client from the history-taking's treatment planning (Phase 1) to a state of stabilization, preparing the client for assessing and reprocessing designated disturbing memories. Phase 2 is designed to accomplish three objectives: (a) setting up the mechanics; (b) providing informed consent; and (c) ensuring the client's ability to self-regulate, that is, regain control should they become upset and need to calm down (F. Shapiro, 2018). These objectives are encapsulated between introducing the client to EMDR as a model of psychotherapy and concluding with the client's demonstrated ability to self-regulate. The duration of this phase is determined by the client's ability to accomplish those three objectives. Stable, healthy clients can move through preparation in half of a session or less. Severely dysfunctional clients may require several months to achieve the necessary stabilization. This chapter discusses each of the Phase 2 objectives as well as provides examples in treating complex cases with successful treatment outcomes.

## INTRODUCING EMDR THERAPY

Once an EMDR therapist learns the client's presenting issue(s) and treatment goals, the appropriateness of EMDR therapy is evaluated. Using the Adaptive Information Processing (AIP) model, the therapist conceptualizes the situation, keeping in mind that EMDR treats memories, both positive memories of achievements and disturbing memories of events, which continue to interrupt the client's quality of life. If EMDR therapy is deemed an appropriate approach, the therapist introduces EMDR therapy to the client as a means of resolving the identified treatment goals. At some time, an explanation of EMDR therapy and the AIP model is provided to the client. When, and how, the explanation is provided to the client is determined by the needs of the client at the time.

It is important the recommended treatment approach relates to the client's presenting issues. The introduction of EMDR therapy to the client may occur in a number of approaches.

### Recommendation of EMDR to the Client

I frequently use an introduction similar to this:

> *I use EMDR therapy in my therapy practice. Are you familiar with it? It is a model of psychotherapy I frequently provide to many of my clients. Its effectiveness is recognized by numerous professional organizations*

*including the World Health Organization (WHO), the Department of Veterans Affairs, and the Department of Defense, and numerous organizations world-wide. It has been found to be helpful for many persons dealing with similar issues as yourself. I think it could be helpful to you in achieving your treatment goals, if you are willing to give it a try.*

With the client's response I mention additional printed materials are available should they wish information. Any questions the client might have are encouraged.

Parenthetically, the mention of EMDR therapy receiving a "Category A" rating in the *VA/DoD Clinical Practice Guideline for the Management of Post-Traumatic Stress* (Department of Veterans Affairs & Department of Defense, 2017) is helpful for many military clients. As the therapist, my focus is on introducing an effective treatment approach that addresses the client's presenting needs.

## REVIEW OF THE VA/DoD CLINICAL PRACTICE GUIDELINES

Some military mental health providers introduce EMDR therapy by referring to the VA/DoD Clinical Practice Guideline (2017) while reviewing EMDR therapy as one of the four recommended treatments for adult trauma.

## REVIEW OF THE NATIONAL CENTER FOR PTSD'S LIST

Reference to the Department of Veterans Affairs National Center for PTSD's list of the three most researched treatments for posttraumatic stress disorder (PTSD; U.S. Department of Veterans Affairs, 2019) in which EMDR therapy is recognized as one of the three most widely researched treatments, can be used to introduce the therapy to clients.

Some clients, when introduced to EMDR therapy, want to know details about the treatment approach. Clients frequently will do their own research on the therapy between clinical appointments. Other clients don't want to be bothered by the treatment details; they accept the recommendation of the therapist. All clients are briefed on the EMDR process during the informed consent period. It is a clinical judgment as to when EMDR is suggested to the client. The timing is determined by the client's needs during their clinical presentation.

Hensley (2016) explains the need for clients to have a general understanding of EMDR therapy's theoretical basis including how the brain manages information. This information is provided during the Preparation phase. It is important for the EMDR therapist to have a working understanding of the theoretical basis of the therapy with a developed presentation to the client; one that is basic, succinct, and both therapist and client are comfortable in discussing.

CONCEPTUAL AND EXPERIENTIAL INTRODUCTION OF EMDR THERAPY

There are four categories of clients who are introduced to EMDR psychotherapy:

- persons who know about EMDR therapy as previous clients;
- those who have heard about EMDR therapy but have no experience with its treatment;
- persons who have no knowledge of EMDR but are skeptical or reactive; and
- those who know nothing of EMDR therapy but operate within optimal self-regulation and open to EMDR therapy treatment.

Therapists have options of presenting both conceptual understanding of the EMDR process as well as an experiential component in which the client has a positive experience of the use of bilateral stimulation (BLS) in reducing stress levels. Clients who already have knowledge of the EMDR approach will evaluate the current therapist's work based on their past experience. If the previous treatment was successful, it can be beneficial to learn what was the most beneficial aspect of the treatment. In cases where previous EMDR therapy was unsuccessful, it is important to learn what contributed to the treatment failure. Clarifying the client's expectations while outlining the treatment process can be helpful to discuss. Others, persons with some familiarity with the EMDR name, but not necessarily the treatment process, have some understanding that the letters "EM" in the name represents "eye movement" as a form of BLS, a paradigm shift in therapy. These clients usually have an openness for the process including setting up the mechanics. Clients who have no knowledge of EMDR therapy but are skeptical or reactive of treatment sometimes benefit with an "experiential introduction," a utilitarian approach that allows the client to focus on stress-related body sensations and notice the shifting and diminishing of the sensations with the use of BLS. This demonstrates the ability of BLS to change the client's experience in a brief time. A few minutes of slow repetitions of BLS, with deep breaths between sets, can help the client relax as their anxiety symptoms are diminished. This is also true for dysregulated clients who have difficulty with cognitive processing, whose memory processing is so fragmented that conceptual understanding does not influence them nearly as much as the positive experience of slow BLS on their dysregulation. EMDR therapy endears itself to the client once the client experiences the application of BLS.

The client who is stable, or functioning within an optimal range of self-regulation, normally welcomes treatment information as a means of making an informed decision. This is a "conceptual" introduction of the therapy to the client. Analogies such as the BLS being similar to rapid eye movement (REM) sleep can be helpful for this group. New information regarding EMDR therapy is often a conceptual introduction with an explanation of the basic description of the EMDR process. Francine Shapiro (2018) offers the following as an example of explaining the EMDR process:

> *Often, when something traumatic happens, it seems to get locked in the brain with the original picture, sounds, thoughts, feelings, and so on. Since the experience is locked there, it continues to be triggered whenever a reminder comes up. It can be the basis for a lot of discomfort and sometimes a lot of negative emotions, such as fear and helplessness, that we can't seem to control. These are really the emotions connected with the old experience that are being triggered.*
>
> *The eye movements we use in EMDR seem to unlock the system and allow your brain to process the experience. That may be what is happening in REM, or rapid eye movement, sleep, when our most intensive dreaming takes place: The eye movements appear to be involved during the processing of unconscious material.*
>
> *The important thing to remember is that it is your own brain that will be doing the healing and that you are the one in control. (F. Shapiro, 2018, pp. 115–116)*

The explanation of EMDR therapy can be offered in printed form such as the information contained in the "EMDR Brochure for Clients" (2009) or Francine Shapiro's book *Getting Past Your Past: Take Control of Your Life With Self-Help Techniques From EMDR Therapy* (2012). The book offers the client a broader description of EMDR therapy along with the AIP model. Clients are encouraged to view videos of what past clients, military personnel, veterans, and their spouses have said about the difference EMDR treatment has made in their lives and that of their relationships (EMDR Treatment Veterans, n.d.).

The handout "An Overview of EMDR Therapy Treatment," available in Appendix A of this book, is designed to supplement a client's conceptual introduction to the EMDR eight-phase approach in treating past events, present triggers, and providing for future situations with the future template. Each client identifies how much information they desires regarding EMDR therapy during the presentation of the model. Too much technical information can enhance a client's anxiety, leaving them feeling overwhelmed.

## SETTING UP THE MECHANICS

Once EMDR therapy has been identified as the designated treatment, the Preparation phase moves to setting up the mechanics as the next step. Setting up the mechanics includes: (a) demonstrating the "ships passing in the night" sitting position; (b) introducing the three modalities of BLS (eye movement [EM], auditory, and tactile); and (c) establishing a stop signal.

The sitting position is established as the "ships passing" position, the therapist uses her fingers to introduce EM. The off-side position allows the therapist to hold up her fingers aligned with the client's nose bridge. The therapist's fingers are on eye level with the client, so the client does not have to look up or down to follow the therapist's fingers. Note, use of technology such as the light bar has the therapist seated to the side of the client.

## EYE MOVEMENT BILATERAL STIMULATION AS A COMPONENT OF EMDR THERAPY

A review of the basics of the mechanics can be helpful. Always inform the client ahead of time what you are going to do in adjusting the mechanics. As few surprises as possible is always beneficial for the client. The seating distance between therapist and client is determined by the client's comfort zone. Many first responders and military personnel are particularly sensitive regarding a person getting too close, sensing their space has been violated. At a time when the goal is ensuring the client is as secure as possible, it is important to ensure setting up the mechanics is in keeping with the client's security. The same is true with the position of the fingers for finger movement (Exhibit 4.1). The therapist should ask the client for feedback regarding the optimal comfort zone for seating location and finger movement. Shapiro's original research described her holding her fingers 12 to 14 inches from the client's face (F. Shapiro, 1989). Most military and veteran clients would find this distance intrusive. Many prefer seats positioned from 2 to 2.5 feet apart. When setting up the mechanics, it is helpful to ask the client what seating and finger distance feels best for them as the therapist positions the chair. When adjusting the finger distance, inform the client that you will begin adjustment with your fingers back by your shoulder and slowly move your fingers forward to the point that is most comfortable for the client.

While there is an emphasis on the use of EM for BLS, there are times when you, as the therapist, may need to change modality. For such occasions it is helpful to have checked the alternative forms of BLS, that is, tactile and auditory with the client before processing. The tactile (tapping) is frequently used for self-regulation. While seated in the "ships passing," I will often introduce BLS with a statement such as:

> *I have learned that if I hold up my fingers and your eyes slowly follow them about 6 to 8 times your body will begin to relax. And, if I speed up the movement you will begin to process your memories faster. Are you okay if I hold up my hand and your eyes follow my fingers slowly to relax?" (Do 6-8 repetitions of EM slowly and gradually increase speed*

**EXHIBIT 4.1 Eye Movement Bilateral Stimulation**

The therapist holds their hand in front of the client's eyes. The client should not have to look up or down to follow the therapist's fingers.

The therapist's fingers follow an imaginary line running across the client's eyes—a straight line, avoiding arching, giving the "windshield wiper" effect.

*for a couple sets.) "Take a breath, let it go. What do you notice? Let's do it again." (Do 3-4 sets having the client take a deep breath after each set. "How was that?")*

(Introduce auditory and tactile BLS)

*"Now, I can change the direction from this horizontal, left to right motion, to a different direction we call diagonal." (Do 3-4 sets of 6-8 repetitions.) "How was that?" (Then introduce the auditory, preferably using headphones.) Do 3 to 4 repetitions of beeps with headphones.*

*"Which one of these—eye movement, auditory, or tactile—work best for you? Now, I would like to establish a stop signal—a nonverbal signal. In case you need to stop, you can give me the signal and I will immediately stop. The signal can be the halt sign (just hold your hand up), the referee time-out (tilted T), or turn your head away. Which one would you like to use?"*

During reprocessing one modality at a time is normally used. However, there are situations where the use of two modalities concurrently is warranted. For example, a soldier with significant physical wounds, a traumatic brain injury (TBI), and complex PTSD had occipital lobe damage while experiencing both visual and auditory intrusions. His occipital lobe damage prevented him from doing EM. He elected to use headphones to override the auditory intrusions while holding the tappers in his hands. This worked well for him.

## WINDOW OF TOLERANCE

Siegel (1999) described an optimal zone of self-regulation where a person can process varying levels of emotional intensity while the system maintains a homeostasis. High levels of emotional intensity can be managed as the client feels in control and comfortable. The intensity of experiencing an aroused emotional state can push a person outside their window of tolerance, creating an interruption in their ability to think or respond appropriately. The extremes, hyperarousal and hypoarousal, both outside the window, are the autonomic nervous system's (ANS's) response to perceived threat (Figure 4.1).

Excessive activity in the sympathetic nervous system can lead to increased respiration and heart rate in preparation for fight or flight as a survival response. Persons in an extreme hyperarousal state can experience fear/panic, rage, feeling overwhelmed, and hypervigilance. Clients stuck in a hypervigilant state lose the ability to change between the states of vigilance and hypervigilance. When persons have been stuck in a state of hypervigilance for some time the prospect of relaxing can

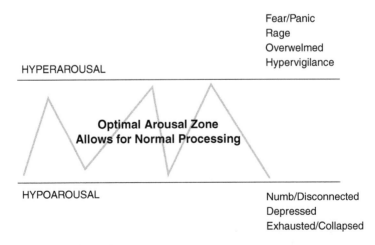

FIGURE 4.1 Window of tolerance diagram.

seem threatening to the person. Some combat soldiers have indicated it has been 7 or 8 years since they were able to relax.

The other extreme outside the window of tolerance is the hypoarousal state. This state is regulated by the parasympathetic nervous system with an energy-conserving response with a decrease in heart rate and respiration along with numbness, being disconnected from reality, feeling exhausted/collapsed and depressed with the neurological regulatory system shutting down. These response patterns are sometimes developed during early childhood experiences. Children who were repetitively scared in their earlier life experiences may allow that fear to become associated with a sense of terror or dread in life, resulting in a present-day experience of feeling out of control or panic. The ability to self-soothe is typically lacking in such clinical presentations.

Ground combat forces may be familiar with the terms "stand-to" and "stand-down" to describe when soldiers are on guard for enemy attack. They are positioned around the perimeter of their base looking out into the dawn of the early morning watching for an enemy surprise attack. As the sun comes up and risk of surprise attack is diminishing, the order to "stand-down" is given, meaning it is secure for soldiers to go about their routine duties. The terms "stand-to" and "stand-down" can be useful in helping soldiers understand there are times it is okay to relax; it is not necessary to be on guard all the time.

Former Army Ranger psychologist David Grossman and retired police officer Loren Christensen (2008) describe the ANS's regulation during life-threatening events such as police operations and military combat. They suggest the sympathetic nervous system is like the front-line troops who are energized for battle. The adrenaline fuels the body's physical operation. Combat military personnel and police officers burn up the adrenaline differently. This is determined by the amount of time used to operate with an adrenaline high. Police officers tend to have more short-term life or death encounters resulting in unused adrenaline, which can keep them hyped up long after the life-threatening incident is over. Combat soldiers often have hours of long combat engagement requiring the consumption of the adrenaline over extended periods. When the adrenaline is consumed, the person is left fatigued.

Grossman and Christensen (2008) describe the parasympathetic nervous system as being likened to support staff who sustain the combatants over a period of time. EMDR therapists who work with these populations benefit from understanding that during the Preparation phase, memories of line-of-duty ANS responses can impact the client's view of relaxation. Following intense life-threatening operations, there is a "parasympathetic backlash" so powerful that, following combat, soldiers sometimes fall asleep once they stand-down. It is a powerful physiological collapse (Grossman & Christensen, 2008, p. 16). This creates a vulnerability that commanders address by keeping reinforcements in reserve to replace those who experience the parasympathetic backlash. In fact, the body's gastrointestinal system shuts down with combat soldiers causing them, at times, to lose bladder control due to the collapse of the digestive system, a condition medically known as having a spastic bowel or colon. Soldiers sometimes defecate and urinate on themselves due to the parasympathetic collapse. They lose control of their bladder functions. EMDR clients may describe these experiences while describing the target memory in which the shut-down occurred. These physical and psychological collapse experiences may become part of the client's implicit memory. Memories of parasympathetic collapse can sometimes be triggered at the suggestion of the client relaxing, leaving the client feeling vulnerable.

It is not uncommon for persons who have lived in the hypervigilance state fueled by adrenaline for an extended period to report feeling vulnerable when relaxation is suggested. It is helpful to ask the client if they would be okay with relaxing for a period. If they report feeling vulnerable, it can be helpful to point out that under normal circumstances a person has choices whether to be on guard or relaxed. We use our risk assessment skills to determine the threat level. We can enjoy a better quality of life if we have the ability to self-regulate. With such clients I will contract with them to relax for 20 minutes in my office with the understanding they can resume an alert status once they leave the office. I convey my job is to help them have more control in their life, so they have choices.

The therapeutic relationship, with sound trust and rapport, can strengthen the client's ability to maintain affect regulation. Clients who are able to glean support from the therapeutic relations are more likely to pursue treatment during challenging periods. Such regulation allows the client's emotional experience to adjust to the present supportive state of the therapist. Alan Schore emphasized the importance of this attunement process (1994, 2003a; 2003b) in influencing regulation of the ANS. The EMDR approach utilizes these concepts with its client-centered approach. The trust and rapport that began in Phase 1, during history taking, continues in this phase. The sitting position in setting up the mechanics, establishing a stop signal, and reminding the client they are in control of the process are all interactive components that make this Preparation phase successful. Later, during Phase 4—Desensitization, the use of cognitive interweaves and adjusting the speed and number of passes during BLS emphasize the importance of attunement and therapist–client alignment to maintain dual awareness throughout the process.

## INFORMED CONSENT FOR THE EMDR CLIENT

Various professional organizations including the American Psychological Association, the National Board of Certified Counselors, and the National Association of Social Workers provide guidelines for providing informed consent to clients. The basic purpose of these guidelines is to ensure the client has the necessary information provided in an understandable language, is knowledgeable of the risks associated with the services, knows the possible limits to the service due to third-party payers, is aware of costs, is aware of possible alternatives, understands the rights of the client to refuse or withdraw from treatment, and is provided with an opportunity to ask questions (National Association of Social Workers, 2017; National Board of Certified Counselors, 2017). The Ethical Standards of the American Psychological Association specify the treating psychologist must obtain informed consent from the client prior to treatment. Psychologists' Ethics Code requires the psychologist to present details about the therapy technique, the professional acceptance of the treatment, and whether a psychologist in training (intern or resident) is providing the treatment (American Psychological Association, 2016).

The EMDR Preparation phase includes providing informed consent to the client. Various agencies and practices may have different forms for providing written informed consent. Verbally describing the mechanics of the EMDR process also provides additional information. Often, since both written and verbal informed consent are provided, a generic informed consent covering the general use of psychotherapy is presented and signed in response to the client's desire for treatment. This is a written document reviewed between the therapist and the client during the initial intake. Then, a more specific EMDR therapy presentation is provided to the client beginning with the offering of EMDR therapy as a viable treatment option. Written information providing a detailed description of EMDR therapy is provided (see Appendix G "Examples of Presenting EMDR Therapy during Phase 2") to the client. Informed consent information is provided to the potential EMDR client during the Preparation phase.

FEAR AND AVOIDANCE

There are numerous reasons a client may wish to avoid aspects of treatment. First, and foremost, the client must feel secure in your office while considering the EMDR therapy process. This is addressed early by asking the client what they need in order to feel secure in your office. Appropriate informed consent is designed to provide treatment information and answer their questions pertaining to their treatment. Identifying the benefits of effective treatment outcome can be helpful. Viewing videos of what other clients, treated with EMDR therapy, have reported (see https://soldier-center.com/what-clients-say---emdr.html; EMDR Treatment Veterans, n.d.) is often reassuring. Clients may have a fear of becoming emotional. Many military personnel have learned to turn down their emotions during deployment as a means of survival. Recognizing emotions, especially fear, can leave the person feeling vulnerable. During combat the only emotion recognized tends to be anger since the energy associated with anger fuels a person's sense of emotional and physical strength. Other persons, due to shame, guilt, or moral injury, may view the target memory as being too painful to address. While supporting the need of the client to feel secure and know they are in charge of the process, it is helpful to identify the source of fear or avoidance with the client. As the therapist, I want to support the client's need to be in charge of their decision-making and point out the benefits of resolving the need represented in the avoidance. Learning when the client first learned to avoid or learned to be concerned about addressing the issues can be identified and usually targeted with reprocessing the source memory. This approach allows the client's avoidance to be addressed and replaced with a more healthy approach without challenging the sole removal of the avoidance with appropriate healthy replacement. Use of the Flash technique is sometimes helpful with fear-based avoidance. (Maxfield, Maxffield, Lovell & Engel, 2017)

STABILIZATION IS REQUIRED

The development of sound clinical skills allows the EMDR therapist to manage how much Preparation time is necessary for the client. As an approved consultant, I have noted some therapists hesitate to begin the reprocessing phases. Some therapists wait for the state change during Preparation to reduce the level of anxiety sufficiently, when reprocessing the material would resolve the anxiety. There is a decision point between using state change of self-regulation to diminish anxiety temporarily or enter the reprocessing phase of Desensitization to resolve the anxiety. In these cases, the clinical skill to move the client through the initial intensity is required. As therapists develop their clinical skills, they increase their repertoire to engage the reprocessing appropriately. In addition, there are clients who are fragile, that is, suicidal possibilities, or dissociative exhibitions with complex PTSD that require extended preparation. First, do not harm.

De Jongh and colleagues (2019) raise the question whether a stabilization period is necessary for treatment. A review of the current literature finds there is no rigorous research to support the belief that adults with cPTSD profit significantly from trauma-focused treatments when preceded by a stabilization phase (De Jongh et al, 2016). It seems the clinical skills of the therapist and the self-regulation of the client determine how much stabilization is needed. If this is partially the case, adequate training and consultation can advance the therapist's clinical abilities.

The EMDR Institute's *Basic Training Course*, Part 2 (2017b), indicates the client may need additional stabilization when the client discloses:

- difficulties managing affect regulation,
- overaction into high levels of arousal by normal life events,
- demonstrated difficulty managing continual reactivity,
- dissociative exhibitions that interfere with personal functioning and relationships,
- acute issues such as self-injury, addictions, suicidality, and violent behaviors.

In response to these challenges, the client may need to work on affect regulation as well as focusing on desensitizing any triggers to daily life events that are dysregulating or disruptive in the client's life.

SELF-REGULATION SKILLS FOR THE CLIENT

EMDR therapy's Phase 2 is designed to introduce the client to a basic knowledge of EMDR therapy, provide informed consent, and ensure the client can self-regulate sufficiently to begin the reprocessing phases (Phases 4–6) of the EMDR eight-phase approach. The therapist determines what is clinically sufficient for the client's self-regulation skills in order to move into the reprocessing phases. Traditionally, there are EMDR therapists who remind me "there is no such thing as too much preparation!" Others, seasoned EMDR therapists, observe that many EMDR therapists tend to "homestead" in the Preparation phase due to hesitation in moving into the reprocessing phases. Some EMDR therapists have the opinion the client must be able to do a specific exercise such as the Safe/Calm Place in order to be ready for reprocessing. Of course, this is not true. The client must demonstrate the ability to self-regulate sufficiently, when paired with the therapist's clinical skills, to manage processing once Desensitization begins as a process. This involves the ability to switch from the alertness of the sympathetic nervous system to the calming regulation of the parasympathetic nervous system. This includes various techniques such as diaphragmatic breathing, slow tapping using the Butterfly Hug (Tactical Tapping), or tapping on one's legs with a couple deep breaths between sets of 1 and 10 repetitions in each set. Any relaxation exercise with which a person can self-regulate is adequate. Remember, the self-regulation is state change, not trait change. The relaxed state will only last a few minutes, hours, or days. Then, life intervenes.

Effective EMDR therapy requires appropriate timing in the Preparation phase. Moving prematurely from Phase 2 into reprocessing, when the client is unable to adequately self-regulate, can leave the client overwhelmed. On the other hand, pausing, or keeping the client unnecessarily too long in doing self-regulation work, can become discouraging for the client. More complex trauma cases, such as complex PTSD, can require extended preparation of several weeks, and sometimes several months, working with the client in developing their self-regulation skills. Keep in mind, with complex trauma, it can be helpful to select the easiest target memory to begin treatment; then go to the next easiest.

SELF-REGULATION TECHNIQUES

EMDR basic training (EMDR Institute, 2017a) introduces training participants to the Safe/Calm Place relaxation exercise during Part 1 of the two-part training. Part 2 training (EMDR Institute, 2017b) suggested additional stabilization skills including autogenic training, meditation, mindfulness, yoga, self-hypnosis skills, Tai Chi, diaphragmatic breathing, Calm/Safe Place, containment technique, and resource enhancement. Stress management techniques listed include the Light Stream technique, Spiral technique, and Breathing Shift. When highly activated clients have difficulty completing exercises such as Safe/Calm Place, relying on the body's basic physical exercises can be effective in engaging the parasympathetic nervous system for relaxing. Having the client do tapping and breathing exercises is very effective for persons whose cognitive processes, including racing thoughts and dissociative experiences such as visual and auditory intrusions, interfere with the success of the Safe/ Calm Place.

# CHALLENGES TO THE SUCCESSFUL COMPLETION OF THE RELAXATION COMPONENT OF PHASE 2

RESOURCE DEVELOPMENT AND INSTALLATION

There are difficult clients, such as those in category 3, who are not yet ready for reprocessing. They lack affect tolerance or the mental strength to engage in the reprocessing phases of EMDR therapy. Korn and Leeds (2002) published their case study using resource development and installation (RDI) in the treatment of persons with chronic PTSD. Now, RDI is included in EMDR basic training, part 2 (EMDR Institute, 2017b). Since RDI is a state change, it does not produce lasting results. Instead, it produces temporary results that can assist a person in using memories of past achievements to address similar challenges in the present. Effective treatment requires getting the client into reprocessing disturbing memories as early as they are able to meet criteria. Doing RDI when not required can leave the client feeling good, but if not necessary, the time could be used more effectively in reprocessing disturbing memories. While RDI is infrequently used in my practice, when the client needs to feel empowered to handle a situation it can be very helpful.

EXTENDED PREPARATION FOR COMPLEX CASES

Many clients enter our offices with a normal ability to self-regulate. Completing a relaxation exercise is an easy process. These are stable persons with the ability to manage affect regulation. Many readily embrace the opportunity to learn additional relaxation skills and view another opportunity to relax as a gift of quiet time. As an EMDR therapist, I basically see three categories of clients who complete the Preparation phase: (a) persons able to self-regulate as a normal daily function; (b) persons who normally operate from a hypervigilant or hypovigilant condition; and (c) persons so dysregulated they need extended work to develop self-regulation skills. Persons who experience hypovigilance are not as behaviorally prominent as hypervigilance in the broader clinical presentation. With the first group of clients, they typically complete the Preparation phase in less than half the session, often in 15 to 20 minutes. During the process, I explain EMDR therapy, set up the mechanics, provide informed consent, and lead the client through the Safe/Calm Place. The second group, persons usually dysregulated, who maintain a hypervigilance or hypovigilance stance, need some additional work such as addressing the vulnerability experienced with relaxing, dealing with dissociative numbing, or focusing on other fear/avoidance concerns. This second category, with appropriate strategy, can usually develop self-regulation in a few sessions. The third category includes persons with severe dysregulation that requires weeks, sometimes months, to adequately prepare the person to self-regulate sufficiently to maintain a present orientation, with the ability to remain in the window of tolerance when confronted with life events. EMDR therapy can be effective in treating each of these categories; it is just a matter of the EMDR therapist providing the necessary clinical strategy.

The first group, category 1, allows for the spontaneous adaptation of relaxation exercises. Category 2 may require the therapist to address blocking beliefs or targeting memories of times when the client learned avoidance or fear responses. Category 3 requires sequential sessions of Preparation work in assisting the client to develop self-regulation abilities as the client recovers from more severe symptoms such as night terrors, flashbacks, depersonalization and derealization, and limitations to maintain present awareness.

Clients in category 3 may have difficulty visualizing themselves at a relaxing place as they attempt to do the Safe/Calm Place exercise. They may report having racing thoughts, or they are so hypervigilant they have difficulty focusing on a relaxing location either real or imaginary. After spending time in combat, some veterans do not believe there is such a safe place anymore. Therefore, I avoid using the word "safe" in Calm/Safe Place. I sometimes refer to a secure place or fortified place. And, I often refer to the Butterfly Hug as "tactical tapping" for military and first responders.

Clients who are "numbed out" (hypovigilant) can often improve their awareness by doing basic exercises beginning with the client noticing differences in body sensations. For example, the client begins with making a fist, then opening his hand, relaxing the tension in the hand. He is asked to notice the difference of sensation and do BLS as the client focuses on the location where the difference is noted. The same is done with breathing. Have the client fill his lungs with a deep breath through the nostrils, hold the breath for 5 seconds, then exhale through the mouth. Call attention to the diffidence in sensation between the full lungs and collapsed with complete exhaling. Do BLS as the client notices the difference. The client is then encouraged to broaden their awareness of sensation differences between sessions. During the session, BLS is used to call attention to those differences. These exercises are done regularly calling attention to differences in body sensations.

## When There is No Safe Place

For clients who have difficulty focusing on a calm/safe/secure place, or who are so hypervigilant they have difficulty relaxing—when there seems to be no safe place for the client—I provide the following:

1. Assure the client, as their therapist, that I am responsible for the security of the room. This is my area of responsibility (AOR).
2. Ask if there is someone who they wish was stationed outside the room to provide additional security. If so, ask them to imagine that person being on guard at the door and what it would be like.
3. Ask them to do a basic breathing exercise: (a) take a deep breath through the nose/nostrils, filling the lungs with air for 5 seconds; (b) hold the breath for 5 seconds; now exhale through your mouth for 5 seconds, emptying your lungs. Then, repeat this exercise two to three times. After each set, ask the client to "just notice the change you feel in your body when you exhale."
4. Now, assign the client to do their own tapping: either the tactical tapping (Butterfly Hug) or tap their legs, doing eight slow tapping repetitions. Having the client do their own tapping can be very enhancing for the client. Assigning this task gives the client something else to focus on and allows the client to feel more in control. This frequently succeeds in getting the client relaxed when Safe/Calm Place does not work.

Based on this technique alone, I have found a sufficient number of my dysregulated clients sufficiently relaxed in preparation of entering the reprocessing phases (Phases 3–8) of EMDR therapy. The approach incorporates a natural neurological process. Slow tapping provides a natural rhythm. The client's own tapping allows for a task to focus on and provides a sense of the client's personal contribution, which provides an element of self-control beyond the passive stimulation of the client responding to the therapist's stimulation.

EXTENDED PREPARATION PHASE

There are times when the client meets selection criteria for EMDR treatment, except the ability to self-regulate. These are persons who fall into the previously mentioned third category, those requiring sequential sessions of preparation work. Such persons tend to be in debilitating conditions psychologically. They present as if they are stuck in dysregulation with constant dissociative exhibitions, easily triggered. Some clients in my office have suffered with constant visual and auditory intrusions based on their unresolved traumatic experiences. Persons with the more extreme symptoms will mentally come and go in their present awareness, in a dissociative process, as they sit in the waiting room. Their ability to be mentally and physically strong enough to do trauma processing is sometimes determined by the few hours of sleep they are able to accomplish during the previous night. Often, there is some suicidal ideation that frequently is like background noise in their mental processing. As long as the client has hope, the suicidal ideation remains in the background. All three categories listed can be successfully treated with EMDR therapy. The length of treatment is determined by the severity of the psychological wounds as well as the frequency of treatment. Effective treatment outcomes are regularly demonstrated at facilities where all clinical staff are seasoned therapists, well trained in EMDR therapy.

## Case Study 4.1: A Narrative of Extended Preparation With a Veteran Who Attempts Regulation By Rocking

The veteran, whom we shall identify as Bryan, entered my office in a highly anxious condition. The office manager reported he had been seated near the window in the waiting room where he continually raised the window blinds in order to monitor any outside activities. At one point, while waiting, he walked outside "to take a smoke" in near-freezing weather. Being outside gave him a break away for the other clients seated in the waiting room. As I met the veteran and led him back to my office, he selected a chair allowing him to face the door entry. While going through the regular intake discussion, Bryan indicated he lived in a housing complex near my office. At one time, about a year previously, he reported sitting in his vehicle in a nearby parking lot with the barrel of a pistol in his mouth, deciding whether or not to pull the trigger. I told him I was glad he chose not to pull the trigger on the weapon and that being in my office seeking healing was a much better choice.

When I inquired about Bryan's history, his hands and legs began to noticeably shake as his voice elevated. He began to rock his upper torso back and forth while sitting in the chair. With his high level of anxiety, I decided to titrate his history-taking by just focusing on an overview of his life, with the focus primarily on his military service. Getting a brief overview of his life was about the best I could accomplish at the time. It was apparent he was having difficulty with his self-regulation. He described feeling that his life was out of control. I described to Bryan that I wanted to first help him regain a sense of control in his life by working with him to learn some skills to manage his anxiety. The treatment plan was presented as beginning with front-loading his self-regulation skills, then discussing the memories of disturbing experiences that seemed to create his current symptoms.

Bryan met with me twice a week during a 4-month period working on his self-regulation skills. We began with basic breathing exercises. Breathing in through the nostrils—inhaling for 5 seconds; holding his breath for 5 seconds; then, exhaling out his mouth—emptying his lungs for 5 seconds. We repeated the process with three breathing exercises. Then we added tapping. I introduced tapping his legs as well as teaching him the Butterfly Hug. He preferred tapping his legs as the Butterfly Hug seemed to constrict his movement, just in case he needed to quickly respond to an immediate situation. From tapping I led Bryan through the Safe/Calm Place. He did not believe there is any place that is safe, so we called the exercise the Secure Place. Bryan was able to work his way through the Secure Place, but his anxiety seemed to interfere with his ability to remember and enact the exercise when outside my office. Next, in subsequent sessions I introduced Bryan to a computerized stress reduction program designed to enhance synchronized coherence between heart rhythm patterns and respiration (HeartMath Institute, 2005). The computerized program is similar to a video game version of biofeedback. It provided basic real-time video games, allowing pictures on the computer screen to begin coloring as coherence is achieved. This provided a sense of achievement to the veteran as his coherence improved. These relaxation exercises were incorporated into Bryan's sessions, allowing for 16 Preparation sessions over the course of 4 months.

Bryan progressively improved his ability to self-regulate. I began to witness his ability to sit in my office and discuss his trauma history while self-regulating without rocking in the chair.

He could control the volume of his voice in recounting his life's incidents. This performance became the indicator he was sufficiently resourced to complete his history-taking and begin treatment on a manageable target memory.

After 4 months of extended preparation, I used a modified EMDR protocol. I asked Bryan to identify a target memory he believed he could manage during the treatment process for 20 minutes, with the understanding we would stop reprocessing after 20 minutes to ensure he was calm and contained at the end of the session. The limited time allowed him to know he could endure the process regardless of the level of difficulty. The remaining time in his session was spent reassuring him there would be enough time to close the session being calm and contained was helpful. He identified a target memory of helplessly watching a young child wearing a suicide vest who was blown up by an insurgent. His subjective unit of disturbance (SUD) was an eight. I changed the TICES (Target = image, cognition, emotion, and body sensation) to viewing the scene from a distance while seeing the incident through a Plexiglas window. Bryan processed through the targeted memory amazingly well. I stopped after 20 minutes as we agreed and immediately went to a prolonged Closing phase, ensuring he had the availability of a container exercise and Safe/Calm Place. Bryan did wonderfully well during his first, short period of reprocessing. The following session we did the Phase 8 Reevaluation and then resumed reprocessing the memory. Bryan was able to complete the reprocessing of the target memory, resulting with a SUD of 0, VOC of 7, and clear body scan.

## Case Study 4.2: Extended Preparation

### TWO-HAND INTERWEAVE FOR A SEVERELY DYSREGULATED VETERAN WITH TBIP

The client, identified here as Robert, is a 38-year-old sergeant first class (E-7), with 18 years of military service and five combat deployments, who is suffering with complex PTSD with severe dissociative exhibitions including auditory and visual intrusions. He has a moderate traumatic brain injury (mTBI) with occipital lobe damage, which prevents the use of EM. His auditory and visual intrusions interfere with his ability to receive and respond to statements and questions. This slows down his response to any communication. The client has been hospitalized on three occasions for attempted suicide while in dissociative states. Due to combat injuries, he lost partial sensation in his right hand. The client's sleep is limited to 1 to 2 hours each night due to night terrors. The night before this session he had 1 hour's sleep, leaving him to dissociate continuously while in the waiting room. He was extremely hypervigilant during this session; he reported difficulty maintaining focus and struggled as he attempted to relax. During this session, my objective was to establish some level of relaxation despite his difficulty since this represents his clinical condition in most sessions.

This script reports the use of the "Two-Hand Interweave" (R. Shapiro, 2005) in addressing the client's ambivalence regarding being on guard and relaxing. Earlier in the session I tossed a ball with the client to get him focused in the present. The ball toss was followed by using the tappers with slow BLS. Once we began to use the tappers, I suggested the client allow one hand to represent that part of himself who wanted to relax, and the other hand represent the part that felt vulnerable and needed to be on guard. I affirmed his need to feel secure while allowing a part of himself to relax. All along I encouraged the client that he was "doing fine."

Therapist: Are you ready to do some relaxation?

Client: My body's just … I just feel like somebody's there and I can't stop watching. I can't stop … I can't close my eyes.

Therapist: Now, would it be okay for you to relax today?

Client: I'm trying, I don't know what the problem is.

Therapist: We're doing different things to help you relax. So, there's no right or wrong to this. We're just working with the way things are. You're doing fine. Okay?

Client: Yes sir.

Therapist: Now let's try these tappers. There we go. (presents Tappers to client)

Therapist: So, what we're working on today is that there's a part of you that feels the need to be on guard and that's okay. Another part of your body is feeling like when you fill your lungs with air, that's helping your nervous system to calm down.

| | |
|---|---|
| Therapist: | So, it's okay for both of those to be there. That's alright. Let's just take a couple more deep breaths. Fill the lungs with air and do it again. And, let's do that one more time. And, when you take those deep breaths, what does that feel like for you? |
| Client: | Seems like I don't have a lot of bad things and I don't.... |
| Therapist: | Yeah, okay. So, let's just do that again, okay? |
| | Now I'm going to turn this on (tappers) very low and let it run just a little bit. |
| | Can you feel that now? |
| Client: | Mm-hmm. |
| Therapist: | Okay. And as you feel that, just take some deep breaths like you're getting those bad things out. And let's do it again please. Just notice how your lungs feel and let's do it one more time. And what does that feel like for you now? |
| | So, like I'm empty on the inside. |
| | Okay. And so, was that like a good or a bad feeling? And let's just do it one more time. |
| Client: | It's good on the inside. |
| Therapist: | Yeah. So just notice that feeling good on the inside and we'll do one more deep breath, okay? Now this is like PT for the inside. |
| | Now, let's just notice that one hand feels relaxed and the other hand feels uptight and on guard. So just notice your two hands. One is relaxed and the other one feels uptight. Let's just take a deep breath and we do it one more time, just cleaning out the inside. (BLS + deep breath) And what's that like for you now? |
| Client: | So, I just feel relaxed on the inside. |
| Therapist: | Well good, is that alright? |
| Client: | Mm-hmm. (Smiles) |
| Therapist: | Now, I'm going to keep guard on the outside to make sure everything's okay too and so we're just |

|  | helping the inside relax a little bit. Now, if you focus on that hand that feels relaxed right now, what does that hand feel like for you? |
|---|---|
| Client: | Just … not really anything, it's just calm. |
| Therapist: | Okay. So just feel that calm hand. |
|  | I'm here to be on guard in this room. I've got the security of this room and I'm standing guard, just feel the calmness in that one hand. I'm going to do this about five times. I just turn it down. Feel the vibration. |
|  | And what do you notice now? |
| Client: | It's like my stomach and my left arm are feeling gray, it's like relaxed, and that's about it. |
| Therapist: | Is that a good feeling? Relaxed? |
| Client: | Yeah, it's a good feeling, it's just weird. It's kind of … That's how it was, it was relaxed. My mind is not relaxed. My mind is … |
| Therapist: | So, a part of your body can be relaxed even when your mind is not? Is that right? |
| Client: | Mm-hmm (affirmative). |
| Therapist: | Yeah. So just feel this sense of relaxation again, and part of your body feels the need to be on guard. And we talked before about the concepts of "stand-to" versus "stand-down." Right? |
| Client: | Mm-hmm (affirmative). |
| Therapist: | Part of your body feels the need to be at "stand-to." The rest of your body knows that now you're at stand-down. So, we want to take a few minutes just to let that part of your body stand-down. But you can be as much on guard as you need to be. So, is there anything that you need in this room in order to feel more secure? |
| Therapist: | What does that feel like? |
| Client: | Relaxed, except for my part of my mind. |

BLENDED PREPARATION: REPROCESSING WHILE SLEEPING

The previous script represents my early approach in developing self-regulation skills with Robert. It was an exploration to see if I could get at least some part of him relaxed. I was looking for change, something that made a difference in his ability to relax. Reducing his level of dissociative intrusions was a primary focus. This was an opening opportunity that allowed additional work in his Preparation phase. Over the course of several sessions, Robert became familiar with the various self-regulation techniques as I continued to work with him. Safe/Calm Place was not an option with his dissociative intrusions and hypervigilance. Instead, I relied on basic techniques of breathing and tapping as a relaxation routine. These had some positive impact on him. I discovered as Robert began to relax the intrusions diminished. In fact, the only time the auditory and visual intrusions diminished was when he relaxed in my office! This indicated the intrusions could be influenced by getting him to relax. Then, on one occasion, Robert arrived for his extended preparation appointment indicating he had only an hour's sleep the night before, uncertain if he could relax at all. I replied, "Let's just give it a try and see what happens." Due to lack of sleep, Robert fell asleep after four to five sets of BLS. He fell asleep with the tappers in his hand still running. Since he needed sleep, I decided to allow his continuing sleep as the tappers continued to operate on slow speed. I let him sleep as long as possible, right up to the time for my next appointment. Placing my shoe next to his boot, I raised the toe of my shoe and swung my foot around, tapping the sole of his boot as I began to say, "Robert, time to wake up. This is Doc. You are secure in my office, you've had a nap." I wanted him to awaken from sleep knowing where he was. I gave him about 10 minutes to awaken and get his bearings regarding his location. When I asked him how he was, he said, "I feel like I've had a power nap. I feel pretty good!"

I continued with this process for another 4 months. Robert would arrive for his appointment; I would get him relaxed using the tapers; and he would fall asleep with the tapers running slowly. He was gaining much needed sleep. After 4 months, he and his family visited his parents. His mother said to him, "I can tell you have made great improvements since I last saw you."

At this point, I asked Robert to select a target memory he felt he could manage getting through. It was an intense memory of when he lost several of his soldiers in combat operations. As he processed through the memory, he began to cry and grieve—for the first time since their death 5 years ago. Robert's experience taught me there are modified techniques, such as this "blended preparation" approach, which can be useful during extended preparation times.

## CONCLUSION

Maneuvering a client through the Preparation phase of EMDR therapy can be challenging, depending on the client's level of stability and self-regulation skills. The three objects for this phase are straightforward: set up the mechanics, provide informed consent, and engage the client in self-regulation responses. Complex cases require additional skills such as those presented in this chapter. Nothing replaces sound clinical judgment as the client is guided from Preparation into the reprocessing of a selected target memory.

### DISCUSSION POINTS

1. What indicators do you use to determine when you introduce EMDR therapy to a client?
2. How does your clinical setting influence your introduction of the therapy?
3. Discuss your introduction of the treatment modalities (eye movement, tactile, and auditory) to the client.
4. How do you present informed consent to your client?
5. What is the average amount of time you take to move a client through Phase 2 Preparation?

### REFERENCES

American Psychological Association. (2016). *Ethical principles of psychologists and code of conduct*. Washington, DC: Author.

De Jongh, A., Bicanic, I., Matthijssen, S., Amann, B., Hofmann, A., Farrell, D., ... Maxfield, L. (2019). The current status of EMDR therapy involving the treatment of complex posttraumatic stress disorder. *Journal of EMDR Practice and Research, 13*(4), 284–290. doi:10.1891/1933-3196.13.4.284

De Jongh, A., Resick, P., Zoellner, L., van Minner, A., Lee, C., Monson et al (2016). Critical analysis of the current treatment guidelines for complex PTSD in adults. *Depression and Anxiety, 33*, 359-369. doi: 10.1002/da.22469.

Department of Veterans Affairs-Department of Defense. (2017). VA/DOD clinical practice guideline for the management of posttraumatic stress disorder and acute stress disorder. Retrieved from https://www.healthquality.va.gov/guidelines/MH/ptsd/VADoDPTSDCPGFinal.pdf

EMDR Institute. (2017a). *EMDR Institute basic training course: Weekend 1 of the two part EMDR therapy basic training*. Watsonville, CA: Author.

EMDR Institute. (2017b). *EMDR Institute basic training course: Weekend 2 of the two part EMDR therapy basic training*. Watsonville, CA: Author.

EMDR Treatment Veterans. (n.d.) Retrieved from https://emdr-veterans.training/what-clients-say-emdr.html

EMDR International Association (2009). EMDR Brochure for Clients. Retrieved from https://www.emdria.org/news-and-announcements/emdr-brochures -for-clients/. (Note: due to Corona-19 the online EMDRIA shop is closed but will reopen in the future.)

Grossman, D., & Christensen, L. (2008). *On combat: The psychology and physiology of deadly conflict in war and peace.* Millstadt, IL: Warrior Science Publications.

HeartMath Institute. (2005). *Learn to access a state of active calm.* Retrieved from https://store.heartmath.org/emwave-pc/emwave-pro.html

Hensley, B. (2016). *An EMDR therapy primer: From practicum to practice.* (2nd Ed.). New York, NY: Springer Publishing.

Korn, D., & Leeds, A. (2002). Preliminary evidence of efficacy for EMDR resource development and installation in the stabilization phase of treatment of complex posttraumatic stress disorder. *Journal of Clinical Psychology, 58*(12), 1465–1487. doi:10.1002/jclp.10099

Maxfield, P., Lovell, J., Engel, L., Maxfield, D. (2017). Use the Flash technique in EMDR therapy: Four case examples. *Journal of EMDR Practice and Research, 11*(4), 195–205. doi:10.1891/1933-3196.11.4195.

National Association of Social Workers. (2017). *Code of ethics.* Retrieved from https://www.socialworkers.org/About/Ethics/Code-of-Ethics/Code -of-Ethics-English

National Board of Certified Counselors. (2017). *Code of ethics.* Retrieved from https://www.nbcc.org/Assets/Ethics/NBCCCodeofEthics.pdf

Schore, A. (1994). *Affect regulation and the origin of the self: The neurobiology of emotional development.* New York, NY: Psychology Press.

Schore, A. (2003a). *Affect dysregulation and disorders of the self.* New York, NY: W.W. Norton & Co.

Schore, A. (2003b). *Affect regulation and the repair of the self.* New York, NY: W.W. Norton & Co.

Shapiro, F. (1989). The efficacy of eye movement desensitization procedure in the treatment of traumatic memories. *Journal of Traumatic Stress, 2*(2), 199–223. doi:10.1002/jts.2490020207

Shapiro, F. (2012). *Getting past your past: Take control of your life with self-help techniques from EMDR therapy.* Emmaus, PA: Rodale.

Shapiro, F. (2018). *Eye movement desensitization and reprocessing (EMDR) therapy: Basic principles, protocols, and procedures* (3rd ed.). New York, NY: Guilford Press.

Shapiro, R. (2005). The two-hand interweave. In R. Shapiro (Ed.), *EMDR solutions: Pathways to healing* (pp. 160–166). New York, NY: W. W. Norton.

Siegel, D. (1999). *The developing mind.* New York, NY: Guilford Press.

U.S. Department of Veterans Affairs. (2019). *Understanding PTSD treatment.* Retrieved from https://www.ptsd.va.gov/PTSD/understand_tx/index .asp

# 5

# EMDR Phase 3: Assessment From Treatment Plan to Treatment

## Introduction

This chapter discusses the role of Phase 3 Preparation within the EMDR eight-phase approach. The review discusses the unique requirements of these special populations in preparing them to enter EMDR therapy's reprocessing phases for resolving the pathology represented in targeted memories. Suggestions are offered to enhance this phase of treatment by asking effective questions to activate the target memory for reprocessing.

## Learning Objectives

- Discuss each of the seven questions used in EMDR therapy's Phase 3 assessment.
- Discuss the impact of attachment issues on the Assessment phase.
- Note how to overcome avoidance issues for effective treatment.
- Suggest ways of managing challenging issues that frequently surface during the Assessment phase.

## MAINTAINING A SECURE THERAPEUTIC ENVIRONMENT FOR ACCURATE ASSESSMENT RESPONSE

The Assessment phase is designed to activate the target memory for EMDR reprocessing. Each question is designed to activate a specific component of the memory including the mental image, cognitions (both negative and positive), emotions, and body sensations. Two baseline measures, the validity of cognition (VOC) and subjective unit of disturbance (SUD), allow for treatment evaluation. Effective treatment means the SUD score (0–10) goes down and the VOC (1–7) goes up during the next phase, Phase 4 Desensitization.

Maintaining a sense of physical and psychological security is important not only for the perceived threat level but also for the sense of security which allows a person to disclose themselves emotionally during treatment sessions. The client needs to know they have the privacy and confidentiality to spontaneously respond to whatever issues might arise during each session. How does your setting contribute to this goal?

A strong therapeutic alliance builds trust and rapport conducive to the healing process. As clinicians, we are continually reminded that a good working alliance is always present in effective treatment outcome results. Meta-analyses confirm that the quality of the client–therapist alliance is a consistent predictor of positive outcome results (Horvath & Bedi, 2002; Norcross, 2002) across multiple therapeutic models. In fact, there is evidence (Castonguay, Constantino, & Holtforth, 2006) suggesting the client's assessment of the alliance is a better predictor of treatment outcome. Dr. Alan Schore (2019, PsychAlive, 2014) describes the therapeutic alliance as being emotional communication, right brain to right brain, between therapist and client. It is described as a deep subject communication using similar mechanisms as the infant–caretaker interaction. Schore (PsychAlive, 2014) notes such intersubjectivity is very different than giving someone advice or telling them what to do. If the subjective right brain is met with left brain objectivity, the mismatch can result in shame and humiliation. Dr. Shore suggests the consequence of such a mismatch between left brain objectivity and right brain subjectivity can create such dysregulation that the consequence can potentially be suicidal. At a time when suicidality is severely high among military and veteran populations, is it possible that suicidal gestures can be influenced by a subjective mismatch that, on the surface, appear to be an uneventful exchange between two humans, one objective left brain–oriented scientist and the other a right brain–focused veteran with posttraumatic stress disorder (PTSD) diagnosis which, at the deeper interactional level, adds insult to injury for persons already emotionally wounded? While there are numerous variables that influence suicidal behavior, Shore's comments deserve evaluation. A solid therapeutic alliance requires an appropriate emotional connection between the therapist and the client.

One of the strengths of EMDR therapy is its focus on maintaining a client-centered approach. This facilitates the therapist's attunement to the needs of the client. Therapists who are comfortable with their own clinical skills, exhibiting a mutual respect toward their clients, make a difference. Experienced EMDR therapists, accustomed to the treatment process, naturally anticipate a significant, positive outcome prior to beginning treatment. Regardless of the clinical complexity, such confidence is based on their previous treatment outcomes with similar clients as well as published research (EMDR Institute, 2019). After all, effectiveness of the treatment is based on maintaining fidelity to the model (Maxfield & Hyer, 2002). I confess, as an EMDR therapist, when I learn of the opportunity to treat another military servicemember or first responder suffering with some aspect of stress response I become excited for the client to experience the difference EMDR therapy can make.

The therapeutic alliance is influenced by attachment styles. Attachment styles are forms of self-regulation influenced by the relational patterns developed in early childhood. Such self-regulation patterns facilitate the therapist in incorporating an alliance to assist the client in pressing through to the resolution of their disturbing memories. Relationships developed in the military are structured around sharing and accomplishing missions together. Bonding is enhanced by managing challenging situations as a team. This is team building to the point where a person's life literally is dependent on the actions of other team members. Military life is based on routines except for the chaos of life in a war zone. There are roles and relational patterns military personnel develop and bring with them into the treatment room. These roles and relational patterns set the stage for the expectations the military client brings to treatment, which facilitates building the therapeutic alliance. Being "squared away" is a term used for a positive evaluation of someone who is organized and well equipped to accomplish the mission. The therapist being "squared away" in your office means you are organized and know what you are doing. The client will follow your lead if you take charge of the treatment direction by helping to guide the process while checking out the needs of the client. Let the client know you are preparing them for doing the treatment work identified in the treatment plan developed in Part 1 History-Taking. The purpose is to help them reclaim their lives by getting over the symptoms they identified when they first came for treatment.

In progressing from the treatment plan to assessment and the treatment process, the therapist asks the client, "In reviewing our treatment plan we agreed this target memory would be what we would work on today. Are you ready to work on it now?" This is the moment of truth in which a disturbing memory is about to be activated from reprocessing. Asking the seven questions of the Assessment phase moves beyond the avoidance strategies the client has relied upon to this time. Remember the client is willing to do this for the sake of being free of those disturbing memories, the subsequent triggers, and their numerous symptoms. Clients are motivated to escape the psychological pain of the trauma memory. While they have relied on avoidance as a coping mechanism in the past, avoidance is not resolution, it is postponing the pain for another time. Effective EMDR treatment resolves the etiology of the pain rather than postponing it.

# THE PURPOSE OF ASSESSMENT PHASE: ACTIVATING A DISTURBING MEMORY

## THE AVOIDANCE BARRIER: WHEN ACTIVATION CREATES RESISTANCE

Avoidance is a common human response for managing distressing memories. It has been identified as a symptom group associated with trauma (Muller, 2010) and specifically with PTSD since the 1980 publication of the American Psychiatric Association's *Diagnostic and Statistical Manual of Mental Disorders* (American Psychiatric Association [APA], 1980) when avoidance and numbing became required categories for diagnosing a person with posttraumatic stress disorder (PTSD). Since the publication of *DSM-III* (APA, 1980), the avoidance category is accepted as a necessary component of the PTSD disorder, including in the latest publication of the *Diagnostic and Statistical Manual of Mental Disorders* (5th ed.; *DSM-5*, APA, 2013). Avoidance is a core psychological process associated with traumatic distress. People don't like to think of unpleasant memories, except for those persons operating from a shame-based orientation where self-loathing is a part of their existence. Even for persons in a shame-based orientation, there is an ambivalence regarding the desire to escape the psychological pain of disturbing memory and the drive to self-loathe from a shame orientation. Experiential avoidance refers to the unsuccessful attempt to avoid experiencing intense psychological distress (Courtois & Ford, 2009). Kelly et al. (2019) defined experiential avoidance as "the tendency to avoid unwanted thoughts, feelings, and bodily sensations, including those experienced in response to interacting with others" (p. 354). This includes cognitive, emotional, and behavioral avoidance strategies. Their research found experiential avoidance to mediate the association between PTSD symptoms and social support.

From the clinical perspective, avoidance may pertain to a particular response, such as avoiding becoming emotional, or it may be a more systemic pattern of avoidance grounded in an attachment style. Lifelong patterns of avoidance are frequently revealed during History-Taking as the therapist notes repetitive coping patterns that have occurred throughout the client's life. Such avoidance patterns are typically identified, including incidents when the client learned to cope that way, and then included in the treatment plan. The focus of avoidance in a discussion on the Preparation phase is not about those lifelong avoidance coping patterns, which are included in the treatment plan already, but the existential avoidance occasions when the client is hesitant or avoidant, believing they cannot deal with a target memory.

Existential avoidance may be due to a fear of what will surface during the processing, becoming emotional, being overwhelmed since so much has been compartmentalized, or a blocking belief such as the client is not supposed to get over an incident. A measure of experiential avoidance can be offset by the therapist's realistic positive description of the treatment outcome results indicating it is necessary to endure an amount of discomfort in order to resolve those disturbing memories once and for all. The right brain support developed with trust and rapport can be helpful in assisting the client to face the discomfort of a disturbing memory.

## ENHANCEMENT FOR RESOLUTION

Sometimes the resistance to treatment develops due to high levels of affect, fears, or blocking beliefs. In such cases, the following clinical responses can be considered:

1.  Flash: If they fear they will be overwhelmed during reprocessing: use the Flash technique (Manfield, Lovett, Engel, & Manfield, 2017) to diminish the SUD to a 4 or less and then treat the target memory.
2.  Motivation/blocking beliefs: Check for blocking beliefs, "Would it be okay for you to get over this?" If the answer is "no," identify when the client first decided it is not okay to get over it and target that memory. If the client agrees it is okay to get over the disturbance, consider using the following steps.
3.  Fear of disclosure: Regarding what will surface such as moral injury issues, assure clients they do not have to disclose information. Keep the focus on the fear of disclosure, not the moral injury. Offer assurance you will help them get through whatever comes up.
4.  Urge to avoid: Use Knipe's (2018) Level of Urge to Avoid for treating implicit memory.
5.  Resource enhancement (Korn & Leeds, 2002) can be used to strengthen the client's perspective in their ability to manage the treatment.

## ACTIVATING THE MEMORY

Military and veteran populations prefer to know what is happening ahead of time. They are trained to conduct risk assessment as they collect information to determine the threat level. Providing your client information, including the concept of assessment in activating the memory and explaining the use of bilateral stimulation (BLS) to neutralize the disturbing charges associated with the memory, can be helpful. Note the end goal is providing the client with the ability to reclaim their life. Therefore, each of the seven questions is directed toward the specific incident being treated: the image, cognitions, emotions, and body sensations in addition to the two baseline measures, VOC and SUD.

Hope versus hopelessness is sometimes determined by the client's knowledge of effective treatment. It is important for the therapist to realize the client probably has not walked down this road before; therefore, the client has limited knowledge of what effective treatment can accomplish. Only the therapist can paint the picture of what can be accomplished and what the outcome looks like. Clients who have not been in therapy before, or who have been in talk therapy frequently, do not have a clue of how much change can occur within a few sessions. They do not know the effectiveness of EMDR therapy. It is helpful for the therapist to ensure the client understands the efficacy of this treatment approach. Metaphorically, I liken it to walking with the client toward a destination. The therapist has been down this road numerous times, but the journey is new to the client. The therapeutic alliance with a strong sense of attunement helps here. Reminding the client about the importance of the destination is essential. Painting a realistic picture of the destination and what it can be like there enhances the client's motivation.

Keep in mind there are occasions, due to highly activated memories, when the client does not need the Assessment questions to activate the memory. Clients who have auditory and visual intrusions are continually activated. An attempt to ask the seven assessment questions only interferes with the process in such cases. The client enters the treatment room, possibly after having night terrors the previous night, and is highly dissociative now. The memory is already active. These are the exceptions to asking the Assessment questions. Remind the client of the incident for focus, and ask as many questions as needed—often it is reminding the client of the incident, calling attention to where they feels it in their body, and begin reprocessing.

When providing the standard Assessment approach, the questions break through the avoidance mechanisms the client has used to manage the disturbing aspects of the memory. There is nothing comfortable about activating a disturbing memory. The client has typically compartmentalized the memory as a means of coping. If the occurrence of the incident happened years ago, the client typically has normalized the memory and avoided the thought, so the SUD level has been normalized and minimalized. A cursory recall does not seem nearly as disturbing as it will once the assessment questions have been asked with an appropriate negative cognition (NC) to activate the affect.

Clients need to be ready to deal with the discomfort of recalling a distressing memory in order for reprocessing to occur. Many are motivated by a desperation to get over the emotional pain connected with the memory. This is the point where the client's motivation is connected with the treatment goals and the outcome potential of effective EMDR therapy. The therapist needs to ensure the client understands the effectiveness of EMDR therapy. What EMDR treatment offers is an effective treatment outcome beyond traditional talk therapy. In a brief period of time the issues the client has lived with for an extensive period can be resolved. It is important to present the potential outcome as being worth the discomfort of recalling the distressing event. The treatment results last a lifetime.

## MEMORY ENCODING, RETRIEVAL, AND ADAPTIVE INFORMATION PROCESSING

Memory involves the process of encoding, storing, and retrieval. van der Kolk once said, "We remember what is important to us" (van der Kolk, 1998). In fact, what is going on in our life at the time, beyond the incident, influences the focus on our attention. The focus of our attention determines what is encoded. Two people observing the same incident on recall of the event will likely report different narratives due to their focus at the time. On an individual basis, research has compared the similarities between encoding and retrieval. Ritchey, Wing, LaBar, and Cabeza (2013), using functional resonance imaging (fMRI) when comparing encoding and retrieval imaging, found that the hippocampus mediated the link between cortical similarity and memory success at the comparison. Emotional arousal was found to be associated with enhanced similarity between encoding and retrieval patterns. Amygdaloid activity associated with the emotional alarm system was found to enhance the similarity of memory patterns. Danker and Anderson (2010) further supported the concept that the same neural regions activated during the encoding process are activated during memory retrieval. When an episode is remembered, the process involves literally returning to the brain state that was present during the encoding of that episode.

This occurs during the Assessment phase as the retrieval of a memory involves returning to the same neural state that was encoded at the time the event occurred. There are some memories so distressing that a person continues to reexperience the event rather than know it is in the past. They react rather than remember. The subjective difference is the emotional charge or reaction a person encounters when they reexperiences the event. In its extreme, people can become so triggered by unresolved past events that they feel they have lost control of their lives. The Adaptive Information Processing (AIP) model, developed by Dr. Francine Shapiro (2018) as the theoretical model behind EMDR therapy, provides an understanding of the impact of distressing life events on memory. The AIP model provides basic tenets (EMDR Institute, 2017) for describing the process:

■ Memories are stored by association. They form memory networks that link present experiences to past experiences.
■ Memory networks are the basis of pathology and health.
■ The physical information processing system, like other body systems, is naturally geared toward health. When an experience is successfully processed, it is adaptively stored, integrating with other similar experiences about self and others.
■ Disruptions to the information processing system due to high arousal states from adverse life experiences result in memories that are inadequately processed and maladaptively stored in a state-specific form.
■ As information from the present situation (unconsciously) links to negative experiences in the past, the similarities can trigger a reaction to the present as if it were the same situation as the past.
■ The past is present. Maladaptive conclusions from past negative experiences that are inadequately processed interpret the present.
■ Inadequately processed memories, and their stored components (images, thoughts, emotions, physical sensations, and beliefs) change, or transmute, during reprocessing.
■ Reprocessing takes place when dual attention on a past memory, combined with BLS, activates an associative process allowing relevant connections to be made.
■ When reprocessing is successful, the previously disturbing memories are neutralized and affectively integrated with other similar experiences.
■ What is useful is stored, available to inform future experiences; what is no longer adaptive is discarded (negative images, feelings, beliefs, etc.).
■ EMDR therapy is designed to:
  □ Access a memory as it is currently experienced.
  □ Stimulate the information processing system in the brain.
  □ Facilitate reprocessing with the goal of adaptive resolution, allowing for linkage to other memory networks.

While the AIP approach is reviewed as part of Phase 1 History-Taking, it is helpful to remind the client the purpose of identifying the target memory, the questions around each component of memory, and the purpose of BLS is to resolve the level of distress associated with the memory.

> *I am going to ask you seven (7) questions about how the incident/event is impacting you now. Each question is designed to access a different part of your memory regarding the incident. I don't need a lot of details about what happened, just what you want to share with me in response to my questions. Following the seven (7) questions I will do what we call bilateral stimulation (EM, tactile, auditory), about 30 seconds each time. I will stop and ask you for feedback such as "What do you notice?" or*

*"What do you get now?" I am asking about what is different about the memory. This is not like talk therapy–all I need is a word, phrase, or a sentence telling me what is changing about the memory. I need as clear feedback as possible. Just observe your experience and report it to me. Whatever you say, I will say, "Go with that," which means resume or start up where you left off a minute ago. We will do this for a period of time until thinking about the incident no longer bothers you. Would this be okay that you are over it and it no longer bothers you?*

## THE TICES SEQUENCE FOR ACTIVATING TARGET MEMORIES

Each of the Assessment questions is sequenced in order to activate various components of a targeted memory in a specific order. Once the target memory is identified for treatment, subsequent questions are asked in sequence of the acronym TICES (Target = Image + Cognitions [negative and positive] + Emotions + Sensations).

### IMAGE

The mental picture can be a very activating component of the targeted memory. Most persons are able to readily retrieve the image as they recall what happened. It can be accessed with a couple of different questions:

*"What picture best represents the experience to you?"*

*Or a question that accesses the most disturbing aspect of the memory can be:*

*"What picture represents the worst part of the experience as you think about it now?"*

A small percentage of people cannot visualize a mental picture, so you can ask them:

*"When you think of the experience, what is the worst part of it now?"*

Activating the mental image brings into focus a conscious awareness of the target memory. The amount of time the client spends describing the mental picture may vary as long as the image is sufficient to activate the target memory. Many clients find it easier to recall the image than other components of the memory. Beginning with the mental picture allows other questions related to the incident to be accessed easier.

### NEGATIVE COGNITION SELECTION CRITERIA

The NC must be:

■ Negative
■ Irrational (to some degree, not necessarily completely irrational)

- Self-referencing (an "I" statement)
- Generalizable (applies to other similar situations)
- Feels relatively true
- Presently held belief about oneself.

The NC is the verbalization of the affect. The importance of identifying the NC cannot be overemphasized. An effective NC activates the affect; that is, it feels like a punch in the stomach when stated. This is a thought the client traditionally avoids thinking because of its level of distress when identified. Nothing is being added to the client's psychological struggles. What has been avoided is faced. The client has lived with the distressing thought continually; they just normally keeps it compartmentalized. It is a statement about the essence of a person, not their action/behavior. For example, instead of the client saying, "I screwed up," which is a performance, the essence of the NC would be similar to "I am a failure" or "I am a screw up." For a medic, the negative cognitive cognition, rather than "I failed him (patient)," would be more like "I am inadequate."

Issues around trust can be vague. For example, if a person says, "I can't trust him," we don't know if the client's struggle is about the client's inability to trust or that the other person is not trustworthy. In such a statement, I would ask, "What does that say about you as a person?" If a person is in a situation they can't trust, what is the essence of who that person is? Frequently, the person would respond, if they are in a situation/relationship they can't trust, then they are vulnerable. The NC would be something like "I am vulnerable" if the person can't trust anyone.

Sometimes identifying an NC can be challenging. At times I ask the veteran, "When you are alone and having negative thoughts you use to beat up on yourself about that situation, what are you thinking?" I stress to the client, "I want to learn what it was like for you to be in that situation (identified target event)." When the client struggles to come up with a NC, it can be helpful to ask, "What does that say about you?" or "What bothers you about being in that situation?" Beyond this, move the focus away from the negative belief about oneself in being in the situation to the focus on how the aftermath is negatively impacting the client now. A medic asked me, "What if you can't come up with a negative thought? I actually helped that person." My reply, "You just mentioned 'I am fed-up.'" His response, "Yeah, I guess that is negative, isn't it?" The focus was adjusted from his appraisal of being in the incident itself to how the aftermath of the situation was impacting him. He was fed-up. "I am fed-up" became the NC. He processed the target memory just fine using that NC.

Likewise, Leeds (2016) credits a mutual colleague, Roger Solomon, PhD, who has significant experience working with first responders, explaining this population of highly trained professionals may not respond to overwhelming emergency events with fear or helplessness but horror.

For first responders and some military, the negative appraisal may be about the nature of the event more than a comment about their coping responses. As long as the affective is up, the NC will normally work.

Referring to the list of negative (NC) and positive cognitions (PC) offered as examples in your EMDR therapy basic training manual can also be used. Ask the client to review the list and see if there is a cognition that appears to be an appropriate fit for the targeted incident/event. Keep in mind the effectiveness of the NC is its verbalization of the affect. Once the affect is activated with the NC and attention is highlighted by asking the other assessment questions, the client is primed for reprocessing beginning with the next phase, Phase 4 Desensitization.

Military personnel and veterans tend to be highly responsible individuals. The sense of responsibility is often revealed in the NCs the client expressed. In the military community it is unacceptable to pass the blame to others. The military chain of command always ensures someone is in charge and someone is assigned the responsibility for the designated tasks. Each person is identified as having their areas of responsibility (AOR). At the same time, the term "stay in your lane" reminds personnel not to interfere with the duties and responsibilities of others. The responsibility theme frequently develops during childhood when persons were taught, due to birth order or roles in the family of origin, to be accountable for specific responsibilities. For these persons, leadership roles are often a very natural assumption.

A strong sense of responsibility also makes the person vulnerable to guilt, shame, and moral injury issues. The person easily views themselves as being responsible/defective or responsible/action in the categories of NCs. The sense of responsible/defective often originates in early childhood, in shame-based environments that facilitate the person developing an overall sense of worthlessness. The sense of worthlessness is easily masked when things are going well in duty performance while the person is able to receive awards and promotions for their service. It surfaces when things go wrong and the person begins to self-loathe, emotionally beating up on themselves. Moral injury is frequently developed out of the responsible/defective orientation.

## POSITIVE COGNITION

*"When you bring up that picture (or experience) what would you prefer to believe about yourself instead?"*

Identifying an appropriate PC sets the direction of EMDR treatment. Remember, once the level of disturbance (SUD) is completely reduced during Phase 4 Desensitization, the following phases, Installation and Body Scan, refer to the PC. Many people who suffer with stress-related issues have never considered an alternative option, such as "What would you prefer to believe about yourself, if you could?" As the NC is the verbalization of the affect, the PC is the verbalization of the "desired state" (Shapiro, 2018, p. 128). The PC opens possibilities for new directions in healing.

Asking about the PC flows smoother when asked immediately following the NC, which is the purpose of the Assessment phase. Identifying the PC activates positive memory networks for possibilities as well as providing a baseline measure for the treatment process (Shapiro, 2018). It represents hope, even if it seems impossible to the client at the time of the Assessment phase.

Selection criteria for a PC include:

- positive
- self-referencing, begins with an "I" statement
- generalizable
- feels relatively untrue
- relates to the same theme as the NC

This question identifies the option for having a positive belief about oneself. This potential PC opens the possibilities about oneself and sets the direction for the treatment. The PC is not merely a negation of the NC but opens new possibilities for the client as the focus is on "What would you prefer to believe about yourself, if you could?" Sometimes, when clients are so stuck in their despair it is difficult to conceptualize a positive response, I suggest, "If you had a magic wand and could change the outcome in a positive way, what would you prefer to believe?" While not wishful thinking, the PC should be the most powerful realistic statement the client can make even if it is difficult to believe at the time. When processing a target memory that had devastating results, a PC might be "I learned from it" or "I am making the world a better place based on that incident!" For a veteran whose target memory was a combat operation in which "collateral damage" occurred with the death of children in the area, and the acknowledgment that the death of children could not be reversed, the PC was "I am making the world a safer place in honor of those children!" Studies have noted EMDR therapy does not allow the client to incorporate anything that is invalid or inappropriate into their belief system.

Once EMDR therapy reprocessing begins, the PC is likely to change. As the perspective associated with the target memory changes, the PC frequently changes. One veteran whose target memory was a combat operation identified the PC as "I am a survivor." This veteran revised the PC after reprocessing Phase 4 to "I am thankful," which expressed his deeper appreciation once the disturbing affect was neutralized.

## VALIDITY OF COGNITION

*"When you think of the memory, how true do the words (repeat the PC above) feel to you now on a scale from 1 to 7 where 1 feels completely false and 7 feels completely true?"*

Dr. Shapiro incorporated two baseline measures in the EMDR Assessment phase. One measure was Joseph Wolpe's Subjective Unit of Disturbance (1956) selected for a measure of the level of disturbance associated with a particular incident. The second measure, the VOC, was designed to measure how true the PC feels to the client when focusing on the target memory. The VOC is designed to use a different numerical scale (1–7) in comparison to the SUD scale 0 to 10. And the directions are different. The VOC is a realistic measure that reminds the client there is a positive possibility in the outcome. In the VOC, the higher the number, the better the results; with the SUD scale, the lower the numbers, the better the improvement.

The VOC follows the client's identification of the appropriate PC. The PC should be realistic, not magical thinking, and based on what the client feels is appropriate to embrace. If the VOC rating is a "1," ensure the PC is realistic to the client, that it is a belief that potentially can be achieved. And, of course, if the VOC is already a 6 or 7 before reprocessing, develop another PC that is not quite fully believable, but one they would prefer to believe, if they could.

## EMOTIONS

*"When you think of the memory and the words (repeat the NC) what emotions do you feel now?"*

Identifying the emotion(s) does two things: (a) activates conscious awareness of an emotional aspect with the target memory and (b) activates any associated memory networks organized with similar emotional connections. The NC is used as a reference since it is the verbalization of the affect. Emotional activation then prepares the client for a more realistic measure of the SUD that follows. The recognition of emotions and the activation of similar emotionally charged networks help prepare the client for emotional reactivity, which can sometimes occur.

Identifying emotions can be a diagnostic process as persons who struggle to identify what they feel are more susceptible to surprises with their emotions during the later reprocessing phases. The unexpected eruption of emotions out of nowhere leaves the client feeling out of control and only enhances their anxiety with unanticipated events happening. In contrast, the ability to readily label emotions typically indicates the person possesses a greater congruence, being more aware of what they feel.

For clients who have difficulty identifying words to go with the emotion, I sometimes offer four categories for the client to select, "between the words happy, sad, mad, and anxious, which one comes the closest to what you are experiencing now?" For some clients, should they have difficulty using feeling words, I ask, "If you scanned your body for colors, what colors would stand out to you?" This changes the language while calling attention to self-awareness.

## SUBJECTIVE UNITS OF DISTURBANCE

*"On a scale from 0 to 10, where 0 is no disturbance or neutral, and 10 is the highest disturbance you can imagine, how disturbing does it feel to you now?"*

The SUD was developed by Wolpe (1956). A behavioralist, Wolpe developed the SUD as a self-report to measure the client's subject level of disturbance in systematic desensitization treatments. The SUD was included into the EMDR therapy as a baseline measure early in its development. Wolpe incorporated EMDR therapy into his research shortly after Shapiro's (1989) initial research publication. He published a case study (Wolpe & Abrams, 1991) on the efficacy of EMD in the treatment of a 43-year-old female who had been sexually assaulted. A validity study was conducted by Kaplan, Smith, and Coons (1995).

The SUD measures the level of distress related to the memory of the event. During the Assessment phase, the SUD is normally contained to the specific memory being targeted. During later reprocessing, when the SUD is used, the therapist sometimes has to remind the client that the emotional charge associated with the specific targeted memory is being measured, not the overall level of distress. When measuring the SUD, the emphasis is always focused on the present experience with the words, "How disturbing does it feel to you now?"

Sometimes the client will underreport the level of disturbance, particularly if the targeted memory occurred sometime in the past. Often, early childhood memories have been compartmentalized with little or no attention to what happened. Compartmentalization reduces the level of disturbance until the memory is activated. Activation increases the SUD level. A client will say, "Now that we are talking about it, it is more upsetting!" And, during the initial sets of BLS, a client may state "it's going higher now!" This is fairly common and has to do with the success of the avoidance until the memory is activated during Assessment. When there seems to be an incongruency between the SUD number the client is reporting and their nonverbal responses, it can be helpful to state "… how disturbing does it feel to you now in your gut?" This helps get the client out of any intellectualization defense mechanism.

## BODY SENSATIONS

*"Where do you feel it in your body?"*

Identifying the location of body sensations during reprocessing is an important strength of EMDR therapy. This component complements the other aspects of the client's feedback during treatment. Persons who tend to have difficulty with verbalizing feedback during reprocessing (Phases 4–6) can usually identify where they feel the somatic expressions in their body. This aspect works well with those who tend to intellectualize responses; that is, they tend to overthink their responses as they stay in their head. It is efficient for persons concerned about having to come up with the right answer to the other assessment questions. It is easier to identify the locations of sensations in one's body. The assumption behind this question is that there are somatic representations associated with distressing experiences. The client should avoid getting lost in the descriptive details of describing the sensation. Just a brief indication where the sensation is located is all that is necessary.

Some clients report being numb; they can't feel anything. Psychological numbness is a feeling, perhaps an unfeeling, of a local awareness of the absence of sensation. Did it just develop or has the client noticed this for some time? In response, ask the client to focus on where they feels numb. If the lack of feeling is pervasive, it may help the client to have a sensory awareness exercise. Usually this issue is identified during the Preparation phase. Should it develop here during Assessment, and if it is pervasive, it may be necessary to take time to work with the client, asking them to notice differences in their body feelings. I begin with asking the client to make a fist as tightly as possible and then open their hand. Then I ask for the client to describe the difference in their feeling sensations.

After asking the client to do the fist exercise about three times, I move to a breathing exercise, asking the client to take a deep breath, filling their lungs with air, as full as possible. Hold the breath for 5 seconds, then exhale. "What do you notice that is different between your lungs being full of air and totally empty with a full exhale?" Call attention to the difference, have the client focus on the location of the difference, and provide two or three sets (20-25 passes) of BLS. This is the beginning of having the client notice differences in body sensation. Have the client continue doing these exercises throughout the week as they notices the differences.

Clients respond to these assessment questions differently. Some respond very succinctly with their responses. Others will explore the history of the incident as they answer describing the event. Either way, taking time to arrive at the best, most suitable answer is important. For persons who explore the answers as they develop their response, they may need some limited guidance as they move from one memory component/question to the next. Their time to explore the memory ensures the client has activated the memory.

NONVERBAL ASSESSMENT (FOR CLASSIFIED SITUATIONS AND OTHER SENSITIVE CASES)

Another strength of EMDR therapy is its capacity to treat a disturbing memory without the client divulging information about the incident. In fact, I have treated persons whose traumatic events were militarily classified. Nothing about the incidents could be revealed. Since EMDR therapy is considered mostly a nonverbal approach, I treated former CIA officers and Army intelligence officers without knowing anything about their incidents. All that I needed was two words: one word means change/different and the other word means no-change/same. The client is asked to recall the image in her mind without revealing the information to the therapist. From that mental image, all other answers in the Assessment phase are about the present experience, not about details of what happened. The questions about NC and PC use the word *now*. Questions regarding emotions and body sensations are current experiences, not descriptions of the past. EMDR therapy can treat and resolve traumatic symptoms without the client ever revealing anything about the incident(s). Numerous intelligence officers have sought out EMDR therapists for treatment once they learned this fact.

This capacity for EMDR therapy to treat a disturbing memory without disclosing any information is helpful for persons who do not wish to disclose descriptions regarding what happened to them. For example, persons with sexual abuse appreciate the opportunity of receiving treatment without going into embarrassing details of being assaulted. The opportunity of being treated without disclosing such information is a welcomed gift for many.

## CONCLUSION

Assessment is designed to activate the targeted memory. The order of questions is designed to activate the memory, similar to a pilot doing a preflight check according to the checklist. Every question asked is designed to activate a component of the memory. This chapter reviewed the TICES sequence of activating specific components of the target memory. The importance of the NC as the verbalization of the affect is noted. Furthermore, the PC sets the direction of the treatment. This phase activates the target memory in preparation for the reprocessing phases.

### DISCUSSION POINTS

1. What is the purpose of the two baseline measures in the Assessment phase?
2. What if the person does not get a mental picture?

3. What does TICES represent?
4. What does negative cognition represent?
5. What does positive cognition represent?
6. What can you do if the client reports not being able to feel body sensations?
7. What would you do if the client begins to cry during the Assessment phase?
8. How can you tell when the client is prepared to begin the next phase, Desensitization?

## REFERENCES

American Psychiatric Association. (1980). *The diagnostic and statistical manual of mental disorders* (3rd ed.). Washington, DC: Author.
American Psychiatric Association. (2013). *The diagnostic and statistical manual of mental disorders* (5th ed.). Arlington, VA: American Psychiatric Publishing.
Castonguay, L., Constantino, M., & Holtforth, M. (2006). The working alliance: Where are we and where should we go? Psychotherapy, *43*, 271–279. doi:10.1037/0033-3204.43.3.271
Courtois, C., and Ford, J. (Eds.). (2009). *Treating complex traumatic stress disorders: An evidence-based guide.* New York, NY: Guilford Press.
Danker, J., & Anderson, J. (2010). The ghosts of brain states past: Remembering reactivates the brain regions engaged during encoding. *Psychological Bulletin, 136*(1), 87–102. doi:10.1037/a0017937
EMDR Institute. (2017). *EMDR Institute basic training course weekend 1 of the two part EMDR therapy basic training.* Watsonville, CA: Author.
EMDR Institute. (2019). *Research overview.* Retrieved from http://www.emdr .com/research-overview
Horvath, A., & Bedi, R. (2002). The alliance. In J. Norcross (Ed.), *Psychotherapy relationships that work: Therapist contributions and responsiveness in patients.* New York, NY: Oxford University Press.
Kaplan, D., Smith, T., & Coons, J. (1995). A validity study of the subjective unit of discomfort (SUD) score. *Measurement and Valuation in Counseling and Development, 27*(4), 195–199. doi:10.1891/1933-3196.2.1.57
Kelly, M., Kimbrel, N., DeBeer, B., Meyer, E., Gulliver, S., & Morissette, S. (2019). Experiential avoidance as a mediator of the association between posttraumatic stress disorder symptoms and social support: A longitudinal analysis. *Psychological Trauma: Theory, Research, Practice, and Policy, 11*(3), 353–359. doi:10.1037/tra0000375
Knipe, J. (2018). *EMDR toolbox: Theory and treatment of complex PTSD and dissociation* (2nd Ed.). New York, NY: Springer Publishing.
Korn, D., & Leeds, A. (2002). Preliminary evidence of efficacy for EMDR resource development and installation in the stabilization phase of treatment of complex posttraumatic stress disorder. *Journal of Clinical Psychology, 58*(12), 1465–1487. doi:10.1002/jclp.10099
Leeds, A. (2016). *A guide to the standard EMDR therapy protocols for clinicians, supervisors, and consultants.* New York, NY: Springer Publishing Company.
Manfield, P., Lovett, J., Engel, L., & Manfield, D. (2017). Use of the flash technique in EMDR therapy: Four case examples. *Journal of EMDR Practice and Research, 11*(4), 195–205. doi:10.1891/1933-3196.11.4.195

Maxfield, L., & Hyer, L. (2002). The relationship between efficacy and methodology in studies investigating EMDR treatment of PTSD. *Journal of Clinical Psychology, 58,* 23–24. doi:10.1002/jclp.1127

Muller, R. (2010). *Trauma and the avoidant client.* New York, NY: W.W. Norton.

Norcross, J. (2002). *Psychotherapy relationships that work: Therapist contributions and responsiveness to patients.* New York, NY: Oxford University Press.

PsychAlive. (2014). *Dr. Allan Schore on therapeutic alliance and emotional communication, right brain to right brain* [Video file]. Retrieved from https://www.youtube.com/watch?v=fI9fxZRtjdU

Ritchey, M., Wing, E., LaBar, K., & Cabeza, R. (2013). Neural similarity between encoding and retrieval is related to memory via hippocampal interactions. *Cerebral Cortex, 23,* 2818–2828. doi:10.1093/cercor/bhs258

Shapiro, F. (1989). Efficacy of the Eye Movement Desensitization procedure in the treatment of memories. *Journal of Traumatic Stress, 2*(2), 199–223.

Shapiro, F. (2018). *Eye movement desensitization and reprocessing therapy (EMDR): Basic principles, protocols, and procedures.* New York, NY: Guilford Press.

Schore, A. (2019). *Right brain psychotherapy.* New York, NY: W. W. Norton.

van der Kolk, B. (1998). Trauma and memory. *Psychiatry and Clinical Neurosciences. 52,* S52-S64. doi:10.1046/j.1440-1819.1998.0520s5s5S97.

Wolpe, J. (1956). *The practice of behavior therapy.* New York, NY: Pergamon Press.

Wolpe, J., & Abrams, J. (1991). Post-traumatic stress disorder overcome by eye movement desensitization: A case report. *Journal of Behavioral Therapy and Experimental Psychiatry, 22*(1), 39–43. doi:10.1016/0005-7916(91)90032-Z

# 6A

# EMDR Phase 4: Reprocessing Phases

## Introduction

This chapter offers a description of memory networks with the encoding of intense life experiences being different than other memories. The origin of symptoms such as flashbacks is discussed with a distinction between implicit and explicit memory. The unique challenge of introducing EMDR therapy to veterans with chronic trauma seeking care within the Department of Veterans Affairs (DVA) and community mental health systems is noted. A discussion of an EMDR treatment continuum ranging from EMDR to limited processing to restricted processing (EMD), as well as providing the EMDR intensive daily treatment, is presented.

## Learning Objectives

- Present a basic overview of the neurobiology of distressing memory.
- Note the impact of PTSD on the functioning of regions of the brain noted by brain imaging.
- Discuss EMDR therapy's processing continuum from the Flash technique, EMDR, limited processing, and restricted processing.
- Describe the structure of EMDR 5- and 10-day intensive treatments.

## THE NATURE OF MEMORY IN EMDR REPROCESSING

EMDR therapists learn to appreciate the many nuances of human memory since this psychotherapy works with memory, both healthy memories of positive past experiences and the treatment of disturbing memories, as the basis of pathology. Therapists focus their treatment efforts on identified memories designated in the treatment plan for the purpose of resolving the client's presenting issues.

Memories with sensory information, images, cognitions, emotions, and body sensations are all processed simultaneously. During the reprocessing of memories, using bilateral stimulation (BLS), EMDR therapists witness the client's spontaneous activation of memory networks where similar memory components have been neurologically organized and stored. The organization and storage of those memories develop the associated memory networks, which will be spontaneously processed with the target memory. This organization of memory allows for the clustering of similar memories during treatment.

Witnessing the client's profoundly disturbing memories change within a brief period is validating for the therapist and healing for the client. This chapter addresses the reprocessing of memories using EMDR therapy. The reprocessing phases, Phases 4 to 6, provide the BLS to reduce the subjective units of disturbance (SUDs), enhance the validity of cognition (VOC), and provide a clear body scan. A brief overview of the types of memory and their apparent distinctiveness during EMDR processing is presented in this chapter.

## LATERALIZATION OF THE BRAIN

An anatomical view of the human brain reveals functional asymmetries of the left and right hemispheres. Studies have found functional differences within the lateralization of the hemispheres (Purves et al., 2012; van der Kolk, 2014). Brain imaging research featuring persons with psychological distress such as posttraumatic stress disorder (PTSD) have frequently found the right hemisphere to be highly active with limbic system activation while the left hemisphere revealed difficulties with the hemisphere's analytical functioning. Early brain imaging research by van der Kolk (1997) was reported through VPro Noorderlicht, a public media outlet in the Netherlands. The program presented his research, which found persons diagnosed with PTSD had highly active amygdala activity in the right hemisphere while the left hemisphere revealed minimal activity in areas such as the Broca and the anterior cingulate. The amygdala, the center of emotion, judges the information as valuable. High activity in the amygdala at the time of experience predicts the emotional valence of those events, measuring the importance of their recall later. The amygdala signals to other parts of the brain that an event is significant—it gives a value judgment decreeing the event is worthy of remembering. The greater the value, the more effort the brain puts into consolidating the information (Ludmer, Dudai, & Rubin, 2011). When its activity is diminished, the Broca area, being the speech center, impairs a person's ability to express verbally what they experience. Clients with PTSD frequently state, "I'm so tired of being lost for words!" Furthermore, the role of the anterior cingulate includes facilitating putting thoughts (knowledge) and feelings together. With diminished activity in the anterior cingulate, conscious thought is left with the inability to read the emotional response of the amygdala, leaving strong emotions to erupt without the person's awareness that such emotions are about to erupt until the client has overreacted and left, feeling their life is out of control. The lateralization problems, with a breakdown of interaction between the two hemispheres, leave persons struggling to cope with dysregulated symptoms. Lateralization has been described by some researchers (Scaer, 2005; van der Kolk, 1997, 2014) as being the primary problem with PTSD due to the lack of interaction between hemispheres. A function of EMDR therapy with its BLS seems to be the enhancement of action between hemispheres allowing the hemispheres to begin interacting with each other again. This is supported by research presented by Pagani et al. (2011, 2012, 2015) who used neuroimaging (EEG) to demonstrate the ability of EMDR therapy to normalize emotional hyperarousal and cortical activation.

## LEARNING AND QUALITATIVE FUNCTIONS OF MEMORY

The capacity of the human brain to gather information, store it, and retrieve the information at a later time is remarkable. This neurological process is accomplished at both conscious and unconscious levels. "Learning" is the process by which new information is gathered by the nervous system with observable changes in behavior. Every time a person learns something new, a new synaptic connection is made in the neocortex part of the brain. As a person learns new information, that learning pattern is hardwired into the cerebral architecture. As an EMDR therapist, I sometimes ask learning-focused questions to identify the beginning of pathology, such as asking a person who is in an avoidance response, "When did you first learn to cope with things by avoiding them?" or with someone who is being hard on themselves struggling with a moral injury or shame, I might ask, "When did you first learn to be so hard on yourself?" Many patterns of behavior, both psychologically and physically, have times of learning—they are points of decision—which can become target memories during EMDR treatment. Once treated with EMDR therapy, those points of decision are neutralized for the person to make choices in a healthier manner.

Human memory is concerned with the process of encoding, storing, and retrieving learned information (Purves et al., 2012). Remembering is based on developing and sustaining synaptic connections. Memories have qualitative functions with two primary categories: declarative (conscious) memories and nondeclarative procedural (unconscious) memory. Declarative memories relate to the conscious recall of events and facts that have been experienced by the person. Memory is associated with numerous areas of the brain where life experiences are recorded; however, there appears to be specific activity associated with each hemisphere of the brain. Declarative or explicit memory includes the details of a past event, as well as information such as a person's date of birth, phone number, or the location where an event occurred. All these events are usually associated with the left hemisphere. Persons rely on the left hemisphere to explain experiences and place them in proper sequence. Explicit memory including conscious learning is organized by the hippocampus in collaboration with the cerebral cortex and amygdala (Cozolino, 2002). LeDoux (1996) explained that explicit memories in the left hemisphere are not mirror copies of the original experience, but reconstructions when recalled. The state of the brain at the time of recall can influence the way the memory is remembered. Therefore, the recall of explicit memories is based on reconstructionist versions. Memory is valid but not necessarily accurate.

The nondeclarative or implicit memory is closely associated with the limbic system, including the amygdala and its affiliated components. Such memory is not available in conscious awareness but includes skills, habits, sensations, emotional responses, unconscious associations, classically conditioned responses, and even the intuitive recognition of patterns. We fall in love with our right brain and experience as well as experience sadness through our right hemisphere. While the majority of the tasks a person performs require activity in different cortical and limbic systems, on both sides of the brain, the two hemispheres have gradually differentiated over time, allowing for specialization in each. The right side of the brain is considered the dominant hemisphere for emotional and social functioning. Memories of smell, sounds, and touch, as well as the emotions they evoke, are stored in the right hemisphere (Purves et al., 2012). Survival skills and muscle memory developed through practice drills are included in this category, enabling persons to respond without thinking during times of crisis. It includes information for responding to threatening situations without having to consciously think. Early research (Schacter, 1987; van der Kolk, 2002) determined observations made during scientific studies are included within the context of implicit memory. This is in contrast to the facts learned from the research being stored in declarative memory. As unconscious implicit memory, it provides storage for somatic memories including unconscious body sensations. LeDoux (1996, 2002) distinguished between two types of emotions: emotion of memory, which is processed in the hippocampus and associated structures; and emotional memory, which is processed in the amygdala in the limbic system. Emotional memories are typically reexperienced as flashbacks, whereas memories of emotion are likely to be verbalized as a recalled memory of emotions. The seat of implicit memory is the amygdala (McGaugh, 2004). While recognized as part of the limbic system, which includes both left and right hemisphere activity, the amygdala is primarily associated with right hemisphere activity in PTSD-related studies. It is attuned to the early developmental patterns of attachment (Bowlby, 1988; Cozolino, 2002).

Memories of traumatic events are experienced differently by the individual. They are stored as state-specific implicit memories consisting of affect, body sensations of affect, body sensations, images, and behaviors. Regular memories, even memories of sad or challenging situations, are stored in a manner so when recalled the individual knows the event happened but is now in the past. The client may make a comment such as, "It was a hard, difficult time but it's over now!" In contrast, memories of traumatic experiences, are stored as frozen in time. Rather than being remembered as something that happened in the past, they are re-experienced as if the event is happening again in the present. During the neurobiological process the thalamus serves as a key processing component (van der Kolk, 2002). Sensory information enters the central nervous system (CNS) through the sensory organs—eyes, nose, ears, and skin—as the information is received by the thalamus. The thalamus, in turn, passes the information to the amygdala and the prefrontal cortex, which provides further evaluation. The amygdala, as the brain's alarm, interprets the emotional valiance of the information being received. That information is evaluated and passed to the brainstem, which controls the autonomic and neurohormonal response systems. By this process, the amygdala transforms the sensory stimuli into hormonal and emotional signals. This process allows for the cuing and controlling of emotional responses. Traumatic memories are encoded as memory differently from the typical memory of daily activities. This marking of memories with a high emotional charge allows such memories to become stored in a state-dependent format in the amygdala. Such memories are frozen terror. The encoding of these highly charged memories at the time of encoding produces implicit, somatic memories consisting of sensations, affect, and behavior, leaving the person with difficulty verbalizing the experience. The emotional charge in the amygdaloid process frequently creates a vividness of the image associated with the memory. In fact, both the mental picture and the sounds of the event often stand out.

Sometimes during EMDR therapy reprocessing, the client will report a sudden change in temperature: their hands become sweaty, and they report the room suddenly has become hot. Often the client removes a vest or sweater due to the reported hot temperature. As the therapist, however, I have experienced no change in temperature during these times. As an EMDR therapist, I recognize the client has tapped into aspects of their memory, which has activated the somatosensory regions of their brain processing. Within 10 minutes, the client's condition will be back to a comfortable range. The somatosensory cortex located in the parietal lobes processes information regarding body experiences. Functioning with the anterior cingulate and insula, it provides multiple representations of the body's experiences that are processed. They organize body experiences such as temperature, touch, pain, joint position, and the visceral state. Neurobiologically, visceral responses, including organs of the chest and abdomen, adjust to the reprocessing of distressing memories. Therapists often witness these adjustments as the involuntary or autonomic activity involving the visceral pathways is reprocessed. These areas are regulated by an unconscious process. Areas of regulation include basic physiological regulation such as the circulation of blood, respiration, digestive and excretory functions, the respiratory tract, body temperature control, endocrine hormone secretions, and functions of the immune systems (Scaer, 2005). The thalamus also receives signals through the spinothalamic and spinoreticular pathways. Neurons in the thalamus relay visceral sensory information to the visceral sensory cortex in the insula lobe for conscious perception. Visceral sensory information also reaches and influences the visceral control centers in the hypothalamus and medulla oblongata (Marieb, 2015).

During EMDR therapy, as the processing of the memory is completed, the physical reactions will readjust to normal levels of operation. For example, a soldier recalled being on a forward operating base (FOB), which was attacked by an insurgent driving a vehicle carrying a vehicle-borne explosive device (VBED), a bomb in a vehicle. The bomb killed 28 Iraqi soldiers on the base. He, a truck driver in a transportation unit, volunteered to help clean up the body parts. During his reprocessing, the memory began to make him sick to his stomach. He was remembering the disturbing smell of the stench of body parts related to the memory of the mass casualty event. What he had to eat during those dates was recalled. The memory with its sensory memory and explicit memories of food he had eaten that day, 5 years earlier, were activated and processed during the recall of the event. He left the office feeling better, laughing that he had recalled what he had to eat 5 years ago.

A lieutenant colonel, while being treated for her PTSD symptoms, was reprocessing a memory of physical abuse by her former partner who had knocked her to the floor in their apartment. During reprocessing of her abuse memory, she began to hold her side as if she was experiencing physical pain generated at that moment. In fact, she was experiencing the pain, but it was a somatic memory from 8 years previously, when the abuse occurred. Between sets of BLS, when asking for feedback, I asked, "Did he hurt you there?" She replied, "After knocking me to the floor, he kicked me there." The memory of the pain had not been resolved until then. After another 15 minutes of reprocessing, the pain dissipated and the memory was resolved with her SUD being a 0, her VOC being a 7, and a clear body scan.

Todd, Talmi, Schmitz, Susskind, and Anderson (2012), while researching how emotion keeps some memories vivid, found the brain's amygdala was more active among research participants when they viewed vivid images. This in turn increased activity in the visual cortex and in the posterior insula (which integrates sensations from the body).

Their findings noted that increased perceptual vividness is part of wider sensory activation. The research found that activity in the dorsolateral prefrontal cortex and the posterior parietal cortex was negatively correlated with vividness. Findings reveal that when emotion is involved in stressful situations it does more than increase one's focus; it changes the focus, reducing the executive processes of the prefrontal cortex in favor of perceptual perspectives. This process provides a different flavor to the memory. Emotion sharpens our attention as the amygdala marks aspects of a memory as important. The findings of Todd et al. (2012) suggested that a person's current view of memories is stored primarily in the brain regions originally involved in the processing of each kind of information. State-specific sensory memory recall can be activated by associated memory components such as sounds, smells, or images—even similar weather or room temperature can activate state-dependent memories. Body states including physiological arousal, such as heart rate and breathing patterns, emotional states, and physical posture, can trigger the activating of state-dependent disturbing memories. For example, a soldier arrived home to learn his spouse was cooking shrimp. The smell of shrimp triggered his olfactory components of his memory, taking him back to combat in Iraq with the smell of burned human flesh. As a result, the client had to leave the kitchen. As with many somatic expressions during EMDR reprocessing, the sensations shift in location and then dissipate. Soldiers frequently recall the sensation of body armor with a protective collar around the back of the neck. While not paying attention to the neck sensation during the firefight, the sensation was unconsciously encoded in implicit sensory memory and became noticeable during reprocessing the memory.

While the memory can be out of mind for long periods of time, the memory can quickly and vividly be retrieved with similar state-specific experiences or stimuli. The same neural patterns active in the encoding of the event activate in memory retrieval. Remembering the event reactivates the same regions of the brain with similar neural patterns (Danker & Anderson, 2010).

## EMDR THERAPY'S ADAPTIVE INFORMATION PROCESSING MODEL

The theoretical basis of EMDR therapy known as the Adaptive Information Processing (AIP) model, is sometimes referred to as the AIP approach (Shapiro, 2007, 2018). The AIP theoretical model recognizes memory networks are part of a physical system (Shapiro, 2006). The physical system is composed of approximately 100 billion neurons in the brain. As Hebb (2002) stated, "Neurons that fire together, wire together."

Like the rest of the body, the brain has a propensity toward healing itself except when the healing process is inhibited. Due to the high arousal state, with inhibited processing, a memory can be maladaptively stored in its inadequately processed state. Such stored memory is "stuck" or dysfunctionally encoded, leaving the memory of the event/incident frozen in time with all the associated memory components including sights, sounds, tastes, thoughts, and emotions. It is the nature of such memories to remain in this dysfunctional state until resolved. They do not diminish with the passing of time. The person may compartmentalize the memory or use other avoidance coping strategies, but the memory remains unresolved. Such memories frequently manifest themselves with nightmares, flashbacks, or triggers. When a client enters EMDR therapy, dormant memories can become activated during the processing of other associated memories and surface as additional nightmares or frequent flashbacks until treated. Once treated with EMDR therapy, the dysfunctional aspects of the memory are resolved. The memory is integrated into other similar experiences about oneself and others as the pathology clears.

The AIP approach reminds us that maladaptive conclusions from inadequately processed past negative experiences are used to interpret the present. Since the memory has been processed the first time in an inadequate manner, the memory can be reprocessed when the client links present awareness with the past memory and the therapist provides BLS. BLS activates the target memory, allowing it to be reprocessed. When done successfully, the previous disturbing memories are neutralized— they lose their emotional charge—and are integrated into other memory networks with similar experiences. As this process happens, what is useful is stored and what is not healthy, no longer adaptive, is discarded.

## THE USE OF EMDR BILATERAL STIMULATION TO REPROCESS INADEQUATELY-PROCESSED, MALADAPTIVELY-STORED MEMORIES

In 1987, Dr. Francine Shapiro, PhD, discovered a connection between eye movement and the neutralizing of a disturbing memory. While out for a walk she made the chance discovery that a distressing memory had lost its emotional charge following her eyes moving in a manner similar to what seems to happen during REM sleep. As a result of eye movement (EM), her reoccurring, disturbing thoughts were changed with some disappearing others seemingly neutralized. This awareness placed her on the path to conduct the first research on the eye movement (EM) procedure she called Eye Movement Desensitization (EMD). Her research was later published in the *Journal of Traumatic Stress* (Shapiro, 1989). The procedure was considered a technique at the time rather than a model of psychotherapy. Dr. Shapiro (1989) described the use of EM as a procedure generating rhythmic, multi-saccadic EMs as the client recalls the target memory. Her initial research reported her holding her finger 12 to 14 inches from the client's face and moving her fingers rapidly from left to right for 10 to 20 passes each time. The range of movement was about 12 inches in length. Direction of the EM was either horizontal or diagonal in front of the client's face. By 1990, there was the realization that more than desensitization is occurring; an actual reprocessing occurs with a shift or change in perspective due to the process. Since the early development of EMDR therapy, EM has demonstrated its efficacy in adequately stimulating targeted memories for reprocessing. This modality of BLS has been the subject of more research than any BLS modality. Lee and Cuijpers (2013) in a meta-analysis evaluated 26 randomized controlled trials (RCTs) in which EMs produced a significantly superior effect in the reduction of imagery vividness and negative emotions.

When a client finds EM psychologically or physically uncomfortable, either tactile or auditory stimulation can be used. Tapping can be done in a number of ways. EMDR basic training teaches that the client can sit with his hands positioned on his knees with palms upward. The therapist taps the client's palms using one or two fingers, alternating right and left tapping with the same speed as doing EM. Some therapists provide an alternate approach by tapping the client's knees instead of hands. Keep in mind that many clients prefer not to be touched by the therapist. Many military and veteran clients find such touching somewhat uncomfortable due to personal boundary concerns. I have found it effective to have the client do their own tapping, similar to the Butterfly Hug, except among military personnel I introduce the tapping as "tactical tapping." Another approach is to have the client tap their legs while the therapist taps the therapist's own legs. The client is instructed to pull their elbows back to their side, place hands on each of their legs, and lift the tips of their fingers, tapping as they observe the therapist doing the same tapping on their own legs. I have found having the client do their own tapping, either Butterfly Hug (tactile tapping) or tapping on their own legs, assists clients who have dissociative tendencies to stay grounded during reprocessing. Concurrent use of EM along with tapping can also be effective on occasion when both are warranted in special situations. The client, doing their own tapping, cues off the therapist when to begin and stop the tapping as they engage their working memory during the task. I have observed this procedure to sometimes make the difference between keeping the client present and successfully reprocessing when otherwise they would dissociate significantly, resulting in the client feeling overwhelmed and stopping processing.

Auditory BLS is an alternative with the use of headphones and appropriate equipment. While it is suggested in EMDR basic trainings that the therapist can snap their fingers to the side of the client's head, this is not very realistic in most situations with military personnel. To do this would require the therapist to physically position himself close to the client, probably too close for the client's comfort. Most therapists would not be able to snap their fingers for a full session. The use of EMDR equipment that utilizes headphones allows for auditory BLS.

It is helpful to introduce the client to all three modalities at the time of setting up the mechanics during the Preparation phase. This avoids having to interrupt the treatment process to introduce an alternate modality of BLS when needing to change the modality during reprocessing, such as when the client begins to tear up significantly and needs to change to tapping or auditory. Having introduced the modalities beforehand allows for a smooth transition. EMDR basic training teaches participants to introduce EM as the primary modality with tapping and auditory modalities being alternatives. While all three modalities are effective, anecdotally, EM is considered by many therapists to access memories at a deeper level with effective processing.

Traumatic brain injury (TBI) with damage to the occipital lobe can prohibit EM. A senior noncommissioned officer (NCO) presented clinically with physical injuries in which he nearly bled out during a combat firefight. Being wounded in both legs, he had tourniquets on his two legs to keep him from bleeding to death. His physical wounds cause him continual pain. His complex PTSD symptoms include auditory and visual intrusions, causing him to view and hear the sounds of his last firefight during all his wakened moments. And, he suffers with such moral injury that he attempted suicide on three occasions. With the client's occipital lobe injuries, he could not do EM comfortably. He discovered headphones with the beeping would override the intrusions. We used the tappers for the primary BLS in the processing of his disturbing target memories. This combination worked well in his treatment.

The administration of BLS allows for adjustment in speed, number of passes, and modalities. It is this adjustment that provides the therapist with the ability to regulate the intensity of the reprocessing. Regulating the reprocessing prevents the client from being overwhelmed with too much stimulation or understimulated for reprocessing the target memory. Proper adjustment of the BLS can assist the client in being sufficiently grounded for reprocessing in spite of their tendency to dissociate.

## MANAGING MEMORY NETWORKS DURING REPROCESSING

Clients report their memories with components representing the senses (images, sounds, smells, taste, and touch). Memory networks are associated through similarities of these senses. Smells and tastes can be very strong components of memory. A senior medic chewed cherry-flavored cough drops continuously. The cherry flavor offset the olfactory memory that he smelled nonstop, the smell of burned flesh and human feces. As a medic, he was responsible for the medical care of an insurgent incarcerated in Abu Ghraib prison. The insurgent was building a bomb, an improvised explosive device (IED), when it detonated on him, burning over 70% of his body. He was arrested, imprisoned, and given a prognosis of less than 30 days to live. As the insurgent's organs shut down, he would lay in feces until the medic attended to his burns and defecation daily. The memory of those putrid death smells became embedded in the medic's olfactory memory. The smell was a part of him continuously. Suffering from complex PTSD, the medic was referred to me at Soldier Center to be treated with EMDR therapy in our 10-day EMDR intensive program (Hurley, 2018). He was treated with EMDR therapy twice a day for a 10-day period.

The medic processed his memories effectively. The memory of the insurgent at Abu Ghraib processed completely in two sessions. Twenty minutes into the second session, the medic exclaimed, "I smell bread!" After a couple more sets of BLS, he stated, "I smell hot bread, I'm hungry for some." After another set of BLS he stated, "I am hungry for some hot bread with butter on it!" These comments were particularly significant since Soldier Center's offices were next door to a donut shop and what he was smelling was the fresh bread used in making donuts. The Soldier Center staff has become desensitized to the smell of the fresh bread. As the therapist, I knew the medic's olfactory memories had processed when he was noticing the present scents rather than past memories. After 10 days of EMDR treatment, the medic was ready to return home with a fresh outlook on his military tours. A painting he had hidden away in storage since it reminded him of negative experiences in his Iraq deployment was hung in his home as a symbol of his positive experiences during his deployment.

When either smell or sound memories emerge, it is beneficial to focus on processing them with successive sets of BLS until they clear. Should they process through without accessing associated memories, the therapist should take the client back to the original target to access any remaining material for treatment. During normal processing, the client taps into other associated memory networks as fragmented memories are being integrated. After each set of BLS, the therapist asks for feedback. If the feedback seems too vague, it can be helpful to provide a couple more sets of BLS to see if the feedback clarifies the processing. If the feedback continues to be vague, take the client back to the original target memory. Should the client appear to become overwhelmed by accessing material, returning the client back to the target memory frequently can control how much material can be accessed for reprocessing.

## EMDR STANDARD REPROCESSING

Often, EMDR therapy will spontaneously reprocess disturbing memories using the standard EMDR procedure. I began using EMDR therapy in the early days of Operation Iraqi Freedom (OIF) and Operation Enduring Freedom (OEF) when military personnel would return home for a 2-week rest and relaxation (R & R). Those soldiers who demonstrated acute stress and simple PTSD regularly identified a single combat incident contributing to their symptoms. Having provided previous couples therapy for many of the military couples, their spouses would refer them to me for help with the obvious changes the soldiers had made since spending 6 months in combat. Their symptoms were those of typical acute stress and simple PTSD including irritability, hypervigilance, social withdrawal, and emotional distance. Children would avoid the newly returned parent by staying in their rooms. Spouses complained they were arguing all the time, and the soldiers acknowledged the situation was not the way they wanted their limited time with their family to be spent. As a newly trained EMDR therapist, I was amazed at the efficacy of the therapy model with little effort on my part.

One of the first soldiers I treated with EMDR therapy was an Army E-7, sergeant first class, medic home for 2 weeks R & R. Since I had provided couples therapy for him and his wife 6 to 8 months previously, I had a functional baseline of his ability to self-regulate and manage life. I asked what had happened in his life since we last saw each other. He reported responding to a mass casualty as a flight medic. A National Guard convoy had hit an IED. As the "bird" (UH-60 Blackhawk helicopter) landed, the first thing he noted was the National Guard markings on the vehicle indicated they were from his region back home. He felt he was caring for neighbors. As he began doing triage, assessing the dead, the wounded, and those who could be returned to duty, the insurgents detonated a second IED. He felt the wind blast in his face as his ears began to ring. The pilot on the Blackhawk motioned him to get back on the helicopter so they could extract, allowing another medevac to complete that mission. This was his target memory. I had 9 days to treat him before his return to the combat zone. The mass casualty response was the past incident. It was treated first as the past incident. He processed the target memory. There were two disturbing parts of the memory, the arrival on scene as he saw the mass casualty situation and the guilt that he had failed to remain and care for the wounded due to the detonation of the second IED. He processed through those fine. In one session his SUD of 9 reduced to 0; his negative cognition "I am a failure as an NCO" resolved to his positive cognition, "I am a good NCO who takes care of my people." His VOC, which had been a 3, increased to a 7 with a clear body scan. The first session had resolved his basic target memory.

Next was the need to treat any triggers that might surface during interaction with his spouse and children. A follow-up appointment was scheduled 4 days later. On arrival for his follow-up session, the medic conveyed that his wife was very pleased with the positive improvement in their time together. His outcome measures (SUD, VOC, and body scan) were maintained. We targeted his present reactivity as being current triggers. His reaction to adjustments at home was identified and processed with similar results from the previous session. The target was reacting when he could not find his gloves and cover (cap) since the spouse had moved them. The SUD was a 6 and processed to 0. The negative cognition was "I am a misfit" with the positive cognition, "I am a caring member of the family" having a VOC of 4. With reprocessing the VOC increased to 7 with a clear body scan. Then, 2 days before his departure back to Iraq, we worked on a future template for the medic. With the future template he imagined himself effectively responding to the next nine-line call and his response as a flight medic. His positive cognition for the future template was I am a good NCO taking care of my people. The VOC was a 4, which increased to 7 with reprocessing. When a challenging situation was entered, the VOC dropped to a 5 as he imagined stepping off another Blackhawk helicopter and feeling challenged. With a few sets of BLS his VOC increased to 7. This is an example of how an EMDR standard processing can be effective in providing EMDR's three-prong protocol in treating someone within a limited period of time, in this case less than 2 weeks.

## LIMITED PROCESSING

Keep in mind the treatment objective is to reprocess a maladaptively stored memory. With this in mind, the standard EMDR approach is desired when the client is stable for reprocessing. However, when treating clients with various levels of self-regulation and stability, therapists learn to adjust the BLS as well as manage the focus on the target memories to keep the client within the window of tolerance. There are times when limited access to the associated memory networks is necessary for the client to successfully resolve a disturbing memory. Limiting the access to the client's memory networks can be done by selecting a target memory the client is able to reprocess, such as selecting the easiest target first. We do this frequently in treating complex PTSD by selecting the client's easiest memory to process first. On occasion, I ask the client to identify a target memory they are confident in treating for the session. And it is possible to select a segment of a memory such as treating a moral injury incident in which the client could not mentally look at the remains of a dead woman and children. We processed everything but that part of the memory by placing that component in a container and reprocessed the remainder of the memory down to a SUD of 0, VOC of 7, with a clear body scan. With the majority of the memory out of the way, we processed the moral injury component with its disturbing image and blocking belief. The second session dedicated to that memory allowed the client to resolve the moral injury issue. The Flash technique can be helpful when a stable client has strong avoidance responses toward addressing a disturbing memory (Manfield & Engel, 2018). Once the avoidance is diminished, the EMDR standard protocol can be used with stable clients. For clients more fragile in their stability, both limited processing and restricted (EMD) processing evolved. Limited processing developed two intermediate approaches for limiting the number of memory networks accessed during reprocessing. The limited processing includes two approahces (a) target-focus and (b) a procedure called EMDr (contained processing). The first is simply "target-focused," a basic step of returning the client back to target every set or every few sets as a means of limiting access to the broader memory network. This approach is basic and keeps the client's reprocessing focused narrowly on the target memory. The frequency of returning back to target is a clinical judgment as determined by the therapist. Sometimes it requires taking the client back to target after each set of BLS; other times it requires taking the client back to target every three or four sets of BLS as determined by how much associated memories the client is accessing. The therapist varies the number of BLS passes to diminish the stimulation.

A more structured intermediate approach for contained processing is known as EMDr (Kiessling, 2015).

## EMDr CONTAINED PROCESSING

EMDr is an approach that restricts the processing of associations primarily to focus on a specific incident within the client's associated memory networks. It allows for "contained processing," accessing connections to those channels of association related to the target. The client can choose what aspect of the treatment plan is ideal for processing. Selection ensures the client can manage the affect as well as the overall target memory. The therapist assists the client in containing the process by taking the client back to target after every set of BLS. The assessment phase is the same as the standard EMDR assessment except the question on body location is a clinical judgment based on the presence of strong body sensations. The therapist may or may not include the body location question since the question can activate components of the broader memory networks. This keeps the focus primarily on the targeted memory component. The Desensitization phase uses 10 to 15 seconds. The BLS with client feedback continues until the SUD is 0 or there is no change. Accepting where the client stops changing, the therapist goes to the Installation phase to increase the VOC as strongly as possible. Neither the SUD nor VOC has to necessarily go the maximum number. Phase 6 Body Scan is focused on the restricted target for evaluating. The therapist checks to ensure the reported body sensations are also confined to the memory component, which has been the focus of EMDr treatment. This containment prevents the processing from freely connecting to broader memory networks, which can threaten the client's ability to remain stable while processing the target memory.

Conceptually, both of the limited approaches listed here provide a contained approach allowing for both desensitization and reprocessing of associated memories connected with the target memory while at the same time restricting access to the client's broader memory networks. It narrows the field of processing.

## EMD RESTRICTED PROCESSING

Restricted processing has been effectively incorporated in the treatment of complex trauma (Gelinas, 2015). The approach allows for clinical work with fragile clients who in regular reprocessing might risk being overwhelmed by continually maintaining focus on the target memory without access to broader memory networks.

EMD, as restricted processing, is the original approach developed by Dr. Shapiro (1989), which repeatedly took the client back to the targeted event that contained the processing to the activated network of the event. It is helpful when sensory disturbance interferes with functioning. EMD is a narrowly focused process allowing for brief contained processing while mostly allowing for desensitization of the memory with minimal benefits of the reprocessing (Figure 6A.1). This confined approach is not intended to replace EMDR but, rather, provide the client who is somewhat fragile an opportunity to desensitize a disturbing memory. It is to be used in fragile situations to reduce arousal and increase stability. This confined approach provides for symptom reduction while limiting spontaneous associations with other memories

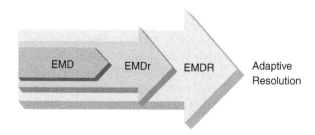

FIGURE 6A.1 EMD restricted processing approach.

(EMDR Institute, 2017). Due to this limitation, it is best to resume the regular EMDR reprocessing as soon as possible.

While the approach uses the standard Phase 3 Assessment with its seven questions, the EMD process (Phase 4) begins by applying short sets of BLS, starting with 12 to 15 passes, and increasing the number of passes as the client demonstrates their ability to engage the process. Return to the target memory with the negative cognition, after each pass is done with the checking of the SUD. When the desired treatment effect is achieved, a positive belief that represents the client's shift in experience is identified and enhanced until it reaches a VOC of 7. Following each set, the therapist states, "Take a deep breath. Let it go. What are you noticing now?" After the client's feedback, the therapist states, "When you bring up that picture and those negative words, on a scale of 0 to 10, where 0 is not disturbance and 10 is the highest disturbance you can imagine, how disturbing does it feel to you now?" The therapist continues until the SUD is as low as it will drop or it appears to be ecologically valid and then moves on to the Installation phase.

## EMDR INTENSIVE APPLICATIONS

The flexibility of EMDR's clinical application allows it to be provided in an intense daily format, twice weekly, weekly, or biweekly. Following Dr. Shapiro's suggestion that I offer EMDR therapy to veterans and military personnel on an intense daily basis, I developed a 5- and 10-day EMDR intensive format (Hurley, 2018). The intensive treatment began as a 5-day treatment program. Since recipients were active duty military personnel and referred veterans from out of state, offering treatment twice a day made use of the client's time at Soldier Center. This approach ensured the client had a minimum of hours between each daily session.

Acceptance into the EMDR intensive treatment program requires the person to complete a PTSD packet of assessments including the PTSD Checklist for *DSM-5* (National Center for PTSD, 2016), the Impact of Events Scale-II (Beck et al., 2008), Beck Anxiety Inventory (Leyfer, Ruberg, & Woodruff-Borden, 2006), Beck Depression Inventory (Ambrosini, Metz, Bianchi, Rabinovich, & Undie, 1991), and the Dissociative Experiences Scale-II (Bernstein & Putnam, 1986). While participants have been previously diagnosed with PTSD by the referring agency, measures in the PTSD packet must support the diagnosis. Participants must demonstrate their ability to self-regulate to the referring therapist prior to arrival for the 10-day intensive program.

EMDR therapy standard protocol is provided twice daily, once in the morning and, with a 3-hour break, a second session in the afternoon. Sessions are 90 minutes each. Research outcome studies found the treatment, both weekly and twice daily, produced similar outcome results with significant results being maintained at 1 year later. In fact, other clients who participated in treatment 5 years previously reported their results being maintained. Some veterans stated "EMDR saved my life" when contacted at 5-year follow-up.

This chapter has focused on providing an introduction to the reprocessing sections of EMDR therapy (Phases 4–6) followed by discussions on Closing and Reevaluation, the last two phases of the EMDR eight-phase protocol. Military, veteran, and first responder clients present varying levels of dysfunction. Recognizing the varying nature of learning and memory due to the brain's encoding of incidents explains the variance in clinical presentations. EMDR therapists must be prepared to work with various levels of clinical complexity. The following discussions are designed to empower therapists in the further development of their clinical skills with EMDR therapy.

## CONCLUSION

This chapter has focused on the Desensitization phase, Phase 4, with the goal of reprocessing a target memory. Reprocessing results in neutralizing the level of disturbance associated with the target memory. We discussed the therapeutic skills of keeping the client within the window of tolerance. The impact of dissociative exhibitions during reprocessing is noted since this is a frequent response in treating clients with complex PTSD. Limiting access to target memory networks by using the EMD, EMDr, and EMDR therapy protocols allows clinical options for keeping the client's focus on the presenting target.

### DISCUSSION POINTS

1. Are flashbacks associated more closely with the hippocampus or the amygdala?
2. Are areas of the brain impacted by PTSD as revealed by brain imaging studies?
3. Would you use the Flash technique with unstable persons who might be overwhelmed during processing or stable persons who might be overwhelmed or exhibit strong avoidance?
4. When would you use EMD instead of EMDR?
5. What is the difference between limited reprocessing models (target-focused and EMDr) and restricted processing (EMD) when comparing desensitization and reprocessing in each model?
6. Based on research (Hurley, 2018), how does treatment outcome for EMDR 10-day intensive treatment compare to weekly treatment?

## REFERENCES

Ambrosini, P. J., Metz, C., Bianchi, M. D., Rabinovich, H., & Undie, A. (1991, January). Concurrent validity and psychometric properties of the Beck Depression Inventory in outpatient adolescents. *Journal of the American Academy of Child and Adolescent Psychiatry, 30*(1), 51–57. doi:10.1097/00004583-199101000-00008

Beck, J., Grant, D., Read, J., Clapp, J., Coffey, S., Miller, L., & Palyo, S. A. (2008). The impact of event scale-revised: Psychometric properties in a sample of motor vehicle accident survivors. *Journal of Anxiety Disorders, 22*, 187–198. doi:10.1016/j.janxdis.2007. 02.007

Bernstein, E., & Putnam, F. (1986). Development, reliability, and validity of a dissociation scale. *The Journal of Nervous and Mental Disease, 174*(12), 727–735. doi:10.1097/00005053-198612000-00004

Bowlby, J. (1988). *A secure base: Parent attachment and healthy human development.* New York: Basic Books.

Cozolino, L. (2002). *The neuroscience of human relationships: Attachment and the developing social brain.* New York, NY: W. W. Norton.

Danker, F., & Anderson, J. (2010). The ghosts of brain states past: Remembering reactivates the brain regions engaged during encoding. *Psychological Bulletin, 136*(1), 87–102. doi:10.1037/a0017939

Gelinas, D. (2015, March). *When less is more: Restricted processing in the treatment of complex traumatization.* Presentation at the 11th Western Mass Regional Network Spring Conference, Amherst, MA.

Hebb, D. (2002). *The organization of behavior: The organization of psychological theory.* New York, NY: The Psychology Press.

Hurley, E. (2018). Effective treatment of veterans with PTSD: Comparison between intensive daily and weekly EMDR approaches—Supplement outlining the clinical protocol. *Frontiers in Psychology, 9*(Suppl.), 1458. doi:10.3389/fpsyg.2018.01458

Kiessling, R. (2015, April). *The processing continuum.* Presentation at the EMDR Canada Annual Conference, Vancouver, BC, Canada.

LeDoux, J. (1996). *The emotional brain: The mysterious underpinnings of emotional life.* New York, NY: Simon & Schuster.

LeDoux, J. (2002). *Synaptic self: How our brain became who we are.* New York, NY: Penguin Group.

Lee, C., & Cuijpers, P. (2013). A meta-analysis of the contribution of eye movements in processing emotional memories. *Journal of Behavioral Therapy and Experiential Psychiatry, 44*(2), 231–239. doi:10.1016/j.jbtep.2012.11.001

Leyfer, O. T., Ruberg, J. L., & Woodruff-Borden, J. (2006). Examination of the utility of the Beck Anxiety Inventory and its factors as a screener for anxiety disorders. *Journal of Anxiety Disorders, 20*(4), 444–458. doi:10.1016/j.janxdis.2005.05.004

Ludmer, R., Dudai, Y., & Rubin, N. (2011). Uncovering camouflage: Amygdala activation predicts long-term memory of induced perceptual insight. *Neuron, 69*(5), 1002–1014. doi:10.1016/j.neuron.2011.02.013

Manfield, P., & Engel, L. B. (2018, October). *The Flash technique, an advance in EMDR processing.* Presentation at the 23rd EMDR International Association Conference, Atlanta, GA.

Marieb, E. (2015). *Essentials of human anatomy and physiology* (11th ed., pp. 467–487). Retrieved from https://www.pearsonhighered.com/content/dam/region-na/us/higher-ed/en/products-services/course-products/marieb-8e-info/pdf/marieb-0134215036-chapter15.pdf

McGaugh, J. (2004). The amygdala modulates the consolidation of memories of emotionally arousing experiences. *Annual Review of Neuroscience, 27,* 1–28. doi:10.1146/annurev.neuro.27.070203.144157

National Center for PTSD. (2016). *PTSD checklist for DSM-5 (PCL-5).* Retrieved from https://www.ptsd.va.gov/professional/assessment/adult-sr/ptsd-checklist.asp

Pagani, M., Di Lorenzo, G., Monaco, L., Daverio, A., Giannoudas, L., La Porta, P., … Siracusano, A. (2015). Neurobiological response to EMDR therapy in clients with different psychological traumas. *Frontiers in Psychology, 6,* 1–12. doi:10.3389/fpsyg.2015.01614

Pagani, M., Di Lorenzo, G., Monaco, L., Niolu, C., Siracusano, A., Verardo, A., … Ammaniti, M. (2011). Pretreatment, intratreatment, and posttreatment EEG imaging of EMDR: Methodology and preliminary results from a single case. *Journal of EMDR Practice and Research, 5*(2), 42–56. doi:10.1891/1933-3196.5.2.42

Pagani, M., Di Lorenzo, G., Verardo, A., Nicolais, G., Monaco, G., Lauretti, G., … Siracusano, A. (2012). Neurobiological correlates of EMDR monitoring—An EEG study. *PLoS One, 7*(9), e45753. doi:10.1371/journal.pone.0045753

Purves, D., Augustine, G., Fitzpatrick, D., Hall, W., LaMantia, A., & White, L. (Eds.). (2012). *Neuroscience.* Sunderland, MA: Sinauer Associates.

Scaer, R. (2005). *The trauma spectrum: Hidden wounds and human resiliency.* New York, NY: W. W. Norton.

Schacter, D. (1987). Implicit memory: History and current status. *Journal of Experimental Psychology Learning Memory and Cognition, 13*(3), 501–518. doi:10.1037/0278-7393.13.3.501

Shapiro, F. (1989). Efficacy of the eye movement desensitization procedure in the treatment of trauma memories. *Journal of Traumatic Stress, 2*(2), 199–223. doi:10.1002/jts.2490020207

Shapiro, F. (2006). *EMDR: New notes on adaptive information processing with case formulation principles, forms, scripts, and worksheets.* Watsonville, CA: EMDR Institute.

Shapiro, F. (2007). EMDR, adaptive information processing, and case conceptualization. *Journal of EMDR Practice and Research, 1*(2), 69–87. doi:10.1037/0278-7393.13.3.501

Shapiro, F. (2018). *Eye movement desensitization and reprocessing (EMDR) therapy: Basic principles, protocols, and procedures* (3rd ed.). New York, NY: Guilford Press.

Todd, R., Talmi, D., Schmitz, T., Susskind, J., & Anderson, A. (2012). Psychophysical and neural evidence for emotion-enhanced perceptual vividness. *Journal of Neuroscience, 32*(33), 11202–11212. doi:10.1523/JNEUROSCI.0155-12.2012

van der Kolk, B. (1997). *Bevroren Angst* [Video]. Produced through public media VPro Noorderlicht, Omroepvereniging VPRO, Rotterdam, The Netherlands.

van der Kolk, B. (2002). Trauma and memory. *Psychiatry and Clinical Neurosciences, 52*(S1), 1–27. doi:10.1046/j.1440-1819.1998.0520s5S97.x

van der Kolk, B. (2014). *The body keeps the score: Brain, mind, and body in the healing of trauma.* New York, NY: Viking/Penguin Group.

# 6B

# EMDR Phases 5 to 7: Installation to Closing

## Introduction

This section explores the importance of the client's positive memory networks throughout the EMDR therapy process in enhancing the client's self-efficacy once the emotional charge, as measured by the subjective unit of disturbance (SUD), is neutralized. The client's positive cognition (PC), used during Phases 5 to 7, is examined phase by phase as the interaction and efficacy of positive memories are studied. Use of the future template as a further extension of positive memory networks are noted as the PC is extended throughout the EMDR third-prong approach. A case study of providing EMDR therapy's third-prong approach to a military client during a 2-week R & R period is provided.

## Learning Objectives

- Provide an overview of positive memory networks utilized in the EMDR therapy's three-prong approach.
- Recognize the importance of positive life experiences (resources) for development and the use of the therapeutic alliance when resources do not exist or present with limited availability.
- Explore the use of the PC in EMDR therapy's Phases 5 to 7 as representative of the client's positive memory network.
- Review the importance of EMDR therapy's future template in extending the PC as far as possible.
- Illustrate the importance of the positive memory networks with a case example.

## POSITIVE MEMORY NETWORKS

Beginning with the Installation phase, the therapist turns his attention to the world of positive memory networks. Now that the SUD has been reduced to 0, or ecologically valid (during the previous Desensitization phase), the next phases focuses on the PC as identified during Phase 3 Assessment. *The positive cognition (PC) sets the direction of the EMDR therapy process.* In reality, the identification of positive memory networks begins early in the treatment process. There are four EMDR phases that evaluate the client's access to positive memory networks: (a) History-Taking's treatment plan assesses for positive memory experiences (resource list); (b) Assessment phase asks the client to identify a PC appropriate for the target memory; and (c) the use of the PC during Installation and (d) the Body Scan. Due to the focus on reprocessing disturbing memories (Phase 4), there is an inherent awareness of distress, with negative beliefs associated with those disturbing memories. At the same time, the influence of positive memory networks is an important part of the EMDR process. The role of positive memory networks is examined in Box 6B.1 with their contributions to the healing process.

While not everyone can identify positive memories from their childhood, every person who has served in the military has a memorable story to tell. Some are war stories—accounts of both good and bad experiences. Harsh, difficult times frequently build close relationships in adulthood as evidenced by veterans who often speak of their valued relationships. Except for loss with its potential for complicated grief, most close memories last a lifetime in the form of stored positive memories even if the people have not seen each other for decades.

I once participated in a reunion celebration for members of a World War II unit who had not seen each other for 50 years. The Army captain during the war was of short stature, and his military bearing had been

---

BOX 6B.1 **Positive Memory Networks**

Phase 1: History-Taking identifies positive memories of achievements and supportive interactions known as resources.

Phase 3: Assessment develops a positive cognition "… what would you prefer to believe about yourself?" A baseline measure is developed of the validity of cognition (VOC).

Phase 5: Installation links the target memory with the PC. Reprocessing is performed to get the VOC to 7 or ecologically valid.

Phase 6: Body Scan pairs the PC of the target memory with a search for somatic sensations associated with the target memory.

lost to years of civilian lifestyle. There were two members of the unit who had gone on to become Army generals. I observed during their reunion the retired generals still treated the WW II captain as if he was in charge. Military relationships, particularly those chiseled in combat conditions, remain the same as when they were last together. Perhaps there is some sense of wanting to maintain the past as last remembered rather than pursuing ongoing current updates. Given any opportunity, a therapist who asks, "What was the funniest thing that happened to you during the deployment?" is likely to elicit a smile and positive shift in physical and emotional response. Most military personnel have reservoirs of positive memory networks. While these networks may be obscured by layers of serious events in the person's life, a basic question during History-Taking can activate those positive memories.

Dr. Shapiro (2018, p. 110) noted the role of positive memories in facilitating processing and preparation. Persons with limited positive experiences during childhood have often encountered adverse life experiences that have been normalized over time. They often underreport the impact of those normalized early memories until activated for reprocessing. Then the SUDs begin to increase during the first few sets of bilateral stimulation (BLS). While the client may not disclose the nature of the adversity, the absence of positive memories is revealing. Sometimes what is not stated is as revealing as the information reported. Persons with limited positive memories typically need longer preparation time. The themes of responsibility/defectiveness, safety, and choices/power/control are established early enough in life for the sensitivity to one or more of those themes to provide distorted perceptions through various life experiences. Whereas, persons with sufficient networks of positive memories tend to have greater coping and problem-solving alternatives as well as an enhanced sense of self-worth.

## FACILITATING POSITIVE MEMORY NETWORKS

Dr. Shapiro taught that a client must have at least one positive memory for EMDR therapy to be effective (Shapiro, 2006). In clinical situations where a client does not have one positive memory, the therapeutic alliance can be used as one. The client's mental capacity for recalling positive memories is first addressed during EMDR therapy's History-Taking phase. The ability to access healthy memory networks reflects on the client's internal resources for facilitating their healing process (Silver & Rogers, 2002, p. 81). This is first evaluated during History-Taking's treatment planning when the availability of positive experiences is listed. The development of a resource list, a list of positive memories consisting of achievement and supportive comments said to the client that support the client's sense of self-efficacy, is completed by the conclusion of the History-Taking phase. The resource list may be included as a 10–10 list (10 memories of adaptive resources and the 10 most disturbing memories) and can be used to list and organize both adaptive and maladaptive memories. When there are limited positive memory networks recalling healthy resources, the therapeutic relationship can be used to strengthen the client's internal strengths.

The second occasion for evaluating the client's ability to access positive resource networks occurs during Phase 3, the Assessment phase, as the client is asked to identify a positive belief which they would like to accept for themselves (Figure 6B.1). During this phase the therapist has an opportunity to observe the client's access to positive memory networks again. The therapist observes the ease or difficulty the client demonstrates in identifying a positive self-reference statement about themselves in contrast to the negative cognition (NC; Leeds, 2016, p. 148). Persons who can readily access positive, healthy memory networks tend to demonstrate stronger problem-solving skills in comparison to clients who have limited resources and inhibited problem-solving skills. During the Assessment phase, the PC can be somewhat flexible since there is time to revise the cognition during Phases 4 to 5. However, it must "fit" enough to be appropriate and set the direction for treatment. Rather than magical thinking, it must be real. Self-referencing statements provide the ownership of the belief. The generalization of the application is warranted as well as being applicable. Remember, the PC feels relatively untrue while relating to the same theme as the NC. The positive cognition—developed during the Assessment phase (Phase 3)—sets the direction of the treatment (Figure 6B.1).

FIGURE 6B.1 Setting the direction of treatment.

# INSTALLATION PHASE: ENHANCING THE PC

The Installation phase is designed to enhance the PC. In reality we are not installing the PC since it is always in the memory system; rather, we enhance the possibility of the positive belief being true as we associate the target memory with the PC and provide sets of BLS.

> *The Installation phase begins with the question, "Do the original words* _____ *still fit, or is there another positive statement that fits even better?"*

This third occasion for observing the client's ability to access healthy networks occurs at the beginning of Phase 5, the Installation phase. Positive networks are activated by asking about the PC. Asking such a basic question at this phase provides a very subtle but influential activation of positive possibilities within memory networks. At this point in reprocessing, as the SUD rate is diminished, healthy memory networks are free to find expression with the integration with other memory networks. The PC continues setting the direction of the treatment as appropriate memory networks establish positive possibilities. As this occurs, the PC also allows for the establishment of a baseline measure.

At the beginning of the Installation phase, the therapist checks to see if the original PC still fits or if there is a more suitable statement the client would like to use. Frequently, as the SUD has reduced to 0, the PC represents a shift in perspective and the client may desire to revise the positive belief applicable to himself. When the client revises the PC, the new revision is usually high in level of belief (usually 5–7). Often it takes a few sets of BLS to achieve the score of 7 on the validity of cognition (VOC). Once a 7 is reported, an additional set of BLS is warranted to strengthen the PC.

There are occasions when residual unprocessed material surfaces during the Installation phase. EMDR therapy, like all other models of psychotherapy, will only do what the client wants done. On occasion, a client may disclose an unprocessed component of memory that surfaces during the Installation phase. I first learned this while treating a special operations noncommissioned officer (NCO) who had fought during the battle at Roberts Ridge; he had processed the memory, achieving a SUD of 0. We moved into the Installation phase as I continued to provide 35 passes of

---

**BOX 6B.2  Residual Unprocessed Material**

There are occasions when residual unprocessed material surfaces during the Installation phase. When this happens, taking the client back to target is usually sufficient to complete reprocessing, allowing the VOC to be strengthened.

BLS. After about six sets of BLS, he exclaimed, "Oh, an image just popped up which I have tried not to think about. After combat, as we were doing an extraction, they placed us on the same MH-47 (military Chinook helicopter) where the dead bodies of our buddies were stacked." I replied, "Go with that!" and the memory processed clear, allowing the resumption toward enhancing the PC. As we finished the Installation phase, the disturbing memory from Roberts Ridge had been processed and cleared, allowing the session to achieve a VOC of 7. Always be ready for distressing components to surface during Phases 4 to 6 of EMDR therapy.

## WHEN THE VOC IS NOT GOING TO A 7

When a client becomes dissociative, the SUD will diminish to 0, since the client is disengaged from the disturbing memory; however, the VOC does not increase since the processing has stopped. In other words, when the client dissociates, they are disconnected from the memory, so it does not distress them. Being disconnected from the memory means the memory stopped processing at the time of the dissociative response. When this is the case, the therapist is not ready to begin the Installation phase, but is required to get the client grounded back in the present, ensuring the client is maintaining dual awareness, then return to target to complete the reprocessing. The therapist needs to assess how much assistance the client needs to maintain dual awareness, recalling the memory from the past while maintaining present awareness in order to resume reprocessing the memory.

Sometimes the VOC does not increase due to the client experiencing blocking in the processing of the PC. Most EMDR basic texts and treatment guides address this possibility (Hensley, 2016; Leeds, 2016; Shapiro, 2018). The cause of the blocking can be revealed by asking the client, "What would it take to get your positive belief - what you would prefer to believe about yourself, to a 7?" And, of course, regardless of what the client says, the therapist responds with, "Go with that!" Often this will reestablish the reprocessing as the blocking belief is resolved. When this is not the case, the therapist can ask, "When did you first learn this (blocking belief)?" and target that event for reprocessing. Additionally, the therapist can use a cognitive interweave, similar to when blocking stops processing during the Desensitization phase. A cognitive interweave is a very powerful means of resolving blocking beliefs.

Cognitive interweave questions such as "Would it be okay to get over this?" or "How much of this do you need to hold on to?" can be helpful. Sometimes asking, "What will be different when you are over this?" followed by a few sets of BLS can be effective. Keep in mind the three themes of responsibility/defectiveness, safety, and power/control/choices as you utilize appropriate interweaves.

Sometimes the Installation processing becomes blocked due to an unresolved issue from another memory network (Leeds, 2016). When this is the case, it needs to be identified and addressed as a target memory. Identifying memories within other memory networks can be identified using the three techniques of Direct Questioning, Floatback, and Affect Scan. Once the VOC has reached a 7 or is considered ecologically valid, the therapist goes to Phase 5 Body Scan as time permits.

## PHASE 6: BODY SCAN

The Body Scan is designed to identify and eliminate any residual somatic expressions noted in the body as the client connects the target memory with the PC and scans the body, beginning at the top of the head and scanning downward to their toes. The Adaptive Information Processing (AIP) model views the dysfunctional psychological material as frequently exhibiting somatic representations of the memory. Any identified sensations are identified and processed using BLS. When body sensations are reported, they frequently will spontaneously process out in a rather short term. On occasion, processing somatic material will take a few sessions. An NCO, whose personality tended to internalize his experiences, required two sessions for processing his somatic sensations. He was a junior ranking sergeant (E-5) who had led his team on 28 missions in retrieving body parts. He stated he would not ask his soldiers to do something he, himself, was not willing to do. The client had achieved a 0 SUD and VOC of 7 with normal reprocessing while his target memory was treated. The Body Scan was part of the process of restoring safety to his own body. It became apparent his having retrieved so many body parts on the battlefield had resulted in his disorienting himself from the somatic expressions of his body. As we began the Body Scan, he reported feeling sensations in his chest. With a set of BLS the sensations moved to his visceral area, then his back, then his neck, then back to the chest. The sensations continued to move in location for the remainder of the first session. For a few minutes his upper torso was jerking up and down. He asked, "Is my body jerking?" I replied, "Yes! It is your body's way of dealing with what sensations you are feeling. It will process out." He replied, "I feel like I am on a C-130" (a military transport aircraft known for its bumpy flights). At the beginning of the second session of the Body Scan, I provided brief psychoeducational information on the neurophysiology of trauma and dissociation with a focus on how the body is wired to protect us. Then we did an exercise for building safety in the body (Schwartz & Maiberger, 2018, p. 162) before resuming the processing of somatic sensations. The body sensations began to move in body location again. I assured him the fact the sensations were moving indicated they were connected to the memory being targeted for treatment. By the end of the session, the body sensations were cleared and the client was in a peaceful, restful state.

During EMDR basic training, we emphasize the importance of allowing sufficient time for closing down a session. We do not want to activate additional material while at the same time we are closing down the neurological system. Our clients teach us as we provide a healing process for them. I learned from this client the importance of allocating sufficient time to complete the Phase 6 Body Scan.

## CLOSING: PHASE 7

It is vital that your client has sufficient time to end the processing session with adequate time for achieving a state of calmness and the ability to manage themselves on leaving your office. With severe pathology, such as c-PTSD and frequent dissociative exhibitions, it sometimes requires up to one-third of the time to close down the session. This means, if necessary, I will take up to 20 minutes for closing as the client switches from the activated sympathetic nervous system to the relaxing parasympathetic nervous system. There are two types of closing: complete (requiring a SUD = 0, VOC = 7, and clear body scan) and an incomplete session in which the session has not achieved a 0, 7, clear body scan.

## CLOSING A COMPLETE SESSION

A complete EMDR session has achieved a SUD = 0, VOC = 7, and a clear body scan. In most cases, this leaves the client in a stable state of relief with the emotional charge neutralized and a sense of calmness with appropriate self-regulation. There is usually no need for additional closing techniques except to remind the client the processing may continue following the session. If there are other unprocessed memories to be treated, a complete session can sometimes activate other material, causing nightmares. The closing usually consists of three statements:

1. We are almost out of time. How are you doing?
2. Is there a positive statement you might make about anything you have learned or gained from today's session?
3. I want to remind you, the processing you have done today may continue. You may, or may not, experience new insights, thoughts, memories, dreams, or sensations. Anything that comes up, make a note of it and we will include it in our next session. You have your relaxation exercise with cue word. I want to encourage you to use it regularly. Let's schedule your follow-up session (Hensley, 2016, pp. 136–139).

## CLOSING AN INCOMPLETE SESSION

An incomplete session sometimes requires additional time for clos-ing. Closing an incomplete session requires the therapist's clinical judgment in evaluating if additional time is needed for self-regulation exercises and/or use of the container exercise to ensure the client's well-being. While transitioning into closure, the therapist should do nothing to activate additional disturbing of unprocessed material. A statement similar to the previous Statement 1 can be used. Does the client need additional time using the cue word to go to their Safe/Calm Place or does the client need to contain unprocessed material using the container exercise? Once the client is determined to be calm, con-tained, and able to self-regulate appropriately, the therapist can then incorporate comments such as Statements 2 and 3 in closing. The clini-cal judgment determining the amount of time needed for closing down is based on the client's processing during the session, including their processing speed and self-regulation abilities.

As discussed previously, many veterans do not believe there are any places that are safe. Referring to the relaxing exercise called "Safe/Calm Place" is somewhat of a disconnect with many veterans. I fre-quently refer to the exercise as a "Secure" place. Other providers refer to the exercise as a "place of strength" or "place of power." Military per-sonnel know a secure place can be established even in a combat zone, so this terminology works well with the population.

Sometimes, additional calming exercises are needed. An infantry soldier who had just processed a gory incident of finding his fellow soldiers beheaded was still physically reeling from processing the memory. At the beginning of the session he had shown me a picture of himself and his two sons dressed in camouflage on their way for some recreational time in a paintball game. On presentation, he laughed and discussed how proud he was of his sons and the fun they shared the previous weekend. Now, at the end of a particularly gruesome session while his physiology was adjusting from the intensity of the session, I did the Safe/Calm Place exercise with him. He completed the exercise but was still impacted from the session. I asked the client if he would show me the picture of his sons again. He smiled and pulled up the picture on his cell phone as he began to laugh. Viewing the picture ac-complished what was needed! It grounded him in the present with a focus on the joy of life with his two sons.

Other clients may need other assistance during closing, such as breathing exercises with or without doing their own tapping on their legs or the Butterfly Hug. All exercises are efforts designed to enhance the client's parasympathetic nervous system. The client should never be allowed to leave the session while in an extreme level of disturbance. At Soldier Center we have a "Preparation Room," a quiet place with no windows specifically designed in the construction of the building to provide a quiet secure place for clients. If necessary, we invite the client to sit in the Preparation Room for a few minutes until they are ready to leave the office.

Clinicians need to evaluate the client for any dissociative responses that could interfere with the client's ability to be present for self-regulation. Caution is warranted when a client is in a euphoric state following the successful processing of a disturbing memory. A colleague and seasoned EMDR therapist told of a client who left his office feeling so good she rear-ended a police vehicle while stopping at a traffic light. That therapist now evaluates clients' functioning in the present while euphoric as well as when distressed over intense memory processing.

Shapiro (2018) notes the importance of debriefing the client at the end of the session. This helps the client to understand what has happened during the session, emphasizing the progress the client has made. Sometimes the processing can activate additional unprocessed material. For example, 2 days following the treatment of an infantry soldier resulting in a complete session (SUD = 0, VOC = 7, and clear body scan), the soldier called indicating he was having intrusive memories about the suicide of a friend's daughter in an adjacent bedroom occurring the night he and his wife spent with his friend and friend's family. He had forgotten about the incident, not recalling it during his History-Taking phase. My lunch hour was available, so I invited the soldier to come in to address the intrusive memory. He did, and 20 minutes into the reprocessing of the memory, it was clear with the SUD down to a zero (0)! Completing the session to achieve a VOC of 7 and clear body scan, the memory was neutralized, never to intrude again. While the suicide of a friend's daughter was sad, and always will be, the emotional charge associated with the memory never returned. It is helpful to explain to the client that any continuation of memory images or thoughts is the product of the continuing of memory processing, the brain's attempt to complete the processing. Sometimes this includes increase in nightmares for two or three nights before subsiding. While this seldom occurs, for safety, it is important your client has contact information should they need additional care and support between sessions. This further enhances the client's sense of security throughout the treatment process.

## PHASE 8: REEVALUATION

Reevaluation, the last phase of the EMDR standard protocol, allows the clinician to assess the latest experience of the client, allowing for various interactions in the client's life since their last session. Reevaluation is done at two levels: macro and micro levels. At the macro level, the therapist considers the information presented in relation to the total treatment plan. At the micro level, the therapist evaluates the impact from the client's previous treatment.

Macro level of Phase 8 Reevaluation: What has changed and what remains to be accomplished?

1. What is different in your life since our last session?
2. What has changed?
3. Have you noticed any dreams or new insights?
4. Overall, what aspects of memory stand out: image, thoughts, emotions, or sensations?
5. Notice any changes in behaviors, symptoms, or attitudes?

The micro level is specific to the target memory the client worked on in the previous session. This level of reevaluation includes questions such as:

1. As you recall the target memory you worked on during the last session, what do you notice now?
2. What stands out as being different about your experience as you recall the memory now?
3. Any new insights or thoughts about yourself?
4. Any new connections to other memory networks?
5. When you recall the incident now, how disturbing is it to you on a scale of 0 to 7?

The macro level inquiry begins with checking to see if the client notices any changes since the previous session. That is followed by checks for dreams, triggers, and other memories, as well as any new thoughts or insights. Inquiry about the client's primary symptoms should be made. As clients report the successful processing of disturbing memories has lessened the severity of their symptoms, it indicates reprocessing should continue. If the reprocessing of a targeted memory seems to have activated additional distressing memories with intrusions along with additional mood states, increased urges for dysfunctional behaviors, or increased anxiety, consideration should be given to whether more stabilization time is warranted prior to continuing with reprocessing.

A micro focus is aimed at the specific target memory reprocessed from the previous session. If the previous session was incomplete, the entire list of assessment questions is not necessary. The therapist asks, "When you recall the memory you worked on during the last session, what comes to mind?" "What emotions do you notice now?" "As you recall the incident, if you were to evaluate how disturbing it is to you now, on a scale of 0 to 10, where 0 means neutral, no disturbance, and 10 represents the highest disturbance a person could imagine, what number would you give it now?" If the SUD is a 0, the therapist moves to finish any remaining phases before going to the next target memory in the treatment plan. If the SUD is not a 0, resume reprocessing by stating, "Pull up the memory of the incident, notice where you feel it in your body, and follow my fingers (tappers or beeps)."

If the Desensitization phase was completed, and a 0 is still reported, go to the next phase not processed and begin there. This could mean beginning with the Installation or Body Scan phases. If the client has achieved a SUD = 0, VOC = 7, and clear body scan, go to the next target memory listed on the treatment plan.

## THREE-PRONG APPROACH

The EMDR therapy standard protocol calls for the therapist to treat all the past events, then present triggers, along with a future template following each trigger treated. While complex cases sometimes require modification to this sequence, the standard approach begins with the development of a target sequence plan including past events, present triggers, and anticipated future happenings. During the treatment of past events, the treatment plan includes targeting each designated memory (Phases 3 through 8). The same is true with each present trigger; each trigger included in the treatment plan is treated (Phases 3 through 8).

## THREE-PRONG TREATMENT DURING A SOLDIER'S 2-WEEK R & R

A strength of the EMDR approach is its treatment not only of past events that established the early dysfunction, but how it also treats the ongoing triggers that developed out of the past events. An added benefit in the approach is preparing the client to effectively manage future events similar to each current trigger. The first time I used the future template was with an E-7, a senior medic serving with the 101st Airborne Division (Air Assault) who had returned home for his 2-week rest and relaxation (R & R). Since being home, he was continually arguing with his spouse while his two young children would hide in their room to avoid contact with their father. I had treated the soldier and spouse with couples therapy prior to his deployment to Iraq. Having 2 weeks at home before returning to Iraq, the soldier sought therapy with me on his fourth day home. His goal was to improve his quality of time with his family with the time he had left for his R & R. Having provided brief, solution-focused psychotherapy with the couple before his deployment, I knew of their healthy, positive relationship. The only significant event identified during the 6 months prior to his R & R was his response as a flight medic answering a nine-line request for medical assistance for a combat unit with a mass casualty incident. A Tennessee National Guard convoy had hit an improvised explosive device (IED), destroying several vehicles and leaving several soldiers wounded and killed. My client described being on a UH-60 Blackhawk helicopter that landed on site where the convoy had hit an IED. He immediately began to triage the wounded soldiers when a second IED was detonated near him. He felt the percussion of wind blasting past his face with ringing in his ears. This debilitated him, causing him to become nonfunctional as a medic. The pilot on the aircraft witnessed the second blast and motioned the medic to get on the aircraft. He had to be extracted, in order for another medevac to complete the medical duties.

From an EMDR treatment perspective, it was the disturbing memory of a single combat incident. His sense of failure from the incident left him feeling as a failure as a medic. During Phase 3 Assessment he identified his NC as "I am a failure as an NCO." The PC was "I am a good NCO who takes care of his people." His SUD was reported as a 10. He reprocessed the targeted memory within the 50-minute session, resulting in his SUD reducing to a 0, his VOC increasing to 7, with a clear body scan.

A follow-up session was set for 3 days later with just enough time to evaluate the client's change as he interacted with his family. He arrived for his second session reporting his wife had noted the difference in how he was responding to her and the children in the brief time since the previous session. The second session was used to address the trigger, which he identified as his spouse blaming him for being emotionally distant and unavailable. The criticism activated his sense of failure associated with the mass casualty incident. The memory of the trigger was identified and effectively processed using EMDR therapy's Phases 3 to 7.

## Future Template

The future template is an extension of the treatment results accomplished from treating past memories and present triggers. Typically, the future template uses the PC identified while treating the identified trigger memory. The medic had a few days left before returning to his military duties in a combat zone. In fact, as a medic he would likely be called upon for responding to a similar incident involving another convoy hitting an IED soon after his return to Iraq. The future template was used to enhance his anticipated response to the next situation.

Therapist: We have treated your memory of the mass casualty incident and the trigger you experienced on your return home for R & R. Chances are you will be called on to respond to another similar medevac call shortly after you arrive back in Iraq. I would suggest you work on your anticipated response to the next mass casualty call when you are back in-country.

I'd like you to imagine yourself effectively responding to your next nine-line medevac call and your positive thought (PC) you would like to believe about yourself is "I am a good NCO who takes care of my soldiers." What are your noticing?

Client: I see myself getting on the bird, anticipating my response when we touchdown on scene.

Therapist: Go with that! (Three sets of BLS are provided as the client reports positive responses.)

Hold your positive thought, "I am a good NCO who takes care of my soldiers." On a scale from 1 to 7, how true does it feel to you now?

Client: It's a 6.

Therapist: Go with that! (Two (2) more sets of BLS, with 35 passes each, are provided.)

Take a breath, let it go. On a scale of 1 to 7, how true does your positive thought "I am a good NCO who takes care of my soldiers" feel to you now?

Client: It is a 7.

Therapist: Okay, let's do one more set to strengthen the thought as much as possible.

(After a set of BLS) Take a breath, let it go. On a scale of 1 to 7, how true does it feel to you now?

Client: It is a definite 7!

Problem-Solving Situation

| | |
|---|---|
| Therapist: | I'd like you to think of some challenge you may experience in that situation.<br><br>What are you noticing? |
| Client: | I just stepped off the bird, began to triage the survivors, I'm looking for another IED. My threat level is up! |
| Therapist: | Go with that! (Two sets of BLS were provided.)<br>Hold your positive thought, "I am a good NCO who takes care of my soldiers." How true do those words feel to you now? On a scale of 1 to 7? |
| Client: | It is a 5 now. |
| Therapist: | Go with that! (Two more sets of BLS.)<br><br>Take a breath. Let it go. On a scale of 1 to 7, how true do those words feel to you now? |
| Client: | It's a 7! |
| Therapist: | Let's do one more set to strengthen that! (A set of 35 BLS is provided to strengthen the results.) |

The client completed the memory of a single-incident traumatic event, his current trigger, and a future template in preparation of his returning to duty in a combat zone, all completed within a 12-day period. His time home with his family began to improve with the first treatment session and continued throughout his time home for the R & R.

It should be noted, in addition to the use of the future template for standard use, Leeds (2016), who co-authored the resource development and installation (RDI) technique (Korn & Leeds, 2002), lists his additional use of the future template to include (a) a positive template and (b) fostering a new self-concept when using the RDI technique.

The positive template brings together the mental rehearsal of new skills and adaptive behaviors in addressing potential challenges to the client's achievements. Fostering one's new self-concept incorporates the installation of mastery memories that identify current capabilities, values, and goals.

## CONCLUSION

During this chapter, we saw reprocessing continue during Phases 5 and 6—Installation and Body Scan. Reprocessing during these phases involves the application of BLS, maintaining a standard speed and number of repetitions to ensure any unresolved issues are cleared. Any unresolved negative material is accessed and reprocessed before the PC is enhanced. Recognizing the PC, established in Phase 3 Assessment, sets the treatment direction. The Closing phase (Phase 7) allows the client to access a calm state with the ability to self-regulate before leaving the office. Reevaluation (Phase 8) ensures adequate processing of the memory. It is used at the beginning of each session once reprocessing begins in Phase 4.

### DISCUSSION POINTS

1. Is there a relationship between the SUD and VOC during EMDR processing? Discuss.
2. If the SUD goes to 0 but the VOC remains unchanged during Phase 4 Desensitization, what should the therapist evaluate?
3. If the client reports limited or no positive experiences, what should the therapist do?
4. What should the therapist do if the client wishes to revise the PC during Phase 5 Installation?
5. What should the therapist do if the PC in Phase 5 does not reach 7?
6. Discuss the use of the PC throughout EMDR therapy's treatment plan.
7. How is the PC incorporated into the third-prong of the EMDR process?

### REFERENCES

Hensley, B. (2016). *An EMDR therapy primer: From practicum to practice* (2nd ed.). New York, NY: Springer Publishing Company.

Korn, D., & Leeds, A. (2002). Preliminary evidence of efficacy for EMDR resource development and installation in the stabilization phase of treatment of complex posttraumatic stress disorder. *Journal of Clinical Psychology, 58*(12), 1465–1487. doi:10.1002/jclp.10099

Leeds, A. (2016). *A guide to the standard EMDR therapy protocols for clinicians, supervisors, and consultants.* New York, NY: Springer Publishing Company.

Schwartz, A., & Maiberger, B. (2018). *EMDR therapy and somatic psychology: Interventions to enhance embodiment in trauma treatment.* New York, NY: W. W. Norton.

Silver, S., & Rogers, S. (2002). *Light in the heart of darkness: EMDR and the treatment of war and terrorism survivors.* New York, NY: W. W. Norton.

Shapiro, F. (2006). *New notes on adaptive information processing with case formulation principles, forms, scripts and worksheets.* Watsonville, CA: EMDR Institute.

Shapiro, F. (2018). *Eye movement desensitization and reprocessing (EMDR) therapy: Basic principles, protocols and procedures.* New York: Guilford Press.

# II

# SPECIAL ISSUES

# 7

# Treating PTSD Symptoms and Traumatic Brain Injury

## Introduction

This chapter is designed to provide a basic understanding of the symptoms of traumatic brain injury (TBI), familiarization of measures used by the military and veteran agencies in evaluating the level of severity, key questions to address, the overlap of symptoms among TBI and posttraumatic stress disorder (PTSD), and the effective application of EMDR therapy in the treatment of PTSD among persons with both PTSD and TBI diagnoses. A review of PTSD measures is provided for application in military, veteran, and private practice settings. A case example is listed.

## Learning Objectives

- Review the symptoms of traumatic brain injury (TBI).
- Learn the assessment and classifications of TBIs both during deployments and back home.
- Review the evaluative process for PTSD co-occurring with TBI.
- Identify the symptoms of mild TBIs and PTSD as well as their shared symptoms.

## INTRODUCTION TO PTSD AND TBI

This chapter addresses the application of EMDR therapy in treating clients diagnosed with both PTSD and mild to moderate traumatic brain injury (mTBI). Since many therapists treat clients with these dual diagnoses, a review of brain injury assessment is provided while considering EMDR therapy as a treatment modality. mTBI is recognized as being the signature injury among U.S. and allied forces serving during Operation Iraqi Freedom (OIF) and Operation Enduring Freedom (OEF). The term TBI, also known as a "concussion," refers to the actual injury sustained by the injured person. The diagnostic category is known as "Neurocognitive Disorder due to TBI" as listed in both the *Diagnostic and Statistical Manual of Mental Disorders5 (DSM-V)* and the *International Classification of Diseases (ICD-11)* 11th Revision. This category relates to impairments and cognitive symptoms which can be experienced following a brain injury (APA, 2013).

The source of TBIs can be from three different sources: (a) direct trauma; (b) head motion; and (c) overpressurization. With a direct trauma, the head is struck by or strikes something with force. In this situation, the brain experiences an impact and then a counter impact (called a "contrecoup" injury). An injury experienced as a head motion is an indirect trauma such as a sudden acceleration followed by a deceleration of the brain, such as a whiplash. This type of injury typically results in damage to the axonal fibers of the brain. These are the long nerve fibers which relay messages to the distant nerve cells. This type of damage affects the brain's ability to communicate effectively to extended nerve cells. The overpressurization is caused by blasts, explosive munitions, and diffuse damage to the brain. This type of injury receives a significant amount of focus from military research since blasts from bombs represent a percentage of brain injury to military personnel.

Over 370,000 servicemembers were diagnosed with TBI during the 18-year period between January 2000 and December 2017 (Defense and Veterans Brain Injury Center, 2018a). With the requirements to sustain the force, the U.S. military recognized the importance to identify concussions and insure their treatment as early as possible. Since many active duty military and veterans will visit EMDR therapists reporting a history of TBIs, along with their PTSD, an understanding of treating PTSD with co-occurring TBI was important for treating nearly 20% of the veteran population. Knowledge of this material was important for the therapist's continuing professional development.

Brain injury severity is classified as being mild, moderate, or severe based on the person's confusion and disorientation at the time of the incident. The assessment includes the Glasgow Coma Scale (GCS), loss of consciousness (LOC), and posttraumatic amnesia (PTA). A comparison of the categories as determined by the Department of Veterans Affairs (DVA) and Department of Defense (DOD) is listed in Table 7.1.

## EVALUATION AND TREATMENT HISTORY

The assessment of a brain injury should include a physical exam with detailed history, neuroimaging, neuropsychological testing, and a screening review. A complete and thorough history-taking is neces-

**TABLE 7.1 Assessment Criteria for Traumatic Brain Injury**

|  | MILD TBI/ CONCUSSION | MODERATE TBI | SEVERE TBI |
|---|---|---|---|
| Neuroimaging | Normal structure imaging | Normal or abnormal structural imaging | Normal or abnormal structural imaging |
| Glasgow Coma Scale (GCS) | 13–15 | 9–12 | <9 |
| Loss of Consciousness (LOC) | 0–30 minutes | >30 minutes and <24 hours | >24 hours |
| Alteration of Consciousness (AOC) | A moment up to 24 hours | AOC >24 hours | Use other criteria |
| Posttraumatic Amnesia (PTA) | 0–1 day | >1 day and <7 days | >7 days |

TBI, traumatic brain injury.

*Source:* Modified from Department of Veterans Affairs/Department of Defense. (2015). *VA/DoD clinical practice guideline for the management of concussion-mild.* Retrieved from https://www.healthquality.va.gov/guidelines/Rehab/mtbi/

sary for an accurate TBI diagnosis. Brain imagining using fMRI, PET, and SPECT scans can reveal the impact of concussion/mTBI. Yet, their clinical use is normally limited to research. CT scans can reveal hemorrhages and evidence of contusions. Screenings such as the Standardized Assessment of Concussion (SAC), along with the Mini Mental Status Exam (MMSE) can help in noting if further evaluations are needed (VA/DOD, 2015).

The nature of the Global War on Terror (GWOT) exposed U.S. and allied forces to improvised explosive devices (IEDs), rocket-propelled grenades (RPGs), mortars, as well as suicide bombers wearing suicide vests. All of these produce blast wounds, both physically and psychologically. Due to the protection of personal body armor such as Kevlar, servicemembers survive some blasts which in the past would have killed the servicemember. Armored combat vehicles have further enhanced the survivability of the person. The armor has frequently protected the servicemember's body while leaving the brain vulnerable to blasts which can result in TBIs. Physical survival is further enhanced with the quick response of medical teams with advances in emergency medical care. Persons with near fatal wounds have a much greater chance of survival now when compared to previous wars.

Now, with the emphasis on requiring a mandatory evaluation of servicemembers within a 50-meter area of a blast, there has been an increased identification of TBIs. Previously, before the systemic evaluation for TBIs, soldiers would include the acknowledgment of a blast "ringing my bell" as they continued to do the mission. Numerous Special Forces soldiers shared their experiences of placing numerous charges in place to blow an entrance with the pressure from the blast being a normal part of the duty performance. There was no evaluation of TBIs unless severe symptoms were indicated.

DOD guidance for managing concussions diagnosed as mTBI has been outlined in the 2012 police guidance "DoD Policy Guidance for Management of Mild Traumatic Brain Injury/Concussion in the Deployed Setting" (Department of Defense, 2012) insuring the proper response to identify, track, and ensure the appropriate evaluation and treatment of servicemembers potentially injured with concussions. When a blast injury occurs, medical triage attends to the more serious injuries first. Concussions can be overlooked when no obvious signs are observable.

The DOD Policy Guidance (Department of Defense, 2012) requires than an individual who was not in a vehicle and within 50 feet of a blast or had a rollover must be evaluated within one week. Persons who experienced three concussions within one deployment are to be removed from combat status. Command personnel must respond to these situations within 24 hours.

## EVALUATING TBIs DURING DEPLOYMENTS

The U.S. military has developed the Military Acute Concussion Evaluation (MACE) as a standardized mental status exam for evaluating military servicemembers for signs of an mTBI while they are deployed to a combat or other deployed setting. Its purpose is to evaluate servicemembers with a suspected mTBI as well as identify symptoms associated with the diagnosis. The MACE consists of four sections (Defense and Veterans Brain Injury Center, 2007):

- Concussion Screening: Servicemember reports the nature of the head injury and answers questions used to determine the severity of the injury including: LOC, alternation of consciousness (AOC), and posttraumatic amnesia (PTA). Any questions which receive a "yes" response, the evaluator continues to the additional components of the MACE.
- Cognitive Exam: The evaluator calculates the scores for the servicemember's orientation, immediate memory, concentration, and delayed recall. The scores are totaled with a possible of 30 points possible and reported at the end of the MACE form.
- Neurological Exam: Tests for pupil response to the light, speech fluency grip strength, pronator drift (indicating muscle strength/ weakness and compensatory adjustment), word finding, and bal-

ance are provided. Test results indicate a "Go" with a "Green" or abnormal results "Red" at the end of the MACE form.

- Symptom Screening: Screening of symptoms including dizziness, memory problems, headache, nausea/vomiting, concentration, irritability, visual disturbances, and ringing in the ear are evaluated. Further, concussion history over the past 12 months is sought. A number of symptoms are assigned a letter grade, that is, "A" indicates no symptoms; "B" indicates one or more symptoms. The grade is also reported at the MACE form.

It is recommended that servicemembers who have experienced a concussive injury should have the MACE administered within the first 24 hours following an incident to insure they receive appropriate attention in a timely manner. The MACE, when accompanied by a medical exam, assists in determining if the servicemember can be returned to duty or should receive medical monitoring. Enhancing the expectation that a servicemember will improve over time, research suggests that 90% of persons diagnosed with an mTBI get better in 1 week (Center for Deployment Psychology, 2011).

During deployment, blast injuries are the primary cause of TBIs. These four levels of brain injuries are associated with blasts (Barth, Isler, Helmick, Wingler, & Jaffee, 2010):

1. Primary—direct injury to brain cells from the blast pressure.
2. Secondary—brain injury from effects of projectiles such as shrapnel from the blast.
3. Tertiary—brain injury because of being thrown into fixed objects or vehicle accidents such as rollovers.
4. Quaternary—brain injury due to inhaling toxic gases from an explosion or the loss of blood due to traumatic amputation.

## SYMPTOMS OF TBIs

Symptoms of a TBI may be acute or develop later. Acute TBI symptoms can be the LOC, amnesia, headache, confusion, nausea, vertigo, vomiting, changes in vision, or tinnitus. Subacute symptoms can include problems with memory and cognition, disturbed sleep, irritability, and fatigue. Late onset of symptoms may include neurocognitive disorders (NCD) due to Parkinson's disease or Alzheimer's.

### Postconcussive Signs

The majority of TBI servicemembers are able to recover from their head injuries in a matter of weeks to months; however, about 15% to 30% continue to experience symptoms a year following their injury (Hou et al., 2011; Pugh et al., 2019). Persons who endorse physical, cognitive, and affective symptoms a year following their injury are diagnosed with postconcussive syndrome (PCS) or persistent postconcussive syndrome (PPCS). Military personnel with a TBI are more likely than their civilian counterparts to experience PCS.

Physical postconcussive symptoms include sensitivity to light or noise, fatigue and sleep disturbances, dizziness and balance problems, headaches. Moderate-to-severe symptoms include coma, weakness or paralysis, language and communication problems. Cognitive symptoms include forgetfulness, poor concentration, changes in speech, slowed thinking and behavior, poor organization and follow-through, difficulty with information processing speed, and lack of awareness. The person may experience emotional/behavioral symptoms such as mood swings as well as being emotionally labile, lack of motivation, apathy, impulsivity and disinhibition, depression, anxiety, loss of sensitivity and concern.

A neurocognitive disorder may be diagnosed following a TBI event. The cognitive presentation subsequent to a person's TBI diagnosis may demonstrate difficulties with complex attention, executive functioning, learning and memory, information processing speed, and social cognition. Additional neurocognitive deficits with severe TBI may present aphasia, constructional dyspraxia, and/or neglect (APA, 2013).

## TBIs AMONG RETURNING OIF/OEF VETERANS

A national random sample study (Lindquist, Love, & Elbogen, 2017) reviewed 1,388 post-9/11 veterans. From the sample, a total of 17.3% met criteria for TBI during their military service. Half of this number reported multiple head injuries, along with higher rates of PTSD, depression, suicide ideation, and back pain. The most common incidents associated with the head injuries were blasts (33.1%); objects hitting the head (31.7%); and falls (13.5%). Multiple head injuries revealed higher incidents of PTSD, depression, suicidal ideation, violence, headaches, and back pain.

Previously, a U.S. Army brigade combat team was screened for TBIs (Terrio et al., 2007). Of the 3,973 soldiers who served in Iraq (OIF), 1,292 reported injury. Out of this number, 907 were diagnosed with TBI and 385 with other types of injuries. A total of 22.8% of soldiers in the brigade combat team returning from Iraq had confirmed TBIs.

## EVALUATING PTSD WITH CO-OCCURRING TBI

PTSD can predate a head injury, develop concurrently, or have a later onset. The development of co-occurring PTSD and TBI can vary greatly as noted by Carlson and colleagues' review of published studies (Carlson et al., 2011). Hoge and colleagues (2008) surveyed 2,525 Army infantry soldiers at 3 and 4 months after their return from deployment. Out of that number, 4.9% (124 soldiers) reported an incident with the LOC; 10.3% (260 soldiers) reported having experienced an altered mental status; and 17.2% (435 soldiers) reported other injuries. Among soldiers who reported LOC, 43.9% also met diagnostic criteria for PTSD. This study found that soldiers with mTBI, primarily those who had LOC, also missed work, had more medical visits, reported more general health issues, and presented with more somatic and postconcussive symptoms. After adjusting for depression and PTSD, the brain injury was no longer found to be significantly associated with the physical health symptoms or outcomes, except for headaches. Concussions/ mTBI among soldiers deployed to Iraq was found to be strongly associated with PTSD and physical health problems. Both the intensity of combat and LOC were found to be significantly associated with PTSD.

The risk for PTSD was found to increase two and three times after experiencing a mTBI (Bryant et al., 2010; Miller et al., 2015; Stein et al., 2015). Vasterling, Jacob, and Rasmusson (2018) addressed the comorbidity between PTSD and TBI in their review as they note the events leading to a TBI are often psychologically traumatic. A brain trauma can impede the resolution of emotions following psychological trauma. The development of PTSD can develop prior to the TBI event, at the time of the TBI incident, or posttraumatic to the head trauma. When the PTSD developed prior to the TBI incident or as a result of the event in which the TBI occurred, it can complicate the TBI healing process. As expected, persons suffering with PTSD and mTBI often struggle with other difficulties including headaches, suicidal impulses, depression, multiple pain issues, and substance use disorder. Veterans were found to be at an increased risk of suicidal ideation and violent impulses associated with the co-occurrence of chronic pain and PTSD, with or without TBI (Blakey et al., 2018).

Various agencies utilize different evaluation forms in gathering client history as it relates to PTSD. Active duty servicemembers are screened for PTSD during the servicemember's annual health screening. The primary care evaluation may include the Primary Care-PTSD Screen (PC-PTSD), followed, as deemed necessary by the PTSD Checklist (PCL) if the PC-PTSD is positive. Servicemembers who have deployed are required to complete a Post-Deployment Health Assessment (PDHA) within 30 days of their return. A follow-up Post-Deployment Health Reassessment (PDHRA) is required to be completed within 90 to 180 days from their redeployment date back at their home station. Persons who indicate mental health concerns are referred to an appropriate mental health agency within the military, the DVA, or a local mental health provider when additional mental health support is needed as is the case with a community-based center such as Soldier Center. The mental health provider or clinic conducts appropriate diagnostic evaluation for PTSD including instruments such as the Clinician

Administered PTSD Scale, the PTSD Checklist-5 (PCL-5), or the Impact of Events Scale-Revised (IES-R).

The DVA identifies PTSD in veterans during various clinical presentations. A PTSD diagnosis may be part of a previous diagnosis, identified during a primary care screening using the PC-PTSD, or during a clinical interview in which the assessment may include the Clinician Administered PTSD Scale for *DSM-5* (CAPS-5) or for brevity of time, the PTSD Checklist (PCL-5) might be used.

Local practices (nonmilitary and non-DVA) treating military and veteran populations use various measures for PTSD evaluations ranging from the Impact of Events Scale-Revised (IES-R), the CAPS-5, or the PCL-5. Often a local community-based practice will receive a referral with a PTSD diagnosis provided as part of the justification for the referral. At Soldier Center, we compile a PTSD packet (see reference list for resources) which includes the IES-R, the PCL-5, Dissociative Experiences Scale-II (DES-II), the Moral Injury Symptom Scale-Military Version, and the Posttraumatic Growth Inventory. Additionally, the Beck Depression Inventory and Beck Anxiety Inventory are used at Soldier Center as supplemental measures as warranted.

In military populations, both within the range of mTBI and across the range of TBI severities, the risk of PTSD increases with the severity of the TBI (Ruff, Riechers, Wang, Piero, & Ruff, 2012). Vasterling and colleagues noted there is no current evidence to suggest the core elements of evidence-based treatments should be modified in order to treat a broad range of TBI severities (Vasterling et al., 2018, p. 98). Recognizing an unconscious memory associated with the TBI can have aspects of the memory stored in implicit memory; EMDR therapists know the efficacy of this psychotherapy in treating implicit memories if there is some distinctive character to the memory such as a body sensation. Oftentimes, EMDR therapists also treat the memory right before the injury and the memory of regaining consciousness.

## WHAT EMDR THERAPISTS NEED TO KNOW

There are two basic questions EMDR therapists frequently express regarding treating clients with co-occurring diagnosis of PTSD and TBI: (a) "Can I effectively treat a client with EMDR therapy if the person has been diagnosed with mTBI?" and based on a "yes" to the previous question, (b) what does a therapist need to know and do clinically to provide effective treatment to someone with these co-occurring disorders? EMDR therapy treats the client not the diagnosis. The functioning of the brain is an integrated process; therefore the symptoms associated with these specific diagnoses represent the integral processes of a total system. EMDR therapy effectively treats psychological wounds; it does not treat the physical injury of a TBI. However, due to the neuroplasticity of the brain and its interactive processes, the influence of psychological healing on the physical state needs research. Clients with an mTBI who are treated with EMDR therapy report their cognitive processing improving as noted in the Case Study 7.1 in this chapter. As Vasterling and colleagues (2018) noted, there is no evidence to suggest evidence-based treatments need to be modified (Vasterling et al., 2018, p. 98). My experience of treating military and veteran populations with PTSD and mTBI injuries with EMDR therapy supports Vasterling's conclusion. I have successfully treated military personnel and veterans suffering with PTSD and mTBI for many years.

The severity of psychological stress among warfighters evolved with the beginning of OIF and OEF military operations following 9/11. Deployed soldiers were repetitively exposed to life-threatening missions. During early military missions, their clinical presentations were acute stress and simple PTSD resulting from combat incidents. Later, the clinical presentation expanded to include complex PTSD with dissociative exhibitions and moral injury requiring additional clinical skills to process complex cases. Over the span of time, many soldiers who had been exposed to blasts, some from military operations placing explosive charges on doorways to breech entries, others from IEDs, began to notice changes in their cognitive and behavioral functioning. For some servicemembers the changes were subtle, others' symptoms were more distinct. Questions such as "Were you ever exposed to a blast?" and "Have you ever been knocked unconscious?" became helpful identifiers before military organizations began screening for TBIs. A number of service personnel could specifically identify periods of time when their cognitive processing changed. A non-commissioned officer (NCO) told me, "Yeah, I was halfway through my second deployment when I noticed my thinking was fuzzy! I noticed when we (combat unit) came back inside the wire, I became more anxious when I had to think about things. As long as I was doing the routine I had been trained to do, I was okay." Soldiers recalled having their "bell rung" while on a combat mission; when exposed to an explosion, as they lost focus for a few seconds, they experienced ringing in their ears. During this period, I provided EMDR therapy to a broad range of clinical presentations from acute stress injuries to PTSD with associated dissociative exhibitions. As the complexity of the clinical presentations evolved, the treatment required development of clinical skills to treat complex PTSD with dissociative features and suicidal intent. EMDR therapy continued to provide healing to military personnel and veterans with a broad range of psychological wounds.

The efficacy of EMDR therapy in treating trauma has been demonstrated in over 30 randomized controlled trials (RCTs). With three modalities available for use in the treatment (eye movement, auditory, and tactile), the therapist has a repertoire of modalities for treating disturbing memories. Table 7.2 lists the distinct and shared symptoms of both disorders. A number of symptoms overlap between PTSD and TBIs. For

### TABLE 7.2  Distinct and Shared Symptoms of mTBI and PTSD

| DISTINCT SYMPTOMS OF mTBI | SHARED SYMPTOMS | DISTINCT SYMPTOMS OF PTSD |
|---|---|---|
| Headaches | Sleep disturbance | Flashbacks |
| Dizziness/Vertigo | Insomnia/Fatigue | Intrusive memories |
| Balance problems | Irritability/Anger/ Aggression | Avoidance |
| Reduced alcohol tolerance | | Increased startle response |
| Vision problems | Problems thinking/ remembering | Hypervigilance/ Physiological arousal |
| Sensitivity to sound/light | Changes in personality | Nightmares |
| Seizures | Mood swings | Relationship conflict |
| Nausea | Withdrawal from social, work, and family activities | |
| | Hypersensitivity to noise | |
| | Memory problems | |

mTBI, mild traumatic brain injury; TBI, traumatic brain injury.

example, a servicemember diagnosed with both disorders describes anger problems with lack of empathy in his social life. These responses could be caused by either or both disorders. Lack of empathy could be due to physical damage done to the motor neurons after experiencing a frontal blast to the face, or occur as the result of relationship difficulties from PTSD. As an EMDR therapist, I can treat the psychological trauma associated with the PTSD. Future research will evaluate the impact of psychological treatment on the healing of physical wounds.

The second clinical question, "What does a therapist need to know and do clinically in order to provide effective treatment to someone with the co-occurring disorders of PTSD and TBI?" is addressed with the same response a therapist would make to any client. Because EMDR therapy is a client-centered approach, the therapist works to ensure the client's sense of security with appropriate accommodation to the treatment process is addressed. If the client reports a sensitivity to light, the lighting in the treatment room needs to be adjusted to use natural lighting or soft lighting. The same attention is provided when introducing Phase 2 Preparation's step of setting up the mechanics. Treating clients with TBI frequently requires the use of multiple modalities, beyond eye movement (EM). When setting up the mechanics in Phase 2, I always introduce all three modalities of bilateral stimulation (BLS) to the client. With all clients (including non-TBI clients), I note any discomfort with doing EM. While setting up the mechanics, I begin with a slow speed and describe to the client I am going to increase the speed of EM briefly. Then, I stop and ask the client to "take a breath. How was that for you?" I repeat the same for all modalities, checking the physical comfort with all three modalities. Clients with PTSD and TBI frequently have difficulty with EM, preferring auditory or tactile modalities. Perhaps the client's endorsement of EM with TBI clients is dependent on the location of the brain injury.

Clients with a TBI can be sensitive to sound. This can be the result of either PTSD or TBI. Sometimes a client's initial irritation to sounds becomes resolved during reprocessing as the disturbing memory is resolved. For example, a client's initial irritation to the sound of a clock faded into the background during reprocessing and was not an issue by the end of the session. The physical sense of being "off" due to TBI symptoms can contribute to a psychological sense of feeling out of control, enhancing the client's level of anxiety.

## RESOLVING PTSD SYMPTOMS WHEN A TBI IS CO-OCCURRING

The EMDR client selection criteria are the same as noted in the treatment of individual PTSD with additional consideration of the severity of the brain injury. EMDR therapy has been found to be effective in treating PTSD when the brain injury is of mild-to-moderate levels of severity. Treatment of PTSD with persons with severe head injuries should be provided in coordination and consultation with a neurological treatment team who coordinate the client's overall rehabilitation program. While outcome reports are primarily anecdotal from clients, EMDR therapists, and TBI treatment staff, more research is needed in this area. Neurological consultation is always important if in doubt. Treating psychological trauma is the primary focus when an EMDR therapist treats a client with dual diagnoses of mTBI and PTSD. Recognizing the role of various professionals in the rehabilitation of a brain injury is important. The rehabilitation for TBI is provided by other injury specialists. The EMDR approach for these persons with two co-occurring disorders uses the same protocol as treating an individual with a PTSD diagnosis except the target memory treatment plan includes TBI incidents and additional disturbances related to the disorder. Remember to shorten the number of BLS passes and take the client back to the target memory more frequently during reprocessing. This is a process similar to treating someone who has attention deficit concerns. If the client has experienced a loss of consciousness (LOC), I would consider including target memories of experiences just before and after the injury as well as experiences related to adjustments. As an example, a Special Forces NCO was knocked unconscious by a rocket hitting near his position. When he regained consciousness, the NCO realized both his legs were gone. Later, when in my office being treated for his PTSD, we targeted his memory before losing consciousness and the very moment he regained awareness and realized he lost his legs.

The symptom chart (Table 7.2) lists symptoms related to both TBI and PTSD as well as symptoms shared by both disorders. Due to the overlap of some symptoms, the resolution of the PTSD symptoms becomes obvious due to their demise. The EMDR standard protocol, as outlined in earlier chapters of this book, is also used in the treatment of clients with PTSD who also suffer with TBI.

In summary, the standard EMDR eight-phase, three prong approach is used in treating clients with PTSD and TBI diagnoses. Appropriate adaptations are used in selecting the modalities since EM is frequently difficult for persons with TBIs. The treatment plan includes both the standard memories of disturbing events along with the addition of TBI-related incidents. EMDR therapy is indeed effective in treating PTSD wounds among persons with both PTSD and TBI diagnosis. The therapist accommodates the BLS modality to the client while the delivery of BLS is adjusted to the most effective resolution for the client.

## Case Study 7.1: Staff Sergeant (E-6) With TBI and PTSD Treated With 14 EMDR Sessions

Therapist: We reviewed the list of disturbing incidents you have identified. When you think about your experiences, do you know where the TBI may have originated? Is there a specific event that caused the concussion?

Staff Sergeant: Yeah, there was a vehicle rollover that actually put me into the hospital for about a week and a half. It was an actual concussion, a head trauma. We were going 60 MPH in pursuit of the enemy. What happened was I actually was cutting across the median, trying to cut him off. The flow of traffic behind us still, you know, still fully charging and they weren't slowing down. Commo was trying to get them to slow down, they weren't. A vehicle came up and hit my driver's door. I had my arm out and it actually ... crazy thing about it, I had my arm kind of out like this. The vehicle came up and hit the side of the vehicle with my arm ... it threw my arm back in, tossing my body. I actually jerked the steering wheel. And in those M1114s if you're going too fast, especially if you're on unstable ground, any jerk with that wheel, you can flip the vehicle. And that's exactly what happened. It was a full vehicle rollover. My gunner was trapped underneath the shield, the turret shield. I was wearing my helmet, but just the fact of that hard blow, you know, hitting on the door and then hitting again. Um, they actually thought I broke my back so they wouldn't let me get out of the vehicle. They actually cut me out of my uniform and put me on the medevac and flew me out.

So, that was a hard one, because after all this, they were like, you know, the military has to do an investigation on things. Everybody had the same story, but it was like the investigator didn't believe it. He thought that it was a reckless act or whatever and that made me feel like, wow! Where's the trust there? (Pause) When I was in the hospital, I had like severe headaches and things that you would have, you know, blurred vision … when you really lose your focus, when you have like a concussion you're trying to focus. Like after I think the third day or the fourth day I'd asked the nurse if it would be okay if I just started walking around a little bit. I ended up making my way down to the computer center and I realized that it was really a slow process for me to comprehend what was going on with the computer. I'm pretty good with computers, so for me to sit there and just stare at the computer screen, to kind of get my eyes and my mind working again, you know, like trying to be able to focus on everything that's going on.

The thing is, because of the combat situation, because of me being in combat, I was an important part of that team. When my platoon sergeant came in (the hospital), he stressed highly on the fact that he is at the point where he wondered if I could be returned to duty. He is at the point where he realized I had a concussion, where he wonders when I can actually return to duty. I mean, he wanted to take me out of the hospital like the second or third day. He wanted to take me back into the mission.

Yeah, he cared about me. You know what I mean? He cared about me, but he wanted to not see me in the hospital. You know, like if I really didn't have a serious injury. When I left the hospital, I didn't feel like I was completely healed, and I went immediately from leaving the hospital to getting in a vehicle and driving back to my FOB (Forward Operating Base). I mean, there wasn't somebody picking me up and I'm sitting in the back seat. It was, I went straight from the hospital, into the vehicle, and I drove myself back to the FOB. Next day I was back out on mission.

Therapist: And what was that like for you and realizing that you weren't completely back to the way you had been before, but you are still going out on missions?

Staff Sergeant: I mean, I remember going on the missions. You just get into this state of mind of … the second that you leave that FOB to go do a patrol. You know that you're going to be gone for 18 hours plus.

So as soon as you get on the mission, you just know, at first it's a whole new thing or after you get into that repetitious pattern. I think that regardless if you've got a brain injury or something traumatic has happened to you, if you've been blown up or something serious has happened, you go right back into that protective mode of security, security. And, that's what I did. But I felt that it was a little blurred to me.

Yeah, there was, I remember sometimes after that, that traumatic situation that I found myself even like dozing off, falling asleep at the wheel, you know I would say to my squad leader, I'm like, "You know, I'm seriously falling asleep here (laughs). Like I'm not just dozing off, like I'm shutting my eyes and then waking up and realizing that I just, you know, took a ten second nap or whatever." Or him waking me up because going from one side of the road to the next, and this is after I had a full night's sleep.

So, I mean, I can't really think of any other indicators, but that's one. And then, of course, the severe, the Daisy chain IED incident of completely … it was the worst blackout, I guess that's, that's the way to put it. It was the worst blackout. And not only did I black out, but I actually lost control of bodily fluids, you know, and it completely, put my body in shock. That's the reason why I received an award because everybody in that convoy went through the same thing. The first two vehicles got blown up. They were, they were static in this situation. They got blown up to the point of where they were … they actually had to stop, you know, stop in the kill zone. I blacked out, my vehicle was still rolling. I came to a stop with the vehicle and I saw out of my left-hand side, I saw a Bradley pull up and it was my replacement platoon sergeant. He pulled up and our windows were up. I just saw his mouth moving, I was completely in shock. I was just like, I was looking around, like trying, just trying to get everything back. I was still seeing stars and I just looked over at him and without hesitation, I slammed on the accelerator and I just jetted, took straight off through there, and just as I did that last IED blew. We were sitting on top of it. Yeah. If I wouldn't have got us out of there, all of us would have been dead.

And the Bradley ended up taking the blast. My platoon sergeant got tossed out of the turret. I mean, he was seriously injured. He was in the hospital for, I don't know, probably a month and a half, but he got banged up and bruised up, received some shrapnel and he was unconscious for like 15 minutes, I think, from that blast, because they, they basically had sat on it. It was like, he knew that there had to be another one in the area, but he didn't know where it was. And, I think I just, I saw his stress and fear and I reacted. I just got out of there and blew right through the kill zone and they ended up taking the blast. My gunner was actually faced to the rear and as we were leaving it blew up and he got shrapnel all in the face.

Therapist: Pretty intense.

Staff Sergeant: So yeah, but I mean that first explosion, it was like, I don't even know. I know it was a 500-pound bomb, but I don't even know what it was like to go through it. Because I was out of it, it's almost like when you have—like a G force or something like that, you have a rocket that's going through the sky, or actually lightning would probably be a better one. You hear it in the initial hit prior to the actual lightning strike. And that's kind of how this is. It's like you're out, there's the explosion, you don't know what happened, you wake up and it's like, what just happened? You look down, you've messed on yourself, you look around every-body. You still got another guy that's passed out in the back seat. I mean, I mean it's just you're like in a complete confused state at that point.

I would say that, and I mean that had happened to me before, but to this point, I mean I even get like tingles running down the arms because that is the way that it felt is just like everything, it's hard to breathe. You have like these shots of pain, down your chest and tingling down your arms and your whole body is just in complete shock. That's why it had amazed everybody that I was even capable of moving my leg, you know, to put it back on that accelerator and get us out of there. And that's where I think conscious and subconscious....

**10 Sessions later—Reprocessing during session 12 of EMDR therapy:**

Staff Sergeant: Something that popped up in my head other than what I was focusing on, um, is that, uh, I felt things are so much better. That's something that just popped into my head that I don't have all these other things going through my head like I was when we first started these sessions. It's great to experience, like I was focusing and I didn't feel any anything else about it, but I didn't have anything else pop into my head. So yeah. And I feel comfortable with that. I was really frustrated before with all these other things that pop up in my head. So now I can just focus on this one. So, it feels really good.

**Reevaluation before termination:**

Staff Sergeant: As far as the, the EMDR process, I'm finding now that I'm at that stage of clarity where I can actually tell that my mind is processing things better and my memory's getting better. So, every time that I go to TBI (clinic), all they keep saying is "EMDR, EMDR, EMDR." They're like, they're basically saying "our treatment is helping to some point, but nowhere even close to what the EMDR is doing!" Because, I mean, this was my first stop before I started anything else. And so why they see this in me now. They just keep telling me how impressed they are with how far that I've come, and I honestly believe it's because now I'm actually at this point where my brain is actually communicating, so yeah. And that's awesome!

Summary: This staff sergeant completed 16 EMDR therapy sessions over the course of 4 months. He was returned to active duty status and reassigned to another military installation as a drill sergeant using his combat experience to train new recruits. On completion of his treatment, he married his partner who had stood by his side during his treatment and recovery process.

## CONCLUSION

We have reviewed the symptoms of TBI as well as measures used to evaluate the level of TBI severity. Key questions were identified as well as the overlap of symptoms between TBI and PTSD. EMDR therapy is effective in treating persons suffering with mild-to-moderate TBI injury. This discussion was designed to provide the reader with an understanding of treatment issues in providing effective treatment to our client base who suffer with TBI as well as PTSD. Experience has taught us that EMDR therapy is effective in treatment of PTSD and TBI. Understanding the assessment process informs the therapy on the severity of the brain injury.

### DISCUSSION POINTS

1. What are the elements, related to the incident, that determine the severity of a concussion?
2. What would be the level of severity of a person (such as the platoon sergeant mentioned in Case Study 7.1) who has been unconscious for 15 minutes?

3. The MACE consists of four sections: Concussion Screening, Cognitive Exam, Neurological Exam, and Symptom Screening. At what period would the persons experiencing a concussive injury have the MACE administered?
4. What symptoms of PTSD and TBI overlap?
5. In what ways is the LOC similar and different from dissociative exhibitions?
6. In the case example, the client described two incidents in which he experienced TBI. The latter one, with IEDs daisy chained, was intense. Based on the client's description, which information provided by him assists in the assessment of his TBI?
7. How does the concept of neuroplasticity relate to treating PTSD when the client also has a TBI diagnosis?

## REFERENCES

American Psychiatric Association. (2013). *Diagnostic and statistical manual of mental disorders* (5th ed.). Arlington, VA: American Psychiatric Publishing.

Barth, J., Isler, W., Helmick, K., Wingler, I., & Jaffee, M. (2010). Acute battlefield assessment of concussion/mild TBI and return-to-duty evaluations. In C. Kennedy & J. Moore (Eds.), *Military neuropsychology* (pp. 127–174). New York, NY: Springer Publishing Company.

Blakey, S., Wagner, H., Naylor, J., Brancu, M., Lane, I., Sallee, N., … Elbogen, E. (2018). Chronic pain, TBI, and PTSD in military veterans: A link to suicidal ideation and violent impulses. *Journal of Pain, 19*(7), 797–806. doi:10.1016/j.jpain.2018.02.012

Bryant, R., O'Donnell, M., Creamer, M., McFarlane, A., Clark, C., & Silove, D. (2010). The psychiatric sequelae of traumatic injury. *American Journal of Psychiatry, 167*(3), 312–320. doi:10.1176/ajp.2009.09050617

Carlson, K., Kehle, S., Meis, L., Greer, N., Macdonald, R., Rutks, I., … Wilt, T. (2011). Prevalence, assessment, and treatment of mild traumatic brain injury and posttraumatic stress disorder: A systematic review of the evidence. *Journal of Head Trauma Rehabilitation, 26*(2), 103–115. doi:10.1097/HTR.0b013e3181e50ef1

Center for Deployment Psychology. (2011). *Mild traumatic brain injury (mTBI).* Retrieved from https://deploymentpsych.org/disorders/tbi-main

DoD/VA The management of chronic mulitsystem illnesses. Retrieved from https://www.healthquality.va.gov/guidelines/MR/cmi/

Defense and Veterans Brain Injury Center. (2007). *Military acute concussion evaluation (MACE).* Retrieved from https://dvbic.dcoe.mil/material/military-acute-concussion-evaluation-2-mace-2

Defense and Veterans Brain Injury Center. (2018a). *Research review on mild traumatic brain injury and posttraumatic stress disorder.* Retrieved from https://dvbic.dcoe.mil/sites/default//files/dvbic_research_research-review_mildtbi-ptsd_v2.0_2018-06-08_508.pdf

Defense and Veterans Brain Injury Center. (2018b). Research review on traumatic brain injury and suicide. Retrieved from https://dvbic.dcoe.mil/sites/default/files/DHA_J-9_DVBIC_TBI%20and%20Suicide%20November%202018_508.pdf

Department of Defense. (2013). *DoD policy guidance for management of mild traumatic brain injury/concussion in the deployed setting.* Retrieved from https://deploymentpsych.org/content/dod-policy-guidance-management-mild-traumatic-brain-injury-concussion-deployed-setting

Department of Veterans Affairs/Department of Defense. (2015). *VA/DoD clinical practice guideline for the management of concussion-mild.* Retrieved from https://www.healthquality.va.gov/guidelines/Rehab/mtbi/mTBICPGFullCPG50821816.pdf

Hoge, C., McGurk, D., Thomas, J., Cox, A., Engel, C., & Castro, C. (2008). Mild traumatic brain injury in U.S. soldiers returning from Iraq. *The New England Journal of Medicine, 358*(5), 453–463. doi:10.1056/NEJMoa072972

Hou, R., Moss-Morris, R., Peveler, R., Mogg, K., Bradley, B., & Billi, A. (2011). When a minor head injury results in enduring symptoms: A prospective investigation of risk factors for postconcussional syndrome after mild traumatic brain injury. *Journal of Neurology, Neurosurgery & Psychiatry, 83,* 217–223. doi:10.1136/jnnp-2011-300767

Lindquist, L., Love, H., & Elbogen, E. (2017). Traumatic brain injury in Iraq and Afghanistan veterans: New results from a national random sample study. *Journal of Neuropsychiatry and Clinical Neurosciences, 29,* 254–259. doi:10.1176/appi.neuropsy.16050100

Miller, S., Whitehead, C., Otte, C., Wells, T., Webb, T., Gore, R., & Maynard, C. (2015). Risk for broad-spectrum neuropsychiatric disorders after mild traumatic brain injury in a cohort of US Air Force personnel. *Occupational and Environmental Medicine, 72*(8), 560–566. doi:10.1136/oemed-2014-102646

Pugh, M., Swan, A., Amuan, M., Eapen, B., Jaramillo, C., Delgado, R., ... Wang, C.-P. (2019). Deployment, suicide, and overdose among comorbidity phenotypes following mild traumatic brain injury: A retrospective cohort study from the chronic effects of neurotrauma consortium. *PLoS One, 14*(9), e0222674. doi:10.1371/journal.pone.0222674

Ruff, R., Riechers, R., Wang, X.-F., Piero, T., & Ruff, S. (2012). A case-control study examining whether neurological deficits and PTSD in combat veterans are related to episodes of mild TBI. *BMJ Open, 2,* e000312. doi:10.1136/bmjopen-2011-000312

Stein, M., Kessler, R., Heeringa, S., Jain, S., Campbell-Sills, L., Colpe, L., ... Ursano, R. (2015). Prospective longitudinal evaluation of the effect of deployment-acquired traumatic brain injury on posttraumatic stress and related disorders: Results from the Army study to assess risk and resilience in servicemembers. *American Journal of Psychiatry, 172*(11), 1101–1111. doi:10.1176/appi.ajp.2015.14121572

Terrio, H., Brenner, L. A., Ivins, B. J., Cho, J. M., Helmick, K., Schwab, K., ... & Warden, D. (2009). Traumatic brain injury screening: preliminary findings in a US Army Brigade Combat Team. *The Journal of head trauma rehabilitation, 24*(1), 14–23.

Vasterling, J. J., Jacob, S. N., & Rasmusson, A. (2018). Traumatic brain injury and posttraumatic stress disorder: conceptual, diagnostic, and therapeutic considerations in the context of co-occurrence. *The Journal of neuropsychiatry and clinical neurosciences, 30*(2), 91–100.

## RESOURCES

**Psychological Health Center of Excellence. PTSD clinical support tools:** https://www.pdhealth.mil/clinical-guidance/clinical-practice-guidelines-and-clinical-support-tools/posttraumatic-stress-disorder

**Psychological Health Center of Excellence. Suicide risk support:** https://www.pdhealth.mil/clinical-guidance/clinical-practice-guidelines-and-clinical-support-tools/suicide

**Clinician Administered PTSD Scale for *DSM-5* (CAPS-5)**

Department of Veterans Affairs. (n.d.). *Clinician administered PTSD scale for the DSM-5 (CAPS-5).* Retrieved from https://www.ptsd.va.gov/professional/assessment/adult-int/caps.asp

**Dissociative Experiences Scale-II (DES-II)**

Carlson, E., & Putnam, F. (1993). An update of the dissociative experience scale. *Dissociation, 6*(1), 16–27. Retrieved from https://onlinelibrary.wiley.com/doi/pdf/10.1002/9781118093146.app1

**Impact of Events Scale-Revised (IES-R)**

Beck, J., Grant, D., Read, J., Clapp, J., Coffey, S., Miller, L., & Palyo, S. A. (2008). The impact of event scale- revised: Psychometric properties in a sample of motor vehicle accident survivors. *Anxiety Disorders, 22,* 187–198. doi:10.1016/j.janxdis.2007.02.007

**Moral Injury Symptom Scale-Military Short Version**

Koenig, H. (2018). Measuring symptoms of moral injury in veterans and active duty military with PTSD. *Religions, 9*(3), 86. doi:10.3390/rel9030086

**Posttraumatic Growth Inventory**

Tedeschi, R., & Calhoun, L. (1996). The posttraumatic growth inventory: Measuring the positive legacy of trauma. *Journal of Traumatic Stress, 9*(3), 455–472. doi:10.1002/jts.2490090305

**PTSD Checklist-5 (PCL-5)**

Department of Veterans Affairs. (2016). *PTSD checklist for DSM-5 (PCL-5).* Washington, DC: National Center for PTSD.

# 8

# Treating Moral Injury With EMDR Therapy

> The only persons who return
> home from combat without
> some form of shame or guilt
> are persons who bleed out
> —those who die.
> —E. C. Hurley, DMin, PhD

## Introduction

Moral injury is a contemporary term for an ancient malady. This chapter prepares the EMDR therapist to understand the three levels of moral injury complexity, the self-referential emotions of shame and guilt, the use of cognitive interweaves (CIs), and the multidisciplinary approaches of moral philosophy, mental health, and moral theology/spirituality. The use of EMDR therapy in treating the complexities of moral injury is discussed with scripted examples provided.

## Learning Objectives

- Discuss the three levels of complexity in treating moral injury.
- Compare the multidimensional approaches to shame, guilt, and moral injury.
- Recognize EMDR's themes of responsibility in addressing shame and guilt.
- Identify the multidisciplinary approaches including moral philosophy, psychology, and moral theology/spirituality.

## UNDERSTANDING MORAL INJURY

Moral injury is an evolving condition. It is not a mental health disorder; therefore, it does not have a diagnostic category. Neither is there a categorical cutoff score to determine if a person qualifies as having the condition. Its existence is determined by definitions provided from various disciplines as listed in this chapter. In the past we referred to the condition primarily as shame or guilt. It is a violation of a person's values creating an internal conflict, a dissonance within oneself. While moral injury can be a stand-alone injury, it is frequently assessed along with acute stress or posttraumatic stress disorder (PTSD) mental health diagnoses. The memory of the moral injury incident(s), like any other disturbing memory, can be treated with the standard EMDR protocol. It is my experience that persons suffering with moral injury seldom seek relief from mental health providers just for moral injury. The psychological pain of a stress-related disorder is usually the identified problem that brings the client to seek help. When identified as existing with stress-related disorders such as PTSD, the moral injury is typically sufficiently intense with emotional charge (measured by the subjective unit of disturbance [SUD]) and avoidance strategies to interfere with the treatment of PTSD's disturbing memories. When this happens, the moral injury must be treated as part of the overall treatment plan. Due to moral injury presenting in varying levels of complexity, I have found it helpful to conceptualize the moral injury level of complexity on one of three levels. Both moral injury and stress-related disorders can be effectively treated with EMDR therapy. Research has demonstrated the effectiveness of EMDR therapy in treating both moral injury and complex PTSD (Hurley, 2018).

### HOW IS MORAL INJURY DIFFERENT THAN PTSD?

The symptoms of moral injury and PTSD have similarities, but each has its own unique construct. PTSD is considered a mental health disorder requiring a diagnosis, but moral injury is considered a multidimensional problem, a syndrome, with no defined threshold to identify its presence (Griffin et al., 2019).

It is my observation that persons typically do not seek psychotherapy solely for moral injury complaints. There are, of course, exceptions. Most moral injury is treated when identified with other stress-related disorders such as PTSD. Traditionally, help for resolving moral injury dissonance was sought from religious and community authorities. Redefining shame and guilt as moral injury by mental health providers creates a shift in perspective as a moral condition is moved into the purview of psychiatrists and psychologists. It also provides a different context to understand the impact of life when personal values are violated.

Symptoms of moral injury have been listed as shame, grief, meaninglessness, and remorse (Brock & Lettini, 2012). Koenig, Youssef &

Pearce (2018) includes the loss of religious faith, loss of trust, difficulty forgiving, loss of meaning/purpose, and self-condemnation. In contrast, PTSD diagnostic criteria listed in the *Diagnostic and Statistical Manual of Mental Disorders* (5th ed.; *DSM-5*; American Psychiatric Association, 2013) requires the following for diagnosis for PTSD: (a) exposure to actual or threatened death, serious injury or sexual violence; (b) presence of one or more intrusive symptoms associated with a traumatic event; (c) persistent avoidance of stimuli associated with traumatic event; (d) negative alterations in cognitions and mood associated with a traumatic event; and (e) marked alterations in arousal and reactivity associated with a traumatic event. Memories of those morally disturbing incidents, with or without co-occurring disorders such as PTSD, are successfully treated with EMDR therapy.

## THE THREE LEVELS OF MORAL INJURY TREATMENT WITH EMDR THERAPY (TABLE 8.1)

I conceptualize three levels of clinical complexity presented by clients suffering with moral injury: (a) moral wounds that EMDR therapy reprocesses spontaneously with associated disturbing memories; (b) moral wounds with blocking beliefs associated with the wound (level II). Level II wounds are normally reprocessed with effective use of cognitive interweaves (CI); and (c) more severe complexity (level III), which often includes complex PTSD including dissociative exhibitions, in which the level of mental and physical strength for treatment is frequently determined by the amount of sleep the client achieves from night to night. Due to the complexity of level III moral injury, it is sometimes helpful to divide the target memory into sub-targets with the first sub-target being what the client can address in reprocessing with least difficulty and the second sub-target containing the remnant of material more aversive to the client. Treatment of the second sub-target often requires the use of CIs and changes in the TICES (target = image,

### TABLE 8.1 Three Levels of Moral Injury Treatment With EMDR Therapy

| Level 1 | Spontaneous processing of moral injury | Standard protocol provides processing |
| --- | --- | --- |
| Level II | Based on blocking beliefs entrenched with moral injury | Use of cognitive interweaves to shift perspectives and resolve moral injury |
| Level III | Shame-prone moral injury enmeshed in long-term shame vulnerability. Complex PTSD; childhood abuse/neglect | Identify "where did you first learn to be so hard on yourself?" Identify and target memories of shamed-based incidents |

EMDR, eye movement desensitization and reprocessing.

cognition, emotion, and sensations), along with adjustment of the bilateral stimulation (BLS) during reprocessing. These are aspects of treatment necessary for successively treating complex clinical presentations.

While many clients with moral injury openly disclose information related to their moral injury, EMDR therapy provides the means to reprocess a memory without the client needing to verbally disclose details. The EMDR standard protocol allows for therapists to treat persons whose entire traumatic experience is classified information due to the secret nature of military operations. This same approach can be used when the shame of moral injury inhibits the client from revealing the complete details of the event. When necessary, you, as an EMDR therapist, can treat a disturbing memory with only two words—any two words—one word means "same" (the memory is the same, not changing) and the second word means "different" (the memory is changing). The Phase 3 Assessment questions focus on how the memory is affecting the client now; it has little to do with the actual event, but rather how the incident is affecting the client when recalling the incident now. When a client struggles with deeply held matters, the EMDR therapist needs to be comfortable with hearing (bearing witness to) the client's deeply held struggles.

## LEVEL I: SPONTANEOUS REPROCESSING OF MORAL INJURY

Many moral injury memories can be spontaneously processed with the EMDR standard protocol.

During History-Taking, when identifying the target memories for treatment, I ask the client, *"Is it okay to get over this incident?"* If the answer is *"Yes,"* it indicates there is no blocking belief associated at this level; therefore, unless otherwise indicated, I assume the processing of the moral injury, with its psychological distress, will spontaneously reprocess as a level 1 category.

This level I moral injury case, in the text that follows, describes the treatment of a 32-year-old Army medic, who was married and father of a 2-year-old boy at the time of his treatment. He was referred for the 5-day EMDR intensive therapy by a psychologist who had known the client when he out-processed out of the military. Here is an example of a servicemember resolving a moral injury wound with EMDR therapy's spontaneous processing of disturbing memories.

## Script Example—Level I: Moral Injury Spontaneously Reprocessed With EMDR Therapy

| | |
|---|---|
| Therapist: | I want to remind you that you're in control of the process. You have a stop signal should you need to |

stop and you have your safe, secure place with your cue word. As we look at the next target on the list, it's the kid, the 8-year-old Iraqi kid. As you think about that, what picture represents the worst part of it?

Client:        When I looked under the blanket and saw him.

Therapist:     As you think about that, as you focus on that, what words would best describe any negative belief about yourself now?

Client:        Is it alright if it's different than what's written on that board? (an NC written during History-Taking)

Therapist:     Yes, an "I am" statement.

Client:        Well, I mean, I was confused. I was angry; fed up with seeing all this crap. Seeing kids is screwy you know. I don't even remember … he wasn't caught in the cross fire. The Iraqis brought people to us all the time who had medical problems. They didn't know what they were doing. I didn't know what was wrong with him, something serious. But I kept him alive with O2. I just, seeing him under that blanket—He was out of it until I gave my oxygen. So it made me angry that no one on the ground thought to give him oxygen. So I am angry!

Therapist:     Anger is an emotion. What we're looking for is a word that would describe a negative belief about yourself.

Client:        I don't know if I had one, uh, for that situation. I actually helped that kid. People on the ground didn't, just by common sense.

Therapist:     A minute ago you mentioned "I'm fed up with it."

Client:        Oh, I guess it is negative, isn't it? Um, I am short-tempered. I don't want to make things up for you, a lot of things I remember making me angry. Maybe I'm so diluted at this point. I don't see it as negative. Um, I don't feel helpless like I did on the first one (target memory). I did what I could do for that kid as a flight medic with that kid.

Therapist: What bothers you about it in terms of yourself ... I am ...?

Client: I didn't know what was wrong with him, so I'm uneducated? (grimaced facial expression) But I mean .... Maybe this isn't the right one to talk about ... I mean, it just makes me angry that the kid was out there.

Therapist: And you're angry because ...?

Client: I'm volatile, uh, unstable.

Client: Unstable?

Client Yeah. oh, yeah! Unstable. I'm trying to keep my mind focused on this because I don't want this to go away. I really like this method.

Therapist: You don't have to work at this. This process is happening in terms of your treatment. You don't have to keep guard up for this to be there. Just notice the results of the process and report it to me. Okay? So, what would be a different statement you'd like to believe about yourself rather than I am unstable, I am what?

Client: Could I say I'm full of rage or is that not appropriate?

Therapist: Rage is a feeling, intense anger. Um, and we're talking about a positive statement. Maybe "I handled it okay" or "I'm okay?"

Client: Yeah, I did handle it. Okay. But it still makes me mad (draws out word with intensity).

Therapist: So positive cognition would be, um, "I handled it okay?" In terms of what we're looking at is in that situation, the negative belief about yourself was "I'm unstable." So as you think about that situation and what you were feeling at the time, um, the negative belief "I'm unstable," does that fit for you?

Client: No. I could have done more for him. He was just a kid, man. I am not powerful enough.

Therapist: Inadequate?

Client: Yeah.

Therapist: So when you think about the statement of what you would like to believe about yourself in terms of a positive statement, what would it be instead of "I am inadequate," "I am adequate," or "okay?"

Client: Pertaining to that situation as I think about it now?

Therapist: What you would want to believe about yourself now.

Client: I'm effective.

Therapist: Okay. I am effective. And when you think about that situation, how true do those words, "I'm effective," feel to you in the gut right now? Like one is totally false and seven is totally true.

Client: Three, I gave him O2 (oxygen).

Therapist: Okay. And what emotion do you feel?

Client: Confusion, is confusion an emotion?

Therapist: Between happy, sad, mad, scared? I heard you use "rage" a minute ago.

Client: Yeah, rage.

Therapist: How much does that bother you on a scale of 0 to 10?

Client: It's a 12.

Therapist: And where do you feel that in your body?

Client: It's not like the other feelings. I don't have a particular sensation. Okay... (stretches open hands toward the ceiling). I want to grab God by the collar and say, "What the f--k man?" There, I said it, I said it!

Therapist:    And where do you feel it in your body?

Client:    Here (punches himself in the chest).

Therapist:    Okay. So I want you to pull up that image and the words, "I am inadequate," notice where you feel it in your body, and follow my fingers. (35 passes of BLS.) Take a deep breath. Let it all go. And what do you get now?

Client:    Now that I started talking about it, I feel it more.

Therapist:    Go with that! (35 passes of BLS.) Take a deep breath. Let it go. And what did you get now?

Client:    I don't know how to say this. Hmm. That's no reason that child should be hurt, you know. No one can tell me God has a plan for this. I need to understand why. I don't know how to look up people in the eyes knowing that I don't know.

It all just seems so random. All I found when I was over there, there were little kids who on at one point were innocent. I mean you see them everywhere, right? They're gonna grow up to be snobby and insecure and hurtful and they're going to hurt people. That's what they do. I talked with my girlfriend, she told me to just forget about things and get on with my life. But I find it hard to forget.

Therapist:    Go with that! (35 passes of BLS.) Take a deep breath. Let it go. What do you get now? * * * * * 35 minutes into the session * * * * *

Client:    Kind of funny talking about that kid, but thank God I was there. No ground medic would know to go with that.

Therapist:    Go with that! (35–36 passes of BLS.) Take a deep breath. What do you get now?

Client:    He was in good hands. He was in better shape when I dropped him off than when I picked him up.

| Therapist: | Take a deep breath. Let it go. What do you get now? |
|---|---|
| Client: | He's 5 years older now. He has a chance. |
| Therapist: | Go with that! (35 passes of BLS.) Take a deep breath. Let it go. What do you get now? |
| Client: | Even surgeons lose people. I'm not that special. It's not about me. |
| Therapist: | Take a deep breath. What are you getting at? |
| Client: | Um, I picked up the kid, he was really small in the blanket, pretty much covering him. I remember now, he opened his eyes on the flight. That's right! Oh my God! I forgot all about that until this very moment. He opened his eyes on the flight and he looked at me. |
|  | Ah man. When I put him in the bird. His eyes were closed and I put the, uh, I didn't have a baby mask. I didn't feel like the blow-by because he was too old for that. I put it right over him and I didn't have it on very high, but he opened his eyes when the flight, before we dropped him off and I held his hand. Ah (sigh of relief). I dropped him off a lot. His eyes were open. I forgot all about that. I can't believe I forgot all about that. Jesus Christ. I hadn't thought about that until this very moment. He opened his eyes on that flight. |
|  | I got him to open his eyes. Oh, the fools on the ground didn't know what to do. It's like they don't know what to do. Oh, they said the Iraqi that brought him, said he's been unconscious for 3 days and as long as it took us to call you. He had not opened his eyes for 3 days and I got him to open his eyes just by putting the oxygen on him. You know I'm Quincy Jones, MD. No. Oh my God. |
| Therapist: | So let's go with that. (35 passes of BLS.) Take a deep breath, let it all go. What do you get? |

| | |
|---|---|
| Client: | I pictured him under that blanket and now I feel happy because I know what happened. Sometimes all I saw was the blanket and my being mad. I remember that now that makes me feel happy. |
| Therapist: | Take a deep breath. What are you getting now? |
| Client: | I'm okay, with this one. This has haunted me for a long time. |

## Discussion

The moral injury in this case began as a flight medic responding to a medevac call involving an 8-year-old Iraqi boy who was unconscious. The medic did not know the cause of the illness. Individuals at the site stated the child had been unconscious for 3 days. Someone suggested the illness might be meningitis. The initial encounter with the ill child negatively impacted the medic as the experience became a moral wound entrenched with his PTSD wounds. The moral wound kept the memory isolated, inhibited from the medic's full awareness of the actual occurrence. He did not remember giving the child oxygen and keeping him alive to reach the combat support hospital. The medic did not remember the 8-year-old boy reaching out his hand or him holding the child's hand while attending to him in-flight. As I heard the medic's description of the incident, with the level of intensity he demonstrated in my office, it seemed the child must have died in his arms. This was not the case! The medic was trapped in the most fearful thoughts of what could have happened, not what actually occurred. In fact, the medic kept the child alive, but that aspect of memory was not accessible until the memory was stimulated for reprocessing with EMDR therapy. The BLS, while stimulating the targeted memory, activated the memory and access to other associated (similar) memory networks where he was able to recall the full memory, thus resolving the moral wound once the complete memory was reprocessed.

## LEVEL II: MORAL INJURY REPROCESSED WITH EMDR THERAPY USING COGNITIVE INTERWEAVES (CIs)

Level II recognizes the existence of blocking beliefs. During History-Taking, when asking if it is okay to get over the incident, the client answers "No" with responses such as "I have to live with this every day for the rest of my life" or "If I get over this it would mean my friends died in vain." This indicates blocking beliefs inhibiting the processing of the targeted memory. I follow up with *"What would it take to get over this incident?"* or *"How long do you need to beat yourself up over this?"*

While blocking beliefs are not limited to moral injury, the strength of a moral issue brings significant power to the cognition. Dr. Shapiro (2018) understood there are frequently occurring themes of responsibility, safety, and power/control (choices) occurring in adverse life experiences. She developed CIs with use in addressing these three themes. CIs are appropriately used when: (a) processing is blocked; (b) you are running out of time; or (c) when the client is facing intense emotional response. Additionally, CIs are effective in resolving blocking beliefs. Examples of CIs are listed in Appendix H of this book. CIs are effective in treating level II and level III moral injury complexity. CIs accompanied with BLS will often resolve the level II reprocessing of moral injury.

## LEVEL III: MORAL INJURY

The complexity of clinical presentation at this level can vary from one session to the next one. For example, the mental and physical strength required for a client to successfully reprocess a disturbing memory is often determined by the amount of sleep the client achieves from the previous night. This is especially true for clients who have mostly had 1 or 2 hours of sleep each night for years due to nightmares/night terrors. At best, some of these clients have interspersed 4 to 6 hours per night at times with medication. Sleep can influence the client's ability to maintain dual awareness rather than dissociating with the memory when the memory is activated. Clinical complexity at this level may include complex PTSD with auditory and visual intrusions, other dissociative exhibitions, previous history of panic attacks triggered by mental healthcare, and previous suicide attempts (two and three times), as well as the veteran stating, "Suicide is always an option" due to physical, psychological, and moral injury.

Clients tend to identify the most highly charged moral events that stand out for treatment. Level III moral wounds, identified during History-Taking, reveal what they wish to avoid recalling in session or, sometimes, the more intrusive aspects of their deployment memories. Sometimes servicemembers will identify this level of moral injury as "eating away at me." Treating the most highly charged moral injury early is normally sufficient to allow any other similar wounds to be included in the traditional treatment plan. In the event that several moral injuries stand out, they can be clustered together with the most highly charged incident treated first. This allows the generalization effect to significantly reduce the emotional charge and cognitive distortions associated with other similar incidents. I have found, even with infantrymen and pilots who face repetitive moral actions, there are frequently one or two worst moral incidents that, when treated, allow other memories to be processed as usual within the standard treatment plan.

Therapists must determine where the moral injury should be placed in the target memory treatment plan. It can be helpful to treat moral injury as early as possible. Sometimes the target memory containing the specific moral injury can be treated first. When this happens, this treatment sequence can offer relief early in treatment. At other times, a specific moral injury memory has to be treated later in the treatment plan due to issues such as dissociative responses, strong avoidance, and embedded blocking beliefs. In such cases, treating other disturbing memories first can add confidence and momentum to the treatment process. As a general principle, treat shame and guilt expressions of moral injury as early as possible.

## SCRIPT OF PARTIAL SESSION OF LEVEL III TREATMENT

A soldier was referred for EMDR therapy having lived with PTSD and a severe moral injury for several years. As a Bradley gunner, he had followed the rules of engagement (ROE) when an Iraqi vehicle was speeding in his direction. In accordance with the standard operating procedure (SOP), he fired a warning round, a 50 caliber machine gun shot, in front in the vehicle. Instead of stopping, the vehicle increased speed. Next, he fired into the engine block, which disabled the vehicle. The vehicle stopped and caught fire. The soldier operating the machine gun was convinced there was an insurgent inside the vehicle. He watched the vehicle burn and, to his surprise, no one got out of the vehicle. After 2 hours, as the fire died down and the vehicle cooled, he opened the door to the vehicle to discover the charred remains of a woman and two children. He was haunted by what he saw. He did what he was supposed to do in following SOPs, yet, in his mind, the wrong outcome happened. He doesn't want to see himself as a murderer of women and children. And, certainly, he doesn't want his wife and children to see him in that light.

This was a very entrenched moral injury incident. The soldier had originally sought treatment with the Army's embedded behavioral health provider at his unit. As an "old school" noncommissioned officer (NCO), he kept his experiences internalized and compartmentalized during four combat deployments. With uncontrolled emotional outbursts now happening when talking with his soldiers, he began experiencing panic attacks. This old school NCO felt vulnerable after spilling his life history to a therapist in one session. Leaving the therapist's office, he arrived home where he experienced another panic attack, crying and feeling out of control. This continued through the night. Arriving on the military installation the next morning, he dissociated with the intent to hang himself while in his dissociative state. After 3 weeks of inpatient acute care for his suicidal plan, he was referred to me at Soldier Center. After History-Taking with developing a treatment plan, we began treatment. Following the History-Taking and Preparation phases, I attempted to treat this target memory early in the treatment plan. However, due to his fear of treatment, his dissociative responses, and avoidance of the moral injury memory, I decided to treat other disturbing memories first. His other memories were treated with the belief that resolving other disturbing memories would create confidence and momentum. This moral injury memory was the last target memory in the treatment plan.

When I began treating the moral injury incident, I realized the need to break the target memory into two memory components. The client reported he could not bear to recall the image of the charred remains. Recalling the mental picture was abhorrent to him. I decided to separate out the part the client could not bear to view—the charred remains in the burned-out vehicle. I asked the client to place the picture of charred remains in a container where it was sealed until we were ready to work on that aspect of the memory in another session. I focused on the first component of memory the NCO could reprocess and began Phase 3 Assessment. The client reprocessed the first sub-target memory fully (except for the haunting image that was in a container) without difficulty. He achieved a SUD = 0; validity of cognition (VOC) = 7; and a clear body scan within a 50-minute session.

The following session we completed the Phase 8 Reevaluation of the memory from the previous session. The SUD of 0 and VOC of 7 remained from the previous week. I asked the soldier to recall the unprocessed part of the memory, the part of the charred remains that had been in the container. We resumed reprocessing that part of the memory. I began with a CI, "Is it okay to get over this?" with which he responded "Yes, I want to get over this!" Processing continued (35 passes of BLS) with the client reporting change after each set. He reported repeating the CI to himself through the processing, "I want to get over this." We reprocessed several sets. Then, I used another CI, "How long did you look at them?" of which he answered no more than 60 seconds. I responded, "Go with that!" and he continued processing. The client reported an abhorrence/attraction to the image. He did not want to look at the image but was being seduced to look at the image. I allowed this to bring him closer to the image as we continued reprocessing. After a few more sets of BLS, I asked the client, "Who do you need to be standing with you?" He choked up and physically squirmed in his seat as he stated, "This seems weird, but I need my two children standing with me." I replied, "Go with that!" We continued with more sets of BLS. Then, I asked the client, "What do you want your children to know?" He squirmed in his seat, paused, and with a choking voice said, "That I am not a murderer of women and children." I responded with another CI, "They know that, go with that!" and he continued reprocessing. After a few minutes the client reported he was getting excited to go home to see his boys. At this point in the processing I knew the session was almost completed. I completed the session with a SUD = 1 (which I considered ecologically valid due to the death of the woman and children), VOC = 7, and a clear body scan. Here is a partial script of the second session focusing on the intense moral injury.

## Partial Script—Treating Level III Moral Injury With EMDR Therapy

Therapist: So when you think about what you saw—it is okay to talk about it? When you think about what you saw, how disturbing is that for you? When you think about seeing it, 0 to 10, what number?

Client: Um, eight. 10.

Therapist: So would it be okay to get over that?

Client: Yes. I want to.

Therapist: You're doing fine. (35 passes of BLS, stop.) Take a breath. Let it go. What do you notice now?

Client: I notice I started to get that same feeling, that guilt, that anger at myself and kept putting the picture up to the side. I said to myself just what you said. "It's, it's okay to get past this. It's okay to get over it."

Therapist: Go with that. (35 passes of BLS.) Take a breath. Let it go. What do you get now?

Client: That's all I get, I was trying to think and that honestly prevented me from—I was about to break down again, but it's okay to get past it. I just want to get past that. I want to get past that picture.

Therapist: So when you in real-world time, when you saw them, how long did you look at them, would you say?

Client:      As long as they were in my sights, probably to be honest, it couldn't have been more than 1 minute. Because the vehicle was moving. I wasn't the driver. I was the gunner, we just kept going.

Therapist:   Go with that. (35 passes of BLS.) Take a breath. Let it go. What do you notice now?

Client:      Um, I try to focus on the vehicle and just our going past it. We got past it. And I get a couple of flashes of them. I tried to focus more on Dually and him driving and because I only really looked through my actual eye tads (Target Acquisition and Designation Sights) and trying to remember that once we got past, I couldn't even tell you how long it was before we ran into anything else. It was awhile. But as I kept trying to focus on the question, when you ask how long, I don't know my sense of time when it comes to that; it doesn't feel like it was more than 30 to 60 seconds.

\* \* \* \* \* 18 minutes of script edited out for space \* \* \* \* \*

Therapist:   So what about if you put up that window so you can see it, but it can't get to you—for 1 minute. Is that workable? (Client Nods "yes.") Okay, let's go with that. (35 passes of BLS—client begins to squirm in his seat as he continues reprocessing the memory. I offer assurance.) You're doing fine. It's a memory from the past. It's over. Take a breath, let it go. And what do you notice?

Client:      I noticed that I can, as long as I keep it at a distance. I can see it. I still get angry, feel myself wanting to be mad at me, at the situation, at life. But I can see it, just from a distance.

## IDENTIFYING A SHAME HISTORY
### SHAME AND GUILT IN MORAL INJURY

Core elements of moral injury include shame and guilt. Psychologist Helen Lewis (1971, 1988) made significant contributions toward understanding shame and guilt. She defined the difference between the two constructs as shame is about the essence of a person; guilt is about what the person has done or failed to do (Lewis, 1971, 1988). Three decades after Lewis's publication, Tangney and Dearing (2002) published their studies on shame and guilt as self-conscious emotions while noting their impact on human behavior. Additional publications contributed to understanding the dynamics of shame as a core issue in addictions (Bradshaw, 2005). Shame is a contributing factor in numerous expressions of pathology. Shame, when present, greatly impacts the client's ability to manage life and complete treatment. The debilitating impact of moral injury with its shame component has been found to have a strong relationship with suicidality (Frankfurt, Frazier, & Engdahl, 2017).

I have noted that clinical presentations of shame often exhibit a quality similar to performance anxiety. Shame-prone clients may become anxious anticipating the challenges of doing the job correctly due to their lack of self-confidence. Anticipation of failure then feeds the shame experience and reinforces their belief they are inadequate and a failure. The gut-wrenching visceral sensations connected with shame enhance their visceral nauseating sensation. The embarrassment of shame enhances the client's determination to maintain their shame experience in secret. Shame can generate anger if someone else's actions are interpreted as acting as if they are better than the client. Phase 1 History-Taking can often reveal shame-proneness by asking: *"When did you first learn to be so hard on yourself?"* or *"On a bad day, when you are beating up on yourself, what are you thinking?"* Remember, shame is pervasive; it represents the essence of what a person believes about themselves, along with body sensations (particularly visceral responses in the gut) and nausea feelings. Shame is more than an emotion; it is a total experience that is usually developed on other memories when a person came to believe they are worthless accompanied with subsequent body sensations. Persons who have difficulty recognizing the concept of shame can often identify the visceral sickening feeling in their stomach. Shame often develops during childhood when a child determines they are worthless. This condition can shut down an EMDR reprocessing session with the toxic impact of shame. Once, while in the midst of Phase 4 Reprocessing, the client dropped his head in gaze aversion as his demeanor changed. I saw him shut down before my eyes. Knowing I needed to get him out of his shame, because otherwise the processing was finished for the session, I asked, "What is the funniest thing that happened on that deployment?" He laughed, told me his funny story, and after he told the story, I said, "Go with that!" We did a set of BLS, then I took the client back to target and the reprocessing continued. Humor broke up the shame state.

Guilt is viewed as being about specific acts that are more readily resolved in comparison to shame. As Silver and Rogers (2002) indicated, the impact of guilt is more disabling than anxiety. The resolution of guilt is customarily accomplished by making amends, doing acts to memorialize the deaths of persons while making the world a better place, and receiving absolution or forgiveness granted from a designated authority such as a community or religious leader.

Edward Kubany developed a measure focusing on the impact of trauma-related guilt incidents on veterans (Kubany, 1994, 1996). Kubany identified guilt types as: (a) survivor guilt; (b) "I should have known better"; (c) "impossible choices"; (d) "error"; (e) "I should have done more"; (f) "the pleasure of violence"; (g) "participation in an atrocity"; and (h) "I should have felt worse." Kubany's work served to provide a clear focus on the impact of guilt among combat veterans. Parenthetically, as a long-term servicemember I often say, "Everyone who has been deployed comes back different." Furthermore, "The only persons who do not have some sense of guilt are those who bleed out." Most everyone else falls within Kubany's styles of guilt.

With the increase in the number of servicemembers presenting with PTSD symptoms, Department of Veterans Affairs (DVA) psychologists and military psychiatrists began to define those clinical presentations as moral injury, recognizing shame and guilt as core emotional components for the newly defined construct (Litz et al., 2009; Nash & Marino, 2006; Shay, 1994). Moral injury is a nebulous term with no categorical measure to define it. In fact, it is not considered a mental health disorder, so it cannot be diagnosed. It is a condition. It is often described as an inner conflict—a dissonance—that robs a person of their sense of inner peace or serenity. As such, this internal malady has been recognized and treated with various approaches since the beginning of human history.

Recognizing the contributions of both shame and guilt to the newly defined construct known as moral injury, measures such as the Moral Injury Symptom Scale-Military Version (MISS-M) and the Moral Injury Events Scale (Nash et al., 2013) were developed to assess the degree of moral injury symptoms reported. Since there are not cutoff scores for categorizing the construct, the measures are used comparatively.

Shapiro's (2018) development of EMDR as a model of psychotherapy recognized there are frequently reoccurring themes of responsibility, safety, and power/choices (control). Those three themes became apparent during numerous processing sessions. These themes are laden with emotional and

---

**BOX 8.1 Moral Injury as a Condition**

*Moral injury is a nebulous term with no categorical measure to define it.*

*In fact, it is not considered a mental health disorder, so it cannot be diagnosed. It is a condition.*

*It is often described as an inner conflict—a dissonance—that robs a person of their sense of inner peace or serenity.*

cognitive aspects based on life experiences. The impact of responsibility themes are addressed with responsibility/defectiveness and responsibility/action categories. Responsibility/action is a theme corresponding with guilt produced from a person's actions. In contrast, responsibility/defectiveness corresponds with the sense of worthlessness produced by shame.

It should be noted that a combination of shame/guilt within the context of moral injury can leave the client vulnerable to suicidality. Exposure to killing or witnessing killing has been found to promote moral injury and suicidality (Khan et al., 2019; Purcell, Koenig, Bosch, & Maguen, 2016; Tripp, McDevitt-Murphy, & Henschel, 2016).

## MORAL INJURY MULTIDISCIPLINARY BACKGROUND

Moral wounds have been addressed from various perspectives including moral philosophy, moral theology, and moral psychology. The first noted reference in using the term "moral injury" was ascribed to an Anglican bishop and philosopher.

### Moral Philosophy: Moral Injury as Diminishing One's Dignity

In past centuries, the moral injury concept was considered within the realms of moral philosophy and theology/religion. An early contributor was Bishop Joseph Butler, an Anglican priest who was also trained in law. Butler was influenced by John Locke and Samuel Clarke, whose concept of moral philosophy was characterized by analytic rigor. During the early 18th century, Butler incorporated his knowledge about the philosophy of law to address a moral philosophy approach (Hampton, 1991). His discourses on moral philosophy were published in sermons, often footnotes to sermons, where he began publishing them in 1726, His contributions to the moral philosophy discipline were made 157 years before the founding of the field of psychology (Garrett, 2018) and 283 years before the DVA embraced the term "moral injury" within the discipline of psychology. Butler's moral philosophy is more recently represented by philosophers Jeffrie Murphy and Jean Hampton, who clarified the philosophy of law related to mercy, forgiveness, and retribution (Murphy & Hampton, 1988). Additionally, J. M.

---

BOX 8.2  Moral Injury: A Psychological Perspective

**Moral injury: Psychological perspective on psychological harm resulting from:**

*(a) acting, failing to prevent, or witnessing actions that violate an individual's deepest values and principles or from (b) betrayal by a trusted authority figure in a high-stakes situation.*

Berstein used Hampton's juridical use of moral injury and critical theory to identify moral injury as a form of devastation resulting from extremely dehumanizing violence such as rape or torture (Berstein, 2005). From a moral philosophy perspective, moral injury can result from the everyday interactions with friends, family, and acquaintances (Murphy & Hampton, 1988). It can also result due to daily social interaction with severe violations ranging from hate crimes, torture, and acts such as rape. Moral injury is a form of devastation resulting from extremely dehumanizing violence. Significant degrees of moral injury can happen when a person is demeaned or seriously degraded. Extreme injury is the result of "diminishment" in which an action degrades the person's value, reducing their dignity. The philosophical view of moral injury includes someone's rights being violated, when a person is demeaned or degraded, or when an act degrades a person's dignity. Moral wounds impact a person's dignity when one's self-esteem is deracinated by subjective violence to the person's sense of worth (Berstein, 2005). Any affront to the dignity or value of a person produces harm both to the individual and society since any moral violence to the individual is also an attack against the community (Hampton, 1991).

### Moral Injury From a Psychological Perspective

Shay (1994) defined moral injury as *a betrayal of what is right by leadership in a high-stakes situation*. Two decades after the Vietnam War, Jonathan Shay, an Army psychiatrist, wrote *Achilles in Vietnam* (1994) about the psychological devastation of war as he compared the suffering of Vietnam era veterans with the soldiers of Homer's *"Iliad"* written 27 centuries before the Vietnam era. Using Homeric philosophy, he heuristically introduced the basic concept of moral injury as a character wound during the decade of the 1990s. Shay presented the concept of moral injury as the result of a leader's betrayal of "what's right" in the eyes of the soldier (Shay, 1994, 2002). The concept of moral injury was defined by him as being present when: (a) there has been betrayal of what is right in the soldier's understanding; (b) by someone in authority; and (c) in a high-stakes situation. Shay, a psychiatrist treating Vietnam era military personnel and veterans, emphasized the concept of "injury" rather than "disorder" as a means of recognizing that mental health wounds do not demonstrate a mental health deficit but rather present an injury judged to be as honorable as wounds sustained in combat (Shay, 2011). Shay's definition places moral injury as the result of a failure in military leadership, not the actions of the soldier.

A second wave, following Shay's view of moral injury, offered a different perspective within the context of Operation Iraqi Freedom (OIF) and Operation Enduring Freedom (OEF) operations. *"Acting, failing to prevent, or witnessing acts which violate a person's deepest values"* (Litz et al., 2009, 700–701.) are definitions of moral injury in the second wave. The second wave differed from Shay by identifying their work as the first scientific research regarding what or who defines commissions of moral injury, believing there are two sources: (a) the solider him- or herself; and (b) the combat environment (Litz et al., 2009). The soldier is viewed as being both the source and the recipient of their own moral injury. In addition, a soldier can become morally injured by witnessing an atrocity or managing the remains of the dead (Litz et al., 2009; Nash & Marino, 2006). Moral injury was operationally defined by this second wave as,

> a psychological harm resulting from either (1) acting, failing to prevent, or witnessing actions that violate an individual's deepest values and principles or from (2) betrayal by a trusted authority figure in a high stakes situation. These actions and events are called "morally injurious events." (Seim, 2019, para. 3)

A more recent description of moral injury, posted on the DVA website, focuses on understanding moral injury within the context of war, thereby adjusting the focus to emphasize the nature of combat-related moral injury (Maguen & Litz, 2019). Moral injury with its inner conflict assumes there is both personal agency and an inner capacity to evaluate and respond when there is shame or guilt-prone distress. This component serves as a conscience, an inner ability to evaluate and sound an alarm when one's moral values have been violated.

The EMDR therapy approach includes the ability to reprocess any disturbing memory ranging from moral injury to complex PTSD. When blocking beliefs are present, CIs work well in dismantling those blocking beliefs associated with disturbing memories. In cases where a regretful incident occurred and cannot be undone, that is, the results cannot be reversed—the therapist can have the client select one or more of these options:

- Memorializing the people—The respect and honor of the people involved can be helpful. Having the client perform acts in honorable memory of the people while performing deeds to make the world a better place can equip the client to progress forward in their life. It provides a sense of control.
- Responsibility pie chart—Draw a pie chart that illustrates what percentage of responsibility each identified person has in the chain of responsibility.
- Seek forgiveness from a respected community or religious leader.

## MORAL INJURY FROM A SPIRITUAL/MORAL THEOLOGY PERSPECTIVE

Moral injury includes a spiritual trauma. Spirituality is about the individual and relationships. The wounds of moral injury isolate and alienate people to live among shame and guilt. Religion is about adherence to an institutional structure of faith statements and creeds. Spirituality allows the individual to seek personal peace by accepting acts of contrition, seeking forgiveness, and resolving guilt. In cases where the damage is nonreversible, the individual can do acts to remember and memorialize the memory of those incidents (in which people were killed or wounded) to make the world a better place in their memory.

While spirituality is individual, religion involves subscribing to creeds embraced by a group of people who accept the same beliefs. Both have played a part in the history of military personnel dealing with their internal conflict. Moral theology developed the "just war" theory, determining if a nation's war making is just. Just war is based on the conditions established by Augustine and Aquinas. Augustine provided the foundation for Just War theory. Aquinas then codified Augustine's reflections into the criteria currently used today. These include: *jus ad bellum*—the right to go to war; *jus in bello*—right conduct in war; and *jus post bellum*—compensatory claims after the war (Biggar, 2013; Mattox, 2006). In addition to the resolution of disturbing memories with EMDR therapy, there are spiritual aspects beyond the psychological trauma, which include spiritual and social aspects of life for persons.

Rites of transition, homecoming, and cleansing have been important aspects of many cultures. The ancient Hebrews considered the shedding of blood a source of contamination. A 7-day period of segregation outside the camp was required for warriors returning from battle. This process was required for both the warriors and their clothes (Kelle, 2014). During the ninth century, it was stipulated that, even when a person is blameless in killing in combat, they must nonetheless seek purification; the individual is required to stay away from the church for 1 or 2 weeks, and abstain from meat and drink during that time (Verkamp, 2006). During medieval times, a ritualistic penance was typically imposed on the warriors as a means of helping them reintegrate into their home surroundings. The process was viewed as spiritual healing.

Ceremonial rites of passage have been recognized as important elements for the reintegration of veterans back into a community (Tick, 2005,

---

**BOX 8.3 Moral Theology (Augustine/Aquinas)**

*jus ad bellum—right to go to war*

*jus in bello—right conduct in war*

*jus post bellum—recompense*

**Personally: forgiveness, absolution, making amends**

2014). Junger (2016), while writing "Tribe" reports, noted that recovery from war is heavily influenced by the society to which the servicemember returns. Homecoming and belonging influence the mental health of warriors. These expressions of personal spirituality provide opportunities for transitions such as confession, absolution, forgiveness, and making amends. Purcell and colleagues addressed the role of forgiveness in healing (Purcell, Griffin, Burkman, & Maguen, 2018). Forgiveness has been a key ingredient in resolving moral wounds for centuries and is often administered by religious leaders. Beyond the scope of individual servicemembers seeking forgiveness, community-wide programs, such as the work of Anglican and Catholic leaders in Northern Ireland, have demonstrated the power of communities when forgiveness and remembering are encouraged (Farren & Miller, 2017) among persons who survived the Troubles of Northern Ireland. The ability to understand and apply the forgiveness process is important in addressing the broad concept of moral injury and elements of the grieving process.

Moral injury is more than a mental health treatment issue; neither is it solely a spiritual problem. Effective treatment calls for effective trauma-resolution therapy such as EMDR therapy as well as social acceptance into health communities where veterans can give and receive validation. EMDR therapy allows members to become free to participate in a broader community where social interaction validates their worth in the community and allows for the development of spirituality including acceptance, forgiveness, and making amends, all enhancing the client's posttraumatic growth.

## HEALTHY RESOLUTION OF MORAL INJURY

Moral injury is an evolving construct. It is not a mental health disorder, but a condition that can rob the client of meaning and purpose in life. These are not categorical measures that determine a person has moral injury; rather, the existing measures are comparative measures based on symptoms. All three disciplines discussed here define moral injury. Mental health treatments such as EMDR therapy are effective in resolving the psychological trauma of moral injury. When spiritual concerns related to moral injury are recognized, it is important the therapist maintain awareness of the client's spiritual needs and encourage them to pursue spiritual direction in order to address issues such as relational acceptance, forgiveness, and making amends on the horizontal and vertical relationships in accordance with their faith.

## EMDR TREATMENT PROCESS OF MORAL INJURY

1.  Complete Phase 1 history-taking to include target memory treatment plan.

2. If strong moral injury incidents are identified, assess the strength of inhibitions for treatment. If none are identified, or they are weak, process the memories as level I suitable for spontaneous processing with EMDR therapy.
3. If strong moral injury memories are inhibiting processing, determine level and treat the strongest moral injury memory as early as possible.
    a. Treat level II moral injury with blocking beliefs and use appropriate CIs.
    b. Treat level III moral injury target memories addressing any complex PTSD issues with dissociation. If strong avoidance, consider splitting the memory into (a) components that can be spontaneously processed; and (b) treat components with the most challenging parts last.
4. Recognize the social and spiritual needs of the client beyond the mental health wounds and encourage the client to resolve his or her social and spiritual needs within their frame of reference.

## CONCLUSION

During this chapter, we have discussed the impact of shame, guilt, and moral injury in the lives of military personnel, our clients. We recognize the term "moral injury" as a recent description for a condition that is as old as humanity when a person feels shame or guilt over the violation of their personal values. The term has its origin in moral philosophy dating to the 1700s. Moral injury has philosophical, spiritual, and psychological components. We conclude by recognizing EMDR therapy is effective in treating moral injury by recognizing the levels of clinical complexity and addressing them accordingly. Use of CIs in addressing blocking beliefs is important. More entrenched shame and guilt, based in childhood, need more extensive attention during the treatment of childhood issues of blame and responsibility. We need more research demonstrating the efficacy of EMDR therapy in treating moral injury as a distinct condition apart from stress-related disorders.

### DISCUSSION POINTS

1. Is the author correct, from your experience, that persons with moral injury—no PTSD diagnosis—tend not to seek mental health treatment for their moral injury?
2. What EMDR application is effective in treating blocking beliefs?
3. When should moral injury be treated in the target sequence treatment plan?

4. What discipline first coined the term "moral injury"? What century?
5. What definition of moral injury do you prefer?
6. Is the term "moral injury" synonymous with shame/guilt? Explain.

## REFERENCES

American Psychiatric Association. (2013). *Diagnostic and statistical manual of mental disorders* (5th ed.). Washington, DC: American Psychiatric Publishing.

Berstein, J. (2005). Suffering injustice: Misrecognition as moral injury in critical theory. *International Journal of Philosophical Studies, 13*(3), 303–324. doi:10.1046/j.1440-1819.1998.0520s5S97.x

Biggar, N. (2013). *In defence of war*. Oxford, UK: University of Oxford Press.

Bradshaw, J. (2005). *Healing the shame that binds you*. Deerfield Beach, FL: Health Communications.

Brock, R., & Lettini, G. (2012). *Soul repair: Recovering from moral injury after war*. Boston, MA: Beacon Press.

Farren, P., & Miller, R. (2017). *Forgiveness remembers: A journey into the heart of God*. Watford, UK: The Instant Apostle.

Frankfurt, S. B., Frazier, P. A., & Engdahl, B. (2017). Indirect relations between transgressive acts and general combat exposure and moral injury. *Military Medicine, 182*(11), e1950–e1956. doi:10.7205/MILMED-D-17-00062

Garrett, A. (2018). Joseph Butler's moral philosophy. *Stanford Encyclopedia of Philosophy*. Retrieved from https://plato.stanford.edu/entries/butler-moral

Griffin, B., Purcell, N., Burkman, K., Litz, B., Bryan, C., Schmitz, M., . . . Maguen, S. (2019). Moral injury: An integrative review. *Journal of Traumatic Stress, 32*, 350–362. doi:10.1002/jts.22362

Hampton, H. (1991). A new theory of retribution. In R. Frey & C. Morris (Eds.), *Liability and responsibility: Essays in law and morals* (pp. 377–414). New York, NY: Cambridge University Press.

Hurley, E. (2018). Effective treatment of veterans with PTSD: Comparison between intensive daily and weekly EMDR approaches. *Frontiers in Psychology, 9*, 1458. doi:10.3389/fpsyg.2018.01458

Junger, S. (2016). *Tribe: On homecoming and belonging*. New York: Hachette Book Group.

Khan, A., Li, Y., Dinh, J., Donalson, R., Hebenstreit, C., & Maguen, S. (2019). Examining the impact of different types of military trauma on suicidality in women veterans. *Psychiatry Research, 274*, 7–11. doi:10.1016/j.psychres.2019.02.025

Kelle, B. (2014). Postwar rituals of return and reintegration. In B. Kelle, R. Ames, & J. Wright (Eds.), *Warfare, ritual, and symbol in biblical and modern contexts* (pp. 205–242). Atlanta, GA: Society of Biblical Literature.

Koenig, H. G., Youssef, N. A., & Pearce, M. (2019). Assessment of moral injury in veterans and active duty military personnel with PTSD: A review. *Frontiers in psychiatry, 10*, 443. https://doi.org/10.3389/fpsyt.2019.00443

Kubany, E. (1994). A cognitive model of guilt typology in combat related PTSD. *Journal of Traumatic Stress, 7*, 3–19. doi:10.1007/BF02111908

Kubany, E. (1996). Development and validation of the Trauma-Related Guilt Inventory (TRGI). *Psychological Assessment*, *8*(4), 428–444. doi:10.1037/1040-3590.8.4.428

Lewis, H. (1971). *Shame and guilt in neurosis*. Madison, CT: International Universities Press.

Lewis, H. (1988). The role of shame in symptom formation. In M. Clynes & J. Panksepp (Eds.), *Emotions and psychopathology* (pp. 95–106). New York, NY: Springer.

Litz, B. T., Stein, N., Delaney, E., Lebowitz, L., Nash, W. P., Silva, C., & Maguen, S. (2009). Moral injury and moral repair in war veterans: A preliminary model and intervention strategy. *Clinical Psychology Review*, *29*, 695–706. doi:10.1016/j.cpr.2009.07.003

Maguen, S., & Litz, B. (2019). *Moral injury*. Retrieved from https://www.ptsd.va.gov/professional/treat/cooccurring/moral_injury.asp

Mattox, J. (2006). *Saint Augustine and the theory of Just War*. New York: Continuum Press.

Murphy, J., & Hampton, J. (1988). *Forgiveness and mercy*. New York, NY: Cambridge University Press.

Nash, W., Carper, T., Mills, M. A., Teras, A., Goldsmith, A., & Litz, B. (2013). Psychometric evaluation of the moral injury events scale. *Military Medicine*, *178*(6), 646–653. doi:10.7205/MILMED-D-13-00017

Nash, W., & Marino, C. (2006). Competing and complementary models of combat stress injury. In W. Nash & C. Marino (Eds.), *Combat stress injury: Theory research, and management* (pp. 65–96). New York, NY: Routledge.

Purcell, N., Griffin, B., Burkman, K., & Maguen, S. (2018). "Opening a door to a new life": The role of forgiveness in healing from moral injury. *Frontiers in Psychiatry*, *9*, 1–7. doi:10.3389/psyt.2018.99498

Purcell, N., Koenig, C., Bosch, J., & Maguen, S. (2016). Veterans' perspectives on the psychosocial impact of killing in war. *The Counseling Psychologist*, *44*, 1–38. doi:10.1177/0011000016666156

Seim, R. (2019). *Different paths can lead to moral injury following military trauma* [Blog post]. Retrieved from https://www.blogs.va.gov/VAntage/57448/different-paths-can-lead-to-moral-injury-following-military-trauma

Shapiro, F. (2018). *Eye movement desensitization and reprocessing (EMDR) therapy: Basic principles, protocols, and procedures* (3rd ed.). New York, NY: Guilford Press.

Shay, J. (1994). *Achilles in Vietnam: Combat trauma*. New York, NY: Scribner.

Shay, J. (2002). *Odysseus in America: Combat trauma and the trials of homecoming*. New York, NY: Scribner.

Shay, J. (2011). Casualties. *Daedalus*, *140*(3), 179–188. doi:10.1162/daed_a_00107

Silver, S., & Rogers, S. (2002). *Light in the heart of darkness: EMDR and the treatment of war and terrorism survivors*. New York, NY: W.W. Norton.

Tangney, J., & Dearing, R. (2002). *Shame and guilt (emotions and social behavior)*. New York, NY: Guilford Press.

Tick, E. (2005). *War and the soul: Healing our nation's veterans from posttraumatic stress disorder*. Wheaton, IL: Quest Book.

Tick, E. (2014). *Warrior's return: Restoring the soul after war*. Boulder, CO: True Sounds.

Tripp, J., McDevitt-Murphy, M., & Henschel, A. (2016). Firing a weapon and killing in combat are associated with suicidal ideation in OEF/OIF veterans. *Psychological Trauma: Theory, Research, Practice, and Policy, 8*(5), 626–633. doi:10.1037/tra0000085.633

Verkamp, B. (2006). *The moral treatment of returning warriors in early medieval and modern times.* Scranton, PA: University of Scranton Press.

# 9

# EMDR Therapy and Military Sexual Trauma

## Introduction

This chapter is designed to familiarize the reader with military sexual trauma (MST), as well as its definition, assessment, and procedures in addressing the trauma by the active military and the Department of Veterans Affairs (DVA) agencies. Distinctions between restricted and unrestricted reporting are noted along with MST risk factors among populations. Treatment options, based on the client's goals, are discussed.

## Learning Objectives

- Define military sexual trauma (MST).
- Identify the roles of the U.S. military and the Department of Veterans Affairs in identifying and intervening with survivors of MST.
- Describe the differences between restricted and unrestricted reporting.
- Identify clinical issues in treating MST with EMDR therapy.

## EMDR THERAPY AND MST

This clinical guide discusses the use of EMDR therapy in the treatment of MST. It is designed as a resource for clinicians who treat active duty servicemembers, those clinicians within the Department of Veterans

Affairs (DVA/VA) clinical teams, and therapists in private practice who treat military and veteran personnel. An overview of MST within the military and veteran populations is provided along with the application of EMDR therapy in the treatment of MST.

MST is a term used by the branches of the U.S. military and the DVA/VA to refer to experiences of sexual assault or the repeated threatening of sexual harassment made to persons while serving within the military. Occurrences of these wounds within the military and VA are monitored by the U.S. Congress, which adopted a "zero tolerance" in 2013 (Vanden Brook, 2019). Each branch of the military annually reports the number of occurrences while providing education, support, and intervention through established sexual assault prevention and response offices.

Reasons to consider EMDR therapy in the treatment of MST include:

- It is an accelerated treatment process. Research shows single-incident trauma can be resolved in three to six sessions.
- EMDR therapy requires limited disclosure of details regarding the disturbing incident.
- No homework is required.
- The client maintains control of the treatment process. They maintain a stop signal should they need to stop and self-regulate cue words to enhance self-regulation.
- EMDR therapy requires the client to focus on the disturbing memory approximately 30 seconds at a time.
- EMDR treatment diminishes the level of disturbance through the treatment as the brain spontaneously resolves the disturbance rather than intentionally maintaining the high levels of disturbance.

## THE MILITARY AND VA RESPONSES TO MST

### ACTIVE DUTY MILITARY AND MST

The Deployment Risk and Resilience Inventory (DRRI) is a self-report measure designed to identify the risk and protective factors military personnel experience before, during, and after deployment (King, King, & Vogt, 2003). A sexual harassment scale is included in the measure as a means of identifying any sexual harassment or sexual assault the servicemember may have experienced. Legal processing of MST charges for active duty personnel is outlined by the Uniform Code of Military Justice (UCMJ). The UCMJ is implemented through orders of the president of the United States codified in Title 10 of the United States Code. Those orders form the *Manual for Courts-Martial* (MCM), which explains the purpose of military law as existing to "promote justice, to assist in maintaining good order and discipline in the armed forces, to promote efficiency and effectiveness in the military establishment, and thereby to strengthen the national security of the United States" (U.S. Army, 2014). The UCMJ defines sexual assault classification under Articles 120 and 125. Guidance is provided for the appropriate response when a MST report is filed accusing a servicemember of a sexual assault offense. Once a report is filed, an investigation and adjudication of the offense follows within the military command. Investigators from either the U.S. Army Criminal Investigation Command, the Naval Criminal Investigative Service (NCIS), or the Air Force Office of Special Investigations normally pursue the investigation. Investigators present their findings to the commanding officer of the accused for disposition (Department of Defense & Department of Veterans Affairs, 2013). Studies found 5% to 6% of active duty women have experienced military sexual assault with approximately 78% experiencing military sexual harassment. These numbers significantly increase among the veteran population with 23% of women reporting military sexual assault in a national survey with 55% of veteran females reporting sexual harassment. The reported MST incidents occurred while the women were serving on active duty (Department of Defense & Department of Veterans Affairs, 2013).

## Department of Veterans Affairs and MST

Any veteran who believes they have experienced MST can report an incident to any VA facility including medical facilities, Vet Centers, or Veterans Benefit Office for counseling and treatment. The VA clinician does not need to determine the validity of the claim, since the veteran's statement is sufficient to begin the process. A VA-licensed healthcare provider is tasked with determining if the veteran's physical or mental health problems are the result of such trauma and that the incident occurred while the veteran was on active duty. MST counseling is available regardless of whether a MST claim is lodged within the VA system.

Historically, there has been a steady decline in the number of reported MST between 2006 and 2016 when the trend was reversed with a marked 38% increase during a 2-year period (2016–2018). The statistics are based on screenings of all veterans who seek care through the VA system. Each veteran is asked; (a) "Did you receive uninvited and unwanted sexual attention, such as touching, cornering, pressure for sexual favors, or verbal remarks?" and (b) "Did someone ever use force or threaten to use force to have sexual contact with you against your will?" (Maguen, Cohen, Bosch, Kimerling, & Seal, 2012). These questions reflect one of the VA's mandated missions, which include identifying veterans who have suffered from MST. MST is defined by federal law (Department of Veterans Affairs, 2015; Legal Information Institute, n.d.). The MST, as a category, includes both the psychological wound of sexual harassment and the physical and psychological wounds of physical assault when one person imposes their power and will on another person. As a "psychological trauma, which in the judgment of a VA mental health professional, [MST] resulted from a physical assault of a sexual nature, battery of a sexual nature, or sexual harassment which occurred while the [service member] was serving on active duty, active duty for training, or inactive duty training" (terDepartment of Veterans Affairs, 2015, p. 1).

## ACCOUNTABLE AGENCIES

The United States Congress requires the Department of Defense (DoD) to provide an annual report on sexual assaults involving the U.S. military personnel. The DoD in the 2012 *Department of Defense Annual Report on Sexual Assault in the Military* (Department of Defense, 2013) suggests less than 15% of MST victims report the incident to their military command. Assessment and methodological differences in data collection provide varying data results. It is estimated that between 9.5% and 33% of females report experiences of sexual trauma (Kintzle et al., 2015).

Information is gathered from the DVA's national screening program, which allows for every veteran seen in the VA system to be screened for MST. The screening revealed that nearly 1 in 4 women and 1 in 100 male veterans reported experiencing MST when screened by a VA provider (Department of Veterans Affairs, 2015). The figures represent a percentage of the total number since, according to the Congressional Research Service (Bagalman, 2014), only 42% of veterans are enrolled in the VA healthcare system. It is anticipated that a significant number of MST wounded decide to suffer in silence rather than going through the difficult, awkward process of an investigation and legal proceedings.

Studies from the National Health Study for a New Generation of U.S. Veterans (Barth et al., 2016) were conducted within the VA. The 2013–2014 study reported a prevalence of 41% women and 4% men acknowledged being survivors of MST. An increased risk for MST was reported by veterans in combat during deployment.

Other military forces report MST difficulties within their ranks. Canadian armed forces define MST as "unwanted sexual touching, sexual attacks and sexual activity to which the victim is unable to consent" (Galloway, 2016, para. 8). Unwanted touching was, by far, the most common complaint among Canadian respondents. More than 27% of military women reported being sexually assaulted at least once during their military careers (Galloway, 2016). In the United Kingdom, there is a reported rise in Ministry of Defence sexual offense investigations. Recent publications have raised questions regarding the appropriate recording of sexual harassment and assaults among the military forces in the United Kingdom (The Conversation, 2017).

## REPORTING

Each branch of the U.S. military has military sexual assault response programs established. This begins with the DoD's Sexual Assault and Prevention Response (SARP), and filters through each branch of the military. The U.S. Air Force, U.S. Navy, and U.S. Marines base their sexual assault and prevention programs similar to the DoD's SARP. The Army's program is known as SHARP (Sexual Harassment Assault Response Prevention). Other programs include the U.S. Coast Guard's Sexual Assault Prevention Response & Recovery (SAPRR) Program.

Therapists who treat active duty clients will hear references to two different categories of reporting the MST incident. Each category allows the sexual violation to be handled differently by the military command.

*Restricted reporting* provides a means for the sexual assault victim to report an assault incident without activating an official investigation. The restricted report does not personally identify the victim but does provide access to appropriate care, advocacy, support, and treatment. When a report is made, a victim advocate is assigned. The response coordinator and VA meet with the victim. Within 24 hours of receiving a Restricted Report, the sexual assault response coordinator (SARC) notifies the appropriate command. This type of report is designed to protect the identity of the victim, provide appropriate treatment and support, and provide information to the command for preventive measures, training, and education.

*Unrestricted reporting* includes any reporting of a sexual assault made through reporting channels such as the victim's chain of command, military, or civilians law enforcement or the military's special investigation offices, the sexual assault coordinator, or healthcare providers when the report is provided as unrestricted.

Chaplains, as staff officers who serve on the commander's staff, have privileged communication status. They are a source of pastoral guidance and support. Information provided to chaplains is considered privileged communication; it is not considered a Restricted Report under the DoD policy.

## THE MST CLIENT

MST is a traumatic experience that can impact the person's total sense of self, both physically and psychologically. It is a violation of the individual, including a violation of their personal space, physical being, emotional security, and self-efficacy, as well as power and control of one's life and body. It takes away a person's sense of being safe in their own body. A single-incident sexual assault can leave a person feeling vulnerable, robbed of their sense of identity, often with a sense of embarrassment and shame. More chronic sexual assault experiences (ranging from childhood to the military) can leave the client feeling life is out-of-control with limited models of healthy decision-making.

While the treatment of MST can be approached similar to treating memories of other disturbing events, the therapist needs to listen and learn from the client the unique nuances of how the assault has impacted the servicemember or veteran. What has changed since the episode? How does the client view themselves now? What do they need in order to feel secure? What are the symptoms associated with the assault or harassment? Have there been other incidents in the client's life? Like other adverse life experiences, MST can be treated effectively with EMDR therapy using similar protocols as those used in treating other disturbing experiences. EMDR therapy resolves the emotional reactivity with accompanying trigger responses connected with the memory. The therapy can also empower the client to take charge of their life again as the client's positive memory networks are enhanced.

## RISK FACTORS

Risk factors for experiencing MST (Sadler, Booth, Cook, & Doebbeling, 2003) include:

- Persons younger in age
- Enlisted rank
- Have not completed college

Sadler and colleagues found the likelihood of the servicemember being raped almost doubled when they were 19 years of age or younger and had experienced childhood physical or sexual abuse or rape prior to entering military service.

Much of the research literature focuses on data collected from female veterans. Most male sexual assault victims do not formally report sexual assaults. Men tend to cope with their traumatic experiences in isolation. Among all the health problems, male sexual assault has been underreported and misunderstood (Tewksbury, 2007). Men who have experienced MST tend to have a greater range of interpersonal difficulties, affect dysregulation problems, and negative self-concept including issues around masculinity and sexual orientation identity (Elder, Domino, Rentz, & Mata-Galan, 2017). Skinner and colleagues (2000) discovered women who were sexually assaulted in the military were significantly younger than veterans who did not report sexual assault. The younger age group of assaulted veterans reported their motivation for entering the military at a young age was based on a desire to escape dysfunctional family environments (Schultz, Bell, Naugle, & Polusny, 2006). Veterans with a history of childhood sexual abuse were found to be more frequently abused by a parental figure with longer durations of sexual abuse. They reported experiences of more severe adult sexual abuse than civilians. Sadler's (Sadler et al., 2003) research found 49% of respondents reported their motivation to escape from their home environment was a significant factor in affiliating with the military. Sadler and colleagues' (2003) study of 520 women veterans found 26% had been raped prior to entry into the military.

In contrast, research among the nonmilitary general population found 22% of women and 3.8% of men reported adult sexual abuse. Risk factors for sexual assault and harassment in the civilian population included the person being younger in age, being female, divorced, history of childhood sexual abuse, and having experienced physical assault in adulthood (Elliott, Mok, & Briere, 2004). Both veteran and nonveteran populations are similar in identifying age and history of childhood sexual abuse as being contributors to the risk for adulthood sexual abuse.

## MST AND THE BETRAYAL OF TRUST

Military personnel who have been assaulted frequently struggle with a sense of betrayal. Since the perpetrators are frequently persons known by the victim, there is a betrayal of trust. The betrayal is exacerbated when the perpetrator is a member of the military, especially someone with a leadership position within the survivor's unit. Freyd (1996) and colleagues (Smith & Freyd, 2014) suggested that abuse that happened within close relationships is more distressing due to the violation of trust required in the relationship. If there has been a history of betrayal trauma experienced earlier in the client's life, a developmental theme with a sensitivity toward vulnerability and safety can develop.

Betrayal within the military is a form of institutional betrayal. Institutional betrayal occurs when an individual becomes the recipient of harm caused by an institution upon which the individual trusts and depends for safety and well-being (Smith & Freyd, 2014, p. 578). Studies of institutional betrayal, such as those within the military, found women who experienced MST displayed more health difficulties when compared with a similar population in the civilian sector (Smith & Freyd, 2014). Freyd (1996) lists the symptoms of betrayal trauma as being similar to other traumatic experiences: anxiety, hypervigilance, feeling overwhelmed, withdrawal and isolation, concentration difficulties, emotional dysregulation, flashbacks, numbness, detachment, disturbances in sleep and appetite, somatic symptoms including tremors, and headaches.

## CONSEQUENCES OF MST

Childhood sexual abuse can negatively impact the developmental process in a child. Emotional regulation, coping abilities, and cognitive style can be impaired with lasting consequences (Wolfe, 2007). Consequences from childhood abuse include depression, low self-esteem, fear, nervousness and anxiety, dissociative responses, guilt, denial, confusion, isolation, grief, somatic problems, and symptoms of PTSD. Trickett, Noll, and Putnam (2011) found that sexual abuse, particularly when more invasive, is associated with a sexualized behavior and sexual risk taking, eating disorders, self-harm, drug and alcohol abuse, and risks of revictimization (Trickett et al., 2011). Psychologically, MST is a trauma that can produce strong emotional responses, numbness, sleep difficulties, memory problems, abuse/dependency on alcohol or other drugs, being easily triggered, feelings of vulnerability, relational difficulties, and physical health problems. Studies by Maguen and colleagues report persons with a history of MST are more likely to have at least three co-occurring mental health diagnoses (Maguen et al., 2012).

Persons who have experienced MST were found to have increased vulnerability to PTSD. A VA study completed by Suris and colleagues (Suris, Lind, Kashner, Borman, & Petty, 2004) found female veterans with a history of MST were nine times more likely to have PTSD when compared with a population group with no sexual assault histories. Fe-

## TABLE 9.1 Consequences of Childhood Sexual Abuse Exhibited in Adulthood

| PSYCHOLOGICAL CONSEQUENCES | RELATIONAL CONSEQUENCES |
|---|---|
| ■ Depression | ■ Less trusting of others |
| ■ Anxiety | ■ Commitment issues |
| ■ Dissociation | ■ Relational conflict |
| ■ Posttraumatic stress disorder symptoms | ■ Isolation |
| ■ Self-mutilation | ■ Fear of intimacy |
| ■ Suicidal thoughts, attempted or complete | ■ Relationship dissatisfaction |
| ■ Drug and alcohol abuse | ■ Marital conflict |
| ■ Don't trust own judgment | ■ Spousal violence |
| ■ Poor coping skills | ■ High-risk sexual behavior |
|  | ■ Absence of relational model/template |

Sources: Children's Bureau. (2019). *Long-term consequences of child abuse and neglect.* Retrieved from https://www.childwelfare.gov/pubPDFs/long_term_consequences. pdf#page=3&view=Psychological consequences; Cure Cervical Dystonia. (n.d.). *Child abuse: Potential adverse long-term effects.* Retrieved from http://curecervicaldystonia.com/wp-content/uploads/2012/05/ChildAbuseLongtermEffects2.png; Ferguson, D., Boden, J., & Horwood, I. (2008). Exposure to childhood sexual and physical abuse and adjustment in early adulthood. *Child Abuse and Neglect, 32,* 607–619. doi:10.1016/j.chiabu.2006.12.018; Liang, B., Williams, L., & Siegel, J. (2006). Relational outcomes of childhood sexual trauma in female survivors: A longitudinal study. *Journal of Interpersonal Violence, 21*(1), 21–47. doi:10.1177/0886260505281603

male veterans with a history of childhood sexual assault (CSA) were seven times more likely to have PTSD. Female veterans with PTSD and a history of MST were more likely to present with depression, anxiety, and eating disorders. In Maguen' s study (2012) with Operation Iraqi Freedom (OIF)/Operation Enduring Freedom (OEF) veterans, females with PTSD and MST were significantly more likely to present with comorbid depression, substance use, anxiety, alcohol use, and eating disorders.

Research that studied 18 male MST survivors (Elder et al., 2017) found consequences following sexual assault include: (a) fear of abandonment by a loved one if the person learned about the occurrence of a MST; (b) substance use/abuse; (c) fear of interpersonal violence, believing other people might attack them; (d) conduct problems due to lack of concentration and interpersonal problems; (e) insecurity regarding sexual performance; (f) anger management; and (g) posttraumatic growth.

## EFFECTIVE APPLICATION OF EMDR THERAPY IN THE TREATMENT OF MST

MST clients exhibit various clinical presentations. Some clients are experiencing adverse symptoms related to a recent assault. These clients are often seeking relief from their immediate psychological pain. Other clients have lived with their MST experiences for years and arrive at your office presenting other psychological concerns ranging from anxiety, depression, PTSD, and duty performance to relationship difficulties. They have developed coping mechanisms around the sexual violations, believing they have learned to live with the wounds. Some clients demonstrate PTSD symptoms and disclose MST during their History-Taking process. They frequently express their reason for seeking treatment by describing the symptoms they want to eliminate, such as not being so "jumpy" (hypervigilant), stopping flashbacks, or they want the anxiety/panic attacks to stop. The treatment plan for a MST survivor may vary from being a single-incident or multiple-incident presentation. Multiple target events may include several MST-related memories as well as early childhood sexual abuse being a touchstone event.

## EMDR THERAPY: AN EIGHT PHASE—THREE-PRONG APPROACH

EMDR therapists provide a client-centered treatment approach (Hurley, 2016). It is important that survivors of sexual harassment and assault feel secure in your office. It can be helpful to ask the client, "What do you need in order to feel secure in this room?" Monitoring the client's clinical presentation includes observing the client's walk as they enter the treatment room. Observe their military bearing, how they physically carry their body, how they walk in the hallway. On entrance

### TABLE 9.2 Examples of Target Events in Treatment Plans

| PTSD-FOCUSED TREATMENT | MST-FOCUSED TREATMENT |
| --- | --- |
| 1. Parents divorced when client was 7 years of age | 1. Childhood sexual abuse |
| 2. Best friend killed in a vehicle accident during high school | 2. MST while ROTC cadet |
| | 3. Abusive marriage with sexual abuse |
| 3. Sexual assault during high school | 4. First marriage abusive/used (divorced) |
| 4. Assigned to the U.S. embassy that was bombed | 5. MST in first military assignment |
| | 6. Alcohol dependency |
| 5. In OIF military convoy that hit IED | 7. Raped at apartment by military servicemember neighbor |
| 6. Divorce after returning home | |

IED, improvised explosive device; MST, military sexual trauma; OIF, Operation Iraqi Freedom; PTSD, posttraumatic stress disorder; ROTC, Reserve Officer Training Corps.

into the treatment room, I monitor how the client claims their space, where they sit, and if their body posture is open or closed. How open is the client in disclosing information regarding what brings them to your office? Is the client positioned to monitor the doorway entrance? Do they continually glance at any windows in the room? Whether I am treating a single-incident MST or a life of extensive sexual abuse, I want to know as much about the client's history as possible within a reasonable amount of time. It is important to allow the client to establish the pace for disclosing their history, including MST. Be mindful that persons who internalize or "keep things to themselves" can easily feel overwhelmed or vulnerable at the end of the session if they disclose too much information too soon. They have avoided facing the uncomfortable information due, in part, to embarrassment and other shame-related symptoms. Now that they are finally talking about it, they may have an attitude of "let me get through this as quickly as possible," which promotes *"spilling their guts"* along with a raw feeling of vulnerability at the end of the session. Pacing the client's disclosing of information is important, with the pace determined by the client's sense of safety and security in your office. Remind the client that EMDR therapy is different; you only need as much information as they feel the need to share in order to provide effective treatment.

## EMDR THERAPY'S ADAPTIVE INFORMATION PROCESSING APPROACH

EMDR therapy's theoretical model, the Adaptive Information Processing (AIP) model, provides the lens through which the therapist views the clinical issues the client presents. Basic tenets of the AIP model include: (a) memory networks are the basis of pathology and health; (b) pathology is the result of inadequately processed, maladaptively stored memories; (c) the past is present; (d) memory networks are associated by similarities (similar emotions, cognitions, sensations, participants, etc.); (e) EMDR therapy provides the accessing of disturbing memories, stimulates the targeted memory, and provides for adaptive resolution of the disturbing memory (Shapiro, 2018).

The three-prong EMDR approach provides for the treatment plan to include treating memories of past events, present triggers, and the anticipated future (future template). The treatment plan is collaboratively developed with the client. A single-incident claim focuses on the solo event while incorporating the EMDR eight-phase approach: (a) History-Taking; (b) Preparation; (c) Assessment; (d) Desensitization; (e) Installation; (f) Body Scan; (g) Closing; and (h) Reevaluation (Luber, 2009). The three-prong approach includes treating any current triggers and future template. While treating a single incident, an EMDR therapist is wise to check to see if there are other incidents that might be activated during the reprocessing of the incident. Using Direct Questioning, Floatback, and Affect Scan can be helpful to identify memory networks.

## MAPPING THE TARGETS FOR TREATMENT

The use of the Direct Question, Floatback, and Affect Scan assists in identifying memories that are associated with the presenting target memory. These techniques used during the history-taking phase and later during the processing phases (when the processing becomes blocked) assist in revealing the connectedness of memory networks. These memory networks are connected with similar memory components in other networks. Identifying these memory incidents allows for a mapping of the interactive connections among memory networks that provide you, the therapist, with a clinical map of the unresolved memories that are likely to be activated during the reprocessing of other memories. Similarities tend to attract during reprocessing.

The clinical goal is to assist the client in processing through these interactive memory networks as they achieve adaptive resolution. Similar unprocessed memories, when activated, interact with one another. For example, beginning the treatment process with a recent sexual assault may activate the client's recall of an untreated childhood sexual abuse incident with all that earlier memory's associated components and level of disturbance. An advantage of beginning treatment with the earliest memories first allows for the processing of those memories while the process taps into more recent memories for reprocessing. Those earliest memories contain the initial distortions that frame perspective in later experiences. Clearing the earlier distortions assists in the development of healthy perspective as other memory networks are reprocessed. Sometimes a client only wishes to address the recent MST incident, stating they have learned to live with the earlier abuse. While I would prefer to include earlier sexual assaults in the total treatment plan, EMDR therapy is client centered. If the client's treatment goal is to only address the recent MST incident, the therapist can control for the accessing of other memories by taking the client back to the target following each set of bilateral stimulation (BLS), that is, "*When you go back to that original incident, what do you get now?*" Or, taking the client back to the targeted memory every three or four sets of BLS allows some accessing of other memory networks while providing some restriction in the spontaneous accessing of memory networks. For clients more severely dysregulated, who become emotionally overwhelmed, using the EMD procedure confines the access of other memories, helping the client avoid being overwhelmed by allowing desensitization with little or no reprocessing of other memory networks.

The EMD protocol, first used in Shapiro's early research (EMDR Institute, 2017; Hensley, 2016), limits access to associated memory networks, thus reducing the symptomatic reactions to the designated target memory. The approach provides desensitization with minimal reprocessing benefits. Emotional reactivity is reduced since the client is repetitively returned to the target memory. Limiting access to other memory networks in EMD inhibits the reprocessing component as the reactivity to the targeted event is desensitized while accessing other memories is contained.

In contrast, the standard EMDR therapy protocol allows access to the full range of associated memory networks that may be activated during the processing. This full processing with the standard EMDR approach provides the treatment to include whatever associated memories may surface during reprocessing. Both single incidents and multiple target events require the therapist to establish a three-prong approach with a treatment plan for treating past, present, and anticipated future events.

Persons with early childhood abuse frequently have difficulty recalling memories of events that occurred during periods when the abuse occurred. An amnestic block occurs when highly charged abuse memories are not accessible. As EMDR therapy reprocesses the disturbing memories, the survivor is frequently able to access additional positive memories, allowing the client's self-concept to spontaneously improve.

Processing memories associated with sexual assault can be particularly intense for the client. It is important the client demonstrates the ability to self-regulate and is reminded they are in control of the process. During reprocessing (Phases 4–6), the client can move from present awareness to the intensity of painful memories rather quickly. Pacing the processing with appropriate stimulation is important. Begin the first sets of BLS at moderate speed with 20 passes and gradually increase the speed and number of passes as the client demonstrates their ability to maintain dual awareness remaining within the window of tolerance. Memories of sexual assault may include somatic components when physical pain was included as components of the memories. Clients sometimes taste semen when an oral assault occurred. It is helpful to remind the client that this is all part of the memory and it will clear out during the processing. Use cognitive interweaves to remind the client that it is a memory, it's over—in the past and they are safe in your office. On occasions when physical abuse was part of the memory, the client may experience the somatic component as the memory is processed. While treating a client whose abuse included being knocked to the floor and kicked, the servicemember began holding her side as she began to double over while seated on my couch during BLS. In order to ensure it was a somatic memory I asked, "Did he hurt you there?" The client responded, "He knocked me down in the floor, and while I was down, he kicked me there." I said, "Go with that!" and continued reprocessing, doing approximately 35 passes in each set. After about 18 minutes, the somatic memory was cleared out. The client achieved a 0 SUD, 7 VOC, and clear body scan. The client thanked me for continuing the process rather than stopping treatment when the somatic sensations became painful.

## EMDR THERAPY AND LEGAL PROCESSES

Clients whose MST involves legal proceedings should understand the nature of memory transmutation during EMDR processing before being treated with EMDR therapy. Specifically, aspects of the memory may change, and the image may fade, blur, or even disappear during reprocessing. Or, the client may view the mental picture more vividly as a result of EMDR reprocessing. While the client will be able to recall the incident and describe its occurrence, the details will be different. There is no way of predicting before treatment how the client will process the memory. Sometimes, when legal processing is anticipated, a deposition can be made beforehand allowing the recording of information followed by treatment. The client's consulting with their legal counsel regarding treatment with EMDR therapy is important when legal proceedings are anticipated.

## EMDR THERAPY PROCESSING WITH LIMITED DISCLOSURE

EMDR therapy can treat an identified target memory while requiring limited information from the client. This approach can be particularly helpful when the client is uncomfortable with disclosing information associated with a MST incident. Some clients appreciate the therapist briefly describing the mechanism of action, informing the client that their job is to recall the event in their mind, the therapist provides BLS, and the client's brain transmutes the memory. This process allows the therapist to treat the memory without knowing the incident, where it happened, or what happened. The client identifies the incident with a term or phrase they decide to use. The identification can be with a number, word, or phrase, something to ensure the client knows the incident they are addressing for processing.

This ability is welcomed among clients who wish to avoid disclosure of details relating to sexual traumas. In using this approach, the therapist introduces Phase 3 Assessment to the client, explaining the process while identifying the two words to use during reprocessing:

> *I am going to ask you seven (7) questions about how the memory of the incident/event is impacting you now. Each question is designed to access a different part of your memory regarding the incident. I don't need a lot of details about what happened, just what you want to share with me in response to my questions. Following the seven (7) questions I will do what we call bilateral stimulation (EM, tactile, auditory), about 30 seconds each time. I will stop and ask you for feedback such as "What do you notice?" or "What do you get now?" I am asking about what is different about the memory. This is not like talk therapy—all I need is a word indicating whether anything about the memory is changing.*
>
> *Let's establish two words, one word means "something about the memory is changing," the other word means "nothing is different from the last time I asked the same question."*
>
> *What words would you like to use—one for change; the other meaning no change?*
>
> *(It can be words like "yes" and "no" or "Yen" or "yang"—"Red" or "Green") What two words would you like to use? Okay. We will use those two words. _____ means "change"; and _____ means "no change."*
>
> *I need as clear feedback as possible. Just observe your experience and report it to me. Whatever you say, I will say "Go with that," which means resume or start up where you left off a minute ago. We will do this for a period of time until thinking about the incident no longer bothers you. Would this be okay that you are over it and it no longer bothers you?*

This approach can be helpful for persons who are hesitant to reveal the details of their sexual assault yet are allowing the reprocessing of disturbing memories.

## SUMMARY

MST can interrupt a person's quality of life permanently unless treated. It often redefines how a person views themself by adding shame to a diminished sense of worth. Effective treatment, such as EMDR therapy, can assist a person in reclaiming their life within a brief period of time. This therapy provides effective treatment while requiring little information from the client. We recognize that associated memory networks can interact in the treatment process, thereby challenging the EMDR therapist to regulate the treatment by using the appropriate EMDR protocol (standard EMDR therapy, restricted processing by adjusting the BLS and returning to target frequently, and EMD). Childhood sexual abuse can add additional complications to adult survivors of MST clinical presentations. As an EMDR therapist, you offer hope and healing to your clients.

## CONCLUSION

The goals of this chapter included identifying and defining MST: What it is as well as the roles the military and VA serve in intervening with the survivors of MST. Distinguishing the difference between restricted and unrestricted reporting is important to understand both for your client and for you as the therapist. EMDR therapy can be very effective in helping people reclaim their lives. Sometimes MST is presented as the primary event for treatment, whereas other times it is presented as one of many events in the person's life that needs resolution. Assessing for earlier abuse history is important in developing a treatment plan. Establishing trust, while recognizing the MST survivor has experienced betrayal among those they trusted, establishes the basis for effective treatment. With EMDR therapy, we offer effective treatment with a sense of security.

### DISCUSSION POINTS

1.  Women tend to report MST more frequently than men. Is the reason because men experience less MST, they simply report it less, or both?
2.  In what ways are the processes to identify MST among active military personnel similar/different than assessing the veteran population for MST?
3.  In what ways is unrestricted reporting different than restricted reporting of MST?
4.  Identify the characteristics associated with MST survivors abused as children.

**5.** How does the concept of "associated memory networks" relate to treating a recent MST when previous incidents have also occurred?
**6.** What legal concerns does your client need to be aware of when their MST is under investigation or legal proceedings?
**7.** Your client has a history of several MST incidents, but only wants to work on the most recent event. What EMDR protocol would you use (EMD, EMDR restricted processing, or EMDR)? Discuss.

## REFERENCES

Bagalman, E. (2014). *The number of veterans that use VA health care services: A fact sheet*. Washington, DC: Congressional Research Service.

Barth, S., Kimerlind, R., Pavao, J., McCutcheon, S., Batten, S., Dursa, E., ... Schneiderman, A. (2016). Military sexual trauma among recent veterans. *American Journal of Preventive Medicine, 50*(1), 77–86. doi:10.1016/j.amepre.2015.06.012

Children's Bureau. (2019). *Long-term consequences of child abuse and neglect*. Retrieved from https://www.childwelfare.gov/pubPDFs/long_term_consequences.pdf#page=3&view=Psychological consequences

The Conversation. (2017). *Sexual harassment is a real problem in the Armed Forces and offences are not being properly recorded*. Retrieved from https://theconversation.com/sexual-harassment-is-a-real-problem-in-the-armed-forces-and-offences-are-not-being-properly-recorded-120619

Cure Cervical Dystonia. (n.d.). *Child abuse: Potential adverse long-term effects*. Retrieved from http://curecervicaldystonia.com/wp-content/uploads/2012/05/ChildAbuseLongtermEffects2.png

Department of Defense. (2013). *Department of Defense annual report on sexual assault in the military: Fiscal year 2012*. Retrieved from https://www.sapr.mil/public/docs/reports/FY12_DoD_SAPRO_Annual_Report_on_Sexual_Assault-VOLUME_TWO.pdf

Department of Defense & Department of Veterans Affairs. (2013). *Complete guide to military sexual assault and trauma (MST): Senate hearings, victim testimony, military justice and investigations, VA study course, and guidelines, harassment and rape*. Washington, DC: U.S. Government Printing Office.

Department of Veterans Affairs. (2015). *Military sexual trauma*. Retrieved from https://www.mentalhealth.va.gov/docs/mst_general_factsheet.pdf

Elder, W., Domino, J., Rentz, T., & Mata-Galan, E. (2017). Conceptual model of male military sexual trauma. *Psychological Trauma: Theory, Research, Practice, and Policy, 9*(S1), 59–66. doi:10.1037/tra0000194

Elliott, D., Mok, D., & Briere, J. (2004). Adult sexual assault: Prevalence, symptomatology, and sex differences in the general population. *Journal of Traumatic Stress, 17*(3), 203–211. doi:10.1023/B:JOTS.0000029263.11104.23

EMDR Institute. (2017). *EMDR Institute basic training course: Weekend 1 of the two part EMDR therapy basic training*. Watsonville, CA: Author.

Ferguson, D., Boden, J., & Horwood, I. (2008). Exposure to childhood sexual and physical abuse and adjustment in early adulthood. *Child Abuse and Neglect, 32*, 607–619. doi:10.1016/j.chiabu.2006.12.018

Freyd, J., Klest, B., & Allard, C. (2005). Betrayal trauma: Relationship to physical health, psychological distress, and a written disclosure invention. *Journal of Trauma and Dissociation, 6*(3), 83–104. doi:10.1300/J229v06n03_04

Galloway, G. (2016). *High levels of sexual assault among Canadian military members: Survey.* Retrieved from https://www.theglobeandmail.com/news/politics/soldiers-almost-twice-as-likely-to-be-sexually-assaulted-statistics-canada-says/article33066760

Hurley, E. (2016). Treating military sexual trauma with EMDR therapy. In L. Katz (Ed.), *Treating military sexual trauma* (pp. 155–173). New York, NY: Springer Publishing Company.

Hensley, B. (2016). *An EMDR therapy primer: From practicum to practice* (2nd Ed.). New York, NY: Springer Publishing.

King, D., King, L., & Vogt, D. (2003). *Manual for the deployment risk and resilience inventory (DRRI): A collection of measures for studying deployment-related experiences of military veterans.* Boston, MA: National Center for PTSD.

Kintzle, S.., Schuyler, A., Ray-Letourneau, D., Ozuna, S., Munch, C., Xintarianos, E., … Castro, C. (2015). Sexual trauma in the military: Exploring PTSD and mental health care utilization in female veterans. *Psychological Services, 12*(4), 394–401. doi:10.1037/ser0000054

Legal Information Institute. (n.d.). *38 U.S. Code § 1720D. Counseling and treatment for sexual trauma.* Retrieved from https://www.law.cornell.edu/uscode/text/38/1720D

Liang, B., Williams, L., & Siegel, J. (2006). Relational outcomes of childhood sexual trauma in female survivors: A longitudinal study. *Journal of Interpersonal Violence, 21*(1), 21–47. doi:10.1177/0886260505281603

Luber, M. (Ed.). (2009). Single traumatic event. In M. Luber (Ed.), *EMDR scripted protocols: Basic and special situations* (pp. 121–132). New York, NY: Springer Publishing Company.

Maguen, S., Cohen, B., Bosch, R., Kimerling, R., & Seal, K. (2012). Gender differences in military sexual trauma and mental health diagnoses among Iraq and Afghanistan veterans with posttraumatic stress disorder. *Women's Health Issues, 22*, e61–e66. doi:10.1016/j.whi.2011.07.010

Sadler, A., Booth, B., Cook, B., & Doebbeling, B. (2003). Factors associated with women's risk of rape in the military environment. *American Journal of Industrial Medicine, 161*, 342–345. doi:10.1002/ajim.10202

Schultz, J., Bell, K., Naugle, A., & Polusny, M. (2006). Child sexual abuse and adulthood sexual assault among military veteran and civilian women. *Military Medicine, 171*(8), 723–728. doi:10.7205/MILMED.171.8.723

Shapiro, F. (2018). *Eye movement desensitization and reprocessing (EMDR) therapy: Basic principles, protocols, and procedures* (3rd ed.). New York, NY: Guilford Press.

Skinner, K., Kressin, N., Frayne, S. Tripp, T., Hankin, C., Miller, D., & Sullivan, L. M. (2000). The prevalence of military sexual assault among female Veterans' Administration outpatients. *Journal of Interpersonal Violence, 15*(3), 291–310. doi:10.1177/088626000015003005

Smith, C., & Freyd, J. (2014). Institutional betrayal. *American Psychologist, 69*(6), 575–587. doi:10.1037/a0037564

Suris, A., Lind, L., Kashner, T., Borman, P., & Petty, F. (2004). Sexual assault in women veterans: An examination of PTSD risk, health care utilization, and cost of care. *Psychosomatic Medicine, 66,* 749–756. doi:10.1097/01 .psy.0000138117.58559.7b

Tewksbury, R. (2007). Effects of sexual assaults on men: Physical, mental and sexual consequences. *International Journal of Men's Health, 6,* 22–35. doi:10.3149/jmh.0601.22

Trickett, P., Noll, J., & Putnam, F. (2011). The impact of sexual abuse on female development: Lessons from a multigenerational, longitudinal research study. *Development and Psychopathology, 23*(2), 453–476. doi:10.1017/ S0954579411000174

U.S. Army. (2014). *Military justice.* Retrieved from https://www.army.mil/ article/128749/military_justice

Vanden Brook, T. (2019). Shanahan calls for reforms as military sexual assaults rise by 38%; highest for young women. *USA Today.* Retrieved from https://www .usatoday.com/story/news/politics/2019/05/02/military-sexual-assaults -climb-2016-2018-pentagon-army-navy-marines-alcohol/3625405002

Wolfe, V. V. (2007). Child sexual abuse. In E. J. Mash & R. A. Barkley (Eds.), *Assessment of childhood disorders* (4th ed., pp. 685–748). New York, NY: Guilford Press.

# 10

# Suicidality in the Treatment of Veterans

## Introduction

Suicide is a major concern in treating military personnel and veterans. Therapists who treat these populations are confronted with suicidality, how to assess for it and recognize the warning signs, what questions to ask, and how to best manage clients who struggle with potential suicide as their reality. Issues discussed in this chapter include theories of suicide, the desensitization to death during combat, the impact of war wounds, the influence of traumatic brain injuries (TBIs), moral injury, and the influence of dissociation on suicidal ideation. The impact of military sexual trauma (MST), unresolved grief, and moral injury can impact a person's will to live or die. Three key questions for assessing suicide are presented. A scripted session of a military client who describes a veteran's experience during a dissociative suicide attempt with subsequent EMDR treatment is presented.

## Learning Objectives

- Identify three key questions for assessing suicide.
- Discuss a theoretical understanding of suicide.
- Identify the roles dissociation, moral injury, and TBI play on suicidal behavior.
- Review the verbatim script of a veteran describing why veterans consider suicide.

# SUICIDALITY AMONG MILITARY AND VETERANS

This chapter is designed to familiarize EMDR therapists with an understanding of suicide among military and veteran populations, as well as its background, warning signs, and prevention. The chapter also details the impact of dissociation, TBI, and moral injury on suicidality. An average of 129 Americans in the general population die of suicide each day (Centers for Disease Control and Prevention, 2019). The number of veteran suicides has maintained a rate of 17 to 22 suicides daily in the United States. The 2019 *National Veteran Suicide Prevention Annual Report* (Department of Veterans Affairs, 2019b) reported the number of veteran suicides exceeded 6,000 a year between 2008 and 2017. An additional 919 suicides of former National Guard and Reserve members who were never activated for deployment occurred in 2017. Previously, between 1999 and 2010, a VA study indicated approximately 22 veterans per day were dying by suicide—that's one veteran committing suicide every 65 minutes. Active duty personnel suicide rates are also concerning. The branches of active duty military, using data collected through 2018, indicated there was a total of 321 deaths including 57 Marines, 58 airmen, 68 sailors, and 138 soldiers (Kime, 2019). In 2012 alone, there were more active duty servicemembers who died by suicide than who were killed in combat (Stewart, 2013).

Building hope by providing effective treatment is essential for our military and veterans. This chapter outlines an effective approach for keeping veterans alive while helping them reclaim a quality of life with EMDR therapy.

## DEFINING SUICIDALITY

### TERMINOLOGY RELATED TO SUICIDALITY

Suicide—an act motivated by the person's intent to die by a lethal means, resulting in a deadly outcome.

Suicide attempt—possess (a) self-initiated, potentially injurious behavior; (b) intention to die; and (c) nonfatal outcome.

Nonlethal attempt—suicidal attempts (intent on dying) resulting in a nonfatal outcome.

Near-lethal attempt—describes the intent of the person to die by a lethal means which, by chance, the person survived.

Self-harm—actions of harm to oneself without the intent to die.

Suicidal risk factors—conditions serving as indicators of causal processes that lead to suicidal outcomes. These include relationship conflict, mental health disorders, physical illness, previous suicide attempt, social isolation, change in employment, change in income, alcohol and other drug abuse, and sleep disturbance.

## UNDERSTANDING SUICIDE

*We don't try to take our lives because we don't feel loved, we want to die to end the pain, knowing our families are taken care of.*

*—Veteran who attempted suicide three times before finding effective treatment with EMDR therapy.*

Suicide is the most extreme form of self-directed violence. French sociologist Emile Durkheim provided a sociological perspective on suicide in his book *On Suicide: A Study in Sociology,* published in 1897. He believed crisis and change (either positive or negative) can be disruptive and thereby increase the suicide rate. Social changes negatively impact social bonds. The lack of social bonds with other people and groups can erode a person's sense of identity, meaning in life, purpose in living, and sense of belonging.

Existing psychological models have been used to understand suicidality from their various psychological perspectives. Those theoretical models provide a lens for studying suicide from psychoanalytical, cognitive, dialectical behavior therapy (DBT), neurobiological, existential/humanistic, genetic, systemic, and evolutionary perspectives.

Other models of suicide were developed specifically for understanding suicide. Blumenthal and Kupfer (1986) proposed that suicide risk factors should be viewed across five domains: biology, psychosocial life events and chronic medical illness, personality traits, family history including genetics, and psychiatric disorders. In this model, the greatest risk for suicide is represented when all five domains overlap. Maris (1991, 2002) conceptualized a suicidal model from a developmental perspective. Suicidal risks are at their greatest when multiple interacting life experiences occur in a person's life course. Shneidman (1998) developed a model around the presence of three simultaneous factors necessary for suicidal behavior: psychache, press, and perturbation. The presence of all three factors represents the strongest and most lethal desire for suicide.

Biological theories suggest suicidal behavior is the result of a biologically based medical condition accompanied by a psychological stressor (Gunn, 2017; Rubenstein, 1986). De Catanzaro's (1991, 1995) evolutionary theory of suicide posited a person is more likely to commit suicide when there is: (a) a dramatically reduced ability to contribute to his or her own inclusive fitness; and (b) a reduced capacity, including poor future health and chronic infirmity, that has the person view themself as a disgrace or failure, has poor prospects for mating, and has perceptions of being a burden on one's genetic kin.

Joiner (2005) published his initial theory on the reason people commit suicide, which he called the interpersonal theory of suicide (IPTS). Joiner identified three factors that seem to identify those persons who are most at risk of killing themselves. These factors are: (a) the feeling of being a burden on loved ones; (b) the sense of isolation; and (c) the learned ability to hurt oneself. Van Orden et al. (2010) proposed fearlessness about death and pain tolerance as requisite for suicidal ideation and suicidal intent. This model perceives the desire to act on suicidal behavior as being based on the simultaneous presence of the interpersonal constructs of "thwarted belongingness" (the belief one does not belong) and "perceived burdensomeness" (the belief one's existence poses a burden to loved ones) with the acquired capacity for suicide (increased capacity for engaging in lethal self-harm). The authors distinguish between the ideation to end one's life and the means to do it. Acquired capacity to commit suicide comprises two components: elevated pain tolerance and lowered fear of death, experiences many veterans confront. Through the lens of the IPTS model, the risk for suicide attempt and death is postulated to be highest in thwarted belongingness and the presence of burdensomeness, along with elevated pain tolerance and fearlessness about death.

The concept of thwarted belongingness, the belief one does not belong, becomes painfully interpreted through basic attachment needs. Unmet attachment needs (thwarted belongingness) are easily viewed through a deficit perspective, which enhances perceived burdensomeness (one's existence is a burden to loved ones). One construct corresponds with the other. Among military personnel and veterans, the strongest sense of belonging is often expressed as the bonding among unit members during combat deployments. Unresolved grief connected to the loss of those relationships accompanied by social isolation exacerbates the thwarted belongingness.

Interpersonal theory views the concept of "perceived burdensomeness" as being actively developed through life circumstances. Loss of meaningful employment, relationship conflict, or physical and mental limitations can create a sense of burdensomeness. These factors provide strong associations with suicide. Many veterans who suffer with physical injuries and mental health problems have a greatly diminished sense of self-efficacy. The accomplishments of military life, with its rank structure, award systems, and challenges to train for the next mission or readiness for promotion, become lost during a major life adjustment, leaving veterans struggling to find meaning and purpose in their life.

The IPTS model has been researched with a number of military studies. Military sexual trauma (MST) survivors participated in a study (Monteith, Bahraini, & Menefee, 2017) evaluating the interpersonal–psychological theory of suicide. Exposure to MST may present an increase in suicidal ideation, vulnerability for posttraumatic stress disorder

(PTSD), and chronic depression (Klingensmith, Tsai, Mota, Southwick, & Pietrzak, 2014). Survivors of MST may be at risk for increasing risky behavior including fearlessness about death, when there is unresolved past abuse, current substance use, and non-suicidal self-injury. Shame-proneness further enhances issues of burdensomeness. The IPTS theory includes fearlessness of death and pain tolerance as requisite for suicidal ideation to become suicidal intent. Perceived burdensomeness, thwarted belongingness, and fearlessness about death were each associated with suicidal ideation as predicted by the theoretical model.

IPTS theory was used in a study of 934 military personnel (Anestis, Khazem, Mohn, & Green, 2015) mostly from the National Guard while at the Joint Forces Training Center, Camp Shelby, Mississippi. The study was part of an ongoing longitudinal study examining possible predictors of suicide risk and suicide behaviors within military personnel. Survey results indicated the interaction between thwarted belongingness and perceived burdensomeness predicted suicidal ideation as well as resolving any plans and preparations for suicide.

Two clinical samples among persons deployed to Iraq were studied—one group consisted of persons seeking treatment for a TBI; the second group consisted of persons seeking outpatient mental health treatment (Bryan, Clemans, & Hernandez, 2012). Results in both samples found perceived burdensomeness and acquired capability were significant in relation to suicidality. These results emphasize the perceptions of burdensomeness, when combined with fearlessness about death, correspond to an increase in suicidality among deployed military personnel. The fact that thwarted belongingness was not significant in this study raises the question regarding differences in attachment among deployed soldiers in a combat zone.

### Perspectives on Military and Veteran Suicide

Each of the theories listed provide a perspective for understanding the major influences in a person's life, including factors considered suicide risks. I suggest there is a danger in assuming all suicidal behavior is the same. For example, most of my suicidal clients attempted suicide prior to seeking treatment for their PTSD. Dissociation played a role for many. Each client described going into a dissociated state, an altered state of consciousness where they attempted to kill themself. Their suicidal acts were impulsive; they were not planned out over the course of weeks. As wounded warriors they lived in a state of emotional and physical pain for months when impulsively they made a suicide attempt. Impulsivity is a significant factor in many veteran suicidal gestures. The possibility is always in their mind, the probability of taking one's life is short lived, and spur-of-the-moment impulsivity is regulated by the state of their mental health at the time. Such impulsivity can move the veteran from a window of suicidal possibility to a window of suicide probability.

Servicemembers who have spent months deployed to a combat zone can become desensitized to death. Facing death becomes such a normal part of combat that the fear of dying no longer exists. For veterans experiencing physical and emotional pain with no fear of death, suicide becomes a possible option; sometimes death becomes enticing as a means of escaping the pain. Add to this situation the element of unresolved grief due to the death of close friends in combat with the inclination to join their deceased battle buddies in the bivouac of the dead. One veteran experienced audio and visual intrusions associated with memories from the last firefight when his men were killed. He believed the intrusions were his men summoning him to join them beyond the grave. During three hospitalizations with each hospitalization lasting 30 days or longer, no mental health professional explained to the veteran his intrusions were dissociative experiences tied to his traumatic combat memories. Each of his three suicide attempts was viewed by the veteran as a response to his intrusions—the perceived invitations of his deceased battle buddies summoning him to the grave.

The honor displayed in memorial services and military funerals is intended to demonstrate respect, honor, and appreciation of a grateful nation to the deceased servicemember and surviving family members. The rendering of military honors speaks to the living while honoring the dead on behalf of a grateful nation. Most servicemembers going into combat do not think about what it would be like if they were wounded. The desire is to live and accomplish the mission. It would be antithetical to the mental preparation for battle to worry about being wounded. Each warrior is focused on who has their "back" while honoring their responsibility as a member of the armed forces to accomplish the mission.

After the battle, those who are wounded are introduced to a crash course in living with limitations. No warrior anticipates the question of what it would be like to live the remainder of one's life with physical and mental limitations. The focus is on accomplishing the mission. The Stoic principle "focus on what can be changed, don't spend time and attention on what you can't change" is a survival mechanism when going into battle. It is only after battle that the wounds of war become the new reality. The tolerance for physical and mental pain changes. Sometimes thoughts of suicide arise among servicemembers who struggle to accept the wounds of war. Military medical specialists who treat the severely wounded have told me about their own emotional pain when the medical staff works to save a person's life only to be told by the patient, "Why didn't you just let me die?" Some believe the honor in death would be preferable to life with its limitations and wounds. Sometimes veterans tell me, "It takes more courage to live with the wounds than courage to go into battle." It is with great appreciation that I honor all survivors.

Servicemembers who believe their life is a liability to their family and friends use this belief to further drive their suicidal ideation. This is noted later in this chapter under "Case Study." Social isolation leaves the servicemember to focus on their inner negativity rather than receiving social support while engaging with others. The close bonding of friends who protected each other in combat becomes broken as they are assigned to other units with new locations and missions over time. The support of friends becomes disconnected. Social isolation is a frequent concern during suicidal ideation. Unresolved grief due to death of friends in battle as well as relationships among the living become lost during reassignment. The disconnection with relationships further enhances depression and shame. Survivors' guilt further impacts a person's sense of worthlessness and failure. Shame-proneness from earlier life experiences further exacerbates the person's will to live.

Mental health reviews acknowledge no harm contracts are not effective in suicide prevention (Lewis, 2010; Norton, 2018). It is important to encourage members in the client's social network to check on the client's well-being, especially during vulnerable times such as anniversary dates (when friends were killed), holidays, and Veterans Day and Memorial Day. It is important to look for warning signs such as those listed in Table 10.1.

The more warning signs exhibited, the greater the risk of suicide.

## RISK FACTORS

The largest number of active duty suicides since the Department of Defense began collecting data occurred in 2018. There were 325 active duty deaths (Department of Veterans Affairs, 2019b). Risk factors among Army military personnel with no previous suicide history included gender, education level, years in military, previous deployments, promotion problems, previous combat injuries, previous physical health appointments, and history of family violence (Ursano et al., 2018).

A 2017 study of over 100,000 male Marines who died by suicide found factors such as duty hazards, TBI wounds, and relationship

---

**TABLE 10.1  Suicide Warning Signs**

| | |
|---|---|
| ■ Talking about wanting to die | ■ Feeling helpless or having no purpose |
| ■ Looking for a way to kill oneself | |
| ■ Talking about being a burden to others | ■ Sleeping too little or too much |
| ■ Acting anxious, agitated, or reckless | ■ Increasing use of alcohol or drugs |
| ■ Displaying extreme mood swings | ■ Withdrawing or feeling isolated |
| ■ Previous suicide attempts | ■ Showing rage or talking about revenge |
| | ■ Talking about feeling trapped |
| | ■ In unbearable pain |

*Source:* U.S. Department of Health and Human Services. (2012). *2012 National strategy for suicide prevention: Goals and objectives for action: A report of the U.S. Surgeon General and of the National Action Alliance for Suicide Prevention.* Retrieved from https://www.ncbi.nlm.nih.gov/books/NBK109906/#introduction.s5

counseling to be significant factors (Phillips, LeardMann, Vyas, Crum-Cianflone, & White, 2017). Failing intimate relationships were found to be significant (Skopp, Zhang, & Reger, 2016). Logan et al. (2015) found intimate partner problems were the most common factors precipitating suicide among U.S. Army personnel.

Aaron Beck and colleagues (Beck, Brown, Berchick, Stewart, & Steer, 2006; Beck, Kovacs, & Weissman, 1975) found hopelessness to be a key variable in linking depression to suicidal behavior. Skopp, Trofimovich, Grimes, Oetjen-Gerdes, and Gahm (2012) found suicide was associated with mood disorder. Bipolar disorder was also noted to be significant by Ilgen et al. (2012).

Serotonin appears to influence both suicide and sleep. It is common for many clients with severe stress-related pathology to have difficulty sleeping. Many veterans report 1 to 4 hours of sleep each night, often interrupted by nightmares and night terrors. When this happens, they appear to be more prone to dissociative exhibitions. Disturbed sleep has been associated with suicide attempts. Symptoms of global insomnia were found to be more severe among persons who later completed suicide within a 13-month period (Nadorff, Nazem, & Fiske, 2011). Persons experiencing more frequent nightmares were 105% more likely to die by suicide when compared to persons with no frightening dreams (Tanskanen et al., 2001).

Substance abuse and the communication of suicidal ideation have been found to be common occurrences prior to suicidal acts (Chiles, Strosahl, Cowden, & Graham, 1986). Hendin, Maltsberger, Lipschitz, Haas, and Kyle (2001) identified precipitating suicidal events as being one or more intense affective responses (other than depression) along with either speech or behavior suggesting suicidal plans, negative change in work or social functioning, and an increase in substance abuse. Medication such as benzodiazepines is associated with suicide as noted in a review of 17 studies examining the relationship between benzodiazepines and suicide. The study discovered this class of drugs was associated with increased risks of attempting and completing suicide (Dodds, 2017).

## EMDR THERAPY AND SUICIDALITY

### THREE KEY QUESTIONS IN ASSESSING SUICIDE

A therapist needs to address three questions with clients regarding suicide. Does the client have:

1. Suicidal thoughts—**"Do you ever wish you were dead or have thoughts about hurting yourself or killing yourself?"**
   If "Yes," go to next question (Question 2).
   If "No" and the answer is deemed authentic, move to other History-Taking information.

2. Plan—"Do you have a plan as to how you would do it?"
   If client has thought of a plan, assess the thwarted belonging-ness (belonging) and perceived burdensomeness (burden to loved ones) areas within the IPTS model.
   If "Yes," go to next question (Question 3).
   If "No," ensure client's safety and offer treatment plan for re-solving client's disturbing issues.
3. Means—"How would you do it?" **or *"What means would you use to kill yourself?"***
   Evaluate the client's capacity for suicide including fear of death and pain tolerance. Identify the means (weapons); ensure the means to accomplish suicide are removed from accessibility. If suicidal thoughts, plans, and means are all answered "Yes," refer/escort the client for inpatient psychotherapy. If the answer for the last question is "No," ensure the client's safety and estab-lish a treatment plan to resolve the person's disturbing memo-ries associated with the identified symptoms.

   Some people plan suicide for weeks and months, while many vet-erans are impulsive and spontaneously act on the spur of the moment. Impulsivity is frequently a characteristic of PTSD. If the answer to these three questions is "yes," then an appropriate intervention is warranted. If in doubt, always ensure the client's safety. Persons considering acting on their suicidal ideation need immediate hospitalization. Sometimes the client is angry with me for insisting on their hospitalization; there is also relief that someone took charge to save them. They thank me afterward.
   When outpatient treatment is warranted, it is also important to en-sure the stability of the client. Their stability includes a personal invest-ment in coping with the vicissitudes of life experiences while enhancing the support network of family and friends to maintain frequent contact during their treatment. Potentially suicidal persons need contact infor-mation, a person to call when they become suicidal. Contact information for times of crisis is determined by the local agency. In addition to the national suicide hotline, provide the local on-call number or, when I was in private practice, I provided personal contact information to be used in times of crisis. EMDR therapy resolves the mental and emotional pain described by Bateson (2015). Effective EMDR treatment neutralizes the negativity associated with past traumatic memories, including the debil-itating shame of moral injury, as it enhances one's sense of self-efficacy, diminishing their sense of "burdensomeness" described in interpersonal theory (Van Orden et al, 2010). In addition to treatment for the suicidal client, partners and family members can benefit from education and psychotherapy. Education provides family members an understanding of post-deployment adjustments while familiarizing family members to recognize warning signs and monitor appropriate life-saving responses.

234 PART II Special Issues

A systemic view of family dynamics is provided for understanding healthy options for families coping with the stress as members learn to practice self-care; opportunities for psychotherapy include both individual and group treatment for partners and family members. Some spouses have learned to recognize the signs of suicidality and maintain a support network of friends who are available for suicide intervention.

## EMDR THERAPY FOR EFFECTIVE TREATMENT

1. Risk assessment. What risk factors are operative in the client's life?
2. Three questions—Does client have suicidal thoughts, plans, and means?
3. Assess IPTS factors: (a) Belonging (thwarted belongingness); (b) Burden (perceived burdensomeness); (c) Suicidal capacity (includes fear of death and tolerance of pain)
4. If the client has a suicidal active plan, ensure they get to a stable environment, such as hospitalization, that can contain their instability and provide treatment. If there is no active plan, collaboratively establish the treatment plan based on the client's presenting issues. Ensure stabilization skills and identify target memories for EMDR reprocessing to relieve mental and emotional pain while enhancing self-efficacy during the EMDR reprocessing. Effective treatment offers hope!
5. Diminish the suicidal capacity by restricting access to weapons or instruments that can be used for self-harm. Note TBI history, shame-proneness, moral injury, and dissociative tendencies.
6. Address shame, guilt, and moral injury as early as possible in the treatment.
7. Provide appropriate coordination with the designated person in the client's support network to monitor any suicidal risks (Table 10.2). Consider couple/family session intermittently. Evaluate if partner or other family members can benefit from individual and/or group therapy and education.

### TABLE 10.2 Suicide Risk Factors

| PSYCHOLOGICAL DISORDERS | MEDICAL CONDITIONS | MILITARY SPECIFIC |
| --- | --- | --- |
| ■ Mood or affective disorder | ■ History of TBI | ■ Disciplinary action (UCMJ) |
| ■ Hopelessness | ■ Terminal disease | ■ Reduction in rank |
| ■ Personality disorder (especially BPD and antisocial) | ■ HIV/AIDS | ■ Career threatening change in fitness for duty |
| | ■ New DX of major illness | |

*(continued)*

### TABLE 10.2  Suicide Risk Factors (*continued*)

| PSYCHOLOGICAL DISORDERS | MEDICAL CONDITIONS | MILITARY SPECIFIC |
|---|---|---|
| ■ Schizophrenia<br>■ Anxiety disorders<br>■ Substance use disorder<br>■ Psychological trauma (PTSD, MST)<br>■ Moral injury<br>■ Relationship conflict<br>■ Unresolved grief due to previous loss<br>■ Previous suicide attempts<br>■ Impulsivity | ■ Medical condition: worsening or chronic<br>■ Intoxication<br>■ Substance withdrawal<br>■ Use of prescribed meds with warning for increased suicide<br>■ Sleep disorder | ■ Perceived sense of injustice or betrayal (unit/command)<br>■ Command leadership stress (isolation)<br>■ Transferring duty station (PCS)<br>■ Admin separation<br>■ Adverse deployment experience<br>■ Deployment to combat zone |

BPD, borderline personality disorder; MST, military sexual trauma; PCS, permanent change of station; PTSD, posttraumatic stress disorder; TBI, traumatic brain injury; Uniform Code of Military Justice (UCMJ).

*Source:* Modified from Department of Veterans Affairs. (2019a). *Department of Veterans Affairs (VA) suicide prevention pocket guide.* Retrieved from https://www.healthquality.va.gov/guidelines/MH/srb/VASuicidePreventionPocketGuideSpreads.pdf

## Case Study 10.1  Veteran With Suicide Attempts

A 37-year-old, U.S. Army sergeant first class (E-7) with complex PTSD accompanied with audio and visual intrusions was highly dissociative during and between sessions. He had attempted suicide on three occasions, followed by inpatient hospitalization for a minimum of 30 days with each attempt. The client has experienced a TBI with occipital lobe damage. During treatment, he explained he has to filter out the intrusions in order to hear what I was saying, then develop and verbalize his response. In this session, he began the session describing the lack of mental health assessment and intervention during his military service in the past.

### VETERAN DESCRIBES DISSOCIATIVE "BLACK HOLE" AND SUICIDE

Client:    In the past, if we had (mental health) problems, we didn't get much help. So I've kind of been living with it (PTSD and moral injury). But as I told you before—I'm not going to lie to you, I'm scared.

You know, I used to be afraid to even say that, to tell somebody "I'm scared" or something. I know how hard it is. I've been there and uh, it's, it's hard. It's not easy. Dealing with that stuff is probably harder than being over there and going through it.

I have thoughts everyday Doc. You know, I've had them the last couple of days. Last couple days it's been hard. The physical pain has been overwhelming. And I mean, once again, I'm not gonna sit back and deny, the thoughts have been there. You know, some days you just think that, you know, it's easier just to take the pain away and just, um, the physical, the emotional and physical pain just gets overwhelming and, you know, you get tired and without no sleep or nothing and not having any pain meds to try to help you or anything, it's just, it gets over running, you know? And I catch myself being by myself sometimes and then those thoughts run through my head. You want to act on them. I can't sit back and tell myself I will do it or sit back to tell myself I won't do it because, you know, I went 2 years without, you know, on and off thoughts and I went almost 2 years without doing anything, and the next thing you know, I tried to kill myself. So, it's just one of those things that you never know.

Therapist:     You went to a place, a dark place as I've heard you describe it, a place where you acted on it.

Client:     I just blacked out. I just, my mind, I just went to a place like tunnel vision. I started having thoughts about my guys, I started picturing over there, and then I started picturing their faces and going back through and remembering the blast with their screaming and crying. And then, I started picturing myself, cutting myself with a razor blade, and hurting myself. I started picturing over there; and I just blacked out, like a black tunnel and you couldn't see nothing, and I went into a blackout. And, uh, I don't remember cutting myself at all. And I, I know that's weird. And I've told that to numerous doctors. I told that to the chain of command, to the doctors on post, and they looked at me like I was stupid.

But, uh, I, I told them, I said, uh, I just went to the blackout phase and I don't remember carving my arms up. I don't remember cutting my wrist. Um, I don't remember that. The only thing I remember is when R_____ (wife) came down and she was hitting me, taking the razor blades away from me. Um, and I don't know how much time elapsed between a point of my getting the razor blades to the point of her coming down. Because I had already carved up both of my arms with the razor blades and then started cutting my wrists by the time she had done that (discovered him bleeding out). And, then they rushed me into the hospital. So, I mean it could've been minutes. Uh, I don't know how much time elapsed because I don't remember anything in between time. In the same thing, I don't remember from the point when I got the revolver to when I pulled the trigger.

I just blacked out, so I don't even remember pulling the trigger. When I came to, I just remember crying and I was in pain. You asked yourself sometimes, 'How can people kill themselves? How can they sit back and how can they pull the trigger? And their heads off and stuff and you wonder what goes through their minds.' I've been there. There's nothing that goes through your mind. My mind was blank. It was in a black hole. For me, it was. And so, I don't remember any of it.

Therapist: So, what we're doing in this part of your treatment is helping you to be able to manage things. So you don't need to act out in hurting or yourself.

## EMDR APPROACH—IDENTIFYING SPECIFIC ISSUES TO BE TREATED

Client: The thing is doc—the one thing that goes through your mind—I talked to M_____ (fellow soldier in same firefight). Me and M_____ talk a lot you know, he's tried to commit suicide a couple times. We talk quite a bit. Um, cause he's, he's the closest person to me that I have, you know. Like at S_____ medical center, they tried to tell me, 'You need to think about your family. You need to think about your family. Think about your kids and stuff like that.' I'm not trying to sound selfish; I'm not trying to sound like a father, or a husband who doesn't love his family and stuff. But you know, it's not your family that doesn't run through your mind. It's not that you don't love them, but you don't think about your family through a whole day. Because at that point your family doesn't matter because you have all of these problems.

And your family, to be honest with you, is the last thing that's on your mind. And I know it's bad to say that when I would never tell my wife. Because I don't want her to think of me as a bad person and I would never tell nobody that except for you. Um, and I by no way mean that in a bad way because my family is everything to me. But you don't. They used to tell that to me all the time, 'Think about your family because that'll keep you from doing it.' I wouldn't have done. I tried to do it three times. So there has to be something more than that. And then when you talk to me about working on the problems themselves, it focuses on that and working on the issues and in trying to get the issues themselves dealt with and trying to get rid of some of that guilt and everything, you know. Down there (the medical center), they were trying to get me to focus on my family and focus on this, this and that. But, once again, it wasn't that. Because, if it was all my family stuff, I wouldn't have wanted to try to commit suicide three times.

Therapist:  And that's important for people to understand. Obviously, some don't understand what you are sharing.

Client:  Because that's what they taught us, you know, you need to let your family be your circle. And when you're living with so much trauma and you're living with so much guilt, it's not that we don't love our family or nothing. It's not that we're trying to rescue them; we're trying to rescue ourselves. We know that they're good. We know they're taken care of.

Therapist:  Right

Client:  I know in my heart, if something happens to me, I know they're taken care of. I know this already. I know this before I was ever getting out in the Army. 'Cause I know I have PTSD and I know if something happens to me, they're going to be taken care of. So in my mind, I know this. I know if something happens to me, they're going to be fine, but I'm not trying to rescue them—I'm trying to rescue me. I talked this stuff down there (inpatient, medical center) to them and it was like going in one ear, and going out the other. I felt like I was kinda getting nowhere, you know.

I love my family more than anything, but it's about me trying to save me. You know, and you asked me about hope; you ask me all the time. I do have hope, because if I didn't, I wouldn't be here right now. It gets overwhelming and you get tired of it. You know, I'm not a ..., I'm not a quitter.

I know I'm not missing both arms and both legs and everything else, you know. Everybody gets beat down one way or another ... (15 second pause) I just don't want to be this way for the rest of my life. I'm 36, 37 years old.

Therapist: What we are doing is like creating some safety valves so that you don't have to get to that place where things feel so overwhelmed that your mind goes to that dark place because that's an automatic response when it happens. We're creating some different ways of handling it so you don't have to go there.

Client: Yeah. R_____ (wife) is totally involved. She's noticed me kinda calming down. Mellowing out more than I was before. Everything has kind of slowed down for me.

**Lessons learned:** This client outlined his experience of attempting suicide. He described transitioning from his chronic depression to obsessing with guilt and shame-related moral injury, which was fueled by unresolved grief related to the death of his soldiers. He isolated himself to the basement of his home to view YouTube videos of combat operations. In his chronic depression he feels a thwarted sense of belongingness as he withdraws for hours and days at a time. Waking his spouse up from sleep in the middle of the night, crying, and screaming with his night terrors leaves him feeling burdensome to his family. He frequently dissociated. While watching the videos, he slumped into a dissociated state in which he "imagined" cutting his arms.

I love my family more than anything, but it's about me trying to save me…. You asked me about hope; you ask me all the time. I do have hope, because if I didn't, I wouldn't be here right now. It gets overwhelming and you get tired of it. You know, I'm not a …, I'm not a quitter.

This case is similar to numerous cases with veterans presenting with complex PTSD including dissociative exhibitions. Suicidal gestures were attempted prior to seeking treatment at Soldier Center. Each described their suicidality as never being a long planned out intention, but rather a low-grade, ongoing emotional and psyche pain with suicide always being an option but not a plan. The suicidal acts were spontaneous and immediate. In every suicidal attempt the act was described as being in a dissociative state suffering with shame-based moral injury. This is the nature of clients suffering with complex PTSD who attempt suicide.

While exploring suicidality among servicemembers, a number of factors appear to influence the condition. TBI, moral injury, and dissociation have all correlated with suicidality.

## TRAUMATIC BRAIN INJURY AND VETERAN SUICIDE

It is reported that 360,000 military personnel experienced TBIs between 2000 and 2016 (Defense and Veterans Brain Injury Center, 2017). Military personnel have experienced blasts during numerous wars and military operations. As the military began assessing for TBIs, there has been research regarding the relationship between TBI and other maladies including PTSD and suicidality. Research documents that persons with a TBI represent an elevated risk for suicide. A TBI can trigger headaches, neck pain, dizziness, and difficultly with memory and cognitive processing. The first 6 months following a TBI the risk of suicide more than triples and remains high throughout the person's life (Mozes, 2018).

A review of Danish health and death records including more than 7 million people found that nearly 35,000 died by suicide. The Danish study found that persons who suffer with severe TBI were 2.4 times more likely to commit suicide when compared with the non-TBI population (Goldstein, & Diaz-Arrastia, 2018; Madsen et al., 2018; Rapaport, 2018). This study is credited with establishing a solid association between TBI and suicide.

An additional study (Fonda et al., 2017) involving 273,591 veterans examined the association of attempted suicide with psychological diagnosis (PTSD, depression, anxiety, and substance abuse) and TBI. Findings indicate veterans with TBI are more likely to attempt suicide. Furthermore, veterans with a TBI and a PTSD diagnosis have a higher likelihood for suicidal outcome.

Persons sometimes ask if EMDR therapy treats TBI. It does not treat the physical brain injury. It does treat the psychological distress. EMDR therapy is effective in treating psychological trauma, even the disturbing memories associated with events connected to the TBI injury (Table 10.3). Future research may reveal the interaction of neurobiological change, due to effective psychotherapy treatment, with neuroplasticity.

## MORAL INJURY AND SUICIDALITY

Moral injury has been described as a "war within" (Brock & Kansfield, 2019; Frame, 2015). There is consensus that the internal dissonance described "moral injury" is a condition, not a mental health disorder. It is considered a moral condition primarily perpetuated by shame and guilt (Purcell, Burkman, Keyser, Fucella, & Maguen, 2018). This condition was first identified by philosophers who coined the term "moral injury" to describe acts that "diminish a person's dignity" (Garrett, 2018). Later VA psychologists, noting a condition beyond stress-related pathology such as PTSD, defined moral injury

TABLE 10.3  Treatment Considerations for TBI

| BE AWARE OF WHAT CAN PRECIPITATE SUICIDAL THOUGHTS | THINGS THAT HELPED IN PEOPLE WITH TBI |
|---|---|
| ■ Loneliness | ■ Psychotherapy |
| ■ Lack of connection | ■ Medication |
| ■ Holiday times | ■ Support groups |
| ■ Lack of support | ■ Having accessible providers |
| ■ Social anxiety | ■ Having a belief-system—spirituality |
| ■ Job/employment issues | ■ Distractions, something to do first, computer, TV, self-regulation |
| ■ Lack of resources | ■ Have a responsibility, i.e., pet, job |
| ■ Frustration over tasks | ■ Family/friends that care |
| ■ Bad news about prognosis | |

TBI, traumatic brain injury.
*Source:* Adapted from the Colorado Traumatic Brain Injury (TBI) Trust Fund Education Program and the Mental Illness Research, Education, and Clinical Center. (n.d.). *Traumatic brain injury and suicide* (p. 25). Denver, CO: Denver VA Medical Center.

as the act of "perpetrating, failing to prevent, bearing witness to, or learning about acts that transgress deeply held moral beliefs and expectations" (Litz et al., 2009). Moral injury, with its shame and guilt, can rob a person of their sense of self-worth. A negative belief such as "I am worthless" is common among persons with severe moral injury. With the erosion of self-worth, moral injury can contribute to suicidal considerations.

Maguen and colleagues (2012) suggest killing in combat may be independently associated with suicidal ideation. They note that questioning about killing experiences is not customarily part of a suicide evaluation. They and other researchers (Tripp, McDevitt-Murphy, & Henschel, 2016) found veterans who had higher killing experiences had twice the odds of suicide ideation. In fact, associations have been noted between killing in combat and negative mental health outcomes with hazardous alcohol use (Kelley, Bravo, Hamrick, Braitman, & Judah, 2019). Moral injury related to killing is further exacerbated when women and children are included. Numerous veterans have suffered with moral wounds as they were in a no-win situation where they were being attacked by a group containing women and sometimes children. If they did not kill the attackers, their fellow soldiers would be killed. If they did kill the attackers, they would violate their personal values regarding killing women and children. Even when females are considered as enemy soldiers who voluntarily place themselves in life-threatening situations, the killing of children is almost always a morally haunting experience.

Therapists using other models of psychotherapy have described the challenge of getting the client to discuss the impact of killing during combat operations (Purcell et al., 2018). The EMDR AIP approach allows for the client to identify his or her list of disturbing memories without probing by the therapist. A moral injury incident may be referred to as "that incident which has haunted me for a long, long time." When necessary, the EMDR approach can treat disturbing memories about killing with the client disclosing only limited information, only the information they are comfortable revealing. Since it is a memory encoded in the client's memory system that is being processed, the therapist does not have to know the details of the memory in situations where it is challenging for the client to disclose details. This is one of the strengths of EMDR therapy.

A key question for the client is, "Would it be okay to get over this?" If the client answers "yes," they are ready for reprocessing the target memory. If the answer is "no," the therapist seeks what is inhibiting the processing by asking, "What would it take to get over this?" These are cognitive interweaves that set the client up for reprocessing.

## THE THREE TIERS OF MORAL INJURY TREATMENT WITH EMDR THERAPY

In chapter 8 I addressed treating moral injury with EMDR therapy presenting the concept of a three-tiered treatment approach. Tier I represents those target memories that spontaneously reprocess. Next, tier II represents those moral injury encased memories with blocking beliefs, while tier III represents the most severely resistant moral injuries, often with childhood injuries, shame-proneness, and/or complex PTSD. Remember, many disturbing memories spontaneously reprocess. The tier II moral injury incidents developed around blocking beliefs are effectively treated with cognitive interweaves. The most severe moral injury memories, tier III, sometimes need the memory to be dismantled into those components that are the most entrenched moral wounds and those components that are readily processed. The components that can be most readily processed are treated first, followed by addressing the most resistant component that can be processed as the brain assesses the health of additional memory networks. Persons who are shame-prone may need their early life history of shame memories to be treated as part of the treatment plan. An outline for "Establishing a Treatment Plan for Shame-Based Clients" is posted in Appendix C of this book.

On occasions when the client could not bear to recall the disturbing memory associated with the moral injury, I used Manfield's (Mansfield, Lovett, Engel, & Manfield, 2017) Flash technique, which I refer to as the "blink" technique to my veteran clients. I avoid the term "flash" with military personnel and veterans due to the nature of explosions and aircraft crashes with flash images. A former Marine could not bear to recall an incident when he and three other Marines were attacked by insurgents. Their vehicle was hit by a rocket-propelled grenade (RPG). My client and the other Marines ran to the closest area where the land was depressed enough to provide some cover. The client, an E-7, was the senior non-commissioned officer (NCO) and took charge. The insurgents, 15 to 20 in number, were charging their position. There were women and children among the charging group. My client did not want to kill women and children; to do so violated his values. Yet, if he did not protect his protective position, he and his fellow Marines would be killed. This memory so overwhelmed him, he could not bring himself to describe the incident. When asked about his military history, the former Marine would shut down conversation. Seeing the client's difficulty—he was motivated to be treated, but could not bring himself to recall the incident—I used the Flash technique, which within 20 minutes had reduced his need to avoid the thought from a 10 down to a 4 (scale of 10 to 0). At the level of a 4 he was relieved the memory had sufficiently lost its power, so he was ready to address his moral injury. This enhanced his confidence in the EMDR process. The following session he reprocessed the moral injury incident, achieving a 0, 7, clear body scan within 45 minutes.

## DISSOCIATIVE EXHIBITIONS AND SUICIDALITY

The client in this chapter's "Case Study 10.1" described his experience of missing four of his deceased soldiers killed in his last firefight. His guilt and grief were obvious, along with his chronic depression. In his dissociative state he attempted suicide.

The dissociative state is common among a number of veterans who have shared their stories of attempted suicide prior to beginning treatment. Varying degrees of dissociation is common among many servicemembers and veterans with complex PTSD. At Soldier Center, my caseload seldom includes persons meeting criteria for dissociative identity disorder (DID); rather, they present across a wide spectrum of dissociative experiences ranging from the loss of dual awareness during reprocessing to the more severe diagnostic category of "other specified and unspecified dissociative disorders" described in the *Diagnostic and Statistical Manual of Mental Disorders* (5th ed.; *DSM-5*, American Psychiatric Association, 2013). Similar clinical patterns involving dissociation and suicidality have been noted by other clinicians. Israeli researchers (Shelef, Levi-Belz, & Fruchter, 2014) studied the relationship between dissociation and suicide among Israeli soldiers. They concluded that recognizing suicide-like dissociation and habituation may contribute to a better understanding of suicidal behavior among soldiers. Recognizing this pattern, I have learned to particularly evaluate the client's ability to self-regulate to maintain present awareness. The Dissociative Experiences Scale-II (DES-II; Carlson & Putnam, 1995) can help identify the client's propensity to dissociate. Also, observation of the client's presentation in the waiting room and in the treatment room reveals the client's ability to maintain current awareness. In treating these cases, an EMDR therapist must ensure the client's ability to self-regulate and adjust the mechanics (bilateral stimulation [BLS] speed, number of passes, and modality) to keep the client within the window of tolerance for processing.

## EMDR AND SUICIDE PREVENTION

### THE THERAPIST AND FAMILY MEMBERS IN SUICIDE PREVENTION

For suicide prevention, family members are taught to look for signs indicating potentially suicidal behavior. Has the person moved from the *"possibility"* of suicide to the *"probability"* of taking their life? It is important to assess for unusual behaviors, changes in behavioral patterns, the person giving away prized possessions, intense expressions of rage, or signs of significant depression for the past few days. Is the person going out at unusual times during the day or night or demonstrating a change of interest or disinterest in religion? Does the person make statements about killing themself or talk about having no reason to live? It is important to engage a network of friends and family to address the client's current status by checking on the person's well-being, particularly when they tend to isolate or present questionable behavior. Asking if they have thoughts of harming themselves or killing themselves provides an opportunity for the client to discuss these concerns.

Sometimes the system becomes part of the problem rather than the solution. Some veteran clients have been hospitalized two and three times for their suicidality. They spend 30+ days as an inpatient each time before being discharged. When their physical and emotional pain, which drives their suicidal ideation, does not resolve, they repeat their suicidal cycle. Repeating the suicidal cycle includes: (a) recognizing the pain of living is intense enough to consider suicide as an escape (this happens as the will to live is diminished); (b) being hospitalized for stabilization; (c) having medications evaluated; (d) participating in inpatient psychotherapy; and (e) after 30 days being discharged. Their suicidal drive is regulated by their pain. When the pain level does not diminish, they repeat the cycle of suicidal gestures. They explain their suicidal ideation to me by saying, "Suicide is always an option"; yet at the end of a session they sometimes say, "I don't want you to give up on me, doc!" I respond, "I won't give up on you if you don't give up on me." The veteran responds, "Roger that!" Providing treatment once and twice a week with each session presented as part of a veteran's healing plan allows the client to know they are changing for the better. Measurable improvement is demonstrated as the client reclaims their life. On occasion, when a veteran continued to grieve over the death of his battle buddies, as he visited their graves weekly, I provided an EMDR session at the military cemetery. After accompanying the veteran to the grave of his friend, we located a bench in an area where I could provide an EMDR session using the tappers for BLS. Hope is established one session at a time.

## SUICIDE PREVENTION PROGRAMS

As psychotherapists, we treat persons who unsuccessfully attempted suicide as well as provide suicide prevention to clients who have yet to act on their suicidal ideation. There are a number of intervention training programs available to both professionals and interested non-professionals. The VA offers online suicide prevention training in collaboration with the Psych Armor Institute. The training, known as S.A.V.E., is developed for persons who work with, live with, or care for servicemembers.

The Suicide Prevention and Resource Center (SPRC) is funded by the U.S. Department of Health and Human Services' Substance Abuse and Mental Health Services Administration (SAMHSA). The SPRC provides trainings in suicide prevention such as Assessing and Managing Suicide Risk: Core Competencies for Mental Health Professionals (AMSR), a training program for behavioral health professionals with a graduate degree (masters and above).

Applied Suicide Intervention Skills Training (ASIST) is a 2-day training program, also offered through the SPRC as a means of teaching suicide first aid for persons at risk. Training participants learn a suicide prevention model to identify persons with suicidal ideation, establish a shared understanding of reasons for dying and living, develop a safety plan, and prepare for follow-up.

Question–Persuade–Refer (QPR) is a suicide prevention program offered through the QPR Institute that teaches how to question an individual if you suspect they are possibly suicidal, persuade them not to end their life but rather seek help, and refer them to an appropriate professional.

Effective mental health treatment offers hope. A number of my clients described times, before seeking treatment, they parked in their vehicle with a pistol in their seat, struggling with the decision whether or not to end their life. Thankfully, instead of taking their life, they decided to seek treatment. Ineffective treatment can push a person further into hopelessness. Effective treatment expands hope, allowing them to discover reasons to live, reclaiming their life in the process. The work we do is life-saving!

## CONCLUSION

In conclusion, I have learned there are two therapeutic approaches regarding suicide: prevention as a means of preventing suicide attempts and treatment for persons who have attempted suicide and survived. While I noted that research concluded "No harm contracts" have not been found to be effective, there are therapists who shared their stories of occasions when a contract has helped prevent a suicide act. For this population, the suicide act is frequently an impulsive, spur of the moment reaction. An important takeaway in this chapter is the awareness that numerous clients I treated after previous suicide attempts reported being in a dissociative state, with no awareness of their actions at the time. Intervention requires a support network of family and friends to check on the person of concern during those dark times. Asking three questions regarding (a) suicidal thoughts, (b) a suicidal plan, and (c) is there the means to carry out a plan is important. Effective treatment offers hope. Hope presents the person with a reason to live.

## DISCUSSION POINTS

1. What are the three key questions to ask the client for assessing suicide?
2. Discuss the suicidal factors identified in the interpersonal theory of suicide (IPTS).
3. Name the warning signs for suicide.
4. What three conditions are discussed in this chapter that can influence suicide?
5. Name the VA's online suicide prevention program.

## REFERENCES

American Psychiatric Association. (2013). *The diagnostic and statistical manual of mental disorders* (5th ed.). Arlington, VA: American Psychiatric Publishing.

Anestis, M., Khazem, L., Mohn, R., & Green, B. (2015). Testing the main hypothesis of the interpersonal-psychological theory of suicidal behavior in a large diverse sample of United States military personnel. *Comprehensive Psychiatry, 60*, 78–85. doi:10.1016/j.comppsych.2015.03.066

Bateson, J. (2015). *The last and greatest battle: Finding the will, commitment, and strategy to end military suicides.* New York, NY: Oxford University Press.

Beck, A., Kovacs, M., & Weissmen, A. (1975). Hopelessness and suicidal behavior. *Journal of the American Medical Association, 234*(11), 1146–1149. doi:10.1001/jama.1975.03260240050026

Beck, A., Brown, G., Berchick, R., Stewart, B., & Steer, R. (2006). Relationship between hopelessness and ultimate suicide: A replication with psychiatric outpatients. *Focus in Psychiatry, 4*(2), 291–296. doi:10.1176/foc.4.2.291

Blumenthal, S., & Kupfer, D. (1986). Generalizable treatment strategies for suicidal behavior. *Annals of the New York Academy of Sciences, 487*, 327–340. doi:10.1111/j.1749-6632.1986.tb27911.x

Brock, R., & Kansfield, A. (2019). The war inside: America's veteran suicide epidemic has a silent, unaddressed cause. *USA Today.* Retrieved from https://www.usatoday.com/story/opinion/2019/10/18/veteran-suicide-increase-first-responders-moral-injury-column/4008852002/

Bryan, C., Clemans, T., & Hernandez, A. (2012). Perceived burdensomeness, fearlessness of death, and suicidality among deployed military personnel. *Personality and Individual Differences, 52*(3), 374–379. doi:10.1016/j.paid.2011.10.045

Carlson, E., & Putnam, F. (1995). An update on the dissociative experiences scale. *Dissociation, 6*(1), 16–27. Retrieved from https://psycnet.apa.org/record/1994-27927-001

Centers for Disease Control and Prevention. (2019). *Suicide facts and figures: United States 2019.* Retrieved from https://chapterland.org/wp-content/uploads/sites/13/2017/11/US_FactsFigures_Flyer.pdf

Chiles, J., Strosahl, K., Cowden, L., & Graham, R. (1986). The 24 hours before hospitalization: Factors related to suicide attempting. *Suicide and Life-Threatening Behavior, 16*, 335342. doi:10.1111/j.1943-278X.1986.tb01015.x

Colorado Traumatic Brain Injury (TBI) Trust Fund Education Program and the Mental Illness Research, Education, and Clinical Center. (n.d.). *Traumatic brain injury and suicide* (p. 25). Denver, CO: Denver VA Medical Center.

De Catanzaro, D. (1991). Evolutionary limits to self-preservation. *Ethology and Sociobiology, 12,* 13–28. doi:10.1016/0162-3095(91)90010-n

De Catanzaro, D. (1995). Reproductive status, family interactions, and suicidal ideation: Surveys of the general public and high-risk groups. *Ethology and Sociobiology, 16,* 385–394. doi:10.1016/ 0162-3095(95)00055-0

Defense and Veterans Brain Injury Center. (2017). *Research review on TBI and suicide.* Retrieved from https://dvbic.dcoe.mil/sites/default/files/DHA_J -9_DVBIC_TBI%20and%20Suicide%20November%202018_508.pdf

Department of Veterans Affairs. (2019a). *Department of Veterans Affairs (VA) suicide prevention pocket guide.* Retrieved from https://www.healthqual ity.va.gov/guidelines/MH/srb/VASuicidePreventionPocketGuideSpreads .pdf

Department of Veterans Affairs. (2019b). *2019 national veteran suicide prevention annual report.* Retrieved from https://www.mentalhealth.va.gov/docs/ data-sheets/2019/2019_National_Veteran_Suicide_Prevention_Annual _Report_508.pdf

Dodds, T. (2017). Prescribed benzodiazepines and suicide risk: A review of the literature. *Primary Care Companion CNS Disorders, 19*(2), 16r02037. doi:10.4088/pcc.16r02037

Fonda, J., Fredman, L., Brogly, S., McGlinchey, R., Milbert, W., & Gradus, J. (2017). Traumatic brain injury and attempted suicide among veterans of wars in Iraq and Afghanistan. *American Journal of Epidemiology, 186*(2), 220–226. doi:10.1093/ajekwxo44

Frame, T. (Ed.). (2015). *Moral injury: Unseen wounds in an age of barbarism.* Sydney, Australia: NewSouth Publishing.

Garrett, A. (2018). Joseph Butler's moral philosophy. *Stanford Encyclopedia of Philosophy.* Retrieved from https://plato.stanford.edu/entries/butler-moral

Goldstein, L., & Diaz-Arrastia, R. (2018). Traumatic brain injury and risk of suicide. *Journal of the American Medical Association, 320*(8), 554–556. doi:10.1001/ jama.2018.10825

Gunn, J. (2017). Editorial: The social pain model: Understanding suicide through evolutionary psychology. *Crisis, 38*(5), 281–286. doi:10.1027/0227-5910/ a000510

Hendin, H., Maltsberger, J., Lipschitz, A., Haas, A., & Kyle, J. (2001). Recognizing and responding to a suicide crisis. *Suicide and Life-Threatening Behavior, 31,* 115–128. doi:10.1521/suli.31.2.115.21515

Ilgen, M., Bohnert, A., Ignacio, R., McCarthy, J., Valenstein, M., Blow, F., & Blow, F. (2012). Psychiatric diagnoses and risk of suicide in veterans. *Archives of General Psychiatry, 67*(11), 1152–1158. doi:10.1001/archgenpsychiatry.2010.129

Joiner, T. (2005). *Why people die by suicide.* Cambridge, MA: Harvard University Press.

Kelley, M., Bravo, A., Hamrick, H., Braitman, A., & Judah, M. (2019). Killing during combat and negative mental health and substance use outcomes among recent-era veterans: The mediating effects of rumination. *Psychological Trauma: Theory, Research, Practice, and Policy, 11*(4), 379–382. doi:10.1037/tra0000385

Kime, P. (2019). *Military suicide rates hit record high in 2018*. Retrieved from https://www.military.com/daily-news/2019/09/26/military-suicide-rates-hit-record-high-2018.html

Klingensmith, K., Tsai, J., Mota, N., Southwick, S., & Pietrzak, R. (2014). Military sexual trauma in US Veterans: Results from the National Health and Resilience in Veterans Study. *Journal of Clinical Psychiatry, 75*(10), e1133–e1139. doi:10.4088/JCP.14m09244

Lewis, L. (2010). No harm contracts: A review of what we know. *Suicide and Life Threatening Behavior, 37*, 50–57. doi:10.1521/suli.2007.37.1.50

Litz, B., Stein, N., Delaney, E., Lebowitz, L., Nash, W., Silva, C., & Maguen, S. (2009). Moral injury and moral repair in war veterans: A preliminary model and intervention strategy. *Clinical Psychology Review, 29*, 695–706. doi:10.1016/j.cpr.2009.07.003

Logan, J., Skopp, N., Reger, M., Gladden, M., Smolenski, D., Floyd, F., & Gahm, G. (2015). Precipitating circumstances of suicide among active duty U.S. Army personnel versus U.S. civilians, 2005-2010. *Suicide and Life-Threatening Behavior, 45*(1), 65–77. doi:10.1111/sltb.12111

Madsen, T., Erlangsen, A., Orlovska, S., Mofaddy, R., Nordentoft, M., & Benros M. (2018). Association between traumatic brain injury and risk of suicide. *JAMA, 320*(6), 580–588. doi:10.1001/jama.2018.10211

Maguen, S., Metzler, T., Bosch, J., Marmar, C., Knight, S., & Neylan, T. (2012). Killing in combat may be independently associated with suicidal ideation. *Depression and Anxiety, 29*, 918–923. doi:10.1002/da.21954

Mansfield, P., Lovett, J., Engel, L., & Manfield, D. (2017). Use of the Flash technique in EMDR therapy: Four Case Examples. *Journal of EMDR Practice and Research, 11*(4), 195–205. doi:10.1891/1933-3196.11.4.195

Maris, R. (2002) Suicide. *The Lancet, 360* (9329), P319–326. https://doi.org/10.1016/S0140-6736(02)09556-9. Retrieved from https://www.thelancet.com/journals/lancet/article/PIIS0140-6736(02)09556-9/fulltext.

Mental Illness Research, Education, and Clinical Center. (n.d.). *Traumatic brain injury and suicide*. Denver, CO: Denver VA Medical Center.

Monteith, L., Bahraini, N., & Menefee, D. (2017). Perceived burdensomeness, thwarted belongingness, and fearlessness about death: Associations with suicidal ideation among female veterans exposed to military sexual trauma. *Journal of Clinical Psychology, 73*(12), 1655–1669. doi:10.1002/jclp.22462

Mozes, A. (2018). *Suicide risk higher in people with brain injury*. Retrieved from https://www.webmd.com/brain/news/20180814/suicide-risk-higher-in-people-with-brain-injury#1

Nadorff, M. R., Nazem, S., & Fiske, A. (2011). Insomnia symptoms, nightmares, and suicidal ideation in a college student sample. *Sleep, 34*(1), 93–98. https://doi.org/10.1093/sleep/34.1.93

Norton, K. (2018). *No harm contracts and suicide prevention*. Retrieved from https://theconnectprogram.org/wp-content/uploads/2018/11/NoHarmContracts.pdf

Phillips, C., LeardMann, C., Vyas, K., Crum-Cianflone, N., & White, M. (2017). Risk factors associated with suicide completions among US enlisted Marines. *American Journal of Epidemiology, 186*, 1–11. doi:10.1093/aje/kwx117

Purcell, N., Burkman, K., Keyser, J., Fucella, P., & Maguen, S. (2018). Healing from moral injury: A qualitative evaluation of the impact of killing treatment for combat veterans. *Journal of Aggression, Maltreatment and Trauma, 27*, 645–673. doi:10.1080/10926771.2018.1463582

Rapaport, L. (2018). *Traumatic brain injury tied to increased risk of suicide.* Retrieved from https://www.reuters.com/article/us-health-headtrauma-suicide-idUSKBN1KZ2A2

Rubinstein, D. H. (1986). A stress-diathesis theory of suicide. *Suicide and Life-Threatening Behavior, 16*(2), 182–196. doi:10.1111/j.1943-278x.1986.tb00351.x

Shelef, L., Levi-Belz, Y., & Fruchter, E. (2014). Dissociation and acquired capability as facilitators of suicide ideation among soldiers. *Crisis: The Journal of Crisis Intervention and Suicide Prevention, 35*(6), 1–10. doi:10.1027/0227-5910/a000278

Shneidman, E. (1998). Perspectives on suicidology: Further reflections on suicide and psychache. *Suicide and Life-Threatening Behavior, 28*, 245–250. doi:10.1111/j.1943-278X.1998.tb00854.x

Skopp, N., Trofimovich, L., Grimes, J., Oetjen-Gerdes, L., & Gahm, L. (2012). Relations between suicide and traumatic brain injury, psychiatric diagnoses, and relationship problems, active component U.S. Armed Forces, 2001-2009. *Medical Surveillance Monthly Report (MSMR), 19*(2) 7–11. Retrieved from https://www.health.mil/Military-Health-Topics/Combat-Support/Armed-Forces-Health-Surveillance-Branch/Reports-and-Publications/~/link.aspx?_id=534E26BD8E5D4ECC8CAA8ABA47679691&_z=z

Skopp, N., Zhang, Y., & Reger, M. (2016). Risk factors for self-directed violence in US soldiers: A case study. *Psychiatry Research, 245*, 194–199. doi:10.1016/jpsychres.2016.08.031

Stewart, P. (2013). *U.S. military veteran suicides rise, one dies every 65 minutes.* Retrieved from https://www.reuters.com/article/us-usa-veterans-suicide/u-s-military-veteran-suicides-rise-one-dies-every-65-minutes-idUSBRE9101E320130202

Tanskanen, A., Tuomilehto, J., Viinamäki, H., Vartiainen, E., Lehtonen, J., & Puska, P. (2001). Nightmares as predictors of suicide. *Sleep, 24*, 844–847. Retrieved from https://psycnet.apa.org/record/2001-05349-006

Tripp, J., McDevitt-Murphy, M., & Henschel, A. (2016). Firing a weapon and killing in combat are associated with suicidal ideation in OEF/OIF veterans. *Psychological Trauma: Theory, Research, Practice, and Policy, 8*(5), 626–633. doi:10.1037/tra0000085

Ursano, R., Kessler, R., Naifeh, J., Herberman, H., Nock, M., Aliaga, P., ... Stein, M. B. (2018). Risk factors with attempted suicide among US Army soldiers without a history of mental health diagnosis. *Journal of the American Medical Association, 75*(10), 1022–1032. doi:10.1001/jamapsychiatry.2018.2069

U.S. Department of Health and Human Services. (2012). *2012 National strategy for suicide prevention: Goals and objectives for action: A report of the U.S. Surgeon General and of the National Action Alliance for Suicide Prevention.* Retrieved from https://www.ncbi.nlm.nih.gov/books/NBK109906/#introduction.s5

Van Orden, K., Witte, T., Cukrowicz, K., Braithwaite, S., Selby, E., & Joiner, T. (2010). The interpersonal theory of suicide. *Psychological Review, 117*(2), 575–600. doi:10.1037/a0018697

## RESOURCE CONTACTS

ASIST Training: https://www.sprc.org/resources-programs/applied-suicide
-intervention-skills- training-asist

QPR Institute: https://qprinstitute.com/professional-training

S.A.V.E. online Suicide Prevention Training (PsychArmor Institute): https://
psycharmor.org/courses/s-a-v-e

VA Suicide Prevention: https://www.mentalhealth.va.gov/MENTALHEALTH/
suicide_prevention/index.aspNadorff, M., Nazem, S., & Fiske, A. (2013).
Insomnia symptoms, nightmares, and suicide risk: Duration of sleep
disturbance matters. *Suicide and Life-Threatening Behavior*, *43*, 139–149.
doi:10.1111/sltb.12003

# 11

# When EMDR Therapy Does Not Work (With Some Therapists)

## Introduction

Occasionally, a client reports they were unsuccessfully treated with EMDR therapy in previous treatments. In contrast, the same client was treated successfully with EMDR at other locations with different therapists. This chapter explores the difference between successful and unsuccessful treatment experiences with the same client. Believing the model always works when fidelity to the EMDR therapy protocol is maintained, we review what can be learned from our client's reports. This chapter presents lessons learned from clients who compare EMDR effective treatment with their previous unsuccessful treatment experiences.

## Learning Objectives

- Recognize the efficacy of EMDR therapy as reported in the Maxfield and Hyer (2002) meta-analysis.
- Illustrate some common failures in treatment delivery when therapists fail to follow the EMDR therapy protocol.
- Highlight the importance of learning from our clinical challenges.
- Illustrate the importance of seeking EMDRIA-approved consultation when working with "stuck" cases.

## FIDELITY TO THE EMDR PROTOCOL

Maxfield and Hyer (2002) found the greater the fidelity to the EMDR protocol, the more effective the outcome. Effective EMDR therapy is dependent on matching the clinical skills of the therapist with the clinical presentation of the client. There are many cases where the client processes a disturbing memory spontaneously. Little response is needed from the therapist in these cases. During EMDR basic training, newly trained participants are encouraged to take what they have learned in the training and begin to use it with clients where there is the most appropriate fit. Effective clinical skills in using EMDR therapy are developed as the therapist provides successful treatment.

What makes an effective EMDR therapist? And, what do the most effective EMDR consultants and trainers provide that sets the quality of their work apart? Dunne and Farrell (2011) explored this question regarding how newly trained EMDR therapists integrate their training into their practice. They raise the question whether EMDR therapy should be considered an integrated approach or a distinct psychotherapy approach. This is an ongoing question that a number of EMDR therapists, trainers, and researchers continue to evaluate. Listed here are examples of cases in which EMDR was unsuccessfully used to treat a client, when later, the same person was successfully treated with a different therapist providing the same therapy.

### WHEN EMDR THERAPY DID NOT WORK
#### Staff Sergeant (E-6) Treated at a Military Post, Unsuccessfully

The noncommissioned officer (NCO) had sought treatment for his posttraumatic stress disorder (PTSD). During the first appointment, he disclosed he had been unsuccessfully treated with EMDR therapy by an active duty officer, at his military post. The mental health officer proceeded with treating him with EMDR therapy until the client experienced an intense response that stopped the process. EMDR therapy did not work with him the first time it was provided on post. As I heard this NCO's description of his treatment experience, I was concerned for him as well as the therapist who unsuccessfully treated him.

At my office the Army staff sergeant (E-6) presented as a high energy, highly motivated person. He reported for treatment with a strong desire to resolve his PTSD symptoms. During Phase 1 History-Taking, I established his treatment plan, noting he was suffering with combat-related incidents. He was able to provide self-regulation (Phase 2) during the Preparation phase. As I did Phase 3 Assessment, he was cooperative and easily developed appropriate responses to the assessment questions. Then, we moved into Phase 4

Desensitization. He sat in the chair with hands resting comfortably on his lap as we began bilateral stimulation (BLS). After two sets of BLS, I observed the sergeant's hands (resting in his lap) begin to make a fist. I stopped the BLS and asked for feedback. He responded, "I'm getting lost in the memory." I assured him I would adjust the BLS to keep him present, allowing for dual awareness during processing. I was doing 18 to 20 passes in each set. I resumed reprocessing again and noticed if I exceeded 12 to 14 passes, the client would dissociate becoming lost in the memory. Normally, we teach that reprocessing requires at least 24 passes of BLS for the memory to be sufficiently stimulated for reprocessing. Yet, he was processing the disturbing memory with 10 to 12 passes. I continued processing, doing the 10 to 12 passes and using cognitive interweaves to keep him within the window of tolerance. Within 20 minutes, his SUD had dropped to 0. He was present and well-grounded in the treatment room. Another 15 minutes and the NCO's VOC was 7 with a clear body scan. At the end of the session, he said to me, "This sh*^ really works. Before, on post, the therapist turned the light bar on and just let it run. I got lost in the light—thought it was an insurgent. My knuckles are probably still scarred where I got lost in the lights, thought it was an insurgent and I attacked it!" Within 4 weeks, the NCO brought his spouse with him to discuss the change in his life as a result of the EMDR therapy.

**Solution:** The key to effective treatment using EMDR therapy required the therapist monitoring the client (attunement) to notice when he began to show his hands making a fist. The next requirement for successful treatment was keeping the BLS passes within a manageable range, allowing him to be present while using cognitive interweaves to keep him present and offer support during the reprocessing.

## Safe/Calm Place From Across the Room

Another soldier described his unsuccessful treatment with EMDR therapy. He was in Phase 2 Preparation and could not relax. The therapist was seated across the room from him doing the "finger thing," which was not working from that distance. He described sitting on one side of the room and the therapist across the room attempting to provide BLS for doing the Safe/Calm Place. All the client knew was that sitting across the room did not work—and that was part of EMDR therapy. Failure in the process activated the soldier's shame, believing he was different if it wasn't working.

**Solution:** Seating positions too far removed from the client can render the BLS ineffective. The client's field of vision becomes distracted with the larger view and easily distracted by any sounds or movement in the room. And, the distance was too far to allow for the slow eye movement (EM) to be effective. Adjusting the seating, so the therapist was positioned in the "ships passing in the night" position, close enough for the client to maintain visual focus, made a tremendous difference. It was a matter of the therapist positioning himself/herself within a distance for attunement, usually 2 to 2½ feet from the client.

The objective in the Preparation phase (Phase 2) is to allow the client to self-regulate. Of course, if a client cannot do the Safe/Calm Place, having the client do breathing exercises along with doing their own tapping nearly always works for self-regulation when timed appropriately. Clients doing their own tapping (with Butterfly Hug or tapping on their own legs) assigns them something to do, tasks their working memory, and helps them to feel more in control of the process.

## A Helicopter Crash and Lightbar

The soldier sought treatment at an out of state inpatient program for his PTSD with symptoms that began after the crash of a helicopter carrying elite special operations personnel. Loaded on one CH-47 helicopter, an entire group of America's best was killed when the helicopter was shot down. The impact of such loss of life became a moral injury that haunted the soldier for years. He sought treatment at a facility that offered EMDR therapy. The therapist, working with the client, completed Phase 1 History-Taking, Phase 2 Preparation, and Phase 3 Assessment as they moved into the Desensitization phase, reprocessing the memory of the crash. Memory of the helicopter crash included a bright flash of light when the helicopter hit the ground. Now, the therapist began reprocessing, using a lightbar where lights are moving across the bar. The lights of the lightbar connected with the flight of the helicopter when the memory of the crash was activated. The client felt overwhelmed and signaled to stop. Consequently, he lived with the emotional pain for another 5 years before the veteran sought treatment again.

**Solution:** When the veteran sought treatment 5 years later, his therapist described the new EMDR therapy process while providing informed consent during Phase 2 Preparation. His therapist informed the client he was in control of the process. Most importantly, the therapist informed the client that the lightbar may not have been the best choice for BLS in his previous treatment due to the flash of light from the helicopter crash standing out in the disturbing memory. Informing the client that there are three modalities for BLS was helpful. Other options included the manual EM in following the therapist's finger thus avoiding the lightbar, or the other modalities of auditory and tactile. The veteran chooses to use the tappers, allowing him to hold the stimulating devices in his hand as they alternated stimulation. As it turned out, attempting to use the lightbar for someone whose target memory includes a flash of light was not a good choice for this case. This particular client was treated with five sessions of EMDR therapy, resulting in his no longer meeting criteria for PTSD. He is free. A video of his success in EMDR therapy is available online from Soldier Center (https://vimeo.com/358532826).

The Army specialist (E-4) was referred for treatment. He was previously treated by an off-post psychologist near the Warrior Transition Unit (WTU) where the specialist was assigned. The psychologist had attempted to treat him with EMDR therapy. The client reported the psychologist began treating him (Phase 4 Desensitization) and concluded EMDR therapy would not work with the client. The psychologist reported to the WTU commander that EMDR therapy would not work with the soldier. However, the commander, a Medical Service Corps colonel who had been trained in EMDR therapy, knew the potential of EMDR therapy. The colonel knew of my work and the intensive treatment programs for active military and veterans offered at Soldier Center (www.Soldier-Center.org). The soldier was referred to our 5-day EMDR intensive therapy provided twice a day during a 5- or 10-day program. The soldier arrived with military orders to spend 5 days in Soldier Center's intensive program.

On arrival, the soldier settled in his lodging at Ft Campbell, then reported to Soldier Center for his treatment. This was one of the angriest clients I had ever treated. And, he was highly dissociative. Being informed EMDR therapy did not previously work with the client, I was eager to see if his target memories would reprocess with me. As we began the first reprocessing, focusing on his first target memory, the client was solemn, with no emotional warmth displayed. However, he was cooperative and committed to the treatment process. During the first few sets of BLS the client reported no change. I began to change the mechanics, altering the speed and elevating the horizontal directions of EM slightly. Next, the client began to sweat and his head jerked from time to time. He removed his outer jacket, commenting that he was hot, his body was sweating. I began to adjust the BLS and use cognitive interweaves to keep him present. Throughout much of the reprocessing of his first target memory, his head continued to jerk as he continued to process the memory. He was on the clinical border between being present and dissociated (lost in the memory) as he continued to report change during the process. While seated 2½ feet from me, during processing, the client lunged in my direction, being in a dissociative state. He immediately was grounded and said to me, "I had a flashback; I was grabbing for my M-16. My battle buddy was saying, we are under attack, grab your weapon." He continued processing; his body temperature began to cool down and toward the end of the first reprocessing session, he achieved a SUD of 0, a VOC of 7, with a clear body scan.

**Solution:** Rather than speculate on why EMDR therapy did not work with his previous psychologist, this report discusses what I did to facilitate the processing. I believe in the EMDR process, so my first goal was to get the soldier processing. If the disturbing memory is active and BLS is provided, the memory will begin to change, unless something is blocking the process. Getting the memory activated meant I was willing to stimulate an already angry soldier and sit with him as he worked on his trauma. Once I learned what he had endured during his deployment, not only combat threat, but abuse and betrayal by his leadership, I recognized the basis of his anger. I had a repertoire of responses for getting the processing going and maintaining the processing. The repertoire is what is taught during EMDR basic training when processing stops: (a) change the mechanics; (b) change the TICES (Target = Image, cognitions, emotion, and sensations); (c) check for blocking beliefs; (d) check for feeder memories; and (e) use cognitive interweaves. Additionally, in working with the client's dissociative responses, I was intent on keeping the client present and grounded for dual awareness during processing. I was willing to sit with him, in his anger, even to elevate his anger by focusing on the target memory and further stimulating memories that were the basis of the anger. My commitment to the client was to learn and incorporate what was needed in order to get the client effectively through treatment. My objective was to provide an environment in which the client's disturbing memory could process productive change. During his dissociative exhibitions, I adjusted the BLS and used cognitive interweaves. I continued to keep the processing going. I worked to maintain dual awareness. After about 20 minutes, the client reported his body was cooling down. After another 12 minutes, he reported watching my fingers (during the EM, which was no longer stressful). At the end of the first reprocessing session (Phases 3–7), he was calm and used the word "refreshed" to describe his state of being. He was smiling as he left the office.

SUMMARY

Unfortunately, we continue to learn of incidents when persons were unsuccessfully treated with EMDR therapy. There are far too many military personnel and veterans who need effective treatment. When it does not work—for whatever the reason—it leaves an already struggling individual to live with their psychological pain even longer. This impacts the hope or hopelessness of those we respect. In every situation I have explored, the treatment failure was found to be due to the therapist's failure to maintain fidelity to the EMDR protocol. The ramification is that the client's emotional pain is extended and the failure of the treatment is shared with buddies who usually suffer with similar wounds, therefore discouraging their motivation to seek help. And the therapist is left discouraged.

These concerns remind EMDR trainers and approved consultants of the importance of preparing newly trained clinicians to ensure they maintain fidelity to the protocol. EMDR therapists can benefit from continuing to develop their clinical skills. There is an ethical responsibility to continue the development of clinical skills in caring for military personnel and veterans whose clinical presentations can be demanding. And, whenever there is a failure such as those listed here, seeking consultation and attending EMDR International Association (EMDRIA)-approved advanced training and EMDRIA conferences for continuing education are important.

## CONCLUSION

Remember, meta-analysis (Maxfield & Hyer, 2002) found that fidelity to the EMDR protocol produced greater treatment results. In every case I have known, unsuccessful treatment results were the result of the therapists not following the EMDR protocol as taught in the standard EMDR basic training, approved by the EMDRIA. A therapist who is not achieving successful outcome would benefit from consulting the EMDR basic text (Shapiro, 2018), or a commentary on the EMDR process (Hensley, 2016; Leeds, 2016). Additional consultation with an EMDRIA-approved consultant (listed on the EMDRIA website [www.EMDRIA.org] can be helpful.

### DISCUSSION POINTS

1. What role does accurate assessment (Phase 3) play in effective treatment?
2. Some of the cited cases reported in this chapter note the misuse of the lightbar for reprocessing. What could these therapists have done differently both in using the lightbar as well as using alternative modalities?
3. Do you offer your clients all three modalities? If not, why? If so, what modality is most commonly selected by your clients?

### REFERENCES

Dunne, T., & Farrell, D. (2011). An investigation into clinicians' experiences of integrating EMDR into their clinical practice. *Journal of EMDR Practice and Research, 5*(4), 177–188. doi:10.1891/1933-3196.5.4.177
Hensley, B. (2016). *An EMDR therapy primer: From practicum to practice* (2nd ed.). New York, NY: Springer Publishing Company.

Leeds, A. (2016). *A guide to the standard EMDR therapy protocols for clinicians, supervisors, and consultants* (2nd ed.). New York, NY: Springer Publishing Company.

Maxfield, L., & Hyer, L. (2002). The relationship between efficacy and methodology in studies investigating EMDR treatment of PTSD. *Journal of Clinical Psychology, 58*(1), 23–41. doi:10.1002/jclp.1127

Shapiro, F. (2018). *Eye movement desensitization and reprocessing (EMDR) therapy: Basic procedures, protocols, and procedures* (3rd ed.). New York, NY: Guilford Press.

# 12

# EMDR Early Intervention Programs During Military and Community Operations

## Introduction

EMDR early intervention (EEI) protocols are used worldwide to treat persons who have experienced major life-threatening events including war, earthquakes, tsunamis, hurricanes, and mass shootings. EEI protocols are known to build resiliency while providing effective and brief interventions to acute stress and PTSD developments. This chapter describes the protocols and their applications. Application to military behavioral health in treating combat and operational stress is discussed. Research conducted in the application of EEI in various traumatic events is noted. EEI protocols are suitable for behavioral health use during military deployments, as well as treating veterans at local veterans' affairs medical centers and community-wide interventions during disasters.

## Learning Objectives

- Review the development of treatment principles of proximity, immediacy, expectancy, and simplicity with mental health applications.
- Become familiarized with the military's programs for combat and operational stress.
- Review the development of EMDR early intervention (EEI) protocols.

- Identify a plan for integrating EEI protocols into needs in your community.
- Review EEI protocols for enhancing resiliency and intervening with acute stress and PTSD-related problems.

## PRINCIPLES FOR EARLY INTERVENTION

The need to preserve the military force on the battlefield was recognized during World War I (WWI) when a paradigm shift occurred regarding combat stress. Psychiatric casualties had not been considered a major source of personnel loss at the beginning of the war. Combat stress casualties were viewed as medical injuries, a physical impairment in the brain caused by artillery shelling. Soldiers were evacuated from the battlefield as having sustained wounds similar to other physical wounds. While some soldiers were returned to combat, the majority were evacuated home accompanied by a psychiatric attendee. There was no stigma associated with the wounds at the time. Over time, the number of soldiers reporting combat stress wounds began to increase as word was circulated about stress casualties being sent home.

Over time, WWI stress casualties came to be known as victims of "shell shock." Shell shock was considered a temporary response to stress that could always be reversed with rest and encouragement. As combat continued, the medical concept of shell shock changed as it came to be viewed as a weakness in character. A new understanding of shell shock developed as it was associated with artillery shelling on the front lines. Shell shock came to be seen as a character weakness as the soldier faced the demands of combat. Soldiers were not allowed to see themselves as sick or injured. They were separated from war casualties who suffered with physical combat wounds. Medical providers expressed the expectation that soldiers wounded with stress would soon be returned to combat following a brief rest. Expectancy that the soldier would resume combat duties rather than being sent home changed the direction of treatment. This became the beginning of a new model for treating combat stress response.

The importance of *"proximity"* in treating combat stress near the front lines was developed by the British and French forces who were treating the wounded in forward positions, as close to the battlefield as possible. By 1917, psychiatrist Thomas Salmon, an emissary of the U.S. Army surgeon general, had observed the practices of the British and French treating soldiers close to the front lines. He conceptualized an U.S. military program for treating "war neurosis." When fully developed, three principles—*proximity, immediacy,* and *expectancy*—became the basis for psychiatric casualty treatment in the military (Jones, 1995). The concept of *"simplicity"* was included to acknowledge the importance of providing rest, food, and perhaps a shower. Together, these concepts created the acronym *PIES*.

Proximity and immediacy are deemed important for maintaining bonds with members of the soldier's unit. The longer the soldier is away from the unit, the greater the chance for self-blame, such as, "If I am not physically sick then I must be worthless as a person and member of my unit."

WWI established the forward assignments of behavioral health providers on the front line of combat in order to treat combat operational stress. Since WWII, division-level mental health providers have been utilized in both the home post and deployed operations (Warner et al., 2007).

This concept was tested by researchers in the Israeli Defense Force (IDF; Z. Solomon & Benbenishty, 1986) as they studied the principles of proximity, immediacy, and expectancy during the Lebanon War. They found all three principles were associated with a higher rate of soldiers who returned to their military unit for continuing operations.

In more recent times, during the global war on terror, the U.S. Army began a restructuring process, which is considered the largest restructuring of the U.S. military since WWII. The process was designed to make the Army a more modular force as it increased efficiency, combat power, and the number of brigade combat teams (BCT). A new mental health structure evolved as the BCT restructured. The mental health structure was organized into the division mental health activity (DMHA). The DMHA component was organized to include a psychiatrist, a senior noncommissioned officer (NCO) with the division surgeon at division headquarters level, a brigade behavioral health officer (BCT BHO), a psychologist or social worker, and an enlisted mental health specialist assigned to each BCT. With multiple BCT teams under control of the division, five or six mental health providers (psychiatrists, psychologists, and social workers) can be assigned to the DMHA. The restructuring allows for more providers to be available as well as the projection of resources to commanders at lower levels of command down to battalion and company levels. With the restructuring, the role of the military mental health provider became more diverse (Warner et al., 2007). The reorganization of the military provided a more flexible response to the behavioral health needs of military units. The military missions during Operation Iraqi Freedom (OIF) were particularly impacted with combat and operational stress. Up to half of all battlefield casualties were found to be accounted for within combat and operational stress response (COSR; Busher, 2011). Loss due to such stress responses decreased significantly as the combat and operational stress control (COSC) components were brought online within the military structure.

## MILITARY POLICIES FOR MENTAL HEALTH EARLY INTERVENTION

There was a time when treatment of combat and operational stress primarily consisted of removing the soldier from the front lines for a period while providing "three hots and a cot," meaning three meals and rest for a period. There are much more effective options for treatment these days. Effective intervention strategies now include resolving the pathology of unresolved stress while enhancing resilience. Based on current understanding, COSC missions are designed to make the most of community support by reducing a person's vulnerability to additional stress-related disorders. Prevention programs begin at pre-deployment, at the time when servicemembers first learn they are being deployed, and continue during deployment operations and the aftermath post-deployment adjustments. Studies indicate 20% to 30% of the U.S. military personnel have psychological symptoms on return from combat operations (Hoge, Auchterlonie, & Milliken, 2006).

For persons unfamiliar with military directives and regulations, I have included the specific titles of military regulations, pamphlets, instructions, and their numbers related to this discussion. Military regulations discussed are available online for downloading. The chapter reference list contains the access information.

In the U.S. Marine Corps unit, leaders helped to create the Marine version of the COSC model to address the challenges faced by unit members (Naval Center for Combat and Operational Stress Control, 2018). Retired Navy psychiatrist Dr. William Nash, MD, is credited with being the primary author of the Navy's COSC doctrine (Nash, 2011) published as Marine Corps and Navy publication MCRP 6-11C/NTTP 1-15M, COSC. A stress continuum model was developed to recognize the spectrum of stress responses and outcomes ranging from green (adaptive coping and wellness), which is considered the "Ready" zone; yellow (mild and reversible distress), the "Reacting" zone; orange (more severe and persistent distress or loss of function), the "Injured" zone; and red (mental disorders arising from stress and unhealed stress injuries), the "Ill" zone (Nash, 2011).

The U.S. Air Force guidance on mental health concerns is covered in a number of directives including Air Force Instruction 44-153 and 44-172. Disaster mental health response and COSC are addressed in the U.S. Air Force Instruction 44-153. The publication augments a broader mental health directive described in Air Force Instruction 44-172, Air Force Mental Health Procedures. This latter publication provides a more general perspective for mental health, while the former publication is more specific to COSC. The COSC guidance lists the goal of preventing and managing stress reactions through increased psychological resilience and skill building both before and after exposure in a wartime environment (Department of the Secretary of the Air Force, 2014, p. 10).

Mental health prevention is addressed (Chapter 3), noting the importance of developing awareness to organizational and individual mental health issues including trends and threats to mission readiness. Both early intervention strategies and psychological first aid policies are addressed as means of providing evidence-based practices. The management of Combat and Operational Stress Reactions (COSRs) exhibited in physical, mental, and emotional signs, due to exposure to combat or military operations, are identified for treatment. The Air Force's approach to the treatment of PTSD is based on the Department of Veterans Affairs (DVA)'s *Clinical Practice Guidelines* (2017). The guidelines recommend four models of psychotherapy—prolonged exposure, cognitive processing therapy, EMDR therapy, and narrative therapy—as being preferred treatment modalities. Within these two documents are the authorization for the U.S. Air Force to provide response to stress reactions and reference to the DVA's list of four psychotherapies recognized as being Category A in the treatment of PTSD.

Department of the Army (DA) guidance for COSC is provided in field manuals FM-6-22.5 *Combat and Operational Stress Control Manual for Leaders and Soldiers* and FM 4-02.51 *Combat and Operational Stress Control*. Army FM 4-02.51 directs all mental health sections, regardless of their location within the organization, to provide stress control (COSC) for their assigned units. This approach ensures stress control teams are available throughout Army organizations regardless of their level. The stress control mission is accomplished through prevention, training, education, consultation, and restoration programs for soldiers. COSC has the purpose of (a) enhancing adaptive stress reactions; (b) preventing maladaptive stress reactions; (c) assisting soldiers with controlling COSRs; and (d) assisting soldiers with behavioral disorders (Department of the Army, 2006, p. 1-1). The goal of the stress control team (COSC) is to return soldiers back to duty as expeditiously as possible (Busher, 2011). Building upon the principles learned in WWI, COSC incorporates brevity, immediacy, contact, expectancy, proximity, and simplicity (BICEPS) when managing soldiers with stress response (COSR) or behavioral disorders. Warner and his military colleagues (2007) provide insight into the wartime experiences of mental health staff serving with a division-level mental health activity within Task Force Baghdad. The mental health unit attended to more than 5,542 clinical encounters during the period of January 2005 through January 2006.

The concept of COSC is a joint-service program provided within each branch of the U.S. military. Caring for the well-being of our military servicemembers enhances mission readiness. Stress control is considered a force multiplier as assessments are performed and interventions provided to military personnel. The following discussion is intended to educate readers in the evolving wave of EMDR therapy's early intervention protocols, which offer significant potential in the building of resiliency and providing effective intervention to service-members both at home base and those deployed to combat zones. The same EMDR resources have been invaluable in treating survivors in both man-made and natural disasters.

## TREATING MILITARY PERSONNEL WITH EMDR BRIEF TREATMENT

### EMDR THERAPY AND 2-WEEK R & R PROGRAM

When I first learned of EMDR therapy, I was very skeptical. I had been an independently licensed psychotherapist for 20+ years by then, trained in most models of psychotherapy. I believed I had no need to learn one more treatment model since the psychotherapy treatments I was providing seemed to be working reasonably well. All this changed with the 9-11 attack and the beginning of military operations known as Operation Iraqi Freedom (OIF) and Operation Enduring Freedom (OEF). Soldiers from the 101st Airborne Division (Air Assault) at Fort Campbell began seeking me for treatment of their acute stress disorder (ASD) and acute PTSD symptoms when they returned home for 2-week rest and relaxation (R & R). These were combat soldiers who had completed 6 months of their combat tour and returned home for 2 weeks. I had known most of the soldiers prior to their initial combat deployment. We had established trust and rapport from previous interactions, so it was natural for them to turn to me with the newly developed symptoms. They were home for 2 weeks and things were not going as they planned. While home for their R & R, they reported daily conflict with their spouse. If they had children, their children hid in their bedrooms avoiding their dad, the infantry soldier. They showed up in my office, many ranting and raving, so hypervigilant, they literally would not remain seated more than 2 minutes before jumping up and pacing across my office blaming everyone and everything for their condition. This is when I learned *"Talk therapy doesn't work if a person doesn't listen!"* The soldiers were so hypervigilant that they would not hear what I was saying. For most who sought treatment at my office, I had less than 10 days to treat them before their return to Iraq. At this time, a colleague at Soldier Center was treating soldiers with EMDR therapy. Our adjacent offices allowed me to see the results of her work and her excitement as a therapist providing effective treatment each session.

Viewing the effectiveness of EMDR therapy as I witnessed my colleague's work, I sought the next EMDR training. I attended a training that weekend. On return to my office, after the EMDR part 1 training, the first soldier I treated with EMDR therapy had two sessions with me. I already knew his history, except for the single-incident combat trauma he revealed to me. During the first session of EMDR therapy (second therapy appointment during his R & R), he identified the events that had happened during his deployment. During that session, I worked with him to master a relaxation exercise for self-regulation. The second session, 2 days later, I treated the single-incident combat trauma. The soldier processed through Phases 3 to 7 of the EMDR standard protocol. His level of disturbance (SUD) was 0 when he left my office, with his positive thought, the idea he would like to believe about himself (positive cognition), ranking the highest possible, a 7 (on a scale from 1 to 7). He achieved a clear body scan. He was calm and felt in control of his life again. Four days later, for his third appointment, I went to the waiting room to meet him. As he arrived for his third appointment, he was accompanied by his spouse who said, "I wanted to come by and thank you. I don't know what you are doing with my husband. I just want you to know, whatever you are doing is working. I have him back the way he was before he deployed to Iraq!" With two sessions of EMDR therapy, his spouse was noticing his improvement!

During the third session, I reevaluated the results from the previous session; he reported the same consistent results as his previous session. During the third session, I treated his triggers, the things happening that created his reactions. Again, he completed processing the targeted memory, Phases 3 to 7, in that session and left my office feeling calm and in control of his life again. The fourth session—the last one before returning to Iraq—we focused on the third prong of EMDR therapy, the future template, as he viewed himself in the future returning to duty in Iraq while effectively managing his life in similar situations (such as what he had worked on). He left my office with a new sense of resiliency having resolved the memories associated with his acute PTSD and feeling in control of his life as he was managing any triggers. He was prepared for a positive response for his future.

This was the first soldier I treated with EMDR therapy. I learned this particular therapy can be effective in a brief period of time. This began my approach of treating soldiers who were home for 2 weeks' R & R, who were suffering with acute stress or acute PTSD, to treat them for three sessions focusing on past event, present trigger(s), and effectively preparing for the future. The results were always significant.

## ONE SESSION RESULTS WITH EMDR THERAPY AT A NAVY FIELD HOSPITAL

Psychologist Mark Russell, a retired Navy commander, published the results of his work providing brief treatment to Marines and soldiers, as well as Iraqi war casualties who were temporarily at a Navy hospital in Rota,

Spain, in transit to medical care in the United States (Russell, 2006). With the PIES guidance for treatment, Commander Russell treated four service-members while they were waiting to return to stateside care. They had been wounded in Iraq and scheduled for imminent return to the United States. Due to the wounded's concern of returning home with continuing ASD or PTSD symptoms, they were strong enough to request treatment while at the Navy hospital in Spain. All the patients treated had requested EMDR therapy treatment. Dr. Russell reported one session of EMDR therapy was sufficient for eliminating the pronounced symptoms. However, all patients were referred for additional follow-up treatment stateside.

The psychologist noted the appropriateness of EMDR therapy in forward-deployed areas in comparison to other models of psychother-apy. EMDR therapy requires no homework and can be administered twice daily or once every week or two as determined by availability. This forward-deployed psychologist, with his experience in treating military personnel in combat areas, suggests EMDR therapy is an im-portant addition to the standard treatment for frontline personnel. A version of EMDR therapy could be used in addition to BICEPS to pro-cess traumatic experiences rapidly and effectively as they occur and within a short period of time.

He provided one session of EMDR therapy as they awaited their transfer to the states. Results of a single session of EMDR therapy made a significant improvement in their acute stress disorder and acute PTSD disorder.

## BRITISH FORCES USED EMDR THERAPY—A CASE STUDY DOWN RANGE

Wesson and Gould (2009) affirmed the frequent use of EMDR therapy by the United Kingdom armed forces in treating military personnel suffering with acute stress and PTSD symptoms. They present a single case report describing their frontline treatment of a soldier suffering from acute stress after he medically treated another soldier who was a landmine casualty.

Usual treatment procedures would require the injured soldier to be treated at home rather than the proximity of the incident. Treatment at home either interrupts the soldier's tour of duty if they are treated in a

---

A version of EMDR therapy could be used to process traumatic experiences rapidly and effectively as they occur or within a short period of time—when forward deployed.

timely manner, or the treatment is prolonged if the soldier waits to complete the deployment before seeking treatment. Neither is advantageous, for the individual and needs of the military. Furthermore, when psychiatric casualties are evacuated, there is evidence suggesting the evacuees have a poor chance of later returning to duty (Rundell, 2006). Wesson and Gould (2009) note that clinicians stationed at the combat front line are in a position to detect and provide early intervention to presenting symptoms. Proximity, immediacy, expectation, and simplicity continue to be the recommended posture in caring for the wounded (Lee, Gabriel, & Bale, 2005).

The solider was 4 months into his second tour with 7 years in the military. His colleague had stepped on a landmine. The soldier presented in the study was the medic who attended to the wounded soldier, worked to stabilize him at the scene, and was with the wounded soldier during the medevac to the hospital. He later learned the wounded soldier, his colleague, had died. Symptoms presented included intrusive thoughts, smells, and nightmares of the event. The medic had been assigned to a location in the rear area and the thoughts of returning to the area where the friend was wounded exacerbated his anxiety. The first author of this article was a member of the British unit's Field Mental Health Team. They treated the medic with EMDR therapy's Recent Traumatic Event protocol for four sessions of treatment. Two additional review sessions occurred over the next months to ensure the medic's well-being. The treatment results remained consistent. At the 18-month follow-up, the effective results remained consistent.

Treatment in this case study was provided at a forward-located military base in the military theatre, which allowed effective results to be achieved in proximity to the incident. This allowed the soldier to return to duty following treatment. Measures used to evaluate the effectiveness of treatment included the PTSD Checklist–Civilian (PCL-C) version. The medic rated a score of 35 on the PCL-C. Following four sessions of treatment with EMDR therapy, the score was reduced to 21. At an 18-month follow-up, the soldier's PCL-C's score had diminished to 17. It is not unusual the benefits of EMDR treatment continue after the treatment is concluded. Following treatment and follow-up, Wesson and Gould (2009) concluded EMDR therapy is effective both at the home post as well as in deployment locations. Not only is EMDR therapy effective within a brief period of time, it requires no homework and allows for treatment while the person remains in the area (proximity).

## EMDR EARLY INTERVENTION PROTOCOLS

The purpose of this chapter is to recognize the need of many military personnel as well as community service personnel, that is, law enforcement officers, paramedics, and firefighters who present with ASD and acute PTSD who can benefit from EEIs. Interventions early in the development of pathology resolve the impact of stress while prohibiting later development of more severe pathology. And, from a military perspective, early intervention frequently allows the person to be returned to duty while remaining in close proximity to their duty assignment. In this sense, effective early intervention is a force multiplier. A familiarization of EEI protocols is provided.

## IMMEDIATE STABILIZATION PROCEDURE/EMERGENCY RESPONSE PROCEDURE

Developed by Israeli psychiatrist Gary Quinn, MD, this protocol was developed for persons experiencing high levels of "fight, flight, or freeze" after the danger is over (Luber, 2014; Quinn, 2018). These are people suffering with acute stress reaction (ASR), which can last from the immediate present to 3 days after a traumatic event. Fear can continue increasing beyond a SUD level of 10 as survivors go into a high state of agitation or a silent terror. Such a state leaves the person with no ability to communicate with their external world. The Immediate Stabilization Procedure/Emergency Response Procedure (ISP/ERP) approach is based on EMDR therapy using bilateral stimulation (BLS), with both negative and positive cognitions. ISP was developed primarily for first responders or non-psychotherapists who can immediately stabilize a survivor on site of the event. Dr. Quinn explains ISP as fitting into the framework of acute stress disorder (ASR/ASD) with psychological first aid (PFA).

This protocol initially became known as the ERP and later known as the ISP with the goal of stabilizing the person sufficiently to resume routine function.

## EYE MOVEMENT DESENSITIZATION

Eye movement desensitization (EMD) is the original protocol developed by Dr. D. Shapiro in 1987 with published research on the approach (1989) indicating its effectiveness. It differs from the EMDR standard protocol by restricting the treatment focus on desensitizing the intrusive sensory image by returning to the original sensory image after each set of BLS. EMD is noted for its ability to process fragmented sensorimotor fragments of traumatic memories. In comparison to the EMDR standard protocol, the negative cognition (NC) is mentioned and subjective units of disturbance (SUD) is checked following each set. This protocol is used primarily for treating intrusive symptoms of ASD.

Elan Shapiro and Brurit Laub (2008) present a case example of a woman, a mother of three children exposed to a traumatic event during the Lebanon war. The traumatic event was a missile striking in the yard near the family as they were on their way to a bomb shelter. The woman's leg was injured by shrapnel as she was knocked to the ground from the blast. The daughter, who was walking hand in hand with her mother, was thrown in the air by the blast, landing in another location. After a few minutes to regain their bearing, both mother and daughter made their way to the shelter. Her symptoms included nightmares and sleep disturbances several weeks following the attack.

Using the EMD approach, the disturbing memory of the mother had been neutralized; she recalled the event without experiencing emotional disturbance. Before the session ended, she was thinking of positive events, such as her older daughter's wedding in the same courtyard. The level of disturbance (SUD) dropped from 10 (highest possible) to a 0 (lowest possible) with one session of EMD. The disturbing memory was neutralized of its emotional charge with positive thoughts for the future.

## RECENT EVENTS PROTOCOL

Dr. Francine Shapiro developed her EMDR recent events protocol in initial response to survivors of the 1989 San Francisco Bay Area earthquake (F. Shapiro, 2018). Dr. Shapiro, while treating survivors of the recent earthquake, noted memory recall following a disaster was different. Recent event memories seemed more fragmented, less consolidated, and less integrated. Due to such fragmentation, memory components have not been adequately integrated; therefore, a single memory component, such as image, may not adequately represent the complete memory episode. Francine Shapiro (2018) estimated that it took 2 to 3 months for a memory to consolidate normally. Therefore, to adequately treat a memory before total consolidation required the identification of various components of the memory. Recent event unconsolidated discrete memories are targeted with the recent events protocol. The protocol separates each component of the target memory to be identified as separate targets for reprocessing. Each component of the disturbing memory is reprocessed before installing the positive cognition and completing the body scan. Next, the present trigger(s) is processed followed by incorporating the future template. The three-prong approach treating past, present, and future is included in the recent events protocol.

Studies found the EMDR recent event protocol to be effective in the treatment of acute stress and PTSD resulting from natural disasters such as Hurricane Andrew (Grainer, Levin, Allen-Byrd, Doctor, & Lee, 1997) and the New York City 9-11 attacks (Silver, Rogers, Knipe, & Colelli, 2005). Similar results were demonstrated in treatment for survivors of Hurricane Katrina, the Maramara earthquake in Turkey, and persons caught in the 2004 Indian Ocean tsunami that hit the coast of Sri Lanka

(Jayatunge, 2008). The number of treatment sessions varied from three to eight in response to survivors of these disasters. Fernandez (2008) documented her treatment of a tsunami survivor suffering with acute PTSD with three sessions including all eight phases of the EMDR standard protocol with the three-prong approach of addressing past, present, and future issues.

As a volunteer coordinator in the EMDR Humanitarian Assistance Program's response to survivors of Hurricane Katrina, I can attest we used both the EMDR standard protocol (single incident) and the EMDR recent events protocol in treating first responders working the Katrina disaster response. Both protocols were effective in treating first responders with one or two sessions.

Following the 9-11 attacks in New York City, EMDR therapy was provided by therapists residing in the region who volunteered to treat survivors. Silver et al. (2005) reported the use of EMDR therapy as a time-limited early intervention project with children, adolescents, and adults. The treatment, with a brief, time-limited approach, was found to be useful in treatment of persons aged 6 to 65 years.

When responding to events where the normal conditions have not been restored, such as natural disasters, the Protocol for Recent Critical Events (PRECI) or the Recent Traumatic Episode Protocol (R-TEP) is recommended by Francine Shapiro (2018).

## PROTOCOL FOR RECENT CRITICAL EVENTS

The PRECI is recommended for treating survivors as long as 6 months following the man-made or natural disaster where conditions have not returned to normal (F. Shapiro, 2018). This approach, based on Dr. Shapiro's Recent Traumatic Events Protocol, was developed in response to critical incidents with modifications to include associated events that have occurred since before the event until the present. Ignacio Jarero and Lucina Artigas included their clinical experience in the modifications for the EMDR PRECI protocol. They introduced the *"Butterfly Hug"* as an alternative to the standard modalities for BLS. The model has been used for treatment as part of a Disaster Mental Health Continuum of Care response to survivors of a 7.2 earthquake in Mexico and North Baja, California. The EMDR PRECI was also used in treating first responders who responded to a human massacre situation in Mexico. Research using this early intervention approach demonstrated diminished PTSD symptoms as well as scores on self-report measures. An increase in psychological and emotional resilience was reported. Scripted protocols of this model and other models discussed are available (Luber, 2014).

A modification of this version has developed for paraprofessionals to use in acute trauma situations known at the EMDR PROPARA (Jarero, 2013). The approach is focused on providing mental healthcare to survivors who live in areas that have limited mental health providers. The approach is focused on reducing the severity of symptoms of posttraumatic stress as well as somatic distress; coping; and social, family, and work impairment. Outcome results determined that participants demonstrated immediate benefits after treatment. Values in the self-measurement score continued to decrease as noted in the second follow-up conducted 3 months later. Findings on this study using paraprofessionals as treatment providers are promising, particularly since many communities rely on first responders during times of crisis.

## RECENT TRAUMATIC EPISODE PROTOCOL

The Recent Traumatic Event Protocol (R-TEP) developed as a means of addressing what E. Shapiro and Laub (2008) viewed as an ongoing trauma continuum with fragmented components of the memory not yet consolidated. In their view, experiences associated with the original event extend to the present. There can be multiple targets that need inclusion in treatment. In order to address the broad spectrum, the R-TEP protocol incorporates the narrow focus of EMD and a wider focus of the parts of the event memory to a wide focus addressing the entire episode. This approach is designed to provide brief intervention results rapidly, normally within two to four sessions.

R-TEP begins with History-Taking, gathering as much information as possible, including others, in gaining an account of the event if necessary. Evaluating for complex PTSD is warranted. Main features of the R-TEP include: (a) stabilization; (b) focusing on the episode; (c) episode narrative with dual attention stimulus (DAS); (d) a "Google search" process; (e) regulation of associated networks; and, (f) providing a bridge between the episode and the theme processing levels of recent traumatic event(s). When treating persons recently impacted by war, as well as first responders, the four elements exercise (E. Shapiro, 2007) for stress management is helpful in ensuring the survivor's ability to self-regulate. R-TEP focuses on processing the series of events or experiences that are part of the entire episode.

The episode focus allows the client to verbally express a narrative account beginning before the event happened, all through the episode until it was over and they felt safe in the present. As the client presents the narrative account verbally, the therapist provides continuous BLS. This process provides an opportunity for the client to move through the memory without needing to become lost in high arousal prematurely. The client is discouraged from going into details during this period, but urged to provide more of a narrative overview of the experiences.

After completing the episode narrative with continuous stimulation, the next phase is directing the survivor to review mentally the points of disturbance. Clients are asked without speaking to search their memory of the entire episode for points of disturbance, those components of the recent event memory that continue to be disturbing. As each point of disturbance (POD) is identified, the EMDR standard protocol's Phases 3 and 4, Assessment and Desensitization, are provided. The goal is to get the SUD as low as possible. The client resumes the Google search after processing each POD until no additional PODs are identified. Then the therapist directs the client to the episode level of the entire trauma to install the episode-level positive cognition (PC), complete a body scan, and go to closure.

E. Shapiro, Laub, and Rosenblat (2018) report on using the R-TEP in response to an Israeli community event where a missile hit a building in a crowded part of the community. Seventeen survivors with PTSD were treated with the EMDR R-TEP protocol. Treatments were provided by volunteer therapists on 2 successive days. Using a waitlist/delayed treatment for half the group and R-TEP for the other half, treatment measures of the R-TEP group significantly improved compared to the waitlist/delayed treatment group, which indicated no improvement. The results remained consistent at 3-month follow-up among civilian survivors of war hostilities in their local community.

Other instances where the R-TEP has been effective in treating trauma survivors include an earthquake in Northern Italy the summer of 2012 in which over 1,000 survivors were treated; a terrorist bombing in Istanbul, Turkey, in 2009 (Kaya, 2010); and Syrian refugees who lived in a large refugee camp after escaping Syria

## R-TEP WITH OKLAHOMA NATIONAL GUARD AND FIRST RESPONDERS

In 2013, I provided EMDR treatment, using the R-TEP protocol, for treating first responders and National Guard personnel near Moore, Oklahoma, following an EF 5 tornado that ravaged the area. With winds peaking at 210 mph, a total of 24 people were killed and another 212 injured. Volunteering my services, I worked out of a conference room in a nearby National Guard armory where I treated an average of 8 to 10 first responders and National Guard personnel each day during a 6-day period. The R-TEP proved itself to be invaluable in helping these people reclaim their lives. First responders had searched for missing bodies, including infants where the tornado had sucked an infant out of a mother's arms as she was running for shelter. Some responders had worked the Oklahoma City bombing at the Murrah Federal Building as well as the Moore tornado. They had cumulative traumatic events to process. Some first responders who were in the Moore tornado described the experience as the proverbial "straw that broke the camel's back" before they learned about treatment. I completed treatment for all persons who had signed up for treatment by the mental health officers. Two weeks later, I returned for follow-up reevaluation. Meeting with each individual for the second week, I discovered the sessions completed during the first week had completely resolved their ASR symptoms; no person needed a second R-TEP session. A R-TEP-trained EMDR therapist can operate out of any room, such as a conference room in a National Guard armory, to provide effective treatment of ASR/ASD.

In addition to military personnel, I use the R-TEP in treating law enforcement officers referred for EMDR therapy by regional police agencies in Kentucky and Tennessee. Soldier Center staff provides treatment to firefighters and medics from throughout the state of Tennessee who travel to our location for EMDR R-TEP treatment.

## EMDR POST-DEPLOYMENT SEMINAR

Psychologist Roger Solomon, PhD, an EMDR Institute trainer and longtime psychologist with law enforcement agencies, developed an assessment and brief intervention, which is used with both law enforcement and military personnel internationally. Known as the Post Critical Incident Seminar (PCIS) with law enforcement, it is identified as a Post-Deployment Seminar (PDS) in working with military personnel. Dr. Solomon utilized the multiday model with a number of organizations including the Federal Bureau of Investigations (McNally & Solomon, 1999), also following a critical incident with the railroad (R. Solomon & Kaufman, 2002), and NASA following the loss of the space shuttle (Solomon, 2008).

The Post-Deployment Seminar is provided at several international locations. Two psychologists in Norway, Drs. Kjersti Vangberg Sordal and Hanne Kristine Haarset, both mental health providers with extensive clinical experience providing clinical interventions with soldiers and veterans, were trained to provide the EMDR Post Deployment Seminar in Norway for veterans and active military personnel. With the cooperation of veterans' organizations in Norway, they recruit veterans who can benefit from the early intervention program. The program includes peer facilitators who previously benefited from participation in a similar program, EMDR-trained mental health providers (the number of providers attending is in proportion to the number of attendees), and, during several events, as the professionals were being trained, the senior trainer was present.

Research completed in the United States found the following selection criteria important for the Post-Deployment Seminar: (a) Each participant has the ability to listen to others and tell their story without being overwhelmed; (b) each participant should be able to provide support to others; (c) participants were primarily capable of performing duty or active in other areas such as interacting in peer support; (d) person needs to be motivated to resolve their situation as well as help others. Often participants are more motivated to help others than pursue their own clinical work since they tend to minimalize their own difficulties. This is sufficient; (e) substance use should be under control; and (f) active suicidality is considered an exclusion. The seminar is designed to address a particular critical incident, which often includes moral injury.

Participants in Norway are screened with the Beck Depression Inventory (BDI), the Beck Anxiety Inventory (BAI), the Posttraumatic Stress Inventory-5 (PCL-5), the Drug Use Disorders Identification Test (DUDIT), the Alcohol Use Disorders Identification Test (AUDIT), and the Moral Injury Questionnaire. Psychologists conduct a phone interview with each participant. The interview provides information about the seminar to the prospective participant, answers any questions, and gathers overall history regarding military service and number of military missions.

The Post-Deployment Seminar is typically scheduled over a 3-day period. On arrival, participants settle in their rooms, then gather for an initial meeting that includes a degree of socializing and familiarizing themselves to their environment for the next 3 days. Seminar leaders welcome participants during the opening session. Peer support is a strong component and provided throughout the seminar for both the large group, small groups, and one-on-one format. The group format provides a secure environment for participants to share among other peers who have similar experiences. Recognition of one's issues with nonjudgmental acceptance among others becomes a powerful experience in itself. The peer interaction breaks the illusion that "nobody would understand if I talked about it." The seminar provides a supportive, accepting environment that provides possibilities for psychological and emotional healing during the 3 days. Post-Deployment Seminar attendees provide a range of feedback ranging from enjoying better sleep, having more energy, more daily happiness, and less aggression. Some participants shared that their partner and children recognized the "old me" again.

Likewise, the PCIS program for law enforcement officers provides similar peer support, acceptance, and opportunities for healing with EMDR sessions provided during the 3 days. The PCIS program in Columbia, South Carolina, began with the guidance of Dr. Solomon and the local leadership of Dr. Eric Skidmore. I have been fortunate to participate in a PCIS hosted in Columbia, South Carolina. Dr. Skidmore, program coordinator of the South Carolina Law Enforcement Assistance Program, has been instrumental in coordinating and promoting both the PDS and the PCIS seminar, along with other key volunteer staff who represent several agencies and years of law enforcement experience. The PCIS is a means of offering support, care, and healing to officers as EMDR therapy is a core component for healing for law enforcement attendees who wish to participate in the therapy component for resolving their psychological wounds. The South Carolina PCIS seminars have become a model for other similar programs offered through several law enforcement agencies at state and regional levels throughout the United States.

Colonel McCarty, U.S. Army War College, and Dr. Sokolowski, Old Dominion University (McCarty & Sokolowski, 2011), evaluated the Post-Deployment Seminar. Colonel McCarty's conclusion noted the joint cooperation of the South Carolina National Guard (SCNG) State Family Programs and the South Carolina Law Enforcement Assistance Program (SCLEAP) in working together to assist the reintegration of National Guard soldiers on return from deployment.

## EMDR EARLY INTERVENTION GROUP PROTOCOLS

Two EMDR group protocols have proven effective: the EMDR-Integrative Group Treatment Protocol (IGTP) and the EMDR Group-Traumatic Episode Protocol (G-TEP). The origins of the IGTP began in Mexico and the G-TEP began in Israel in response to significant crises. Both protocols are now used internationally.

### EMDR-INTEGRATIVE GROUP TREATMENT PROTOCOL

The EMDR-Integrative Group Treatment Protocol (EMDR-IGTP) was developed in response to the devastation of Hurricane Pauline, which ravaged the western coast of Mexico in 1997 (Artigas, Jarero, Mauer, Lopez Cano, & Alcala, 2000; Jarero, Artigas, & Hartung, 2006). A modified version of the EMDR standard protocol was used to treat children who survived the hurricane. One of the strengths of this protocol is the ability to provide treatment without the survivor needing to respond with verbal answers. Instead, the person draws a picture as the assessment phase. And, Artigas developed a form of BLS called the Butterfly Hug when working with children survivors of the hurricane, enabling the entire group to be treated as a group approach with the modified EMDR approach structured similar to the eight-phase approach. The Butterfly Hug is done by crossing one's arms close to the chest so the wrist crosses each other and the fingers touch near the collarbone. BLS is done by alternating tapping near the collarbone.

This protocol's effectiveness has been documented with reports and field studies (Maxfield, 2008).

In the initial treatment of children, hurricane survivors are shown a diagram of faces depicting various levels of negative emotions. Each child is directed to draw a personal picture of the traumatic event on a sheet of paper divided into quadrants, then rate his/her level of disturbance (subjective units of disturbance; SUD). Looking at the picture, they provide their own BLS using the Butterfly Hug (Artigas & Jarero, 2009). Children are asked to look at the drawn picture, cross their arms, and tap themselves doing the Butterfly Hug. They then draw another picture related to the disturbing event and rate it according to its level of distress and do the Butterfly Hug. The process is repeated until there are four pictures drawn. The survivor is then asked to look at the drawing that is most disturbing and use the rating scale to determine how disturbing the current SUD is now. For those who did not reach a SUD of 0, additional individual treatment may be warranted. There may be blocking beliefs or other problems needing additional time. The survivors are asked to draw a picture representing their future vision of themselves along with a word or phrase that describes the picture. The picture of the future is paired with a Butterfly Hug for another set of BSL. Then, in completing the treatment, the survivor is asked to do a body scan. The person is directed to close their eyes, scan their body, and do the Butterfly Hug. The person is asked to recall their safe/secure place. Reevaluation then takes place afterward, with the therapy team leader and members conducting an evaluation of any residual symptoms that may need attention.

Originally modified for the treatment of children, the EMDR-IGTP protocol is now used in treating adolescents and adult groups as well. The therapy can be applied over several consecutive sessions as needed. It is nonverbal as persons do not verbalize information about the incident, and it allows the treatment of several persons at the same time, allowing sections to be treated at the same time. In comparison to exposure-based cognitive treatments, which are generally considered inappropriate for emergency situations with chaotic environments, EEIs have been proven effective, as demonstrated in the use of EMDR-IGTP in responding to emergency situations in Italy where three 90-minute sessions were found to be sufficient for 45 survivors of an earthquake in the central region of Italy. At each session, participants were asked to make a drawing connected with the earthquake, to provide a score from 0 to 10 representing the negative emotions associated with the picture, and do BLS four times (Maslovaric et al., 2017). Significant results were demonstrated in treatment using EMDR-IGTP.

The EMDR-IGTP protocol was used in the treatment of a group of Palestinian children who had experienced war trauma 5 days previously. They were exhibiting symptoms of acute stress. After two sessions of EMDR-IGTP, as the children began to improve, they were exposed to another traumatic incident. At the next EMDR session, even though exposed to another wartime incident, the children did not exhibit or report any distress related to the recent incident as their apparent resiliency was increasing with the initial two EMDR-IGTP sessions (Zaghrout-Hodali & Dodgson, 2008).

## GROUP-TRAUMATIC EPISODE PROTOCOL

The Group-Traumatic Episode Protocol (G-TEP) was developed by Elan Shapiro based on his earlier development of the Recent-Traumatic Episode Protocol (R-TEP). The approach is a simplified development that incorporates the basics of R-TEP adjusted for the treatment of groups. The protocol has application both for recent events as well as life-changing events with ongoing consequences. A screening is done for potential participants to ensure they are ready for the trauma processing. In preparation for treatment, group members are introduced to a stabilization and containment exercise known as the four elements (E. Shapiro, 2007, 2012). A worksheet, much like a placemat, is provided to participants. The design of the worksheet presents a meta-communication with the present, past, and future, which are spatially positioned to illustrate the past, present, and future. Participants are asked to identify PODs, much like the R-TEP doing a mental search, which is much like a Google search. Levels of disturbance (SUD) are checked and each POD is listed for processing. Each POD is processed by the individual doing their own BLS by visually following their hand movement, as the hand taps on the worksheet from a place of safety to focusing on the memory of the incident represented by the POD. The EM is done by each participant as they follow their hand moving, tapping from one location on the worksheet to another. After three sets of BLS, the participant goes back to the POD and checks the SUD. After nine sets, a new Google search is done as the participant searches for the next POD and continues similar processing. After processing of all PODs, an Episode Positive Cognition (PC) is installed. In the final session, the closing includes a container exercise.

Advantages to the G-TEP are similar to those of the R-TEP. Participants draw the picture of the incident/event. Little verbalization is required. It is acultural, since it effectively treats people of all cultures and languages. The protocol provides for the reprocessing of several disturbing events (PODs) during the brief treatment. Using tapping on the worksheet provides EM while the person provides their own BLS. Participants doing their own BLS have a greater sense of being in control.

Past use of the G-TEP includes a field study treating refugees in Germany who had fled Syria and Iraq (Lehnung, Shapiro, Schreiber, & Hofmann, 2017). G-TEP was used for treatment of Syrian refugees with PTSD with a randomized controlled trial included. Measures detected a significant decline in depression by the BDI as well as decline in Impact of Event Scale-Revised. A large decline in depression was discovered in addition to significant decline in the IES-R. Results indicated treating refugees with PTSD using the G-TEP approach was effective.

Similar results were noted when treating Syrian refugees located at a refugee center in Turkey, near the Syrian border. Participants in the EMDR-G-TEP study (Yurtsever et al., 2018) included 47 adults who were randomly allocated to treatment ($n = 18$) and control ($n = 29$). Impact of Event Scale-Revised, the BDI-II, and the International Neuropsychiatric Interview (MINI) were used at pre-, post-, and 4-week follow-up. The treatment group received two sessions of 4 hours each due to translation of instructions. After the two sessions, the outcome results found the PTSD diagnosis dropped from 100% to 38.9%. Overall, 61.1% of the treatment group no longer met diagnostic criteria for a PTSD diagnosis. The findings were maintained at 4-week follow-up.

This protocol offers great potential in treating groups such as survivors of school and congregational shootings, veterans adjusting to the distress of civilian life, and members of military units that have recently survived a combat mission once they are in a secure area.

## FUTURE OF APPLICATIONS OF EEI

The use of EEI protocols normally begins with a therapist who recognizes the efficacy of the protocols and is attuned to the mental health needs within their areas of responsibility (AOR). These protocols are effective, they make a difference; key persons think ahead about effective interventions that can be helpful in addressing presenting needs. This is how EMDR early invention protocols were first used downrange, during deployment. Military mental health providers newly trained in EMDR therapy within the Army's Medical Command (AMEDD) trainings took the concept of EMDR recent events with them for implementation during deployment. As the EMDR Institute's trainer to the Army AMEDD, I began to learn the EEI protocols as the mental health officers returned from deployments.

There are numerous opportunities to incorporate these EEI protocols. As an EMDR therapist, a provider, I urge you to become trained in EEI models, if you are not already. Begin to assess how early interventions, such as these protocols, can respond to needs in your AOR. For military personnel, we want to be leaning forward in developing programs to move the PIES concept forward to ASD and acute PTSD as early as possible with treatment that offers a full range of resources. Civilian providers can assess how these protocols can address the needs of first responders in your community. My recommendation is to become trained in these models—trainings are listed on the EMDRIA website under "Trainings." Once trained, begin to identify areas that need such broad range clinical resources. Explore the possibilities with key decision-makers, daring to think of what needs to be, should be, and can be. Remember the words of George Bernard Shaw, *"There are those that look at things the way they are, and ask why? I dream of things that never were, and ask why not?"* (Shaw, 1949).

## CONCLUSION

EEI protocols offer important possibilities to the military and civilian communities in caring for personnel impacted by acute stress and PTSD issues. While the protocols were developed in response to natural and man-made disasters, including war, the protocols offer opportunities for care in combat zones and community disaster response, where PIES are key factors. Military personnel coming back from a mission as well as first responders have benefited from EEI. Their application is a force multiplier in assisting persons to complete their mission and maintain readiness for the next operation. EEI opens new horizons for the care of those who serve.

### DISCUSSION POINTS

1.  Where did the treatment principles of PIES develop?
2.  What is the program that all military branches have in their organizational structure designed to address combat and operational stress?
3.  What EEI protocols allow treatment using drawing rather than verbal narration in the assessment phase?
4.  In which organizations are Post-Deployment Seminars developed? In which organizations are PCIS seminars included in their care of first providers?

### REFERENCES

Artigas, L., & Jarero, I. (2009). The Butterfly Hug. In M. Luber (Ed.), *Eye movement desensitization and reprocessing (EMDR) scripted protocols: Special populations* (pp. 5–7). New York, NY: Springer Publishing Company.

Artigas, L., Jarero, I., Mauer, M., Lopez Cano, T., & Alcala, N. (2000). *EMDR and traumatic stress after natural disasters: Integrative treatment protocol and the Butterfly Hug.* Poster presented at the EMDR International Association Conference, Toronto, Ontario, Canada.

Busher, E. (2011). Combat and operational stress control. In M. Lenhart (Ed.), *Combat and operational behavioral health.* Washington, DC: Office of the Surgeon General, Department of the Army.

Department of the Army. (2006). *Combat and operational stress control, FM 4-10.51 (FM 8-51).* Washington, DC: Author.

Department of the Navy. (2010). *Combat and operational stress control* (MCRP 6-11C; NTTP 1-15M). Retrieved from https://www.marines.mil/Portals/1/Publications/MCRP%206-11C%20%20Combat%20and%20Operational%20Stress%20Control.pdf

Department of the Secretary of the Air Force. (2014). *Disaster mental health response and combat and operational stress control* (Air Force Instruction 44-153). Retrieved from https://static.e-publishing.af.mil/production/1/af_sg/publication/afi44-153/afi44-153.pdf

Department of Veterans Affairs. (2017). *VA/DOD clinical practice guideline for the management of posttraumatic stress disorder and acute stress disorder.* Retrieved from https://www.healthquality.va.gov/guidelines/MH/ptsd/VADoDPTSDCPGFinal012418.pdf

Fernandez, I. (2008). EMDR after a critical incident: Treatment of a tsunami survivor with acute posttraumatic stress disorder. *Journal of EMDR Practice and research, 2*(2), 156-159. doi:10.1891/1933-3196.2.2.156

Grainer, R., Levin, C., Allen-Byrd, L., Doctor, R., & Lee, H. (1997). An empirical evaluation of eye movement desensitization and reprocessing (EMDR) with survivors of a natural catastrophe. *Journal of Traumatic Stress, 10,* 665–671. doi:10.1023/a:1024806105473

Hoge, C., Auchterlonie, J., & Milliken, C. (2006). Mental health problems, use of mental health services, and attrition from military service after returning from deployment to Iraq or Afghanistan. *Journal of the American Medical Association, 295*(9), 1023–1032. doi:10.1001/jama.295.9.1023

Jarero, I. (2013). EMDR individual protocol for paraprofessional use: A randomized controlled trial with first responders. *Journal of EMDR Practice and Research, 7*(2), 55–64. doi:10.1891/1933.3296.7.3.55

Jarero, I., Artigas, L., & Hartung, J. (2006). EMDR integrative group treatment protocol: A postdisaster trauma intervention for children and adults. *Traumatology, 12*(2), 121–129. doi:10.1177/1534765606294561

Jayatunge, R. (2008). Combating tsunami disaster through EMDR. *Journal of EMDR Practice and Research, 2*(2), 140–145. doi:10.1891/1933-3196.2.2.140

Jones, F. (1995). Psychiatric lessons of war. In R. Zajtchuk (Ed.), *War psychiatry* (pp. 1–34). Washington, DC: Office of the Surgeon General.

Kaya, F. (2010, June). *The effects of early EMDR interventions (EMD and R-TEP) on the victim of a terrorist bombing in Istanbul.* Paper presented at the annual conference of the EMDR Europe Association, Hamburg, Germany.

Lee, H., Gabriel, R., & Bale, A. (2005). Clinical outcomes of Gulf veterans medical assessment programme referrals to specialized centers for Gulf veterans with post-traumatic stress disorder. *Military Medicine, 170,* 400–405. doi:10.7205/MILMED.170.5.400

Lehnung, M., Shapiro, E., Schreiber, M., & Hofmann, A. (2017). Evaluating the EMDR group traumatic episode protocol with refugees: A field study. *Journal of EMDR Practice and Research, 11*(3), 129–138. doi:10.1891/1933-3196.11.3.129

Luber, M. (2014). *Implementing EMDR early mental health interventions for manmade and natural disasters: Models, scripted protocols, and summary sheets.* New York, NY: Springer Publishing Company.

Maslovaric, G., Zaccagnino, M., Mezzaluna, C., Perilli, S., Trivellato, D., Longo, V., & Civilotti, C. (2017). The effectiveness of eye movement desensitization and reprocessing integrative group protocol with adolescent survivors of the central Italy earthquake. *Frontiers in Psychology, 8,* 1826. doi:10.3389/psyg.2017.01826

Maxfield, L. (2008). EMDR treatment of recent events and community disasters. *Journal of EMDR Practice and Research, 2*(2), 74–78. doi:10.1891/1933-3196.2.2.74

McCarty, R., & Sokolowski, J. (2011). *The impact of behavioral health issues on soldiers returning from deployment—Assessing the programs for reintegration of South Carolina National Guard soldiers.* Retrieved from https://apps.dtic.mil/dtic/tr/fulltext/u2/a565129.pdf

McNally, V., & Solomon, R. (1999, February). FBI's critical incident stress management program. *FBI Law Enforcement Bulletin, 68*(2), 20–26. Retrieved from https://www.ncjrs.gov/App/Publications/abstract.aspx?ID=176790

Nash, W. (2011). US Marine Corps and Navy combat and operational stress continuum model: A tool for leaders. In M. Lenhart (Ed.), *Combat and operational behavioral health* (pp 107–120). Washington, DC: Office of the Surgeon General, Department of the Army.

Naval Center for Combat and Operational Stress Control. (2018). *Resilience and mental health: U.S. Marine Corps and U.S. Navy combat and operational stress control.* Retrieved from http://www.workplacementalhealth.org/Case-Studies/Naval-Center-for-Combat-Operational-Stress-Control

Quinn, G. (2018). *ISP and ERP: Immediate stabilization in man-made to natural disaster and trauma.* Presentation at the EMDR Canada Annual Conference, Vancouver, BC. Retrieved from http://www.emdrresearchfoundation.org/toolkit/

Rundell, J. (2006). Demographics of and diagnosis in Operation Enduring Freedom and Operation Iraqi Freedom personnel who were psychiatrically evacuated from the theater of operations. *General Hospital Psychiatry, 28,* 352–351. doi:10.1016/j.genhosppsych.2006.04.006

Russell, M. (2006). Treating combat-related stress disorders: A multiple case study utilizing eye movement desensitization and reprocessing (EMDR) with battlefield casualties from the Iraqi war. *Military Psychology, 18*(1), 1–18. doi:10.1207/s15327876mp1801_1

Shapiro, E. (2007). Four elements exercise for stress management. In M. Luber (Ed.), *Eye movement desensitization and reprocessing scripted protocols: Basic and special situations.* New York, NY: Springer Publishing Company.

Shapiro, E. (2012). EMDR and early psychological intervention following trauma. *European Review of Applied Psychology, 62*(4), 241–251. doi:10.1016/j.erap.2012.09.003

Shapiro, E., & Laub, B. (2008). Early EMDR intervention (EEI): A summary, a theoretical model, and the Recent Traumatic Episode protocol (R-TEP). *Journal of EMDR Practice and Research, 2*(2), 79–95. doi:10.1891/1933-3196.2.2.79

Shapiro, E., Laub, B., & Rosenblat, O. (2018). Early EMDR intervention following intense rocket attacks on a town: A randomised clinical trial. *Clinical Neuropsychiatry, 15*(3) 194–205. doi:10.1037/t06165-000

Shapiro, F. (1989). Efficacy of the eye movement desensitization procedure in the treatment of traumatic memories. *Journal of Traumatic Stress, 2*(2), 199–223. doi:10.1007/BF00974159

Shapiro, F. (2018). *Eye movement desensitization and reprocessing (EMDR) therapy: Basic principles, protocols, and procedures* (3rd ed.). New York, NY: Guilford Press.

Shaw, G. (1949). *Back to Methuselah, act I, Selected Plays with Prefaces* (Vol. 2, p. 7). Retrieved from https://www.bartleby.com/138

Silver, S., Rogers, S., Knipe, J., & Colelli, G. (2005). EMDR therapy following the 9/11 terrorist attacks: A community-based intervention project in New York City. *International Journal of Stress Management*, 12(1), 29–42. doi:10.1037/1072-5245.12.1.29

Solomon, R., & Kaufman, T. (2002). A peer support workshop for the treatment of traumatic stress of railroad personnel: Contributions of eye movement desensitization and reprocessing (EMDR). *Journal of Brief Therapy*, 2, 27–33. Retrieved from https://www.researchgate.net/publication/294684934_A _peer_support_workshop_for_the_treatment_of_traumatic_stress_of _railroad_personnel_Contributions_of_eye_movement_desensitization _and_reprocessing_EMDR.

Solomon, R. (2008) Critical Incident Interventions. *Journal of EMDR Practice and Research*, 2 160–165. Retrieved from https://connect.springerpub .com/content/sgremdr/2/2/160.full.pdf.

Solomon, Z., & Benbenishty, R. (1986). The role of proximity, immediacy, and expectancy in frontline treatment of combat stress reaction among Israelis in the Lebanon War. *American Journal of Psychiatry*, 143(5), 613–617. doi:10.1176/ajp.143.5.613

Warner, C., Breitbach, J., Appenzeller, G., Yates, V., Grieger, T., & Webster, W. (2007). Division mental health in the new brigade combat team structure: Part I. predeployment and deployment. *Military Medicine*, 172, 907–911. doi:10.7205/milmed.172.9.907

Wesson, M., & Gould, M. (2009). Intervening early with EMDR on military operations. *Journal of EMDR Practice and Research*, 3(2), 91–97. doi:10.1891/1933-3196.3.2.91

Yurtsever, A., Konuk, E., Akyuz, T., Zat, Z., Tukel, F., Cetinkaya, M., ... Shapiro, E. (2018). An eye movement desensitization and reprocessing (EMDR) group intervention for Syrian Refugees with post-traumatic stress symptoms: Results of a randomized controlled trial. *Frontiers in Psychology*, 9, 1–8. doi:10.3389./fpsyg.2018.00493

Zaghrout-Hodali, M., & Dodgson, P. (2008). Building resilience and dismantling fear: EMDR group protocol with children in an area of ongoing trauma. *Journal of EMDR Practice and Research*, 2(2), 106–113. doi:10.1891/1933-3196.2.2.106

## EMDR EARLY INTERVENTION RESOURCES

EMDR. (2018, April 20–21). *EMDR early intervention and crisis response: Current practices, research findings, global needs and future directions.* Conference recordings retrieved from https://beacon360.content.online/xbcs/S1524/ catalog/product.xhtml?eid=6857

EMDR Research Foundation. (2019). *EMDR early intervention and crisis response toolkit.* Retrieved from https://emdrfoundation.org/resources/toolkit/

Luber, M. (Ed.). (2014). *Implementing EMDR early mental health interventions for man-made and natural disasters: Models, scripted protocols, and summary sheets.* New York, NY: Springer Publishing Company.

Schedule of R-TEP/G-TEP trainings: https://www.earlyemdrintervention.org/ gallery

# APPENDICES

The following supplemental pages have been used in many of my EMDR veteran-focused trainings, EMDR International Association (EMDRIA) presentations and EMDR consultations. Many therapists report finding the pages to be helpful in incorporating EMDR therapy in their work. I have included them here, as a supplement to this book, for persons who may find them helpful.

Best wishes,
E. C. Hurley, DMin, PhD
Soldier Center

# An Overview of EMDR Therapy Treatment for Military Personnel/ Veterans and Spouses

E. C. Hurley, DMin, PhD

## AN INTRODUCTION

**Purpose:** This "Overview of EMDR Therapy Treatment" is designed as a handout for introducing EMDR therapy to clients and other members of their social network with whom they may choose to share their treatment information. Listed first in the handout, the professional recognition of EMDR therapy is provided as a means of recognizing the acceptance of the treatment approach and validating its effectiveness in treating traumas such as posttraumatic stress disorder (PTSD) and other life adjustment issues. Recognitions of EMDR therapy effectiveness range from the World Health Organization (WHO) to the VA/DOD Clinical Practice Guidelines. The single paragraph presents a brief overview, designed to inform without inundating the reader. The eight-phase protocol is presented phase by phase with a brief statement describing each phase. This provides a sense of the flow of the treatment process. A brief statement describing each phase is provided.

**The session** section describes the therapist's agenda during the treatment process. Brief statements are made during this section, allowing the therapist to expand discussion points as needed during the initial introduction of the therapy approach. Phase 1, History-Taking, is described first with the agenda of identifying a resource list of positive life experiences as well as a list of memories of disturbing life events that continue to distress the client when activated. It is a brief mention of the two lists, one a resource list and the other a list of disturbing life events, that acknowledges the role of past events as well as present issues. These lists are then later acknowledged with an overview of the adaptive information processing (AIP) approach.

The Preparation phase is introduced to the client as a period for developing self-regulation skills in order for the client to manage their responses during treatment and between appointments. Self-regulation techniques are described as helping the person to be able to calm down should they become upset. This is a self-control technique that, when described as helping the client "regain more control of their life," is greatly appreciated by the client.

The remainder of the handout provides an overview of the treatment process with questions asked during Phase 3 Assessment and reprocessing of each identified (targeted) memory followed by Installation, Body Scan, and Closing.

**Client:** Provide this handout to the client for their own information or to share with family members or close friends to understand the EMDR therapy treatment process.

The following supplemental pages have been used in many of my EMDR veteran-focused trainings, EMDR International Association (EMDRIA) presentations, and EMDR consultations. Many therapists report finding the pages to be helpful in incorporating EMDR therapy in their work. I have included them here, as a supplement to this book, for persons who may find them helpful.

Best wishes,

E. C. Hurley, DMin, PhD
Soldier Center

## An Overview of EMDR Therapy Treatment
## for Military Personnel/Veterans and Spouses
### E. C. Hurley, PhD, COL, USA (Ret)

EMDR therapy is recognized by the American Psychiatric Association (2004) for the effective treatment of trauma. The VA/DOD Clinical Practice Guidelines (2010, 2017) recognize EMDR as being a category "A" (highest level recommendation) for the treatment of trauma. Its efficacy is recognized by the Substance Abuse and Mental Health Services Administration (SAMHSA, 2012) of the federal government. The World Health Organization (2013) recognizes EMDR as being one of two recommended treatments for trauma for children, adolescents, and adults.

The therapy requires little talk or information and the client does not have to go into detail about the memories of disturbing events which often contribute to nightmares, flashbacks, and being triggered when unexpected events set us off. EMDR therapy is a client-centered approach so the client is in control of the treatment process. The client determines the pace of the treatment which helps ensure the treatment is manageable and effective. There is no homework involved.

The EMDR approach has eight phases:

1. History taking - Initial session the therapist gets to know the client and identifies both positive resources that contribute to resilience as well as the disturbing memories that contribute to the symptoms which bring the client in for treatment.

2. Preparation - Introducing the client to the basic mechanics of EMDR, providing informed consent and insuring the client has the ability to manage self-regulation, i.e., relaxing if they become upset and need to calm down.

3. Assessment - Asking questions about how the incident/event is impacting the client now. The questions are not focused on the details of what happened, but how the event is impacting the client *now*.

4. Desensitization - Using bilateral stimulation (eye movement, headphones or tactile) to process the disturbing memory until it no longer is disturbing.

5. Installation - Strengthening the client's positive belief about themself.

6. Body scan - Identifying and treating any physical/somatic sensations associated with the distressing memory.

7, Closing - Ending the session.

8. Reevaluation - When starting up the next session the therapist learns from the client about any experiences the client may have encountered between sessions which contributes to their state of being while also evaluating where the client is presently in regard to the distressing memory they are working to resolve.

### The Session

First, the therapist talks with the client about both positive life experiences that have strengthened the person's ability to cope in life as well as what kinds of incidents/events that have happened which contribute to the symptoms being experienced. This is considered phase 1 of the treatment.

Next the client is taught a relaxation technique to ensure they are able to manage regulating their responses, i.e., if they become upset they can calm down through self-regulation using relaxation exercises. It is important the client feel safe in the treatment and know they are always in control of the process. The client selects a "stop signal" which can be used at any time throughout the treatment if he/she needs to stop or take a break.

At the beginning of each session the therapist will reevaluate how the client has been since the previous session. Since the treatment is client-centered every session begins with a reevaluation of how the client is doing in order to set the pace for the next session ensuring the treatment is not overwhelming even if disturbing memories may sometimes become intense.  The treatment balances the client's urgent desire to get through the problems and the ability to manage the intensity of the treatment.  The client's stability and sense of safety during treatment sets the pace of the treatment.

Once a distressing event is identified for treatment the therapist will ask seven questions about how the memory of the event is impacting the client now.  The questions are not focused on the details of the event, but how is the event impacting the person now.  This is phase 3 of treatment, called the Assessment phase.

Next comes the treatment of the memory of the disturbing event/incident.  It is the disturbing memories that have created the symptoms the client is experiencing.  When the client recalls what has happened in the incident that memory can become significantly upsetting to the client.  So this phase of treatment has the goal of reducing the client's level of disturbance to "0" and recalling the event no longer upsets them when they remember what happened.  After this phase some clients say, "When I think about what happened it's like I am now an observer looking at the incident from a distance, not a participant."  They remember what happened but the memory has lost its power to upset them.

During treatment (Preparation phase) the client is asked to identify a realistic positive thought they would like to believe about themself, not that they fully believe the positive thought in relation to what happened.  Once they get to this phase (Installation, phase 5) of the treatment, that positive, self-referencing belief is strengthened as strongly as possible.

Before completing treatment of the identified disturbing memory the therapist checks for any stress, tension, or unusual sensations which may be experienced that are connected with the memory of the event.  This is called the Body Scan, which is phase 7 in the EMDR treatment approach.

Once the memory of a disturbing event/incident is no longer upsetting (phase 4, Desensitization), the positive, self-referencing belief about oneself (pertaining to the event) is enhanced as strongly as possible, and the body sensations (connected to the memory) are clear - the EMDR treatment of identified memory is complete.  If there are other disturbing memories to treat, the EMDR treatment moves to the next disturbing memory in the person's experience.

EMDR therapy research, funded by Kaiser Permanente, found that 100% of single-trauma and 77% of multiple-trauma survivors were no longer diagnosed with post-traumatic stress disorder after six 50-minute sessions.

.

www.soldier-center.com

# B

# Presenting EMDR Therapy to Your Client

E. C. Hurley, DMin, PhD

## INTRODUCTION

**Purpose:** This handout is for the therapist, not the client, as it emphasizes basic key points for the therapist to remember in establishing a positive treatment environment and therapeutic relationship with the client. These key points can help avoid early client dropout as well as confusion about treatment.

Recognizing that clients often struggle with the decision to seek treatment, creating a receptive clinical environment facilitates the client's acceptance of the treatment. Often vulnerability and feeling out of control are key issues, particularly with persons suffering with PTSD. Veterans who have been deployed in combat operations often express they never felt safe, and many never feel safe even after they return home. Asking about their security needs in your office, such as "What do you need to feel secure here?," lets the client know you are aware of their needs and clear up any concerns that could be roadblocks to treatment. Notice the word is "secure," avoiding the use of "safe" since many veterans believe there is no safe place anywhere.

**Client:** Explaining the connection between the client's need for change (what brought them to your office) and what you have to offer for resolving their needs is important early in the process. This means connecting the treatment *goals* with the treatment *approach*. The approach is reassuring, as it provides a sense of security while enhancing the client's motivation. Identifying the treatment goals and ensuring the client feels secure in your office allow them to continue with Phase 1, History-Taking, and the remaining phases of EMDR treatment.

## OVERVIEW: CREATING THE SETTING IN YOUR OFFICE FOR EFFECTIVE TREATMENT OF YOUR CLIENT

1. Client feels secure in your office. Client must feel safe/secure in your office to do effective clinical work.
2. Identify what brings the client in for treatment. This becomes the treatment goal(s).
3. Describe briefly how EMDR therapy can help the client achieve their treatment goals (connecting the treatment goals with the treatment plan using the AIP model). Note the past events that provide the emotional charge to the client's current present problem/symptoms.
4. The client's motivation to "get over" the presenting problem is the motivation of treatment.
5. Client provides a broad psychosocial history of what life has been like for.
6. Generate a resource list.
7. Generate a list of memories of disturbing events that continue to impact the client.

## CREATING A SECURE ENVIRONMENT

Assess the client's perceived threat level in your office. How "on-guard" is the client? Can they relax enough to feel comfortable with you? A new client is already anxious, not knowing how the appointment will go. If it is an existing client, they will be introduced to a new approach so the novelty of the session can contribute to their anxiety. Effective treatment requires the client to feel secure enough in your office that they are is willing to be open to participate in the treatment process. Hypervigilant clients require more effort for the therapist in creating a secure treatment room allowing them to feel as calm as possible. Ask the client what they need to feel secure in your treatment environment. Note the client's ability to present their life experiences while self-regulating, even while remaining present and grounded in your office. Those who struggle with stabilization will require additional Phase 2 Preparation. Let the client know you will be working to ensure they are secure in every session.

## IDENTIFY THE TREATMENT GOALS

What brings the client in for treatment? What do they wish to accomplish in coming to your office? Many want relief from being triggered by intrusive events in their life, that is, nightmares, flashbacks, being overreactive to sounds or smells, feeling of being cut off in situations. Recognize *the client's reason for resolving their presenting problem(s) is also their motivation for effective treatment with EMDR therapy.* Assess for secondary gains and the client's motivation for change. Remember, EMDR therapy will only do what the client wants done! If there is avoidance or other defense mechanisms, identify when/where they learned the pattern of avoidance as survival may need to be treated (as the target memory) first. Many therapists think they need to inundate the client with information about why the client needs EMDR therapy, but in reality the client wants relief and trusts you to know what you are doing. Most need brief information, such as EMDR therapy is recognized by leading professional organizations as being effective.

Present the professional recognition of EMDR therapy as an effective treatment for resolving the client's treatment goals. Explain EMDR therapy is recommended as being a treatment choice by the World Health Organization, the VA/DoD Clinical Practice Guidelines, and the Federal Government's Substance Abuse and Mental Health Administration (SAMHSA), among numerous other organizations.

As the therapist, remember EMDR therapy is a three-prong approach for identifying the presenting problem(s) of the client while using the AIP model, identifying those experiences the client wishes to resolve, and identifying what past events energize the present triggers.

In presenting EMDR therapy as a possible treatment, it can be helpful to remind your client, *"EMDR therapy has been helpful for many dealing with similar issues. It might be helpful for you as well."*

## ASSURE CLIENTS THAT YOU WANT TO LEARN WHAT LIFE HAS BEEN LIKE FOR THEM AS A MEANS OF UNDERSTANDING HOW TO BEST TREAT THEIR PRESENTING PROBLEM(S)

The History-Taking phase is where you gather a broad psychosocial view of the client's life. Use your current history-taking approach. It can be helpful to review the attachment/bonding experiences beginning with childhood. The early childhood experiences develop patterns of relationship and problem-solving. Review these questions with clients.

What were their earliest memories of their caretaker responding to their needs?
Were they ignored or were their needs addressed?
How did these early life experiences impact how they manage life?

Who could they count on? Who was there for them? Who believed in them?

Were there times they wished they were somewhere else and invented an imaginary world to cope with their dilemma?

Develop the **resource list** of positive life experiences—events that help clients feel good about themselves when they recall those achievements/accomplishments.

Note that everyone can identify issues that bother (upset) them when reminded. Develop a **list of disturbing challenging memories** of events which, when remembered, still bother them. Use the three techniques—direct questioning, float back, and affect scan—to search for past events, beginning with the presenting problem, and work backward.

From the list of challenging disturbing memories, select those that are connected to the presenting problems which bring the client in for treatment. These selected disturbing memories (connected to the presenting problems) become the treatment plan. Remember, EMDR therapy is a three-prong approach—treat the past events, the present triggers, and future template, unless modification is required.

## COMPLEX TRAUMA WITH HYPERVIGILANCE AND DISSOCIATIVE EXHIBITIONS

1.  Emphasize to the client that your first task is to work with them to relax enough to be calm in your office.
2.  Introduce the client to various relaxation exercises, teaching them to self-regulate until they have some mastery of self-regulation. Sometimes extended preparation is necessary with the client doing tapping and breathing exercises as they learn to self-regulate.
3.  Ask the client to identify one distressing memory connected with their presenting problem in which they feel strong enough to work on the memory.
4.  If the client still has difficulty reprocessing, consider flash technique, addressing the easiest target memory or contract with the client to do 10 to 15 minutes of reprocessing, then stop and review the experience and spend the necessary time for relaxation/containment in Phase 7 Closing.

# C

# Establishing a Treatment Plan for Shame-Based Clients

E. C. Hurley, DMin, PhD

## INTRODUCTION

**Purpose:** A handout for therapists treating shame, guilt, and moral injury. Shame, guilt, and moral injury are common issues in treating veterans and military populations; yet, the basis of the conditions often goes untreated. This handout is designed for EMDR therapists who need to recognize shame-prone memory networks and treat those memories, including early shaming touchstone memories. While many memories will spontaneously process, this handout can assist the therapist in recognizing embedded shame which does not process spontaneously but rather needs to be targeted separately and processed.

Shame-prone individuals will find a reason to promote their shame. Persons with childhood shame will find a reason for self-deprecation. Therefore, an approach to establishing a shame-based treatment plan is offered.

**Information:** All addictions are considered shame based. Shamed-based persons have difficulty identifying the origin of their shame. EMDR therapy is effective in neutralizing the emotional impact of shame. When this is the result, the basis of moral injury is resolved, allowing the full treatment of the veteran's traumatic incidents. This is an important aspect of treating entrenched shame and moral injury since these wounds frequently will not resolve until the basis of shame is resolved.

**Treatment:** Identify the touchstone event (if there is one) which established the shame. Add other incidents which have reinforced the shame as part of the target treatment plan. Reprocess those shame-based/shame-generating events, thereby allowing a fuller treatment plan to be completed. Return to remaining target memories in the treatment plan.

- Most addictions are shame based.
- Persons who grow up in shaming families feel worthless and tend to beat-up on themselves. They don't believe they are worth deserving nurture, love, or positive regard. They have difficulty objectively knowing if they were slighted of basic psychological needs, that is, nurture and affection. Therefore, it is easier for them to identify the pain of disappointing others than their own pain of being neglected or hurt. They frequently believe if a person is worthless, they deserve to be disappointed or hurt.
- They have difficulty believing they have a right to object to being ignored or abused as a child.
- Shame-based persons therefore have difficulty identifying when they were neglected.
- It is difficult to identify an appropriate target memory (TM), since shame-based clients do not have enough self-esteem to believe they have been wounded.
- Rather, they believe they are worthless; therefore, they are aware of their disappointment to others.
- The pain they recognize is not their pain for being wounded but the pain of disappointing others.
- Ask: do you remember the time when you first began to believe you are different? Worthless?
- How did you manage that feeling?
- Did you believe the family you grew up in was different?
- When did you learn to "beat-up on yourself"?
- What incidents/events taught you that you are different or worthless?
- How do those memories impact you now?
- If you rated how much those memories bother you now, 0 to 10, what number would you give each?

# D

# Target Sequence Treatment Plan

E. C. Hurley, DMin, PhD

## INTRODUCTION

**Purpose:** This TARGET SEQUENCE TREATMENT PLAN provides the EMDR therapist with a quick means of identifying where to resume treatment at the beginning of the next treatment session by looking at the sheet.

**Information:** The sheet allows the therapist to review what target memories have been previously treated by a quick view of the circles in the left column. Each circle represents a target memory. They are designed for the therapist to place a number inside the circle indicating the sequence of the target memory, or place a letter in the circle, such as "TE" for touchstone, the earliest memory.

The right side of the form provides for written information identifying the target, the date treatment of the target began, and the client's response to questions from Phase 3 Assessment. The last two lines in each block (next to each circle) provide for both complete and incomplete sessions. Complete sessions (completed 0, 7, clear body scan [CBS]) can be underlined. Incomplete sessions will have underlined the phases completed, allowing the therapist to quickly determine the next phase for resuming reprocessing.

The last line allows the therapist to make a brief note regarding resuming the next session.

**Client:** Resuming the next session with Phase 8 Reevaluation is included at the beginning of each session once reprocessing of memories begins. Check with the client to ask, "Are you okay with resuming treatment by working on this memory (identified) today?"

**Target Sequence Treatment Plan**

Page _____

Target: _____ Date: _____
Image: _____
NC: _____
PC: _____
VOC: _____ Emotion: _____
SUD: _____ Sensation: _____
Session Complete (0, 7, CBS); Incomplete, resume with Phase: (4), (5), (6)
Note:_____

Target: _____ Date: _____
Image: _____
NC: _____
PC: _____
VOC: _____ Emotion: _____
SUD: _____ Sensation: _____
Session Complete (0, 7, CBS); Incomplete, resume with Phase: (4), (5), (6)
Note:_____

Target: _____ Date: _____
Image: _____
NC: _____
PC: _____
VOC: _____ Emotion: _____
SUD: _____ Sensation: _____
Session Complete (0, 7, CBS); Incomplete, resume with Phase: (4), (5), (6)
Note: _____

Target: _____ Date: _____
Image: _____
NC: _____
PC: _____
VOC: _____ Emotion: _____
SUD: _____ Sensation: _____
Session Complete (0, 7, CBS); Incomplete, resume with Phase: (4), (5), (6)
Note: _____

EC.Hurley, 2011

Legend: Target = target memory
Image = mental picture associated with the memory
NC = Client's Negative Cognition
PC = Positive Cognition
VOC = Validity of Cognition
Emotion = The emotion the client associated wtih recalling the memory
SUD = Subjective Unit of Disturbance
Sensation = Where in the body the client experiences the somatic sensation
Complete Session requires SUD = 0; VOC = 7 and a clear body scan (CBS).

# The Three Techniques

E. C. Hurley, DMin, PhD

**Introduction:** This handout presents a ready reference to EMDR therapists who are learning to use the three questions during Phase 1 History-Taking and when the processing stops, presenting the need to check for a FEEDER MEMORY. I refer to these questions as the "three techniques."

**Information:** The DIRECT QUESTION provides an opportunity for the therapist to easily move the search from the presenting issue to those past events. This relies on conscious awareness of those past events. If nothing is indicated, go to the Float Back technique.

FLOAT BACK uses the image, the negative cognitive, along with emotions and sensations to "float back" to an earlier time when a similar experience occurred. Over the course of several evolutions, this version has included images along with emotions and sensations. This is an opportunity to use the negative cognition (NC) to assist in the recall of a similar experience. If nothing is identified, go to the Affect Scan.

AFFECT SCAN focuses primarily on the emotions and sensations the client is experiencing to scan back to an earlier experience that needs to be included in the treatment process.

When used during blocked processing to search for an earlier memory, the affect scan includes aspects of implicit memory that may have been outside conscious awareness.

## DIRECT QUESTIONING

*"When did you first experience this_____ (pattern of response, emotional reaction, belief)?" "How/when did you first learn this?"*

*"Who taught you this?"*

## FLOAT BACK TECHNIQUE

This clinician-guided process (Browning, 1999; Young, Zangwill & Behary, 2002) is designed to access memories that are connected to the client's current experience of the problem that are out of awareness but are driving the disturbance/reactivity in the present.

This technique can be used once the client has agreed to work on the presenting problem and informed consent has been established. It can also be used at any time throughout the course of treatment on any recent experience that is disturbing. Use with caution with clients who have a pervasive history of abuse or neglect or who may be dissociative.

> *"As you bring up the recent experience of _____, notice the image that comes to mind, the negative thoughts you're having about yourself along with any emotions and sensations, and let your mind float back to an earlier time in your life when you may have felt this way before and just notice what comes to mind...."*

*Sources:* Browning, C. (1999). Floatback and float forward: Techniques for linking past, present and future. *EMDRIA Newsletter,* 4(3), 12. Young, J., Zangwill, W., & Behary, W. (2002). Combining EMDR and schema-focused therapy: The whole may be greater than the sum of the parts. In F. Shapiro (Ed.). *EMDR as an integrative psychotherapy approach: Experts of diverse orientations explore the paradigm prism* (1st ed., pp. 181-208). Washington, DC: American Psychological Association.

## AFFECT SCAN (SHAPIRO, 1995)

Note: Affect Scan is particularly useful when earlier memories are not as readily accessible, or the client has difficulty with putting words to negative thoughts or feelings about themselves. It can also be used during reprocessing when the client gets stuck in an emotional state and it doesn't shift on its own with bilateral stimulation.

> *"Hold the experience in mind, the emotions and the sensations that you're having now, and allow yourself to scan back to an earlier time you experienced something similar...."*

*Source*: Reproduced with permission from Shapiro, F. (1995). *The EMDR approach to psychotherapy*. Watsonville, CA: EMDR Institute.

# F

# EMDR Case Conceptualization and Treatment Planning

E. C. Hurley, DMin, PhD

**Introduction:** This therapist handout lists a sequence of questions helpful in conceptualizing the client's presenting case while developing a treatment plan. These questions are developed out of the EMDR Phase 1 History-Taking process.

**Information:** Many therapists have developed their style of taking history as they learn what life has been like for the client. EMDR basic training assumes the therapist is trained to conduct some type of history-taking as part of their graduate training. However, there are many therapists who seek an outline attuned to the adaptive information processing (AIP) approach. This list is in harmony with the standards of the EMDR standard approach outlined in EMDR basic training of the EMDR Institute and the teachings of Dr. Francine Shapiro (2018) presented in the EMDR basic text *Eye Movement Desensitization and Reprocessing (EMDR) Therapy*, Third Edition.

The sequence of questions develop the EMDR three-prong approach beginning with present issues and other recent examples, then checking for past experiences (using the three techniques—Direct Question, Floatback, and Affect Scan), checking for a touchstone memory, listing other past experiences, then identifying the desired future (Future Template). These intake questions help the therapist to gain treatment history within the AIP model.

**Client:** The questions are presented in a natural sequence, allowing the client to disclose important information in a natural flow of life experiences.

**Has the client had previous treatment? Client's attitude toward previous treatment?**

_____

_____

1.   What brings you in today? (Presenting Issues)

**Specifically, what does the client want to change (measurable treatment goal[s])?**

**Connect the client's goals to the treatment plan.**

2.   Have there been other recent examples of your presenting problem?

1.   _____

2.   _____

3.   _____

4.   _____

5.   _____

6.   _____

3.   Identify past experiences using three techniques: Direct Question, Floatback, and Affect Scan

## DIRECT QUESTIONS

*"Does this remind you of similar incidents earlier in your life, perhaps as early as childhood?"*

or

*"When did you first come to think of yourself in this manner?"*

or

*"Do you recall when you first began to believe this about yourself?"*

## FLOATBACK

*"As you bring up the recent experience, notice the image that comes to mind and the negative thoughts you have about yourself (repeat the NC) along with any emotions and sensations, and let your mind float back to an earlier time in your life when you might have had felt this way before and just notice what comes to mind."*

## AFFECT SCAN

*"Hold the experience in mind, the emotions and sensations that you're having now, and allow yourself to scan back to an earlier time you experienced something similar."*

4.  What past experiences established the groundwork for the client's current symptoms?

1.  _____

2.  _____

3.  _____

4.  _____

5.  _____

6.  _____

7.  _____

**Is there a Touchstone memory to be treated first?**

5.  What past experiences established the groundwork for the client's current symptoms?

1.  _____

2.  _____

3.  _____

4. _____

5. _____

6. _____

7. _____

8. _____

6. How would you like to see yourself managing these issues in the future?

_____

_____

_____

## ISSUES THAT MIGHT INTERFERE WITH TREATMENT NEED TO BE ADDRESSED FIRST

Are there immediate issues related to avoidance, including fears, blocking beliefs, and difficulty relaxing (due to fear of vulnerability), that need to be targeted/addressed early in treatment?

**List:**

_____

_____

**Do you begin each session reminding the client of the connection between today's session and the overall treatment goals?**

_____

**Childhood History:** ❑ Uneventful ❑ Childhood abuse
❑ Childhood neglect

Theme(s) (alcoholism, drugs, sexual abuse, etc.):

_____

_____

NOTE: Remember to identify the Future Templates following the treatment of each trigger using Phases 3 to 7.

PHASE 2—Preparing the client for reprocessing of disturbing memories

❏ Meets selection criteria ❏ Demonstrates ability to be present enough for reprocessing ❏ Setting up the mechanics ❏ Informed Consent ❏ S/CP or other relaxation

Therapist has evaluated for dissociative exhibitions (DES-II and clinical demonstration) and prepared to change mechanics and ground client as needed (change bilateral stimulation speed, direction, and modality as needed to keep client present).

## REFERENCE

Shapiro, F. (2018). Eye Movement Desensitization and Reprocessing (EMDR) therapy. *Basic principles, protocols, and procedures.* (3rd Ed.). New York: Guilford Press.

# G

# Examples of Presenting EMDR Therapy During Phase 2

E. C. Hurley, DMin, PhD

**Introduction:** This page provides scripted examples for introducing EMDR therapy to military and veteran clients. The examples are not set in concrete but offer examples that have been used for several years while treating military and veteran clients. They are offered as examples that can be used for therapists to develop their own script during their clinical treatment with these populations.

**Therapist:** The initial introduction emphasizes the recognition of EMDR therapy among international professional organizations. Then, "Phase 2: Setting up the mechanics" presents a way of introducing eye movement to clients who can comfortably perform eye movements (EM). Recognize that some persons with brain damage (TBIs) may have difficulty with EM, requiring other modalities of bilateral stimulation (BLS). Demonstrating the impact of slow EM to the parasympathetic nervous system for calming down or helping the client relax is helpful for the client to gain an experiential understanding of BLS. Presenting an introduction in this manner, during Phase 2, develops confidence in both the use of EM and the client's ability to relax. Of course, when the client feels vulnerable in relaxing, the therapist must first work with security/vulnerability issues before addressing the relaxation of the client.

Informed consent offers the client a basic description of what to expect at the beginning with asking the seven questions in the Assessment phase along with the request for brief feedback, noting that EMDR therapy is unlike talk therapy. You, as the therapist, only need a word, phrase, or sentence to see if the memory is changing before saying, "Go with that!" which means "start back up where you just left off."

**Client:** These scripts provide a basic structure for introducing EMDR therapy with its BLS to the client, allowing them know what to expect next in the treatment process.

## INTRODUCING EMDR THERAPY—USUALLY PROVIDED TOWARD THE LAST PART OF PHASE 1: HISTORY-TAKING

*"EMDR therapy is a model of psychotherapy I frequently provide to many clients. Its effectiveness is recognized by numerous professional organizations including the World Health Organization (WHO), the Department of Veterans Affairs, and Department of Defense, and numerous organizations worldwide. It has been found helpful for many persons dealing with similar issues as yourself. I think it could be helpful to you if you are willing to give it a try."*

## PHASE 2: SETTING UP THE MECHANICS

"I have learned that if I hold up my fingers and your eyes slowly follow them about 6 to 8 times, your body will begin to relax. And, if I speed up the movement, you will begin to process your memories faster. Are you okay if I hold up my hand and your eyes follow my fingers slowly to relax?" (Do 6–8 repetitions of EM slowly and gradually increase speed for a couple sets.) "Take a breath, let it go. What do you notice? Let's do it again." Do this three or four sets, having the client take a deep breath after each set. "How was that?"

(Introduce auditory and tactile) "Which one of these—eye movement, auditory, or tactile—work *best* for you?"

--------------

## E. C. HURLEY'S INFORMED CONSENT WHEN WORKING WITH MILITARY/VETERANS AND FIRST RESPONDERS

*(After the Phase 2 relaxation exercise—just before beginning Phase 3 Assessment)*

*I am going to ask you seven questions about how the incident/event is impacting you now. Each question is designed to access a different part of your memory regarding the incident. I don't need a lot of details about what happened, just what you want to share with me in response to my questions. Following the seven questions, I will do what we call bilateral stimulation (EM, tactile, auditory) for about 30 seconds each time. I will stop and ask you for feedback such as "What do you notice?" or "What do you get now?" I am ask-*

*ing about what is different about the memory. This is not like talk therapy—all I need is a word, phrase, or a sentence telling me what is changing about the memory. I need as clear of feedback as possible. Just observe your experience and report it to me. Whatever you say, I will say "Go with that," which means resume or start up where you left off a minute ago. We will do this for a period of time until thinking about the incident no longer bothers you. Would this be okay that you are over it and it no longer bothers you? (Pause)*

*You are in control of the process. You have your stop signal should you need to stop as well as your relaxation exercise should you need to calm down. You may or may not experience some intense emotional response. Should this happen I will not leave you in the middle of it—my job is to get you through it. It is information you have bottled up and carrying with you. Should it happen, it usually only lasts 2 to 5 minutes and you will be over it. This is like a safety briefing; just because we are talking about it does not mean it will happen, but if it does, we know what to do. Are you okay with this?*

*(Begin Phase 3 Assessment)*

# Cognitive Interweave

E. C. Hurley, DMin, PhD

**Introduction:** EMDR therapists develop a repertoire of cognitive interweaves (CI) when treating military and veteran clients. This list contains examples of some of the most widely used interweaves. It can be used by therapists looking to expand their list. Interweaves are effective when addressing blocking beliefs and moral injury issues.

**Information:** Cognitive interweaves are used when: (a) processing is stopped; (b) you are running out of time; and (c) when the client is experiencing intense emotional processing.

Interweaves can make the difference between success and failure when treating blocking beliefs and moral injury issues. Remember, during EMDR basic training, it was stressed that cognitive interweaves are not a reason for transitioning into talk therapy. The therapist offers the interweave—a brief statement or question—but the client may or may not have a verbal response before the therapist says, "Go with that!" Effective cognitive interweaves can enhance the shifting of perspectives during reprocessing.

**Client:** Cognitive interweaves are used to create a shift in perspective using bilateral stimulation (BLS). The interweave is offered and immediately followed with BLS. Cognitive interweaves are effective in allowing the client to spontaneously respond without thinking through the answer.

## COGNITIVE INTERWEAVE EXAMPLES

What if you had not done it?

Did you plan on it to happen?

How much of it do you have to hold on to it?

Did your action save lives?

Did you do what you were trained/told to do?

What would you want them (deceased/perpetrator, etc.) to know?

What would you like to say?

Is that OK (here or in this office)?

What would the adult in you want that little (boy/girl) to know?

What if it was your (your neighbor's) child?

What would your buddy (friend) say to you?

Did you (die)?

Has it helped others?

Who determines … (whether people live or die)?

Are you so powerful you can override (God's decisions)?

He/she outweighed you by how much?

It has been how long since that happened?

Can you learn from it?

Did you learn from it?

I'm confused, what if …?

Is the world a safer place because of … ?

Are you prepared now?

Have you ever …?

Have there been times you were (did it) alright?

# INDEX

CPSIA information can be obtained
at www.ICGtesting.com
Printed in the USA
BVHW041308240122
627031BV00012B/461

9 780826 158222